# The Returns of Zionism

## Myths, Politics and Scholarship in Israel

GABRIEL PITERBERG

**VERSO**

London • New York

First published by Verso 2008

1 3 5 7 9 10 8 6 4 2

**Verso**
UK: 6 Meard Street, London W1F 0EG
USA: 180 Varick Street, New York, NY 10014-4606
www.versobooks.com

Verso is the imprint of New Left Books

ISBN-13: 978-1-84467-260-8 (pbk)
ISBN-13: 978-1-84467-259-2 (hbk)

**British Library Cataloguing in Publication Data**
A catalogue record for this book is available from the British Library

**Library of Congress Cataloging-in-Publication Data**
A catalog record for this book is available from the Library of Congress

Typeset in Bembo by Hewer Text UK Ltd, Edinburgh
Printed in the USA by Maple Vail

# The Returns of Zionism

*In memory of Edward W. Said (1935–2003),*
*the conscious pariah par excellence*

# TU B'SHVAT

Each spring, sometimes as early as January, when almond trees blossom white and pink, the birthday of trees is celebrated throughout Israel. Thousands of boys and girls in white shirts, and foreign donors congregate at designated sites to plant new starts and expand the forest. One boy in our class, however, called the ceremonies fascist and murderous. He said that pines grow acrid needles and shed them, thereby annihilating all other growth, wild flowers, shrubs, and smaller indigenous trees. He said, obviously repeating words he heard at home, that forestation of land that was not formerly forested, but which seems every year to hold fewer marks of stone terraces, as rubble and orchards disappear among and under the pines, is a part of what he called 'the big lie of our existence.' We had been friends with that boy, but on that celebration of *Tu B'Shvat* did not share with him the customary foods of the holiday, dried figs, dates, and nuts, neatly packed for us by our parents.
(A fragment from Oz Shelach, *Picnic Grounds: A Novel in Fragments*, 2003)

Este es el árbol de los libres.
El árbol tierra, el árbol nube.
El árbol pan, el árbol flecha,
el árbol puño, el árbol fuego.
Lo ahoga el agua tormentosa
de nuestra época nocturna,
pero su mástil balancea
el ruedo de su poderío.
(From Pablo Neruda, 'Los Libertadores',
*Canto General*, 1950)

# Contents

# Acknowledgements

This book is the product of a realization. I grew up in an affluent part of Israel which is strewn with labour Zionist cooperative settlements. The region is called Emeq Hefer. What I came to realize was that underneath Emeq Hefer lay – erased and buried – Wadi Hawarith; and that my joyful and privileged childhood and young adulthood in Emeq Hefer were inextricably intertwined with the destruction of Wadi Hawarith and the removal of its previous inhabitants.

This project was accompanied by an ongoing conversation with Perry Anderson. I am humbled by his intellect and grateful for his friendship.

The writing of the book was associated with two most productive and pleasurable sojourns at Oxford and one in Paris. In the spring of 2005 I was a visiting professor at the École des Hautes Études en Sciences Sociales in Paris, taking advantage of UCLA's exchange programme with the École. I presented parts of the book and continued to work on others. For this fruitful visit I am grateful to Jacques Revel and Hamit Bozarslan.

I spent the 2005–6 academic year as the Alistair Horne Fellow at St Antony's College, where a substantial portion of the book was written. I am deeply thankful to the College for electing me to the Fellowship, to Sir Alistair for his generosity and to the then Warden, Sir Marrack Goulding, for the College's hospitality. The Middle East Centre at St Antony's was, as always, a home, and I extend warm gratitude to Eugene Rogan, the Centre's Director, and to all the fellows, staff and students. Avi Shlaim and Gwyn Daniel are friends who, also as always, opened their home and hearts; simply put, their presence is a reason to visit Oxford. Without the warmth and hilarity of Avishay, Orit and Tal, that year would have been colder and lonelier.

In the spring of 2007 I delivered the 2006–7 Leonard Stein Lectures at Balliol College. This was a propitious occasion for presenting parts of the book and receiving stimulating comments. I am truly grateful to Balliol for electing me to this lectureship, for the magical lodging at the King's Mound, and for exquisite food and wine. The success of my stay at Balliol owes much to the kind hospitality extended by Sudhir Hazareesingh.

As an institution and as a community UCLA has been very conducive to my intellectual work. I benefited much from grants by the University Senate and by the Center for Near East Studies. The Young Research Library is matched by few in its richly infinite collection, and in the efficiency of the service rendered by its staff. I am especially grateful for their invaluable help to Val Rom-Hawkins, and to the Middle East and Judaica Bibliographer, David Hirsch. I was fortunate to enjoy the research assistance of Kent Schull and Jena Gibbs.

Of the numerous individuals with whom I interacted while writing the book, I should like to thank Tami Sarfatti for insisting that Herzl ought to be revisited; Avi Raz for sharing his immense knowledge of the documentation on the 1967 war; Sung-eun Choi for the sustained exchange we have had on settler colonialism; Aaron Hill, for the conversations on and references to modern French and German writers; Klaus Gallo for inviting me to present parts of the book at Universidad Torcuato Di Tella and for big-heartedly 're-admitting' me to Buenos Aires; Ellen Dubois for bringing Patrick Wolfe's work to my attention; Tom Penn at Verso for his dedicated editorial work; Kathleen Micham for the way her keen eye improved parts of the book; and Uri for constantly putting things in perspective.

The book is dedicated to the memory of Edward Said, whom I sorely miss. The passage of time has done nothing to ease the pain. I am still guided by the concluding lines of his memorable essay 'Identity, Negation and Violence', which was fittingly published in *New Left Review* (1988):

> In education, politics, history, and culture there is at the present time a role to be played by secular oppositional intellectuals, call them a class of informed and effective wet blankets, who do not allow themselves the luxury of playing the identity games (leaving that to the legions who do it for a living), but who more compassionately press the interests of the unheard, the unrepresented, the comparatively powerless people of our world, and who do so not in 'the jargon of authenticity' but with the accents of personal restraint, historical skepticism, and consciously, politically committed intellect. It is possible, in short, to negate the stale pieties of identitarian politics with other means than violence.

# Introduction

Two crucially important things happened in Israel in March 1976. One was the uprising of the Palestinian citizens of Israel on 30 March against what amounted to a state-guided looting of their lands that had begun in the aftermath of the 1948 war. March 30th became known as the Land Day and is marked every year by Palestinian Israelis and the few Israeli Jews who are sympathetic to their plight. Earlier that month, Israel Koenig, commissioner of the northern district in the Ministry of the Interior, penned a memorandum that was meant for internal circulation, to which he added a second part in the wake of the Land Day. This document became known as the Koenig Report, and it was leaked to *Al-Hamishmar*, the newspaper of the labour party Mapam, which published it in early September 1976. The Galilee was an area in which the ethnic cleansing of 1948 had *relatively* limited success. In the report Koenig sought to alert the government to the dangerous reality of the Galilee's Arabness, and suggested ways for radically altering that situation through a variety of policies, ranging from accelerated expropriation of land, through enhanced settlement of Jews (what would become known as 'Judaization of the Galilee'), to encouraging Israeli Palestinians to study abroad and then preventing their return.

In a nutshell, the book is an excavation of the intellectual and literary history which, together with the material history of settler–indigenous relations in modern Palestine, accounts for the awareness of the Israeli Palestinians that their removal by the state of which they were citizens continued apace, and the consciousness and political imagination that made the production of something like the Koenig Report possible and the implementation of the policies it recommended feasible.

There is of course a profusion of writing on Israel/Palestine. Among the better studies on Zionism and Israel one particular theme stands out. Pro-Zionist authors are inclined to portray Zionism as an ideological utopia rooted in progressive European sensibilities, whose realization in Palestine could not be as pristine as the founding idea, but is nonetheless highly satisfactory. In this way, the kibbutz is portrayed as an experiment in socialist utopia. Consciously or not, these studies adhere to an Idealist causality, because they privilege not only the ideational sphere but also the intentions of the Zionist settlers (for example, they state that the fact that Zionist settlers had not intended to dispossess the indigenous people is intellectually and ethically decisive, regardless of the facts on the ground). In these authors' narratives the settler community was shaped by dynamics that were exclusively Zionist Jewish. The interaction with the indigenous population, in other words, was ultimately inconsequential for the nature and identity of that community.

On the other hand, writers who are radically critical of Zionism and Israel usually play down the significance of the European ideational background, foregrounding instead the actual process of the colonization of Palestine. In this view, the kibbutz is an instance of the pure settlement colony, bearing structural resemblance to the early seventeenth-century colonies of Virginia and New England. These writers are often suspicious of ideology and literature, which they believe do not reflect social and economic realities; rather, they focus on the material and institutional. For them, intentions matter little, results almost exclusively: the conflict with the indigenous Palestinians is not extrinsic to the contours of the pre-state Yishuv (settlers' community) and the state of Israel; it has shaped both.

This book is not a compromise between the above tendencies, but it does insist on collapsing several alleged dichotomies. First, Zionism, its own historical peculiarities notwithstanding, was both a Central–Eastern European national movement *and* a movement of European settlers which sought to carve out for itself a national patrimony with a colony in the East. To say that it is either one *or* the other phenomenon is an impoverished, restricted interpretation. Second, it is problematic to compare the colonization of Palestine with other settler societies in terms of land, labour and certain institutions, but not in the interpretation of ideological, scholarly and literary texts. On the contrary, it can be shown that these texts express typical settler consciousness and imagination. Third, considering the intentions of settlers should not perforce exclude consequences or result in silencing the indigenous voice, provided the hegemonic story of the settler nation is not permitted to prevail without being critically read. Nowhere is this clearer than in the Zionist Israeli settler nation's construction of its own story as a nation that is unique, impregnable and in no way shaped by the mere presence of an indigenous people and the need to wrest the land away from them. Instead of dismissing this narrative as false consciousness of sorts, it is more interesting to interpret it as one typical of settler nations, albeit with its own historically specific features.

This book's various arguments, then, are underlain by the tension between Europe and its internally and externally colonized groups and territories, and between the historically specific and the historically comparable. The axis around which the book revolves is the Zionist foundational myth, which has three manifestations: the negation of exile (*shelilat ha-galut*), the return to the land of Israel (*ha-shiva le-Eretz Yisrael*) and the return to history (*ha-shiva la-historia*). These three fundamental phrases are, in effect, different registers of what could conceivably be said to constitute one integral foundational myth; they are truly inextricably intertwined. This book argues that the myth is inexorably national and settler-colonial, specific and comparable, shaped by European ideational currents and the reality of colonial strife.

To use a Marxist distinction for the sake of brevity and clarity, this book considers a series of texts that belong in the domain of the superstructure. These texts represent three main discursive fields: the political–ideological, the literary, and the scholarly. It cannot be stressed enough that the source material examined here is drawn from a very large Hebrew corpus, most of which is unavailable in English. And while that corpus cannot of course be fully translated here for reasons of space, it is thoroughly and contextually discussed and quoted in English translation. On a related note, this book strays from the conventions of academic writing, especially in the social sciences, in two important ways: it disregards the distinction between 'primary' and 'secondary' literature or sources; and it has neither an overall stated thesis which it proves, nor a straightforward narrative, even though the first chapter is concerned with *fin de siècle* Europe and the last with Israel in the 1950s and 1960s. The reason for straying from the first convention, in addition to its tediousness, is intellectual rectitude. Since the themes of this study are things like a foundational myth, literary imagination or historical consciousness, that is, constructed abstractions, it is intellectually untenable to argue that current or past scholarly writing on these themes stands outside of them (i.e., is 'secondary' whereas the abstractions themselves are somehow 'primary'); that would also result in collusion with the reification of hegemony.

The book's first chapter sets the stage by challenging one of the foundations of Zionism's hegemony: its ability to disseminate its world view as a self-evident, a priori truth rather than as an ideological perspective. Using and further developing the concept of the conscious pariah put forth by the literary critic and journalist Bernard Lazare and later by Hannah Arendt, I argue that a viable, progressive and at the same time anti-assimilationist alternative to Zionism existed within modern secular Jewry, and that its appearance was not coincidentally concomitant with the birth of – and in opposition to – Herzl's political Zionism. I also suggest that the perspective of the conscious pariah is morally and politically viable even – perhaps especially – today. The chapter uses as a starting point two texts that were entitled 'The New Ghetto' and were written within nine days of each other in Paris in November 1894: Herzl's play *Das neue Ghetto* and Lazare's article in *La Justice*, 'Le nouveau ghetto'.

Chapter Two explains why the burgeoning field of comparative settler nationalism, or colonialism, is the most comprehensive framework within which the Zionist colonization of Palestine, the state of Israel, and the Israeli–Palestinian conflict ought to be understood. It first surveys that field, and emphasizes the hitherto most important attempt to apply its method and language to the early phase of Zionist colonization. The fundamentals of settler nations' hegemonic narratives are identified and shown to exist in the Zionist Israeli case too. Finally, a sustained interpretation is offered of a long – and almost unknown – essay from the mid 1920s by a foremost Zionist leader, Chaim Arlosoroff (killed in Tel Aviv in 1933). I demonstrate how this fascinating piece, which has never been translated into English, evinces white-settler awareness.

Chapter Three launches a thorough discussion of the Zionist foundational myth's three appearances: as negation of exile, as return to the land of Israel and as return to history. It begins by providing a working definition of the myth's three registers, followed by the presentation of its mainstream varieties. This analysis is deepened by looking at the foundational myth from the vantage point of a radical right-wing movement, pejoratively dubbed Canaanism, which made its first appearance in the early 1940s. Canaanite rejection of Zionism is then examined in the 1980s, through an important book by Boas Evron, written from a perspective that can be called neo-Canaanite. What follows is an account of the myth's reiteration by Anita Shapira, the foremost pro-Zionist Israeli historian of Zionism and Israel, dubbed the 'Princess of Zionism'. The chapter concludes with an examination of a recent radical critique of the myth by Amnon Raz-Krakotzkin, informed by Walter Benjamin's 'Theses on the Philosophy of History'.

Chapter Four is the first of two that look at the remarkable careers of the Jerusalem scholars, the first generation of historians and philologists who founded the Institute for Jewish Studies and the Hebrew University in the first decades of the twentieth century, and whose intellectual world was shaped by German romanticism and historicism. It argues that, certain differences notwithstanding, this group gave the foundational myth its ultimate consistency and coherence. Whereas the myth's varieties as discussed in Chapter Three ignored or sidestepped the long period of exile, the Jerusalem scholars created an organic territorial narrative into which the 'interim' period of exile was integrated. Here, I focus particularly on the work of the scholars Yitzhak-Fritz Baer, the ascetic Germanic historian par excellence, and Ben-Zion Dinur, the prominent politician-cum-nationalist-historian, whose term as education minister in the 1950s is the most formative and consequential in the history of Israeli national education. As in Chapter Three, I close with an illustration of the current prevalence of the myth, and hence of Zionism: a keynote address by Anita Shapira at Yad Vashem in 2001, in which she contrasted two perspectives on the Eichmann trial – those of Haim Gouri (a celebrated Sabra poet of the 1948 generation) and Hannah Arendt.

In Chapter Five, Gershom Scholem is discussed separately from his Jerusalem colleagues, simply because his genius is an irresistible challenge. Although he alluded to all three registers of the foundational myth, Scholem emphasized Zionism as a return to history. His life and *oeuvre* are interpreted with the aid of a term – 'the mythology of prolepsis' – borrowed from the Cambridge intellectual historian Quentin Skinner. For its true and authentic meaning to become manifest, the unfolding Jewish history had to await the return to history and return to Zion of Scholem, the Hegelian historian blessed with the keen eye of Minerva's owl. From here, the chapter goes on to engage with other interpretations of Scholem as a modern thinker on themes like Zionism and Israel. There is an attempt in the chapter – my own as well as another scholar's – to relate Scholem's thought to Carl Schmitt in two ways. First, I look at his entire enterprise as a Zionist political theology. Second, I suggest that his obsession with messianism 'exploding' legalistic–rabbinical Judaism in order to vitalize and energize it is a sort of Schmittian moment, in which the constitution is suspended in order for the state to preserve itself. The chapter ends with an intervention in the debate over who 'owned' Benjamin's legacy: the orthodox Marxists? Scholem and/or Theodor Adorno? none of them?

Whereas Chapters Four and Five show how Zionist historiography and historical consciousness could be seen as extensions of German romanticism and historicism, the book's final two chapters 'return' to Palestine and to Zionism as manifestation of settler colonialism. Chapter Six examines the use of the Old Testament by a settler society, starting from a critical engagement with, again, Anita Shapira's work, this time on Ben-Gurion and the Bible and on the Bible's place in Jewish Israeli collective identity. It shows how Shapira reproduces one of the settler fundamentals, namely, the separation of history and identity of the Yishuv and the state of Israel into two discrete and putatively unrelated narratives: one on Ben-Gurion's Bible project and the place of the Bible in 'our' collective identity, in who 'we' are; the other on the 'Arab Question'. This is followed by an intricate examination of the literary production of the most outstanding Hebrew author born in the Yishuv, S. Yizhar (the pen name of Yizhar Smilansky). Instead of categorically deciding whether Yizhar was ultimately a Zionist writer or a truly oppositional one, I keep vacillating between the two poles. The discussion's tone remains undecided because I think that Yizhar himself vacillated ceaselessly. Through Yizhar I show, firstly, that the Bible and who 'we' are on the one hand, and on the other the ethnic cleansing 'we' perpetrated in 1947–8 and the ensuing land-grab, are inextricably intertwined. The chapter also underscores Smilanksy's complexity: both a critic of, and participant in, the cleansing of Palestine; an author who simultaneously lamented the destruction of rural Palestine in one story he wrote in 1949, and eternalized the destroyers as the sacrificial boys of 1948 in another marvellous, epic story he penned in 1958; a critic of Zionism and Israeli statehood who was nonetheless mobilized as an organic intellectual of Ben-Gurion's regime. Finally, the chapter shows how, in their anxiety that Yizhar might be collapsing the wall between who 'we' are and 'our' interaction with the indigenous Palestinians, contemporary liberal settler writers, most notably Amos Oz, hasten to offer explications that force Yizhar back into the nation's bosom, by insisting that he was addressing 'us' and 'our identity' rather than – perish the thought – exploring whether what 'we' have done is actually who 'we' are.

Through an analysis of Ben-Gurion's exegeses, especially on the Book of Joshua, Chapter Seven argues that his understanding of the Old Testament was that of a 'Protestant' settler, and did not emanate in any obvious way from an uninterrupted Jewish tradition, nor did it immanently spring from an organic Jewish history. It explores how Ben-Gurion's exegeses, and his Bible project as a whole, met the immediate need of nation-building in the 1950s and early 1960s and of justifying the appropriation of the land emptied of its indigenous people in the 1948 war. Preceding the examination of Ben-Gurion's exegetical endeavour is a depiction of the context within which it ought to be understood.

1

# The Sovereign Settler versus the Conscious Pariah: Theodor Herzl and Bernard Lazare

I divided a map of Palestine into small squares, which I numbered.
(Joseph Levy, director of the Jewish Exodus from Europe and
colonization of Palestine, in Herzl's *Altneuland*, 1902)

The nobler course would be to insist on a just treatment of the Jews
wherever they are born and bred. The Jews born in France are French
in precisely the same sense that Christians born in France are French.
(Mahatma Gandhi, 'The Jews in Palestine, 1938', *Harijan*, 26 November
1938[1])

The Atlantic City Resolution [October 1944] goes even a step further
than the Biltmore Program (1942), in which the Jewish minority had
granted minority rights to the Arab majority. This time the Arabs
were simply not mentioned in the resolution, which obviously leaves
them the choice between voluntary emigration and second-class
citizenship.
(Hannah Arendt, 'Zionism Reconsidered', *Menorah Journal*, 33 (October
1944)[2])

## Bifurcation

On 8 November 1894 Theodor Herzl reported in a letter to his friend the Jewish Viennese writer Arthur Schnitzler that he had just completed a new play called *Das neue Ghetto*, following an intense period of writing over the previous month. At the time the Parisian correspondent of the prestigious liberal Viennese daily, *Neue Freie Presse*, Herzl intimated that he did not want to be identified as the play's author, and asked Schnitzler to send it for consideration to several major Berlin theatres in a specific order, under the pseudonym Albert Schnabel ('a very ordinary name').[3] I shall later return to Herzl's striking confession in the same letter to Schnitzler: 'In the special instance of this play, I want to hide my genitals more than any other time.'[4] Clearly, what Herzl wanted hidden was his Jewishness. It is important to note already at this point that the moment which is considered the beginning of Herzl's 'conversion' to Zionism is also the moment in which he most strongly wanted to occlude the fact that he was Jewish.

Nine days after Herzl's letter to Schnitzler, on 17 November, Bernard Lazare published an article, 'Le nouveau ghetto', in the leftist French journal *La Justice,* followed on 31 December by another piece, 'Antisémitisme et antisémites', in *L'Écho de Paris*. A French Jew from an old Sephardic family in Nîmes, in the mid 1880s Lazare went like many others to Paris in search of a literary career. He was an anarchist, a socialist, a symbolist *littérateur*, public activist and the first true and undeservedly forgotten Dreyfusard. Bernard Lazare briefly joined the Zionist movement (1896–9) and was close to Herzl, but later left the movement, owing to profound objections to Herzl's politics and style of leadership.

I should at this point say that Hannah Arendt is absolutely crucial to the way in which my thoughts and research on *fin de siècle* Zionism have evolved. The possible pairing of Theodor Herzl (1860–1904) and Bernard Lazare (1865–1903) was suggested by Arendt's brush-stroke survey (1942) of anti-Semitism in modern France, which is brought to conclusion with a section entitled 'Herzl and Lazare'. Arendt notes what the two men shared and then proceeds briefly to explain their disagreement and how they parted ways.[5] In the work of Michael Marrus and Jacques Kornberg, I subsequently came across passing mentions of two texts written in proximity by Herzl and Lazare,[6] and was struck by the fact that the correspondences between these texts had not received greater attention.

The writing of the two New Ghetto texts in the autumn of 1894 may be retrospectively seen as the site of a remarkable bifurcation, something

I would like to theorize under the notion of *Ansatzpunkte*, starting points. In this, I am informed by Carlo Ginzburg's adaptation of a notion he borrows from Erich Auerbach. 'How can a philologist from a single cultural tradition approach a world in which so many languages, so many cultural traditions interact?' Auerbach asked. Ginzburg's response was as follows: 'Auerbach believed that one has to look for *Ansatzpunkte*, that is, for starting points, for concrete details from which the global process can be inductively reconstructed . . . By knowing less', Ginzburg continued, 'by narrowing the scope of our inquiry, we hope to understand more. This cognitive shift has been compared to the dilation and constriction of a camera lens. One might call this approach microhistory; but ultimately labels are irrelevant.'[7]

I see the bifurcation embedded in the two New Ghetto texts as an instance of *Ansatzpunkte*, and explore the variety of themes that it suggests. These include the politics of the sovereign, yet alienated, settler versus the politics of the consciously marginalized pariah, the politics of particularism versus the politics of universalism, the limits of the nation-state in *fin de siècle* Europe, colonialism and utopia in the literary imagination, and the way gender, psychoanalysis and modern anti-Semitism were related. It should be made clear that I do not seek the notion of *Ansatzpunkte* in order to excavate beginnings, but rather – to quote Ginzburg again – in order 'to know less' in the hope of 'understanding more'.

Before exploring the history and implications of the bifurcation, I should register a biographical point of interest. Drawing on references in Herzl's diaries, it is commonly held that Herzl and Lazare met for the first time in 1896. I think that there is evidence to suggest that they may in fact have met in 1894, around the time the two New Ghetto texts were written. It is also worth emphasizing that Herzl's diary alone is not conclusive evidence of their first meeting having occurred in 1896, because Herzl only began to keep a diary in early June 1895.

In a perceptive overview of Herzl's Parisian sojourn, Pierre van Passen commented on the social life of the foreign correspondents in the city. He reports that the more distinguished among them, including Herzl, used to gather for a weekly luncheon at the Restaurant Fuyot near the Luxembourg Gardens, where French journalists would join them. The event normally continued well into the afternoon. Passen notes that '[a]mong the luncheon-visitors during the winter of 1894–1895 appear the names of Anatole France, Arthur Meyer, editor of *Gaulois*, Gaston Calmette of *Figaro*, Victor Basch, Bernard Lazare'.[8]

## A Genealogy of the Conscious Pariah (I)

In the autumn of 1896 Bernard Lazare 'felt utterly deserted and alone'.[9] That November, he published and disseminated his pamphlet *Une erreur judiciaire: la vérité sur l'Affaire Dreyfus*, which earnestly set in motion what became the Dreyfus Affair. Shortly after the pamphlet's dissemination, he confided in his friend Joseph Reinach, author of the seven-volume account of the Affair:

> Je ne dis rien des injures et des insultes, ni des accusations. Rien de l'attitude de la presse qui me fut dès ce jour fermée. *Du jour au lendemain, je fus un paria.* Un long atavisme m'ayant préparé à cet état, je n'en souffris pas moralement. Je n'en souffris que matériellement. Vous savez que cela ne m'a pas découragé, ni ar[r]êté dans l'oeuvre entreprise.[10]

> I will not say anything about the attacks and insults, or the accusations. Nothing about the attitude of the press that was closed to me from that day onwards. From one day to the next, I had become a pariah. Since I had long been predisposed to that state, my morale did not suffer. I suffered only materially from it. You know that it didn't discourage me, nor did it stop me from the work I had undertaken.

Two separate but related questions arise: what made Lazare think of himself as a pariah, and, more precisely, a conscious pariah? And what was it in him that appealed to Arendt? Together, the answers to these two questions constitute a genealogy of a distinctly modern, secular and progressive socio-political type, namely, the conscious pariah.

Lazare was born in Nîmes in 1865. His mother's family came from Toulouse and claimed to have descended from the Languedoc Jewry that had settled in the area in Roman times. His father's family settled in Nîmes in the eighteenth century, and had come from either Alsace or Brandenburg. Lazare's father was a well-off tailor, and his home only mildly observant; he attended state schools with a republican orientation and was an atheist. Developing a passionate interest in literature, Lazare went to Paris in 1886 to become a *littérateur*. There he aligned himself with the symbolists, especially in their positivism-bashing and their intense adoration of Mallarmé. In the first half of the 1890s he was a central figure of the *Entretiens Politiques et Littéraires*, founded in 1890. (Ironically, in view of the Dreyfus Affair, Zola's realism was one of the main targets of criticism for Lazare and his symbolist associates.) Lazare also studied comparative religion at the École Pratique des Hautes Études. At the same time, owing to his dissatisfaction with the aloofness of purely aesthetic symbolism, he became an anarchist, critical of republican bourgeois democracy, and increasingly adopted combative journalism as his main – though by no means only – literary and political tool. The point of contact between symbolism and anarchism was the *Revue Blanche*, where Lazare met another passionate literary critic, Léon Blum.[11] Although some scholarly literature on Lazare exists, the remarkable combination of his life and work has not received the attention it deserves, given the variety of his fields of interest and activity.

An appropriate context within which to situate Lazare is offered by Michael Löwy in his engaging study on Jewish libertarian thought in the Germanic world during the first half of the twentieth century.[12] Developing the concept of elective affinity between seemingly unrelated socio-cultural phenomena, for which he draws mostly on Max Weber, Löwy brings together a substantial and widely varied group of German Jewish thinkers. He argues that, however different they were, these thinkers contributed to the formation of a distinct elective affinity between Jewish messianism and libertarian utopia, between energies they found in the reservoir of non-rabbinical Judaism and the possibility of releasing these energies in order to create revolutionary utopian situations. The group examined by Löwy includes such figures as Gustav Landauer, Martin Buber, Franz Kafka, Gershom Scholem and Georg Lukács, to name just a few; the foundation of Löwy's edifice, however, seems to be Walter Benjamin. The book's final chapter is concerned with 'a French exception': Bernard Lazare.

For Löwy, Lazare is 'the exception that proves the rule', in the sense that he was probably the only French Jewish intellectual, if not the only non-German Jewish intellectual, who combined the Romantic/revolutionary drive and articulated the messianic/libertarian vision, albeit in ways unique to him. He personified the affinity that French symbolism had with German neo romanticism and its anti-capitalism.[13] He also pushed forward the inherent closeness between symbolism and anarchism. 'Bernard Lazare stood at the crossroad of the two movements', Löwy observes. '[H]e was attracted both by Mallarmé's Salon (which he attended) and by Kropotkin's ideas (which he presented in *Entretiens*).'[14] This revolutionary libertarian drive never left Lazare, however much the specific social networks might change. It is not coincidental that in the last years of his life he felt comfortably welcomed only by Georges Sorel, Charles Péguy, and the circle of Péguy's Dreyfusard journal *Les Cahiers de la Quinzaine*.[15]

The year 1894 was crucial in Lazare's life. He had just published a hefty volume on the history of anti-Semitism, *L'Antisémitisme, son histoire et ses causes*,[16] written between 1891 and 1893, which drew on his studies at the Sorbonne's École Pratique and was the culmination of his views in the early 1890s. At that time Lazare thought that assimilation was possible and that it was the only road to emancipation of the Jews. He thought that progress would bring both obstinate Judaism and anti-Semitism to an end, and that the onus to change was on the Jews, for their own sake and in order not to hinder the final integration of the perfectly poised Israelites.[17] An *israélite de France* such as himself, Lazare asserted, had nothing in common with 'these coarse and dirty, pillaging Tatars [i.e. East European Jews], who come to feed upon a country which does not belong to them'.[18] This analysis was not at all in disagreement with anti-Semites like Edouard Drumont, who had reviewed Lazare's book favourably, describing it as 'a fine effort at impartiality',[19] and who invited him to help referee *La Libre Parole*'s competition for the 'best solution to the Jewish Question'; the analysis was also not uncommon among leftists. The initial stages of the Dreyfus Affair in the autumn of 1894, and the accompanying reaction in the press and on the streets, marked the beginning of the dramatic change in Lazare's position on the Jewish Question, to which he brought his anarchist universalism. Within less than a year he was fiercely debating Drumont; indeed, the two were actually involved in a duel from which both emerged unscathed.[20]

Both Löwy and Robert Wistrich discern a textual turning point in Lazare's politics. The turning point, they argue, can be found in the middle of Lazare's history of anti-Semitism. In the first seven chapters, Lazare on the whole adhered to an anti-Semitic understanding of anti-Semitism, in the sense that the latter was understandable given Jews' obstinate reluctance to be self-effacing. However, his attitude and judgment change in the second half of the book, which surveys modern anti-Semitism.[21] It is clear that, by the time Dreyfus was first accused, Lazare sensed that something was profoundly wrong with assimilation and its direction, a perception articulated in his article 'Le nouveau ghetto'. Identifying 'an anti-Semitic mood', he observed that this was a graver sign than an anti-Semitic political party (which indeed did not exist), and that it might have been mistaken to imagine 'that only small armies follow [generals] like M. Edouard Drumont'. Drumont was the editor of the anti-Semitic newspaper *La Libre Parole*, which had a considerable readership. What Lazare meant was that the existence of such readership indicated a rather sizeable support for Drumont's views, and that the anti-Semitic mood evinced by this was in a way more worrying than the hypothetical formation of an institutionalized anti-Semitic party. Then Lazare proceeded to expose what he termed 'the New Ghetto'.

He did not think it likely that the walls of the Old Ghetto would be erected again 'in the civilized West'. Something more insidious was taking place:

> But we see, little by little, a moral ghetto being constituted. The Israelites are no longer cloistered, the streets at the edge of their neighbourhoods are no longer cordoned off by chains, but there is around them a hostile atmosphere, an atmosphere of mistrust, of latent hatred, of unacknowledged prejudices that as such are more powerful. It is a ghetto that is terrible in different ways than the one from which one can escape by revolt or exile.

This moral ghetto, Lazare commented, might recreate the Jewish pariah. He did not conclude 'Le nouveau ghetto' on a pessimistic note however, and was confident that the nation-state's universality would enable inclusiveness to triumph over organic exclusiveness, and would 'destroy the new ghetto as well'. After the publication of this article Lazare's activity as a Dreyfusard intensified. In February 1895 he was approached by Mathieu Dreyfus (Alfred's brother) and decided to help. The main result was *Une erreur judiciaire*, published in November 1896, which set in motion the campaign to prove Dreyfus's innocence, but there were other initiatives, such as the campaign against Drumont, to whom Lazare was now profoundly opposed, in the radical journal *Le Voltaire*.[22]

Although I shall address Herzl's own literary and political world later (including *Das neue Ghetto*), the significance of the bifurcation requires a comment now. For Lazare the first events of the Dreyfus Affair coincided with his own political transformation (the first round of the judicial process took place between 19 and 22 December 1894). Herzl was in Paris at that time as the correspondent of the Viennese *Neue Freie Presse*, but the trial left no impression upon him at the time. A few years later Herzl, now a politician leading the Zionist movement he had founded, understood the importance of obtaining early consciousness of the Dreyfus Affair as transformative prolepsis, which he masterfully proceeded to concoct. What Herzl proceeded to do, in other words, is invent the Dreyfus trial as a moment of Zionist epiphany. Admiring scholars and politicians subsequently portrayed the mythical narrative of the assimilated Jew witnessing the humiliation of Dreyfus and being transformed into a Zionist prophet, a myth convincingly unravelled by Kornberg. In a letter written in 1898, Herzl noted that *Das neue Ghetto* had been composed 'after the first Dreyfus trial and under its impact'. As shown by the above-mentioned letter to Schnitzler, as well as the dates on a draft copy of the play, the writing had begun on 21 October and was completed on 8 November, whereas the trial took place some six weeks later. In an article published in 1899 Herzl was adamant: 'What made me a Zionist was the Dreyfus trial . . . which I witnessed in 1894.' Kornberg shows that 'Herzl had covered the trial for his newspaper, but his reports of the event do not confirm his assertion', for these reports were of an indifferent and matter-of-fact register, rather than one that would indicate an irrevocable, life-changing experience. Crucially, at the time that is justifiably considered the apogee of his conversion to Zionism (May 1895, when he wrote *The Jews' State*), Herzl did not mention the Dreyfus case. What made him aware of Dreyfus's probable innocence and its ramification was his meeting with Lazare in July 1896 and the latter's pamphlet, published four months later.[23]

Arendt was aware neither of the fact that Herzl's embrace of the Dreyfus Affair was retrospective nor of the striking temporal proximity of, but huge differences between, the New Ghetto texts. She did, however, sense what I call bifurcation in the 'Herzl and Lazare' passage, which concludes the essay on modern French anti-Semitism (1942). Arendt's text appears in two contrasting contexts within her *oeuvre*. The text's first appearance is as the conclusion of her remarkable examination of modern French anti-Semitism. The second version appears as a passage in Ron Feldman's collection of excerpts from Arendt's work, one of the most cited sources of Arendt's *oeuvre*, in which it is severed from the thorough discussion of French anti-Semitism that precedes it.[24] In the Feldman edition, the severing of the passage from its original context entails the loss of some of the depth of Arendt's observation, which is compounded by the fact that she did not have the benefit of Kornberg's finding. What is lost is the extent to which Lazare's commitment to the actual world around him was the framework for his politics and, in stark contrast, Herzl's alienation from that world. Lazare did not wish to 'normalize' the Jews but to effect a revolutionary change of the entire society and work with Jews as they were. Herzl accepted the anti-Semitic framing of the Jewish Question, and from this followed the solution of 'normalizing' the Jews by sending them away:

> Herzl's solution to the Jewish problem was, in the final analysis, escape or deliverance in a homeland . . . To him was a matter of indifference just how hostile a gentile might be; indeed, thought he, the more anti-Semitic a man was the more he would appreciate the advantages of a Jewish exodus from Europe! To Lazare, on the other hand, the territorial question was secondary . . . The consequence of this attitude was that he did not look around for more or less anti-Semitic protectors but for real comrades-in-arms, whom he

hoped to find among all the oppressed groups of contemporary Europe. He knew that anti-Semitism was neither an isolated nor a universal phenomenon and that the shameful complicity of the Powers in the East European pogroms had been symptomatic of something far deeper, namely, the threatened collapse of all moral values under the pressure of imperialist politics.[25]

There is an elective affinity between the ways in which Lazare and Arendt interacted with organized Zionism, and with Zionism as a movement of settler nationalism whose purpose was to colonize Palestine and establish a Jewish state. In both cases there was a phase of participation, which coincided with the recognition of the failure of assimilation and Zionism's vehement rejection of it. But, because the moment of recognition was also that at which both Lazare and Arendt became conscious pariahs, they were repulsed by Zionism like magnetic fields whose polarity had been reversed. Arendt wrote in the 1940s about the Herzl/Lazare contrast and the hidden pariah tradition. In her 'Zionism Reconsidered' of 1944 she tried, in alliance with J. L. Magnes, the American Jewish President of the Hebrew University, but to no avail, to create a constituency for the establishment of a binational state in Palestine.[26] Nevertheless, Herzl and Lazare became close during the first years of their acquaintance: Herzl praised Lazare in his diary and to his confidants, and Lazare was willing to help produce a French edition of The Jews' State. Herzl invited Lazare to serve in the Actions Committee of the World Zionist Organization. Lazare attended the Second Zionist Congress in 1898 and, in recognition of his Dreyfusard credentials, was received by the delegates with something approaching adoration.[27]

Less than a year later, however, there appeared an irreparable rift between the two and, by March 1899, Lazare had resigned from the Actions Committee and more or less left the Zionist Organization. Lazare was averse to Herzl's autocratic and condescending style. He saw how Herzl had undermined a democratic discussion on the national bank in the Second Congress, and objected to the very idea of his Jewish Colonial Trust. Moreover, he could not tolerate the path of high diplomacy that ignored the needs of actual Jews as opposed to those who in some future date would be 'normalized' in Palestine, and could not forgive the willingness to ignore the atrocities committed against the Russian Jews and Armenians in order to ease the negotiations with the perpetrators, the Russian tsar and the Ottoman sultan. But, fundamentally, the rift can be attributed to what I called a bifurcation. Lazare cleaved to an anarchist–revolutionary nationalism, which was meant as a foundation for a universal humanist project, whereas Herzl propounded a bourgeois settlers' nationalism, intended to create a Jewish state in a territory inhabited by non-white natives. In February and March 1899 Lazare wrote to Herzl a series of letters that brought to an end his contacts with the budding Zionist establishment and its leader. In one of them Lazare left little room for doubt as to where the fault for the split lay:

> Vous êtes des bourgeois de pensée, des bourgeois de sentiments, des bourgeois d'idées, des bourgeois de conception sociale. Etant tels vous voulez guider un peuple, notre peuple, qui est un peuple de pauvres, de malheureux, de prolétaires . . . Vous agissez alors en dehors d'eux, au-dessus d'eux: vous voulez faire marcher un troupeau . . . Comme tous les gouvernements vous voulez farder la vérité, être le gouvernement d'un peuple qui ait l'air propre et le summum du devoir devenant pour vous de 'ne pas étaler les hontes nationales'. Or je suis moi pour qu'on les étale, pour qu'on voie le pauvre Job sur son fumier, raclant ses ulcères avec un tesson de bouteille.[28]

> You are bourgeois in your thought, bourgeois in your feelings, bourgeois in your ideas and bourgeois in your conception of society. As such, you want to guide the people, our people, who are poor, unhappy, working class . . . You act outside of them and above them: you'd like to have them follow you like a herd of sheep. Like all governments, you want to disguise the truth, you want to be a proper government whose principal obligation is not exposing the national shame. But I want to expose it, so that everyone can see poor Job on his dungheap, scraping his sores with a piece of broken bottle.

Lazare was not a systematic thinker, but his transformation into a conscious pariah did include an attempt to formulate a revolutionary Jewish nationalism.[29] Benedict Anderson has already noticed the paradox of '[t]he political power of nationalisms vs. their philosophical poverty and even incoherence. In other words, unlike most other isms, nationalism has never produced its own grand thinkers: no Hobbses, Tocquevilles, Marxes, or Webers . . . Like Gertrude Stein in the face of Oakland, one can rather quickly conclude that there is "no there there".'[30] What is interesting in Lazare's construction of Jewish nationalism is, I think, the creative tension between the particular and the universal, and the way in which the politics of the conscious pariah emerges out of this tension. In anticipation of the next step of unfolding the pariah's genealogy, I might mention that this tension foregrounds the connection between Arendt's reading of Lazare and her statement (to which I will return later) that 'Rahel [Varnhagen] had remained a Jew and pariah. Only because she clung to both conditions did she find a place in the history of European humanity.'[31]

Lazare first identified the existence of a Jewish nation in a way more or less congruous with prevailing nineteenth-century theories. From that premise he relentlessly, though not always in an orderly and coherent way, emphasized the revolutionary potential of the Jewish nation, especially in its East European manifestation. The proletarian nature of that nation was therefore important not only for the dignity of its own members, but also for the betterment of the society in general, through an alliance of the nationally and socially aware Jews, other progressive groups, and humanity's downtrodden. All along, Lazare continued to attack the bourgeoisie and, with special vehemence, the Jewish bourgeoisie. His observation that the Jewish nation was, as such, revolutionary and proletarian had two articulations. One was an attempt to show that this had been the nation's essence from biblical times.[32] The other drew on an historical and sociological analysis of the various situations of the Jews within different societies throughout contemporary Europe. It was on the basis of this analysis that Lazare fought for the Jewish cause as a national revolutionary movement that was simultaneously particular and universal.[33]

For Lazare the liberation of the Jews and, more generally, liberation of each national society were intertwined: 'Il n'y aura sans doute de guérison que dans la guérison générale: les juifs ne seront libres que quand les pays sont libres' ('There is no cure without a general cure: Jews will be free only when the countries are free').[34] He strongly objected to Zionism's convenient – and false – equation of emancipation with assimilation. The Zionists always argued that emancipation would inevitably result in assimilation because this was the condition – explicit or implicit – presented by the 'host societies', and because as equal and free citizens (assuming that this was at all attainable) the Jews would lose their collective identity. Lazare rejected assimilation and regarded emancipation as a necessary condition, at the level of the individual, for collective liberation: 'To them [the Zionists] we must say: Nationalism and emancipation are in no way contradictory; quite the opposite. One implies the other, and to my mind the emancipation of the Jews is the prerequisite for their nationalization.'[35] In a negative formulation of the same argument, Lazare imagines a dialogue in which an East European Jew says to his West European Jewish interlocutor who offers him emancipation as the ultimate goal: 'What will your emancipation give me? . . . Out of an *unconscious* pariah it will make me a *conscious* pariah.'[36]

Emancipation is crucial, in other words, because to some extent it truly emancipates but at the same time it inculcates the political consciousness of absence and incompleteness, of what is denied and what ought to be achieved.

However crafted, Lazare's commitment to Jewish nationalism made him intellectually and politically engaged with two audiences: the anarchists on the left and the Zionists on the right. He found himself – instinctively perhaps – adapting his nationalist concept to the former. As Nelly Wilson correctly observes, 'He had drunk deeply at the anarchist cup', and Zionism worried him as the 'nationalisme qui a pour base le sol'.[37] Lazare did observe that the Jews were 'une nation sans territoire',[38] but he did not complete the theological-colonial myth, for he did not state that they therefore needed 'une territoire sans nation'. His divergence from Herzlian Zionism within the time span of a single congress is remarkably poignant. As if anticipating the Zionist presupposition that the Passover saying 'next year in Jerusalem' evinced a territorial urge, Lazare conjectured that in its modern guise that traditional statement meant 'L'année prochaine nous serons dans un pays de liberté' ('Next year, we'll be in a free country'). He continues in a way that, I think, encapsulates the conscious pariah's humanist nationalism:

> [L]e Juif qui aujourd'hui dira 'Je suis un nationaliste' ne dira pas d'une façon spéciale, precise et nette 'je suis un homme qui veut reconstituer un Etat Juif en Palestine et qui rêve de conquérir Jérusalem.' Il dira: 'Je veux être un homme pleinement libre, je veux jouir du soleil, je veux avoir droit à une dignité d'homme. Je veux échapper à l'oppression, échapper à l'outrage, échapper au mépris qu'on veut faire peser sur moi.' A certaines heures de l'histoire, le nationalisme est pour des groupes humains la manifestation de l'esprit de liberté.[39]

> The Jew who today says 'I am a nationalist' is not saying precisely and especially 'I am a man who wants a Jewish state in Palestine and who dreams of conquering Jerusalem.' He is saying 'I want to be a man who is completely free, who has his place in the sun; I have the right to be treated as a human being with dignity. I want to escape oppression, escape outrage, escape the disdain that is heaped upon me.' At certain times in history, for certain groups, nationalism represents freedom.

Once such a Jewish nation came into being, where would it exist? Here Lazare palpably resorted to anarchism. In contrast to Herzl, he wished to strive for a pluralist society, in which it was perfectly feasible to have a nation within a nation, even a state within a state. Lazare was reluctant to forsake either his Frenchness or his Jewishness. Moreover, he did not agree that it was necessary to choose between the two, insisting on the right of minorities to retain what could be anachronistically called cultural autonomy.[40] Put differently, Lazare's Jewish nationalism was a progressive foundation from which to challenge the nation-state's assumption of homogeneity. The particular type of Jewish nationalism put forth by Lazare had much to do with the social circles in which he was now moving, and their reaction to *fin de siècle* anti-Semitism and to the Dreyfus Affair.

The late nineteenth and early twentieth centuries witnessed increasing interest in the Jewish proletariat among left-leaning scholars of social studies. An important impetus for this was a study published in Paris in 1898 by a Russian Jew, Léonti Soloveitschik, entitled *Un prolétariat méconnu: étude sur la situation sociale et économique des ouvriers juifs* ('An unacknowledged proletariat: a study on the social and economic situation of Jewish workers'). This book emerged out of a doctoral dissertation at the University of Brussels, a notable site of left-leaning social studies. Soloveitschik concluded from his statistical data that, contrary to the prevailing assumption, the Jews were not a people of merchants and bankers; rather, there existed a higher proportion of proletarians among them than in other national societies. In the same year a group of working-class French Jews organized themselves as the Groupe des Ouvriers Juifs Socialistes de Paris. They drafted an open letter, which instantly appeared as a pamphlet, addressed to the Parti Socialiste Français. The letter complained bitterly that French socialism had not taken a firm stance against anti-Semitism and had not declared its solidarity with the Jewish working class. The letter tried to combine a call for universal class fraternity with assertion of revolutionary and proletarian Jewish nationalism. As Marrus convincingly senses, Lazare's hand was evident in that text, as was the anarchist insistence on the right of minorities to obtain cultural autonomy. This group viewed its mission as a continuation of the Revolution. From their centre of action in Montmartre they issued the working-class Dreyfusard newspaper bearing the clearly revolutionary title *Les Droits de l'Homme*. Henri Dhorr, a known anarchist close to Lazare and contributor to anarchist newspapers like *Le Libertaire* and *Le Journal du Peuple*, thus confirmed the simultaneous commitment to the cultural autonomy of the minority nation within the majority one ('it is salutary, for the purposes of liberty, that peoples, like individuals, preserve and develop their autonomy'), and to the universal tradition of the Revolution: 'In the same way that anti-Semitism is the most powerful diversion from the Revolution, so the Revolution is the sole barrier that one can effectively oppose to anti-Semitism. Jews who are not revolutionaries are traitors to their own cause.'[41]

Dhorr was not the only voice in Lazare's circle to articulate this politically potent position. A Jewish socialist teacher recommended that Jews heed their 'moi supérieur' in order to realize that the Jew truly was 'this immortal pariah'.[42] For such Jews, Bernard Lazare among them, in Marrus's apt formulation, 'the essence of Jewishness was not religious affiliation, was not even an ethnic or cultural identification, but was rather a social perspective on the society in which the Jew found himself. Because they were basically alienated from that society, they perceived their Jewishness in terms of their alienation. For these Jews, Jewish nationalism was thus an overwhelmingly negative phenomenon, a phenomenon of protest and rebellion rather than one of affirmation.'

I have described how, while writing *Antisemitism* in the first half of the 1890s, Lazare underwent a change in his political outlook. Although this change was doubtless significant, I believe that it was underlain by a fundamental continuity: the constant tension between the particular and the universal, the fact that a particularist position is worthy only as part of a universally human cause. In other words, utopian anarchism and commitment to the Enlightenment and the Revolution as he understood them continued to underpin Lazare's politics throughout his life. His final rejection of Herzlian Zionism underscores this continuity. In an unpublished note 'Contre le nationalisme du sol', written some time after 1902, Lazare left little room for uncertainty: 'You want to send us to Zion? We do not want to go . . . We do not want to go there to vegetate like a dormant little tribe. Our action and our spirit lie in the wider world; it is where we want to stay, without abdicating or losing anything.'[43]

It is not a coincidence that this statement, and the idea that Jewish nationalism meant to 'participate in the human enterprise while remaining oneself', not only explain the conscious pariah in a nutshell, but also remind Löwy of the position taken a little later by the most committed anarchist among the German Jews, Gustav Landauer, in his debate with his Zionist friends.[44]

If Löwy provides a pertinent intellectual context within which Lazare was a French exception to a German phenomenon, a series of three articles by Aron Rodrigue offers another pertinent intellectual context that is distinctly French.[45] This context was the interplay between the universalist potential and actuality of the Third Republic, and the particularist sense of Jewishness. Rodrigue presents the experience of bourgeois French Jewish intellectuals in this context. The group includes Léon Halévy, the Saint-Simonean scholar who was active in the early decades of the nineteenth century, Salomon Reinach (brother of Joseph and Théodore), Edmond Fleg and André Spire, who cover the *fin de siècle* and beyond, up to the 1930s. The tension between universalism and particularism was both objective and subjective. Objectively, the Third Republic allowed these intellectuals to benefit from the advantages of their French nationality without having to deny their Jewishness, even if there was an anti-Semitic eruption around the Dreyfus Affair and integral nationalism was gaining momentum in France. Subjectively, they understood their world in a corresponding manner.

Without being overwhelmed by the benefit of hindsight, Rodrigue shows how the Franco-Jewish political orientation that would mature in the Third Republic can be seen to have been anticipated in the historical scholarship of Léon Halévy in the 1820s. He also shows what was distinctly French in that orientation, similarities with the Germanic world notwithstanding:

> Yet one significant difference remains. For French Jewish historians from Halévy onward, the transparence between the ideals of the French Revolution and those of 'civilization' remained total. Whereas in Germany the messianic utopia of universal fraternity was yet to come, this had already begun to take shape in France. The universalism of the French Revolution was in the process of crystallizing, especially with the final victory of republicanism and the creation of the Third Republic. Franco-Jewish historiography was perfectly at home in the latter. The continuing problematic nature of Jewish emancipation in Germany, on the other hand, was not propitious for a lasting Jewish historiography based on the telos of political emancipation.[46]

The work and career of Salomon Reinach, who flourished from around 1880 onwards, embody the full maturation of the process anticipated by Halévy. His *oeuvre* on Judaism was central to the formulation of what Rodrigue calls 'the dominant ideology of Franco-Judaism'. It was 'a particular discourse that saw a symbiosis between it [Judaism] and the post-1789 France of the modern period . . . The identity between the principles of 1789 and of purified Judaism shorn of the superstitions that it had acquired during the centuries of oppression meant that Jews could now partake as full-fledged citizens in the onward path of civilization.'[47] This discourse was accompanied by a more objective institutional reality. Comparatively speaking, the Third Republic enabled upper-class Jews to develop careers in both academia and state service earlier than other European states, without requiring them to forsake Jewish affiliations.[48] In this sense the observation that assimilation and even more so emancipation had failed in *fin de siècle* France was understandable

– given the anti-Semitic eruption in the 1890s – but premature when it came from Lazare and his contemporaries. It is overstated and politically tendentious when penned by Zionist scholars and propagandists. I believe that Rodrigue is correct when he states: 'Given the creation of a Jewish sense of self that was predicated on its transparence with the universalism of the Republic, it was understandable that the leaders of French Jewry did not become involved with the process of revision during the Dreyfus Affair in the name of a particularist collectivity as Jews, but as French citizens.'[49]

The convergence of a subjective discourse and an objective institutional reality also yielded a distinct kind of scholarly discourse on Jews. This is important because it underscores the difference between the French and German contexts. Rodrigue observes that the scholarly view currently prevailing is that the studies by these French Jewish scholars were so dominated by the more original scholarship emanating from the German Wissenschaft des Judentum (the nineteenth-century field of Jewish Studies, which aspired to adhere to strictly scientific methods and concerns, and tried to sustain the position that Judaism was compatible with modernity and Jews could be fully integrated into German society) that their work was fundamentally derivative. 'However, in a social, political, cultural, and institutional context that differed substantially from Germany, the influence of German ideas and methods led to very different formulations and conclusions, most notably in the foregrounding of universalism as a guiding principle, stressing the comparative and the global.'[50]

The most recent of the authors mentioned here, Spire and Fleg (both more clearly *littérateurs* than scholars, who wrote well into the 1920s), are interesting because they manifest a development within Third Republic France itself, the emergence of the twofold allure of Maurice Barrès's integral nationalism and Zionist nationalism, which presupposed the existence of an organic Jewish nation. The positions articulated by both these writers contained a thread of continuity with what had come before, but they departed from the nineteenth century's prevailing philosophy in two important ways. First, unlike their predecessors, they adopted a standpoint in which particularist Judaism and universal republicanism were increasingly not inseparable constituents of a coherent whole, but two poles between which there was constant oscillation. Second, the commitment to Zionism – at least in Spire's case – was much stronger. This change can be illustrated through the friendship of Fleg, from the late 1890s onwards, with Lucien Moreau, who would become a leading ideologue of the far-right counter-revolutionary Action Française movement. In 1898 Fleg, responding to

Moreau's newly found resolve 'to live a social existence' and 'to acquire convictions', wrote to his friend: 'I have felt the need to connect myself to an exciting whole, to a past, to a tradition, to something that is me and more than me, to toil at work begun by others and which will be continued by others . . . The past that I have discovered, sleeping really in the very depth of my being, is the past of my race.' Moreau not only approved but did so in a formulation that evinces the common underlying political or cultural grammar: 'I too am becoming particularist [*Moi aussi je me particulariste*].'[51]

Spire manifested a comparable state of mind. His conversion to Jewish nationalism took an irrevocable turn through his encounter in 1902 with the Jewish working class in London's East End. Bernard Lazare's encounter with similar East European working-class Jews in Paris was crucial to his anarchist–revolutionary type of Jewish nationalism. The contrast with Spire could not have been starker. Spire found in the East End Jews a primordial authenticity, in a way that is somewhat reminiscent of the impact upon Gershom Scholem of his encounter with East European Jews in Berlin and even more reminiscent of the literary encounter with Mordecai of Daniel Deronda – also in the same East End – in George Eliot's eponymous novel. It is not entirely coincidental, I think, that all three encounters are Zionist ones. Here is the gist of Spire's articulation of his nationalist epiphany in Whitechapel, which is also uncannily anticipatory of American identity politics: 'For, to grasp the real Jew, it is not enough not to hate the Jews, nor to have met a few Jews in the well polished garb of the Christian. One has to live among poor Jews, one has to eat with them the *kugel* of Saturday and the *matsa* of Passover. One has to like fried fish, gefilte fish, and kosher meat.'[52]

Rodrigue is perceptively cognizant of the fact that, although such figures as Fleg and Spire admired Lazare as an iconic Dreyfusard and even as an *israélite* who rediscovered his Jewish selfhood, they were not really familiar with his writings. I think that, although Lazare was part of the world that emerges from Rodrigue's essays, his position was unique within that context. He would certainly have found the particularist sojourns of Fleg and Spire objectionable and excessive. But his position was also significantly different from the Franco-Judaism of, for instance, Salomon Reinach. What made the difference was, again, the fact that Lazare's most stable and foundational commitment was above all to anarchism. Without taking into consideration the fact that for him Jewish nationalism was important because of its potentially pivotal role in an anarcho-revolutionary vision, Lazare's politics cannot be truly understood.

Political rivalry has strange manifestations, one such being the touching obituary of Lazare which Drumont wrote in 1903 in *La Libre Parole*: 'Nous ne pouvons que souhaiter une chose, c'est que les chrétiens se fassent de la grandeur et des devoirs du nom de chrétien l'idée que Bernard Lazare se faisait de la grandeur et des devoirs du nom de Juif' ('We can only hope for one thing: that Christians attribute the same importance to the nobility and inherent obligations of the Christian that Lazare attributed to the nobility and inherent obligations of the Jew').[53]

This then was the Bernard Lazare who gave Arendt inspiration for her politics and scholarship, and whom she included in her famous pariah essay as one of four types, together with Heinrich Heine, Charlie Chaplin (who was not Jewish) and Franz Kafka.[54] Lazare's appeal to Arendt was chiefly political. In her genealogy of the modern pariah he 'translated' the predicament that Heine had expressed culturally 'into terms of political significance'.[55] Like Lazare, Arendt also identified the crucial importance, and at the same time insufficiency, of emancipation as the process that transforms the pariah into a rebelliously conscious pariah. 'As soon as the pariah enters the arena of politics, and translates his status into political terms', she observed, 'he becomes perforce a rebel. Lazare's idea was, therefore, that the Jew should come out openly as the representative of the pariah, "since it is the duty of every human being to resist oppression".'[56] She also agreed wholeheartedly with his position that the conscious pariah's politics ought to include an uncompromising struggle against the Jewish parvenu.[57] With the benefit of hindsight, one senses in Arendt's sympathy for Lazare's vitriolic castigation of the Jewish plutocracy the immanence of her own vehement criticism of the *Judenrat* that would erupt in *Eichmann in Jerusalem* two decades later.

## Genealogy of the Conscious Pariah (II)

'If Hannah Arendt had not existed', wrote Ernest Gellner, 'it would most certainly be necessary to invent her. Her life is a parable, not just of our age, but of several centuries of European thought and experience. Providence, however, in its wisdom has decided that Hannah Arendt should actually exist, so there is no need to invent her for the sake of the parable.'[58] As mentioned, the chronology of my research – gaining insight into the late nineteenth-century bifurcation via Arendt's work from the 1930s on – creates a certain tension vis-à-vis the chronology of the historical experience. The significance of Arendt for the present discussion is contained in a helpful metaphor offered by Walter Benjamin, in a passage that Arendt cited in her introduction to *Illuminations*. Benjamin wrote: 'One may liken him [the critic] to a palaeographer in front of a parchment whose faded text is covered by the stronger outlines of a script referring to that text.

Just as the palaeographer would have to start with reading the script, the critic must start with commenting on his text.'[59] For me, the metaphor's palaeographer, Arendt's work is 'the stronger outline of a script', and without deciphering it, I feel that 'the faded text', that is, Bernard Lazare in particular and the politics of the conscious pariah in general, will remain incomplete.

The modern European use of what had originally been the term for the largest lower caste in southern India – pariah – came about in the nineteenth century, even though early knowledge of the term by English travellers dates from the early part of the seventeenth century.[60] In Germany especially it gained currency as an analytical category in the discourse on the Jewish Question. An allegorical use of this category was made as early as 1823. Michael Beer, a young German Jewish playwright and poet, wrote a play called *Der Pariah*, which was staged for the first time at the Royal Theatre in Berlin in December of that year. The play's protagonist was a Hindu named Gadhi, whom his upper-caste oppressors made a pariah. Among the many privileges denied to pariahs was the right to fight and die for the fatherland (we shall later see the importance for Herzl of the right to die heroically). At the very end of the nineteenth century the use of the pariah concept was enhanced in reference to Jews in France and Germany in the wake of the Dreyfus Affair, not least by such figures as Herzl and Lazare.[61]

Two significant scholarly contributions, by Max Weber and Hannah Arendt, were added in the first half of the twentieth century. Arnaldo Momigliano (1908–87, a towering scholar of ancient history and historical writing) notes that Weber was the first to introduce the term 'pariah' to the scientific study of Judaism, that Herzl and Lazare had already applied the term to modern Jews, and that '[m]ore recently, Hannah Arendt has given wider circulation to this word in America'. Momigliano adds: 'Though she used it in her own sense, she specifically borrowed it from Max Weber.'[62] Efraim Shmueli, a Hebrew University historian, seems to be critical of the fact that 'H. Arendt uses very lavishly, perhaps as no other writer in our generation, the term pariah in relation to Jews'.[63] There is no reason to question Momigliano's observation, since Arendt was of course familiar with Weber's work in general and on Judaism in particular (something she acknowledged in her pariah essay),[64] and she also studied at Heidelberg with one of Weber's closest friends, Karl Jaspers. But perhaps one ought to be more cautious about Momigliano's phrase 'specifically borrowed'. Weber's importance notwithstanding, I think that the concept of pariah Arendt developed and deployed was more significantly influenced, as I shall show, by her study of the early nineteenth-century German Jewish writer Rahel Varnhagen and by her reading of Bernard Lazare.

Weber's application of the term 'pariah' to explain the collective history and essence of the Jews, and the debates and objections to which it gave rise, a quite well known. The texts that contain Weber's pronouncements on this issue are *Ancient Judaism* (1917–19) and certain sections on religion in *Economics and Society*, written between 1911 and 1913.[65] In the former text he explained that 'sociologically speaking the Jews were a pariah people, which means, as we know from India, that they were a guest people [*Gastvolk*] who were ritually separated, formally or *de facto*, from their surroundings'. In the latter work Weber leaves aside the notion of 'guest people' that stresses the Jews' conscious choice to be segregated pariahs, and says: 'In our usage, "pariah people" denotes a distinctive hereditary social group lacking autonomous political organization and characterized by prohibitions against commensality and intermarriage originally founded upon magical, tabooistic, and ritual injunctions. Two additional traits of a pariah people are political and social disprivilege and a far-reaching distinctiveness in economic functioning.'[66]

The mindset within which Weber wrote these passages was that of a nineteenth-century liberal German nationalist thinking about the Jewish Question. He concerned himself with the emancipation of the Jews and their possible integration into German society as individuals, as well as the difference between Protestant and Jewish capitalisms.[67] What should be evident is that, first, Weber was thinking about the pariah people as an objective category that faithfully described the position of the Jews in European societies (even if they chose to be a pariah people, as he stated in *Ancient Judaism*); and, second, that he did not see the term pariah as explaining a political stance adopted by certain Jews towards the modern world. That is why I think that, beyond becoming cognizant of the possible use of the Indian term 'pariah' to shed light on the Jews in modern Europe, Arendt did not 'borrow' all that much from Weber. Momigliano himself comments: 'For Arendt, the pariah is one Jewish type . . . to be opposed (and preferred) to another Jewish type, the parvenu . . . Weber had something else in mind.'[68]

I contend that Hannah Arendt was inspired to make the pariah a pivotal category by her reading of Bernard Lazare and her study of Rahel Varnhagen. She was taken by this notion because it offered her such an obvious description of herself: a secular, modern, non-conformist German Jewish woman in the middle decades of the twentieth century. Simply put, Arendt had become a pariah by inclination and preference. Re-establishing contact after the Second World War she wrote to Karl Jaspers from New

York: 'As you see, I haven't become respectable in any way. I'm more than ever of the opinion that a decent human existence is possible today only on the fringes of society, where one then runs the risks of starving or being stoned to death. In these circumstances, a sense of humour is of great help.'[69]

Let us now bridge between Arendt's description of herself in New York in 1946, and a major inspiration for that description – the life of Rahel Varnhagen as Arendt understood it. Born in Berlin in 1771, Rahel Levin was the first child of a wealthy Orthodox Jewish diamond merchant. She belonged to the first generation of German Jews for whom emancipation and assimilation – with all the problems and contradictions entailed therein – had become options, as had the acquisition of German national culture. She is considered a key figure in a special period of openness and interaction in Berlin's cultural history, roughly from the final decade of the eighteenth century until Napoleon's invasion of the city in 1806. Her famous salon in the attic on Jägerstrasse, which was active for a decade and a half from 1790, is considered a very important site for the history of German romanticism and for the birth of the Goethe cult.[70] Many of Berlin's intellectuals attended Rahel's salon: Alexander and Wilhelm von Humboldt, Friedrich Schlegel, Friedrich Genz, Schleiermacher, Prince Louis Ferdinand of Prussia and his mistress, Pauline Wiesel, Brentano, and more. Rahel had several love affairs with European diplomats and upper-class Prussians. In 1814, after a few years of acquaintance, Rahel was baptized (as Antonie Friederike) and married Karl August von Varnhagen Ense, a Prussian civil servant. After von Varnhagen had held several positions in various cities, the couple settled in Berlin in 1819, where Rahel made the acquaintance of the young Heinrich Heine, who became one of her closest friends until her death in 1833. The Varnhagens hosted a salon in Berlin from 1821 to 1832, which seems to have been less intense and adventurous than the one in Rahel's Jägerstrasse attic and whose attendants included Bettina von Arnim, Heine, Hegel and Ranke.[71]

Arendt was first introduced to Rahel's life and work in the mid 1920s by her good friend Anne Mendelssohn. Mendelssohn purchased most of the Varnhagens' published correspondence for sixpence from a book dealer who had gone bankrupt during the hyperinflation, and later gave it to her friend Hannah. It is not coincidental that Arendt dedicated the book 'To Anne'. Initially Arendt showed little enthusiasm for Rahel, but her attitude was to change completely in the late 1920s, when she developed a keen interest in romanticism. This sprang from her studies in Heidelberg with a notable member of the Stefan George circle, the critic and poet Friedrich Gundolf, and from her social and intellectual involvement with a group of students (Benno von Wiese in particular) who were immersed in Romantic literature. Also, unlike Arendt's previous school in Marburg, Heidelberg had something pertinent in common with Rahel's Berlin: its own version of a salon tradition. It centred on Marianne and Max Weber, Gertrud and Karl Jaspers, Gertrud and Georg Simmel, and their students.[72] There, in 1926, Arendt met Kurt Blumenfeld, who came as a guest speaker. Blumenfeld was one of the most effective speakers for German Zionism, whose close friendship would become consequential in all sorts of ways, not least to her writing and politics. It was Blumenfeld who brought to Arendt's attention Bernard Lazare and the distinction between two modern Jewish types, the parvenu and the pariah.[73]

Although *Rahel Varnhagen* is not as well known as other works by Arendt, it has attracted increasing attention in the past decade.[74] Commentators on *Rahel Varnhagen* have faced a certain tension that inheres in that work.[75] On the one hand, it can be justifiably surmised that Arendt meant to write a perfect reconstruction of Rahel's life and world, a reconstruction that would be strictly confined to what Rahel could have known and thought. On the other hand, the impact of Arendt's world on *Rahel Varnhagen* is palpable and highly significant. Is this work then an unsuccessful project of perfect contextual reconstruction because of the intrusion into it of the author's world? Completing the genealogy of the conscious pariah, I would like to bring together the differing attempts to understand *Rahel Varnhagen* by emphasizing three related factors. The first is chronological: there were considerable gaps between the writing of different parts of *Rahel Varnhagen*. The second is the impact on the book of Arendt's interaction with Walter Benjamin. The third is the book's form.

Critics have tended to overlook the significance of the fact that Arendt wrote different parts of *Rahel Varnhagen* in three separate instalments. By 1930, her mind was set on writing a study focused on Rahel rather than on German romanticism more widely. She did most of the research at the Prussian State Library in Berlin, in the company of Blumenfeld and his Zionist circle. This research took her far beyond Rahel's published correspondence, which had been selected and edited by Varnhagen himself, whom Arendt − through textual acquaintance −loathed and despised. The first portion of Arendt's book − the bulk of it, eleven chapters − was written by 1933, before her escape from Berlin to Paris.[76] But the crucial final chapters, entitled 'Between Pariah and Parvenu (1815–1819)' and 'One Does Not Escape Jewishness (1820–1833)', were written in Paris in the summer of 1938, something revealed retrospectively in a letter to Jaspers. He read the whole manuscript for the first time in

1952 (it was first published in 1957), and asked Arendt why the final two chapters had a different register from the rest of the book. She replied on 7 September 1952:

> I wrote the end of the book very irritably in the summer of 1938, because [Heinrich] Blücher and [Walter] Benjamin would not leave me in peace until I did. It is written throughout in terms of the Zionist critique of assimilation which I accepted then and which I have not until this day modified very much . . . I had been as a young woman truly naïve; I found the so-called 'Jewish Question' quite boring. Kurt Blumenfeld opened my eyes to the matter.[77]

It should be stressed that Arendt's statement on Zionism's viable rejection of assimilation is where her acceptance of an important Zionist tenet began and ended; otherwise, as is well known, her objection to Herzl's and Ben-Gurion's Zionism was prophetically expressed in the 1940s and grew exponentially thereafter.[78] The third instalment of the book, its preface, was written in New York in the summer of 1956, with the *Shoah* standing between it and the book proper.[79]

The possible parallels between Rahel Varnhagen and Hannah Arendt have already been pointed out by Arendt's perceptive biographer, Elisabeth Young–Bruehl, and Seyla Benhabib, who, though a bit apprehensive about Young-Bruehl's over-emphasis on these parallels, calls her own essay 'The Pariah and Her Shadow'.[80] Most recently this tension–ridden closeness has been interestingly commented on by Liliane Weissberg and Heidi Tewarson.[81] The affinity Arendt felt towards her subject was indeed special. Her oft-cited statement in the book's preface – 'What interested me solely was to narrate the story of Rahel's life as she herself might have told it'[82] – is striking, as is Arendt's intimating to Heinrich Blücher (her second husband) in 1936, that Rahel was 'my closest friend, though she has been dead for some one hundred years'.[83] Certain scholars have understood the statement in the preface and the book in general as conveying an intention to write a perfect contextual reconstruction of Rahel's life and her world. Thus Ulrike Weckel remarks: 'There is a certain tension between Arendt's interpretation [of Rahel Varnhagen] from the perspective of the end of German Jewry and her approach as a biographer who claimed that she did not want to know any more than her protagonist had. This also led the Jewish Germanist Käte Hamburger to reject the characterization of Rahel's life as one "between a pariah and a parvenu" as a projection on Arendt's part.'[84]

The problem with Weckel's remark is that it assumes *Rahel Varnhagen* to have been a project of perfect reconstruction that got out of hand because the author's world overwhelmed that of her protagonist. The statement in the preface to *Rahel Varnhagen* cannot be taken as a straightforward indication of intention because it was written in 1956, long after the book proper had been completed. Moreover, there is a clear indication to the contrary – that, even from the later perspective of the 1950s, Arendt did not regard *Rahel Varnhagen* as an exercise in perfect contextual reconstruction. Initially rejecting the manuscript, Arendt's publisher Klaus Piper said that it was not a biography since there was no narrative reconstruction of Rahel's contextual world. He later requested that Arendt compress 'the purely epistemological sections' and add a much-needed clarifying narrative. Arendt refused, saying that what she had written was a 'curious book' and she did not wish to render it 'less curious'. This does not sound like an intention to produce a perfect reconstruction, for Piper's suggestion that she try and create one is flatly rejected.[85] *Rahel Varnhagen*'s importance for Arendt and its constant existence in her life from the 1920s to 1974, when the American edition appeared, make it, I think, her *Bildungsroman*. The pre-*Rahel Varnhagen* Arendt was indifferent to politics in general and to the Jewish Question in particular. An immensely gifted young woman carving for herself a niche in the temple of German philosophy, she was, as she herself would presumably say, a parvenu. By the time of the book's completion in 1938, Arendt had become a rebellious pariah: politically conscious and active, she vehemently rejected assimilation in and of itself and as a condition for emancipation, and she insisted that, because her humanity, dignity and citizenship were threatened as a Jew, she would fight to thwart the threat as a Jew, not just as a universal individual.

Although the whole book may be understood as Rahel's oscillation between the parvenu and pariah (I use 'oscillation' advisedly, for Arendt did not deem the passage from parvenu to pariah irrevocable), there appear explicit definitions and bold formulations particularly in the last two chapters.[86] A salient example is Arendt's definition of the parvenu through a vicious quote from Wilhelm von Humboldt's correspondence with his wife Caroline: 'I hear . . . that Varnhagen has now married the little Levy woman. So now at last she can become an Excellency and Ambassador's wife. There is nothing the Jews cannot achieve.' Arendt then continues: 'Here, as elsewhere, Wilhelm von Humboldt was the best, keenest and most malicious gossip of his age. He hit the nail on the head – even though he did put the matter more crudely and more spitefully than was absolutely necessary. Nineteenth-century Jews, if they wanted to play a part in society, had no choice but to become parvenus par excellence, and certainly in those decades of reaction they were the choicest examples of parvenus.'[87] The way Arendt describes Rahel's passage from parvenu to pariah (and the liminal pauses between parvenu and pariah) through her relationship with Pauline Wiesel is – even though many scholars would beg to differ – a most compellingly feminist pronouncement.

Pauline Wiesel was the former mistress of Prince Louis Ferdinand of Prussia and regularly attended Rahel's Jägerstrasse salon. Rahel sought to find Pauline and regain her company in the mid 1810s, precisely when her desire to become a parvenu had been satisfied; precisely at the moment of satisfaction of achieving full parvenu status she began to contemplate the price of passage from pariah to parvenu (which is why I insist on 'oscillation' and 'liminal pauses'); precisely at that point she ordered Varnhagen to find Pauline – 'the most compromised of the friends of her youth'[88] – in Paris. He objected, to no avail. He could not understand why Pauline's attempt to seduce him, in order to 'taste Rahel's husband – like iced punch', not only did not incense his wife, but 'was proof of the liveliest interest in Rahel's own fate'.[89] In the heyday of Rahel's salon there was tension between Pauline and Rahel because both were occasionally courted by – and in turn tried to woo – the same men. The wretched Varnhagen could not comprehend, according to Arendt, why Rahel wanted him to find Pauline in the first place, and even less why she delighted in Pauline's seductive gestures. In fact, only Arendt, Rahel and Pauline seem truly to understand. Rahel's attaining at long last a full parvenu status, her rejection of it and passage to becoming a pariah, and her search for, and pariah partnership with, Pauline Wiesel, which lasted until her death, are all presented in a manner in which narrative coherence is disregarded, indeed seems not to matter.[90] From that point on definitions and formulations of the pariah abound, but none of them are comprehensive and most are simply quotations of Rahel's statements (notably: 'But I am a rebel after all!'[91]). Perhaps the most powerful is Arendt's statement just before ending the book: 'Rahel had remained a Jew and pariah. Only because she clung to both conditions did she find a place in the history of European humanity.'[92]

As mentioned above, the final two chapters of *Rahel Varnhagen* were completed by the summer of 1938 in Paris, in close interaction with Walter Benjamin.[93] What has gone almost unnoticed is that, in addition to Arendt's relating the process of writing the book to Jaspers more than a decade after its completion, there is an intrinsic clue for this interaction: the book's *form*. In an early and perceptive review of the book, the British novelist Sybille Bedford noted the following points about its form: the overwhelming collection of quotations of Rahel's voice used by Arendt, the difficulty of pinning down the book's context, and its 'relentlessly abstract' nature, which she nonetheless found appealing. 'Miss Arendt is content to adumbrate and amplify [Rahel's verbalized experiences]', Bedford comments. 'Reflection caps reflection, comment encompasses comment, and event precedes event; rare factual bones lie muffled in paragraphs of words like coins inside a ball of knitting-wool.'[94] Young-Bruehl is appreciative of Bedford's early review. She further identifies Benjamin's presence in *Rahel Varnhagen* and cites a telling observation Arendt made in her 1968 essay on Benjamin: 'The main work [Benjamin's] consisted of tearing fragments out of their context and arranging them afresh in such a way that they illustrated one another and were able to prove their raison d'être in a free floating state, as it were.'[95] Liliane Weissberg similarly notes that *Rahel Varnhagen* was planned as 'a montage of quotations that would attempt to capture Rahel's voice', and points to Benjamin as the source of inspiration.[96]

There is, I think, no satisfactory explanation for the presence of Benjamin in *Rahel Varnhagen*'s concluding chapters. The period of Arendt's interaction with Benjamin in Paris was the same period that engendered the 'Theses on the Philosophy of History', the manuscript Benjamin bequeathed to Arendt just before he left Paris for the final time. This text is one of the most compelling objections not only to the idea of progress, but also to positivism's desire to reconstruct the past perfectly and comprehensively. I mention the 'Theses' cautiously but with certain confidence, following a recent, Talmudic, study of that magnificent text by Michael Löwy. He emphasizes the fact that, strictly speaking, the 'Theses' was prompted by the Molotov–Ribbentrop Pact, that is, after the summer of 1938 during which Arendt wrote the final chapters of *Rahel Varnhagen*; hence the caution. But Löwy also reconstructs the intellectual and political development of Benjamin that could lead to a text like the 'Theses', and mentions the role in this development played by Blücher, Arendt's husband.[97]

In her introduction to Benjamin's *Illuminations* Arendt explores how his obsession with collecting – first books and then quotations – unfolded, and how the 'montage of quotations' became the form of his writing and the expression of his politics. 'This discovery of the modern function of quotations, according to Benjamin . . . was born . . . out of the despair of the present and the desire to destroy it; hence their power is "not the strength to preserve but to cleanse, to tear out of context, to destroy".' The realization, Arendt continues, was that the power of the quotations to destroy was (and she cites Benjamin) 'the only one which still contains the hope that something from this period will survive – for no other reason than it was torn out of it'. She concludes that, in this form of 'thought fragments' (Benjamin's term, but so apt to describe *Rahel Varnhagen*), 'quotations have the double task of interrupting the flow of presentation with "transcendent force" and at the same time of concentrating within themselves that which is presented'.[98]

The subversive power of collecting in general, and of collecting quotations in particular, is anchored in the present, which preserves the 'pearls and corals' lifted from the past by unavoidably 'doing violence to their context'.[99] When Weckel censures the excessive presence of Arendt's perspective (the end of German Jewry), and when Hamburger rejects as projection on Arendt's part the characterization of Rahel's life as one between a pariah and a parvenu,[100] they unwittingly lend support to my point that the effect of the 'montage of quotations', especially profuse in the concluding chapters, is essentially Benjaminian. Without necessarily denying Rahel voice or agency, it tears her life out of its context and preserves it in the present as the timeless – timeless, that is, within the confines of modernity – passage from the parvenu to the pariah. This decontextualization is politically consequential. It not only preserves a remnant of German and European Jewry, it is what gives the pariah as a political type the Benjaminian 'transcendent force', the universal relevance to the present, even though Rahel emerged from a particular past. What Arendt wished to lift from the past and deploy in the present, I propose, was the conscious pariah as a position that is inherently Jewish and universal. Her project was historical in the sense that she did not understand Jewishness as essence, and that for her the conscious pariah was implicitly a meaningful category only within the confines of European modernity. It was not historical in the conventional sense of contextual reconstruction, because that was neither what Arendt did nor what she had intended to do. Discussing with Piper the title of the German edition (a fascinating affair in its own right), Arendt mischievously suggested a variation on a passage from Rahel's letter to Heinrich Heine: ' "Rahel Varnhagen. The Melody of an Insulted Heart. Whistled after Her Tune with Variations by Hannah Arendt." Because this is precisely what I have done.'[101]

It is fitting to conclude the discussion on 'Arendt's Rahel' by creating a textual link between the first and second parts of the genealogy of the conscious pariah. The mantle of the conscious pariah was transferred from Rahel Varnhagen to Bernard Lazare via Heine (the transference from Heine to Lazare was of course 'established' by Arendt, in her famous essay on the pariah's hidden tradition). Along with Pauline Wiesel, Heine was the closest person to Rahel during her last years. They had first met in 1821 when she was fifty and he was twenty-three.[102] He promised to be 'enthusiastic for the cause of the Jews and their attainment of equality before the law. In bad times, which are inevitable, the Germanic rabble will hear my voice ring resoundingly in German beer halls and palaces.'[103] With this, Arendt says, Rahel could die reassured that she had left an heir to whom she could entrust 'the history of a bankruptcy and a rebellious spirit'. Arendt brings *Rahel Varnhagen* to a closure with a quotation of Rahel, where she almost literally bequeathed 'pariahdom' to Heine from her deathbed:

> No philanthropic list, no cheers, no bourgeois star, nothing, nothing could ever placate me . . . You will say this gloriously, elegiacally, fantastically, incisively, extremely jestingly, always musically, provokingly, often charmingly; you will say it all very soon. But as you do, the text from my old, offended heart will still have to remain yours.[104]

## The Sovereign Settler[105]

> The point is that whether Negro, Jew or colonized, one must resemble the white man, the non-Jew, the colonizer.
> (Albert Memmi, *The Colonizer and the Colonized* [1957] 1965, p. 122)

Although we shall shortly approach Herzl directly, I would like to start with Benny Morris, because of the light he sheds on what is called liberal or humanist Zionism, of which he is a product. Clinging to Herzl and portraying his vision as liberal or humanist is a practice most favoured by that socio-political orbit.

There is something irresistible about the brutal candour of Benny Morris. For two decades he has been a notable historian of the Arab–Israeli conflict. He meticulously and thoroughly documented the ethnic cleansing that was an integral part of the birth of the state of Israel in the 1948 war as well as other episodes in that conflict's history. The 2000 Camp David fiasco caused Morris to shed any lingering inhibitions: he pronounced that the ethnic cleansing of 1948 should be completed, and that Israel is the West's crusading outpost in its clash of civilizations with Islam. This combination of scholarly integrity and authority on the one hand, and on the other an unmasked social Darwinism that would have made Max Nordau blush, prompted the editors of the *New Left Review* to publish verbatim a striking interview Morris gave to *Haaretz* on 8 January 2004 entitled (aptly in both languages) 'Survival of the Fittest' in the English edition and 'Awaiting the Barbarians' in the Hebrew original. The *New*

*Left Review*'s introduction justifiably states that the interview is 'a document of unusual significance in the modern history of Zionism – and reproduced here for that reason. To his shocked interlocutor, Morris lays out two unpalatable truths: that the Zionist project could only be realized by deliberate ethnic cleansing; and that, once it was embarked upon, the only reasons for stopping short of the complete elimination of the Arab population from Palestine were purely temporary and tactical ones.'[106]

More recently Morris reviewed the eminent Zionist historian Anita Shapira's hefty biography of Yigal Allon, the least known of the trio (Dayan, Rabin and Allon) who were the incarnations of Paul Newman's 'New Jew' in the Hollywood film *Exodus*. In the review Morris also mentions Shapira's *Land and Power: The Zionist Resort to Force, 1881–1948*, which had been published in English the previous year. A highly significant addition to Zionist Israeli ideology, the argument of *Land and Power* is conveyed by the Hebrew title, *The Dove's Sword*, which was suggested to Shapira by Amos Oz. It gives scholarly credence to the position of the so-called Israeli peace camp, which was that Zionism had begun as a movement averse to the use of force and to war, and that only the realities of Palestine and the Middle East coupled with increasing anti-Semitism in Europe reluctantly forced it to resort to the use of violence, a 'defensive ethos' that gradually became an 'offensive ethos'. In her familiar moralistic tone Golda Meir took up this position in her observation: 'We can forgive the Arabs for killing our children. We cannot forgive them for forcing us to kill their children. We will only have peace with the Arabs when they love their children more than they hate us.' Enter Morris:

> This is Shapira's thesis. I myself am not so certain that it is valid, though it shouldn't be dismissed completely. In my estimate, if Herzl had had at his disposal five divisions of Marines, he would not have hesitated for a moment to send them to Palestine and conquer it from the Turks, instantly, without procrastination and idle talk. He, and those who followed him in the leadership of the Zionist movement, resorted to convincing and diplomacy mainly because they did not have the [military] power to conquer the country – and in any event in the Mandatory period the British supplied the military umbrella under whose protection the Zionist enterprise grew into a state.[107]

Until recently many Zionists who call themselves 'moderates', 'centrists' or 'leftists' considered Herzl's founding Zionism (adopted successively by Weizmann, Ben-Gurion, Rabin) to be the real Zionism. In this view,

Zionism refers to a progressively liberal or moderately social democrat national liberation movement, which sought a national home for the Jews with the peaceful consent of its neighbours, and which still holds the key for peace and for the perfectly feasible existence of a state that is simultaneously Jewish and democratic. All other formulations are deviations from, and corruptions of, that true Zionism.[108] It is true that there are varieties of Zionism whose differences should not be ignored. I believe, however, that the goal of founding an exclusively Jewish state in Palestine by European Jews is a more or less continuous concept and praxis from Herzl's foundational Zionism, through the settlement movement in the Occupied Territories, to Sharon's wall, regardless of the varieties and as Arendt had already understood, with astonishing prophetic accuracy, in 'Zionism Reconsidered' of October 1944. From the perspective of Zionism's indigenous victims, who have been dispossessed and cleansed by all Zionist varieties, this continuity outweighs the differences. I further concur with Amnon Raz-Krakotzkin that Israeli Zionism is a theological-colonial nationalism regardless of whether a certain shade or variety within it is outwardly religious or secular.[109]

The bifurcation with which this chapter began, between the sovereign settler and the conscious pariah, has thus far followed the latter's path. I would now like to focus on the sovereign settler and thereby follow the bifurcation's other path. I do so through a literary commentary on two Herzl texts: the play *Das neue Ghetto* and the utopian novel *Altneuland* (first published in 1902). I will propose that they contain the two underlying elements that comprised Herzl's political and literary imagination: his acceptance of modern anti-Semitism's framing of the *Judenfrage* (the Jewish Question) and his wholehearted embrace of utopian colonialism.

### Masculinity and anti-Semitism

In his famous study of *fin de siècle* Vienna, Carl Schorske situates Herzl's Zionism in its precise context: the 'Politics in a New Key', an anti-rational, anti-Semitic, anti-liberal and direct appeal to the masses. Schorske not only comes up with this apt term, 'Politics in a New Key', he also identifies 'An Austrian Trio' that devised it: Georg von Schönerer (1842–1921), 'the militant knight-redeemer of the German *Volk*'; Karl Lueger (1844–1910), founder of the Christian Socials and the first anti-Semitic mayor of Vienna; and Theodor Herzl.[110] On two occasions Schorske brings this trio together in a way that conveys this context with special clarity and succinctness:

Several features of Herzl's attitude as he approached his moment of conversion [to Zionism in the mid 1890s] betray his deep kinship with Schönerer and Lueger: his rejection of rational politics, and his commitment to a noble, aristocratic leadership style with a strong taste for the grand gesture. Another tie linking him to his enemies, even though he drew different conclusions from it, was his distaste for the Jews.[111]

And later:

In his appeal to the masses, Herzl combined archaic and futuristic elements in the same way as Schönerer and Lueger before him. All three leaders espoused the cause of social justice and made it the center of their critique of liberalism's failures. All three linked this modern aspiration to an archaic communitarian tradition: Schönerer to the Germanic tribes, Lueger to the medieval Catholic social order, Herzl to the pre-diaspora Kingdom of Israel. All three connected 'forward' and 'backward', memory and hope . . . and thus outflanked the unsatisfying present for followers who were victims of industrial capitalism before being integrated into it: artisans and greengrocers, hucksters and ghetto-dwellers.[112]

Herzl interacted with German culture in numerous ways and at several levels.[113] Born and raised in Budapest till the age of eighteen when his family moved to Vienna, he quickly became a bourgeois Viennese Jew but, as he confessed in his diary in 1895, '[i]n fact, had I wanted to be someone else, I would have chosen to be a Prussian aristocrat from the old nobility'.[114] This desire to have been a Prussian Junker is highly significant for, as I shall show, this was the social type whose acceptance Herzl sought for himself and for the Jews. Another route into German culture for Herzl was the liberating and transformative energy he discovered in Richard Wagner. The inspirational role Wagner's music played in the writing of Herzl's best-known work, the pamphlet Der Judenstaat ('The Jews' state', 1896), was revealingly acknowledged by the author:

Heine tells us that he heard the flapping of an angel's wings above his head when he wrote certain verses. I, too, believe that I heard such a fluttering of wings while I wrote that book. I worked on it every day to the point of utter exhaustion. My only recreation was listening to Wagner's music in the evening, particularly to Tannhäuser, an opera which I attended as often as it was produced. Only on the evenings when there was no opera did I have any doubts as to the truth of my ideas.[115]

It was no coincidence that *Tannhäuser* was ceremoniously played at the opening of the First Zionist Congress in 1897.[116]

Schorske too recognizes the importance of the uplifting impact of the Wagnerian gesture to Herzl's unfolding anti-Liberalism and its translation into Zionism: 'The Zionist movement would be a kind of *Gesamtkunstwerk* [a total artwork] of the new politics. Herzl sensed this when he said, "Moses' exodus would compare [to mine] like a Shrove Tuesday *Singspiel* of Hans Sachs to a Wagnerian opera".'[117] The ultimate lesson in this kind of politics in a new key was drawn from *the* Prussian Herzl had admired. Attempting to lure to the cause of Zionism 'the sober and calculating philanthropist' Baron Hirsch (a German-born Jewish magnate who founded the Jewish Colonization Association, which was active in Palestine and Argentina), Herzl wrote to him: 'Believe me, the politics of a whole people . . . can only be made with imponderables that hover high in the air. Do you know out of what the German Empire arose? Out of dreams, songs, fantasies and black-red-gold ribbons . . . Bismarck merely shook the tree that fantasies had planted.'[118] For Herzl, one of the crucial 'imponderables' in this politics was the will to die (as it was in Michael Beer's 1823 play, *Der Pariah*, mentioned above). Here too Bismarck was a role model. Bismarck, Herzl thought, knew how to harness the 'stirrings, mysterious and undeniable like life itself, which rose out of the unfathomable depths of the folk-soul in response to the dream [of unity]'. He was able to demand great sacrifice from the Germans, who 'joyfully rushed toward unification in war'.[119]

Enter another meaningful Junker, the retired captain of cavalry Count von Schramm, in Herzl's *Das neue Ghetto*.[120] Situated in 1893 bourgeois Jewish Vienna, the play opens at the wedding of Dr Jacob Samuel, a lawyer, and Hermine Hellman, the daughter of a wealthy textile merchant. Count von Schramm is one of the guests. He owns a coal mine in a Slovakian province of the Habsburg Empire and, since he excels in neither work nor frugality, wishes profitably to dispose of it through the services of Samuel's newly acquired brother-in-law, Fritz Rheinberg. The latter has an employee, the *Ostjuden*-like Emmanuel Wasserstein, who is despised but turns out the most successful in the stock market. Rheinberg asks Samuel to prepare the contract for the von Schramm deal.

It then transpires that, some years previously, Samuel had an unrealized (and hence humiliating) duel with von Schramm, who had challenged Samuel over a petty argument. Despondent over the illness of his father, Samuel extended an apology to von Schramm's seconds and the duel was called off, which prompted von Schramm to question Samuel's virility. Von Schramm's reappearance reminds Samuel of this painful humiliation.

Towards the end of the wedding Samuel and Rabbi Friedheimer, a prominent member of the Jewish Viennese community, discuss the exit of the Jews from the ghetto as part of their emancipation, which engenders the construction of a new ghetto – this time, a moral ghetto. The humiliation von Schramm's presence awakened in Samuel is exacerbated by a visit from his friend Wurzlechner some time after the wedding. Wurzlechner wishes to advise Samuel that their friendship, at least the public-social side of it, must come to an end, because Samuel is surrounded by too many Jews. In addition, Wurzlechner intends to enter politics and cannot afford to 'be branded a tool of the Jews first thing!'[121]

Later Samuel, whose dealings with workers' matters have won him a certain reputation, is visited by a coal miner, Peter Vendik, who represents the workers of von Schramm's mine and seeks Samuel's services on the miners' behalf. They are especially anxious about the maintenance and safety of the mine. Samuel visits it and is appalled. After his visit the miners go on a strike that lasts three weeks. When they resume work, disaster follows. The lack of activity in the mine has caused the water to back up and the mine's foundations collapse, resulting in many deaths. This episode drew on Herzl's experience as the *Neue Freie Presse* correspondent in Paris (1891–5), where he covered, among other events, the long 1891 strike at the coal mines of St Etienne in central France that ended in a catastrophic collapse of one of the main mines. Herzl also covered the big miners' strike in 1892 at Carmeaux in southern France, where a miner, Calvignac, was elected mayor of Carmeaux, and the company that owned and ran the mine fired him for allegedly neglecting his work. These reports made Herzl aware of the coal mines as sites of labour disputes and political showdowns.[122]

The collapse of the mine ruins von Schramm financially, whereas Rheinberg's investment is secured thanks to Wasserstein's aptness and timing at buying and selling shares. The irate von Schramm accuses Samuel in particular and the Jews in general of conspiring to destroy him. Samuel strikes him in the face, and in the ensuing duel is killed by the Prussian cavalry captain. Samuel's last words are: 'O Jews, my brethren, they won't let you live again until – until you . . . I want to – get – out! Out – of – the – ghetto!'[123] In place of the ellipsis, the original text contained the following words: 'until you learn how to die'.[124]

At the beginning of the chapter Herzl's striking confession, 'In the special instance of this play, I want to hide my genitals more than any other time', was quoted but commentary upon it deferred. I would like to address it now by bringing into the discussion Daniel Boyarin. Drawing on George Mosse's pioneering work,[125] Boyarin has developed a thought-provoking argument on the gender implications of anti-Semitism, the masculinity of bourgeois Jews in Central Europe and Herzl's Zionism.[126] Discussing the well-known episode of Freud going to the theatre on 5 January 1898 to see *Das neue Ghetto*, after which he claimed to have dreamt his famous 'My Son the Myops' dream, Boyarin comments that this 'intertextual meeting' of Herzl's Zionism and Freud's psychoanalysis was used to understand Freud's 'psychobiography', but thinks that its significance is broader. He proceeds to suggest that

> [o]ne of the most significant aspects of 'My Son the Myops' dream is the way that it produces a conjunction of political and sexual meanings. Freud's dream of a safe haven clearly thematizes a positive affect for Zionism, but Zionism for Freud, as indeed for Herzl, was not simply a political program. It was not even an alternative to assimilation with the culture of Western Europe, but rather a fulfilment of the project of assimilation. Assimilation for these Jews was a sexual and general enterprise, an overcoming of the political and cultural characteristics that marked Jewish men as a 'third sex', as queer in their world. For Freud, Zionism was . . . a return to Phallustine, not to Palestine.[127]

More calmly, Boyarin argues that, formulated in terms of gender, modern anti-Semitism constructed the male Jew as feminine, one whose masculinity was deficient. Such incomplete masculinity was what prevented full integration (within this logic assimilation or emancipation are merely semantic differences) into, and acceptance by, white Christian society, whose members could be German/Aryan, English, ancient Greek or Roman. This is something that haunted the bourgeois Viennese Jews in particular, whose internalization of a putatively feminine masculinity had reached striking depths. Although in significantly differing ways, Zionism was for both Herzl and Freud a way to 'regain' full masculinity, which years of corrupting and degenerating ghetto life, as well as the unbearable presence of *Ostjuden*, had severely undermined.[128] Boyarin is not the first to notice Herzl's alienation from Jews, from himself as a Jew, and his palpable anti-Semitism.[129] In correspondence with Herzl (quoted above), his contemporary Arthur Schnitzler had made disapproving comments about the portrayal of Jews in *The New Ghetto*; Schnitzler reserved a more sharply scathing remark for his 1909 novel *The Road to the Open*, in which a Jewish character confesses: 'I myself have only succeeded up to the present in making the acquaintance of one genuine anti-Semite. I'm afraid I am bound to admit . . . that it was a well-known Zionist leader.'[130]

Boyarin's thesis is important in that it identifies the continuity in Herzl's life and literary and political activity, rather than the alleged rupture of his conversion to Zionism. This underlying continuity is Herzl's obsessive need to prove and render complete his masculinity so that he, and later the Jews who as a collective stood in his way with their obstinate exilic femininity, would be accepted as equal by white Christian men. This does not mean that his recognition – similar to Lazare's – of the erection of a new ghetto was not an important development. Rather, it signifies that all his thoughts about the Jewish Question and about politics – conversion to Christianity, socialism or Zionism, duelling or colonizing – were fundamentally underlain by this one obsession, a central feature of which was the emphasis upon form at the expense of content, upon the vitalizing impact of the aesthetics of the violent gesture itself as an affirmation of masculinity at the expense of the purpose. Whereas for Lazare anarchism was a world view, Herzl wrote in his brilliant feuilleton (29 April 1892) on the trial of the French anarchist Ravachol: 'The ordinary murderer rushes into the brothel with his loot. Ravachol has discovered another voluptuousness: the voluptuousness of a great idea and of martyrdom.'[131]

*The New Ghetto* indeed marked the beginning of Herzl's turn to Zionism, which, at least in literary terms, culminated in *Altneuland*. It was at one and the same time a compensation for Herzl's own past duelling humiliations, and an aesthetic gesture whereby, ultimately, Jews would learn how to die in a manly and honourable manner in duels and thus be accepted as proper white men. Herzl's insatiable attraction to duelling in his student days in Vienna is well documented. He was a member of the ultra-German nationalist duelling fraternity Albia, from which he was expelled, partly because of the fraternity's growing anti-Semitism. But it is quite plausible that the expulsion also stemmed from the fact that he had avoided a duel in the 'dishonourable' manner reminiscent of Jacob Samuel's first avoidance of von Schramm's challenge.[132] Herzl's confession from his student days is revealing: '[T]he peculiar feeling of impotence, the humiliating consciousness of being incapable! Eunuch, away!'[133] All this culminated in the only fitting resolution Herzl could find for the breaking of the walls of *The New Ghetto*: a duel that makes little sense even within the narrowly masculine confines of the logic of duelling. The strikingly intimate comment Herzl made to Schnitzler upon completing the play, with which this chapter opened, can now be revisited. By saying, 'In the special instance of this play, I want to hide my genitals even more than any other time',[134] Herzl sought to acquire, at least in a literary way, the *Mensur*, the scar incurred in a duel and a masculine sign inscribed on the body, one that would erase the scar of circumcision.

The final stage of Herzl's conversion to Zionism and his becoming a sovereign settler, whose literary articulation I will discuss in this chapter's conclusion, was his project of making the Jews acceptable as Western men by colonizing a territory for a Jewish state in the East. As Boyarin powerfully puts it: 'His [Herzl's] final medication resulted ultimately in the inscription of this masculinity on the body of Palestine and on the body of the Palestinians.'[135]

## A settler's utopian colonialism

All the means we need, we ourselves must create them, like Robinson Crusoe on his island – your readers will surely understand this hint. In the days to come the story of Zionism's growth will be like a wonderful novel. (Herzl in an interview to the London Zionist journal, Young Israel, July 1898)

Altneuland begins in fin de siècle Jewish Vienna. Dr Friedrich Loewenberg is a young, professional, well-educated man, with little employment or prospect thereof, who spends most of his time in a Vienna café. His life is centred on the unfounded hope of marrying Ernestine Loeffler, the love of his life and daughter of the wealthy owner of Moritz Loeffler & Co. He is devastated by the announcement of Ernestine's betrothal to another man. On the verge of contemplating the worst Friedrich remembers a strange advertisement his friend Schiffman gave him at the café: 'Wanted, an educated, desperate young man willing to make a last experiment with his life. Apply N.O. Body, this office.' Loewenberg replies and goes to meet the impressively large 'Adalbert von Könighoff, a royal Prussian officer and Christian German nobleman'.

Könighoff is the Junker who will accept the Holy Land Jews as proper men, after his literary ancestor Count von Schramm had rejected their exilic ancestors – even the one who had challenged him to a duel – in The New Ghetto. Könighoff had been to another settlers' colony, America, where he had made a huge fortune, changing his name to Kingscourt in the process. His younger wife having been unfaithful, Kingscourt decides to withdraw from humankind to an island in the Pacific. Since his only company consists of two servants, one 'a mute negro' and the other a Tahitian – not real human solace for a man of such civilized pedigree – Kingscourt seeks a young companion who will commit himself to being at his disposal and who will outlive him. Before leaving Vienna for ever, Loewenberg gives the money he receives from Kingscourt to an immigrant Jewish family, from Lithuania as the name Littwak suggests, who are on the verge of starvation. He disappears before the Littwaks and their children, David and Miriam, get a chance to thank him.

On board the magnificent yacht, at Kingscourt's behest, they stop in Palestine, which, apart from a moonlit Jerusalem, leaves no lasting impression. The two decades spent on the island are glossed over quickly. In 1923 Kingscourt and Loewenberg, on their way to take another glance at Europe, anchor again in the Palestinian port of Haifa. They are identified instantly, though by sheer coincidence, by David Littwak, the little Lithuanian boy whose family had been so generously assisted by Loewenberg in Vienna twenty years ago. The royal hospitality extended by David Littwak and his friends to Kingscourt and Loewenberg is the literary way Herzl chooses to describe the magnificent transformation of the Jews and Palestine within two decades, thanks to the Zionist colonization of that land. At the centre of the project stands the New Society as the umbrella organization that oversaw the exit from Europe and the colonization of Palestine, as well as the current administration of the country. Loewenberg and Miriam Littwak are silently betrothed at the novel's very end as Miriam's mother lies dying. Kingscourt also consents to remain in Palestine, unable to resist the spell cast upon him by David Littwak's baby boy, little Fritzschen.

I believe *Altneuland* was not just a utopian novel, as numerous critical and favourable commentators note,[136] but that it is a utopian *colonial* novel. More generally, I think that such an interpretation of *Altneuland* raises the possibility that colonialism is always potentially present in utopian literature, even though this does not mean that each and every utopian text is perforce colonial. Such potential comes to the fore if the tendency to read utopia almost exclusively in a temporal way is tempered by awareness of utopia's spatial consequences. As Miss Adela Quested reflects in E. M. Forster's *A Passage to India* while the cactus thorns are removed from her skin, 'In space things touch, in time things part.'[137] The importance of the spatial dimension to reading literature is not confined to utopian literature; to cite one notable example, it is evident in Edward Said's insistence on reading *Mansfield Park* not only from the serene counties of the south of England but also from Antigua, whose slave labour sustained Mansfield Park.[138] *Altneuland* contains not only movement in time – from the old biblical land to its putative renewal, and from the early 1900s to the 1920s – but also a movement from Europe to Palestine: just as in the Exodus myth the passage is not just from bondage to freedom but also from Egypt to Canaan. A case in point is a stimulating exchange between Perry Anderson and Fredric Jameson, to which I will now turn.[139]

The exchange itself is focused on the likelihood and desirability of utopian energies as a possible progressive politics, and whether the literary release of such energies corresponds to periods of calm before revolutionary eruptions, to the 'revolutionary whirlwinds themselves', or both. As far as the present discussion is concerned, the point is not the politics itself. It is, rather, that the exchange seems to be underpinned by the assumption that the only dimension that matters is the temporal. Thus Anderson cites Jameson's formulation: 'Ontologies of the present demand archaeologies of the future, not forecasts of the past',[140] and entitles his response 'The River of *Time*'. Among the numerous works mentioned are Edward Bellamy's *Looking Backward* (1888) and Theodor Hertzka's *Freiland* (1890). Anderson is exclusively concerned with the fact that they were composed during the relatively calm period that preceded the first two decades of the twentieth century, and that this therefore supports the correlation Jameson identifies, even though he questions the correlation's comprehensive validity.[141] Yet Bellamy's work and American utopianism, however progressively communitarian it was, cannot be extricated from the spatial drive to colonize the continent's west and all that this entailed. Similarly, Hertzka's utopia was thought to be at the heart of the attempt to build a German Empire. The writing of *Freiland* is inextricable from that attempt. Progressive as it was, the utopian society imagined in *Freiland* the book and Freiland the place too would be realized not only in the future but also in colonial Africa. In other words, the utopian imagination requires not only a time at which better human society will exist but also a place that is construed as sufficiently virginal and unstructured – empty, in the Zionist case – to facilitate its construction from scratch.

Herzl began to conceive his novel in the summer of 1899 and, while travelling in Central Europe, on 30 August decided to call it *Altneuland*, inspired by *Altneusynagoge*, Prague's main synagogue. The book was completed on 30 April 1902, and was published at the end of September by the Leipzig press Hermann, Seemann, Nachfolger. The first English publication was in serial instalments from October 1902 onwards in the US Zionist monthly, *The Maccabean*.[142] Herzl quickly clarified that his book was utopian only in a limited sense in a note attached to the copy he gave to Lord Rothschild: 'There will, of course, be stupid people who, because I have chosen the *form* of a Utopia which has been used by Plato and Thomas More, will declare the *cause* to be a Utopia. I fear no such misunderstanding in your case.'[143] I agree only in part with the Dutch Orientalist L. M. C. van der Hoeven Leonhard and with Muhammad Ali Khalidi that '*Altneuland* was written by Herzl primarily for the world, not for the Zionists. It had propagandistic aims: Herzl wanted to win over non-Jewish opinion for Zionism.'[144] It is problematic, I think, to surmise that Herzl was purely tactical and propagandistic, for, as I showed earlier, gaining acceptance from Christian Europeans, especially Germans, was for him the only acceptance that truly mattered. When M. A. Khalidi points out that a central theme in the novel is to bring Kingscourt, the Prussian Junker who is not innocent of anti-Semitic tendencies, to accept the newly created paradise and even decide to stay, he is absolutely correct,[145] except that in my view Herzl was not thinking in a merely propagandistic way. His belief that having a successful colonial European-like venture in the East was the ultimate path to admission into the West was a genuine one. The need for this admission, which earlier had expressed itself in the duel and honourable death, was too fundamental for Herzl to be ascribed solely to tactical 'marketing' on his part. Of course he addressed it to Christian Europeans, for it was from them, from Kingscourt, that he sought acceptance and approval.

There is another, related, point which is highly significant. Shlomo Avineri, a notable representative of the Zionist position with a veneer of liberalism, not only reinforces Herzl's anxiety about *Altneuland*'s utopian nature, but also points out that the novel evinces its author's 'tolerance and universalistic humanitarianism, characteristic of his Central European outlook and his impeccable vision of civil rights as related to the Palestinian Arabs'. Avineri further notes that Herzl did not anticipate that the native Arabs would resist the Zionist project as a national movement.[146] As M. A. Khalidi observes, however, the distinction between civil and national recognition of the indigenous population ignores the fact that in *Altneuland* Herzl does not explain what happened to that population, which at the turn of the century was by far the majority in Palestine.[147] The argument that the book is fiction is not a sufficient explanation for the fact that between 1903 and 1923 Palestine's Arabs vanish, especially in view of the insistence of Herzl and his followers upon the novel's realist vision. The disappearance of the Arabs in the novel, with very few exceptions such as the Orientalist portrayal of the token Arab, Reschid Bey, is a pivotal point that exposes the literary and political imagination of the *fin de siècle* sovereign settler.

What Herzl did and wrote while intermittently writing *Altneuland* is crucial. First is what Herzl had not issued publicly but was perceptively noticed by van der Hoeven Leonhard in her careful examination of Herzl's diary. 'The existing landed property', she observes, 'was to be gently expropriated, any subsequent resale to the original owners was prohibited, and all the immovables had to remain in exclusively Jewish hands. The poor population was to be worked across the frontier "unbemkert" (surreptitiously), after having for Jewish benefit rid the country of any existing wild animals, such as snakes. This population was to be refused all employment in the land of its birth.'[148] Then there is the rarely noticed contribution (one of many) by the outstanding scholar of early Zionism, Adolf Böhm, who published a remarkable document he had found in the Herzl Archives in Vienna. This document was a draft of a hopeful agreement – the charter Herzl was indefatigably seeking – which never materialized, between the World Zionist Organization and Abdul Hamid II's Ottoman government regarding the 'privileges, rights, liabilities, and duties of the Jewish Ottoman Land Company (JOLC) for the settlement of Palestine and Syria'. The document has been studied by Walid Khalidi who has also provided an English translation.[149]

Although the document bears neither date nor autograph, Khalidi, drawing on Böhm, thinks that it was drafted during negotiations with the Ottomans – and the concomitant writing of *Altneuland* – between the summer of 1901 and early 1902. He asserts that it was written by Herzl and his intimately close friend, the Hungarian Jewish Orientalist Arminius Vàmbéry, who had important contacts in Abdul Hamid's court. The importance of the document is that it reveals Herzl's non-public vision, and therefore complements such public articulations as the Basle Programme (1897), *Der Judenstaat* (1896) and *Altneuland*. What Herzl had in mind, according to Böhm, was 'the form in which in the past the English and also the Dutch government had bestowed on private companies (for instance, the East India Company) rights to a newly acquired territory'.[150] The proposed charter was to grant Palestine and Syria to the JOLC as 'Privileged Territories', in which the company could do, within certain confines, almost anything. For our discussion, Clause III is especially pertinent, for it gave the JOLC complete freedom to transfer the native inhabitants from Palestine to other locations 'procured by it [the JOLC] in other provinces and territories in the Ottoman Empire'. This would be accompanied by financial compensation to the transferred native inhabitants.[151] As is better known, what Herzl offered the Ottoman Empire in return was to rid it of its debilitating Public Debt to European creditors, which had driven it to declare bankruptcy already in the 1870s.

We may now rejoin David Littwak and his friends as they lead Kingscourt and Loewenberg to an election gathering at the most successful and prestigious cooperative settlement established by the New Society, Neudorf (New Village – it must be borne in mind that this utopian society is highly civilized, i.e., German speaking), just above Lake Tiberias. The coming elections in the New Society are a face-off between the party of Rabbi Geyer, who used to be conveniently anti-Zionist but now runs on the platform that non-Jews should not be admitted to the New Society, and David Littwak's party, which is appalled by the idea that something as contrary to the essence and history of the New Society as Geyer's ideology might prevail. To cut short the unbearable suspense, the Littwak party winds up winning and he is elected president of the New Society.

During the gathering, David Littwak delivers a lecture in which he justifies his position through a historical overview of progressive utopia and scientific achievement, of which Neudorf is an example.[152] What is striking in this lecture is, firstly, the complete absence of reference to native Arabs. Making his main point about being a link in the chain of cooperative progress, Littwak says: 'How could we have achieved results that no one else had achieved here before? No one, I mean to say, except the German Protestant farmers who founded several colonies in this country toward the end of the last century.' The Arab peasants do not exist even as an undeveloped backdrop in order to aggrandize the Zionist achievement. 'Don't imagine I am jesting when I say that Neudorf was built not in Palestine', Littwak continues, 'but elsewhere. It was built in England, in America, in France and in Germany. It was evolved out of experiments, books, and dreams.'[153] In the rest of his survey Littwak mentions utopian novels, copies of which Herzl possessed, such as Hertzka's *Freiland* (1890) and Bellamy's *Looking Back* (1888).[154] He also enumerates important land-marks of cooperative history, such as the Ralahine community in Ireland in the 1830s, and the Rochdale Pioneers in Lancashire from the 1840s on, the flannel weavers who laid the foundation for consumers' cooperatives that pervade *Altneuland's* New Society.[155] It is even possible to suggest, thanks to a comment made to Littwak by a boy named Jacob that Neudorf's library holds a copy of the history of the Rochdale Pioneers, that the monograph Herzl read was that of G. J. Holyoake, who also became an important figure in the history of American utopia.[156]

The great extent to which Herzl's world and imagination were ingrained in that complex of European progress, science and colonialism is manifest. A striking example is a visit to the laboratory of the internationally famous Professor Steineck. Asked by Loewenberg what he is working on, the narrator remarks that 'the scientist's eyes grew dreamy' and he replies: 'the opening up of Africa'. When the perplexed Kingscourt repeats the statement, the professor explains that it has to do with finding a cure for malaria. 'We have overcome [malaria] here in Palestine', he says, 'thanks to the drainage of the swamps, canalization, and the eucalyptus forests. But conditions are different in Africa. The same measures cannot be taken there because the prerequisite – mass immigration – is not present. The white colonist goes under in Africa. That country can be opened up to civilization only after malaria has been subdued. Only then will enormous areas become available for the surplus populations of Europe. And only then will the proletarian masses find a healthy outlet. Understand?'[157]

The way the Exodus was re-enacted and the Jews left Europe in order to colonize Palestine is a tediously detailed yet not uninteresting narrative in the novel, which is recounted by Joseph Levy, the overall director of this massive operation, whose voice emanates from a gramophone. This narrative reflects the influence on Herzl's literary imagination of the combined effect of the first wave of capitalist globalization (1870–1914), in which it was possible to envision people and goods being moved across the globe in an orderly and coordinated manner, the centrality of technology for empire, especially of railroads and advanced trains in the German case, and imperialism in which colonies can be carved into rubrics on maps and imagined empty in order to start a new world from scratch.[158]

The prologue leading to the assembly where the Exodus narrative is recounted is the embodiment of what Zionism was in Herzl's consciousness, and what it would become: a sort of amalgamated theology of nationalism and colonialism, comparable, with its own historical particularities, to other instances of white settlers' ventures in the modern era. The party begins at the Passover Seder hosted at the old Littwaks' villa on the shore of Lake Tiberias. The Seder is a United Colours of Benetton à la *fin de siècle*. There is Kingscourt, the Russian priest from Sepphoris, the Franciscan monk who came from Cologne a quarter of a century earlier, Father Ignaz the clergyman, the Reverend Mr Hopkins – but of course no Arab clergy, neither Muslim nor Christian, nor Jewish. At the end of the Seder David Littwak deems it appropriate for everybody to listen together to Joseph Levy, to create continuity between the Old Exodus and the New (and implicitly to negate everything in between). He argues for the continuity by invoking the foundational ingredients of technology, colonialism, the move to the East, and a land empty of natives:

> First we shall finish our Seder after the manner of our forefathers, and then we shall let the new era tell you how it was born. Once more there was an Egypt, and again a happy exodus – under twentieth century conditions, of course, and with modern equipment. It could not have been otherwise. The age of machinery had to come first. The great nations had to grow mature enough for a colonial policy. There had to be great screw steamers, with a speed of 22 knots an hour, to supersede the sailing vessels. In brief, the whole stock-in-trade of the year 1900 was needed. We had to become new men, and yet remain loyal to our ancient race. And we had to win the sympathy of the other nations and their rulers. Otherwise, the whole enterprise would have been impossible.[159]

# Notes

1 I thank Vinay Lal for pointing out this essay.
2 Cited from R. H. Feldman (ed.), *Hannah Arendt, The Jew as Pariah: Jewish Identity and Politics in the Modern Age*, New York: Grove, 1978, p. 131.
3 'Excerpts from the Correspondence Between Theodor Herzl and Arthur Schnitzler (1892–1895)', trans. J. Carmichael, *Midstream*, 6 (1960), pp. 55–6.
4 J. Kornberg, *Theodor Herzl: From Assimilation to Zionism*, Bloomington and Indianapolis: Indiana University Press, 1993, p. 152.
5 H. Arendt, 'From the Dreyfus Affair to France Today', *Jewish Social Studies*, 4/3 (July 1942), pp. 208–40. This was enhanced by a review I was writing of I. Zertal, *Death and the Nation: History, Memory, Politics*, Or Yehuda: Dvir, 2002. See G. Piterberg, 'Hannah Arendt in Tel Aviv', *New Left Review*, 21 (May–June 2003), pp. 137–47.
6 M. Marrus, *The Politics of Assimilation: A Study of the French Community at the Time of the Dreyfus Affair*, Oxford: Oxford University Press, 1971, pp. 179–80, and Kornberg, op. cit., p. 200 n. 25.
7 C. Ginzburg, 'Latitude, Slaves and the Bible: An Experiment in Microhistory', *Critical Inquiry*, 31:3 (Spring 2005), pp. 665–83. For comparison with a previous pronouncement on microhistory see Ginzburg's 'Microhistory: Two or Three Things That I Know about It', *Critical Inquiry*, 20/1 (1993), pp. 10–36.
8 P. van Passen, 'Paris, 1891–1895: A Study of the Transition in Theodor Herzl's Life', in M. W. Weisgal (ed.), *Theodor Herzl: A Memorial*, New York: The Palestine Society, 1929, p. 38. Marrus too feels that the two may have met already in the autumn of 1894. See Marrus, op. cit., pp. 179–80. Marrus also remarks that 'the fact that the two men reached similar conclusions is significant' (p. 180). I agree only in so far as they both concluded that assimilation had failed and that a new and more insidious ghetto had been created.
9 N. Wilson, *Bernard-Lazare: Antisemitism and the Problem of Jewish Identity in Late Nineteenth-Century France*, Cambridge: Cambridge University Press, 1978, p. 144.
10 Ibid., emphasis added.
11 Ibid., pp. 3 65 and 222–53; M. Marrus, 'Bernard Lazare: An Anarchist's Zionism', *Midstream*, 23/6 (June–July 1977), pp. 35–42, and *The Politics of Assimilation*, Oxford: Oxford University Press, 1971, pp. 164–96 and 243–82; E. Silberner, 'Lazare and Zionism', *Shivat Zion*, 2–3 (1951–2), pp. 328–63, and R. S. Wistrich, *Revolutionary Jews from Marx to Trotsky*, London: George G. Harrap, pp. 133–53.
12 M. Löwy, *Redemption and Utopia: Jewish Libertarian Thought in Central Europe. A Study in Elective Affinity*, Stanford: Stanford University Press, [1988] 1992.
13 Ibid., pp. 178–9.
14 Ibid., p. 183.
15 Ibid., pp. 186–7.
16 Appeared in Paris: Léon Chailley, 1894. An early English translation is *Antisemitism, Its History and Causes*, New York: The International Library, 1903.

A partial and because of its modern history unavoidably archaic Hebrew edition is *Ha-Antishemiyyut, sibbotheha ve hishtalshelut hitpathuta*, Vilna: Biblioteka, 1913. Most recent is the English edition introduced by R. Wistrich, Lincoln and London: University of Nebraska Press, 1995.

17 See for instance B. Lazare, 'Juifs et israélites' and 'L'antisémitisme et ses causes générales', both in *Entretiens Politiques et Littéraires*, September 1890 and September 1892 respectively, and 'Juifs et antisémitisme', *Evénement*, 23 December 1893.

18 Cited in Marrus, *The Politics of Assimilation*, p. 170.

19 Marrus, *The Politics of Assimilation*, p. 174. Marrus argues interestingly that at the very end of the book Lazare's view changes somewhat and anticipates his imminent transformation (p. 177).

20 Wilson, op. cit., pp. 86–7 and p. 87 n. 34.

21 Löwy, op. cit., pp. 190–1, and Wistrich, Introduction to the 1995 edition of Lazare, *Antisemitism*, pp. viii–xi.

22 Wistrich, op. cit., pp. 142–3.

23 Kornberg, op. cit., pp. 190–1 and 200.

24 Arendt, op. cit., pp. 195–241, which is concluded with 'Herzl and Lazare', pp. 235–41; cf. Feldman, op. cit., in which only 'Herzl and Lazare' appears on pp. 125–31.

25 Arendt, op. cit., p. 238.

26 See A. Raz-Krakotzkin, 'Binationalism and Jewish Identity: Hannah Arendt and the Question of Palestine', in S. E. Aschheim (ed.), *Hannah Arendt in Jerusalem*, Berkeley: University of California Press, 2001, pp. 165–81, and R. J. Bernstein, *Hannah Arendt and the Jewish Question*, Cambridge: Polity Press, pp. 101–23.

27 See n. 24.

28 Much of the Lazare–Herzl correspondence is presented as an appendix to Silberner, op. cit., pp. 349–61. The letter cited was of 4 February 1899, and is probably the longest and most detailed (citation is from p. 358). For a partial English translation see Marrus, *The Politics of Assimilation*, p. 268, and D. Vital, *Zionism: The Formative Years*, Oxford: Oxford University Press, 1982, pp. 71–2.

29 Most of the writing on this and related subjects was done in the period 1897–9. For a helpful survey of these texts see Wilson, op. cit., pp. 226–30.

30 B. Anderson, *Imagined Communities*, London and New York: Verso, 1991 (revised edition), p. 5.

31 H. Arendt, *Rahel Varnhagen: The Life of a Jewess*, Baltimore and London: The Johns Hopkins University Press, 1997, p. 258.

32 B. Lazare, 'Judaism's Social Concept and the Jewish People', in *Job's Dungheap: Essays on Jewish Nationalism and Social Revolution*, ed. H. Arendt, trans. H. L. Binsse, New York: Schocken Books, 1948, pp. 108–28. Originally appeared in *La Grande Revue*, 1 September 1899.

33 A succinct exposition is offered by Marrus, *The Politics of Assimilation*, pp. 180–95, and Wilson, op. cit., pp. 227–52.

34 Cited in Wilson, op. cit., p. 251.

35 B. Lazare, 'Jewish Nationalism', in *Job's Dungheap*, p. 103. Originally a lecture delivered to the Association of Russian Jewish Students, 6 March 1897, and

published as a pamphlet by Publications du Kadimah [Forward Publications], no. 1 (1898).

36 Ibid., p. 66 (emphasis added).

37 Wilson, op. cit., p. 251.

38 Ibid., p. 228.

39 Lazare, Le Nationalisme juif, cited in Wilson, op. cit., pp. 232–3. Originally a lecture delivered to Jewish students in Paris in 1897, which was subsequently (1898) published by Publications du Kadimah. See an English rendering in Lazare, Job's Dungheap, p. 73.

40 Lazare, Job's Dungheap, pp. 105–7, and Wilson, op. cit., pp. 229–30.

41 Marrus, Politics of Assimilation, pp. 245–51.

42 Ibid., p. 251.

43 Cited in Löwy, op. cit., p. 196.

44 Ibid., pp. 196–7.

45 A. Rodrigue, 'Rearticulations of French Jewish Identities after the Dreyfus Affair', Jewish Social Studies, new series, 2:3 (1996), 1–24; idem, 'Léon Halévy and Modern Jewish Historiography', in E. Carlebach et al. (eds.), Jewish History and Jewish Memory, Hanover and London: Brandeis University Press, 1998, pp. 413–27; idem, 'Totems, Taboos, and Jews: Salomon Reinach and the Politics of Scholarship in Fin-de-Siècle France', Jewish Social Studies, new series, 10:2 (2004), 1–20.

46 Rodrigue, 'Halévy', p. 424.

47 Rodrigue, 'Totems', p. 2.

48 Ibid., p. 3.

49 Ibid., p. 7.

50 Ibid., p. 4.

51 Rodrigue, 'Rearticulations', pp. 10 and 11.

52 Ibid., p. 8.

53 Cited in Wilson, op. cit., p. 271.

54 H. Arendt, 'The Jew as Pariah: A Hidden Tradition', in Feldman, op. cit., pp. 67–91. Originally appeared in Jewish Social Studies, 6/2 (April 1944), pp. 99–122.

55 Ibid., p. 76.

56 Ibid., p. 77.

57 Ibid., pp. 78–9.

58 E. Gellner, 'From Königsberg to Manahattan (or Hannah, Rahel, Martin and Elfriede or Thy Neighbour's Gemeinschaft)', in Culture, Identity, and Politics, Cambridge: Cambridge University Press, 1987, p. 75.

59 Cited in H. Arendt, Introduction to W. Benjamin, Illuminations, trans. H. Zohn, New York: Harcourt, Brace & World, 1968, p. 5.

60 See 'Pariah' in the online Oxford English Dictionary.

61 E. Shmueli, 'The "Pariah-People" and Its "Charismatic Leadership": A Revaluation of Max Weber's "Ancient Judaism"', American Academy for Jewish Research, 36 (1968), pp. 167–247, reference pp. 170–1.

62 A. Momigliano, 'A Note on Max Weber's Definition of Judaism as a Pariah-Religion', History and Theory, 19 (1980), pp. 313–18, citation p. 313.

63 Shmueli, op. cit., p. 171 n. 6.

64 Arendt, 'The Jew as Pariah', p. 68.

65 Momigliano, op. cit., p. 315.

66 Both passages cited in ibid., p. 314.

67 Shmueli, op. cit., pp. 195–213.

68 Momigliano, op. cit., p. 314.

69 The letter (29 January 1946) is partially brought in P. Baehr (ed.), *The Portable Hannah Arendt*, London and New York: Penguin, 2000, pp. 25–31. The citation is from p. 26.

70 Although I cannot discuss it here, I should mention Ulrike Weckel's reservations about the application of the term salon to Berlin of that period, as well as about what is in her view excessively idyllic portrayals of these social circles, whatever label is attached to them. See her 'A Lost Paradise of Female Culture? Some Critical Questions Regarding the Scholarship on Late Eighteenth- and Early Nineteenth-Century German Salons', *German History*, 18 (2000), pp. 310–26. I thank David Sabean for pointing out this interesting article to me.

71 See H. T. Tewarson, *Rahel Levin Varnhagen: The Life and Work of a German Jewish Intellectual*, Lincoln and London: The University of Nebraska Press, 1998.

72 E. Young-Bruehl, *Hannah Arendt: For Love of the World*, New Haven: Yale University Press, 1982, pp. 56 and 67–8.

73 Bernstein, op. cit., pp. 15–17; M. R. Marrus, 'Hannah Arendt and the Dreyfus Affair', *New German Critique*, special issue on the nineteenth century (Autumn 1995), p. 158; L. Weissberg, 'In Search of Mother Tongue: Hannah Arendt's German-Jewish Literature', in S. E. Aschheim (ed.), *Hannah Arendt in Jerusalem*, Berkeley: University of California Press, 2001, p. 155 n. 18; and Young-Bruehl, op. cit., pp. 71 and 73. For a concise presentation of Blumenfeld see Sh. Esh, 'Kurt Blumenfeld on the Modern Jew and Zionism', *The Jewish Journal of Sociology*, 6/2 (December 1964), pp. 232–43.

74 The volume of literature on Arendt amounts by now to a scholarly explosion. I have consulted mainly the following: Peter Baehr's Introduction to his edited *Portable*, pp. ix–xvi; S. Benhabib, 'The Pariah and Her Shadow: Hannah Arendt's Biography of Rahel Varnhagen', in *The Reluctant Modernism of Hannah Arendt*, Thousand Oaks: Sage, 1996, pp. 1–35 (a shorter version appeared in *Political Theory*, 23/1 (February 1995), pp. 5–24); Bernstein, op. cit., pp. 1–46; Marrus, 'Dreyfus Affair', pp. 147–63; J. Ring, 'The Pariah as Hero: Hannah Arendt's Political Actor', *Political Theory*, 19/3 (August 1991), pp. 433–52; Weissberg, op. cit., pp. 149–65; Young-Bruehl, op. cit., pp. 42–115.

75 There are four editions: *Rahel Varnhagen: The Life of a Jewess*, London: East and West Library, 1958; *Rahel Varnhagen: Lebensgeschichte einer deutschen Jüdin aus der Romantik*, Munich: Piper, 1959 (later Ullstein, 1975); *Rahel Varnhagen: The Life of a Jewish Woman*, New York: Harcourt Brace Jovanovich, 1974. The most thorough is *Rahel Varnhagen: The Life of a Jewess*, ed. L. Weissberg, trans. R. and C. Winston, Baltimore and London: The Johns Hopkins University Press, 1997. On the history of the publication of the various editions see Weissberg's Introduction to the 1997 edition, pp. 41–54. All references henceforth are to the 1997 edition.

76 Young-Bruehl, op. cit., pp. 85–6.

77 Cited ibid., p. 91. See also Marrus, 'Dreyfus Affair', p. 150.

78 See especially Raz-Krakotzkin, op. cit., pp. 165–81, and G. Piterberg, 'Zion's Rebel Daughter', *New Left Review*, 48 (November–December 2007), pp. 39–59.

79 Arendt, *Rahel Varnhagen*, p. 83. In a letter to the German publisher Klaus Piper, Arendt explicitly said that she had just written the preface she was sending (p. 44, Weissberg's Introduction to the 1997 edition).

80 For Young-Bruehl see especially op. cit., pp. 85–92, and p. 50 ('Hannah Arendt had to tell someone else's story, had to write *Rahel Varnhagen: The Life of a Jewess*, before she freed herself from Martin Heidegger's spell'); and for Benhabib see n. 74 above.

81 Weissberg, Introduction to the 1997 edition, see especially apt formulations on pp. 6 and 13, and Tewarson, op. cit., pp. 3–5. Tewarson is rather strongly critical of Arendt.

82 Arendt, *Rahel Varnhagen*, p. 81.

83 Young-Bruehl, op. cit., p. 56.

84 Weckel, op. cit., p. 312 n. 7.

85 The revealing exchange between Arendt and Piper (and other employees in his press) is cited in Weissberg, Introduction to the 1997 edition, pp. 46–9.

86 For an interesting interpretation see Ring, op. cit., whose article is an attempt to reconcile two types of seemingly irreconcilable political actors in Arendt's thought: that of the classical Greek tradition, and the conscious pariah.

87 Arendt, *Rahel Varnhagen*, pp. 238–39.

88 Ibid., p. 242.

89 Ibid., p. 243.

90 Ibid., pp. 242–9.

91 Ibid., p. 256.

92 Ibid., p. 258.

93 See again Young-Bruehl, op. cit., p. 91, and Marrus, 'Dreyfus Affair', p. 150.

94 S. Bedford, 'Emancipation and Destiny', *Reconstructionist*, 24/16 (12 December 1958), pp. 22–6, citation pp. 22–3.

95 Young-Bruehl, op. cit., pp. 86–7.

96 Weissberg, 'In Search', pp. 155 and 160–1, and Introduction to the 1997 edition, pp. 50–1.

97 M. Löwy, *Fire Alarm*, London and New York: Verso, 2005, especially pp. 14–16.

98 Arendt, Introduction to Benjamin, *Illuminations*, p. 39.

99 Ibid., pp. 45–6.

100 Weckel, op. cit., p. 312 n. 7.

101 Cited in Weissberg's Introduction to the 1997 edition, p. 50.

102 Bernstein, op. cit., p. 30.

103 Arendt, *Rahel Varnhagen*, p. 259.

104 Ibid.

105 I have not yet found a way to integrate into the discussion, without expanding it to unmanageable proportions, the very important figure of Max Nordau. For a fresh interpretation see M. Stanislawski, *Zionism and the Fin de Siècle*, Berkeley: University of California Press, pp. 36–98.

106 'Benny Morris: On Ethnic Cleansing', Editor's Introduction, *New Left Review*, 26 (March–April 2004).

107 B. Morris, 'Commander Who Was also a Nice Person', *Haaretz Books Magazine*, 21 April 2004.

108 For an Israeli perspective see A. Rubinstein, *From Herzl to Rabin: 100 Years of Zionism*, Jerusalem and Tel Aviv: Schocken, 1997, and for a French one A. Dieckhoff, *The Invention of a Nation: Zionist Thought and the Making of Modern Israel*, New York: Columbia University Press, 2003.

109 A. Raz-Krakotzkin, 'Religious Colonial Nationalism', *Haaretz Books Supplement*, 24 January 1996.

110 C. E. Schorske, 'Politics in a New Key: An Austrian Trio', in *Fin-de-Siècle Vienna: Politics and Culture*, New York: Vintage Books, 1981, pp. 116–81. First appeared as an article in *The Journal of Modern History*, 39 (1967).

111 Ibid., p. 160.

112 Ibid., p. 167.

113 In addition to Schorske, see also Kornberg, op. cit., pp. 35–59 ('Herzl as German Nationalist'). Kornberg, it should be pointed out, disagrees with Schorske on the extent and depth of Herzl's German nationalism (pp. 51–8). I think that, although Kornberg's study as a whole is a major contribution to the understanding of Herzl, this particular argument is a tad apologetic.

114 T. Herzl, *Die Judensache (The Jewish Cause): Diaries 1895–1904*, 3 vols, Jerusalem: Mossad Bialik and the Zionist Library, 1997–2001, intro. Sh. Avineri, Hebrew trans. J. Wenkert, editorial notes M. Heymann. Citation from the entry of 5 July 1895, vol. 1, p. 200. This is doubtless the best edition of Herzl's diaries in terms of annotation and references.

115 T. Herzl, *Zionist Writings: Essays and Addresses*, trans. H. Zohn, New York: Herzl Press, 1973, vol. 1, pp. 18–19.

116 A. Elon, *Herzl*, New York: Holt, Rinehart and Winston, 1975, p. 259.

117 Schorske, op. cit., p. 163.

118 Ibid., p. 165.

119 Ibid.

120 All references are to T. Herzl, *The New Ghetto: A Play in Four Acts*, trans. H. Norden, New York: The Theodor Herzl Foundation, 1955.

121 Ibid., p. 32.

122 T. Herzl, *From Boulanger to Dreyfus, 1891–1895: Reports and Political Articles from Paris*, trans. S. Meltzer, ed. A. Bein and M. Schaerf, 3 vols, Jerusalem: The Zionist Library, 1974, vol. 1, p. 47 (December 1891 on St Etienne) and pp. 157–65 (October and November 1892 on Carmeaux).

123 Herzl, *The New Ghetto*, p. 80.

124 Kornberg, op. cit., p. 146.

125 See especially G. L. Mosse, *Nationalism and Sexuality: Middle-Class Morality and Sexual Norms in Modern Europe*, Madison: University of Wisconsin Press, 1985, and *The Image of Man: The Creation of Modern Masculinity*, New York: Oxford University Press, 1996.

126 D. Boyarin, 'The Colonial Masquerade: Zionism, Gender, Imitation', *Theory and Criticism*, 11 (Winter 1997), pp. 123–44, and 'Outing Freud's Zionism, or, the Bitextuality of the Diaspora Jew', in C. Patton and B. Sánchez-Eppler (eds), *Queer Diasporas*, Durham, NC, and London: Duke University Press, 2000, pp. 71–104.

127 Boyarin, 'Freud's Zionism', p. 72.

128 See especially Boyarin, 'The Colonial Masquerade', pp. 125–32.
129 P. Loewenberg, 'Theodor Herzl: Nationalism and Politics', in *Decoding the Past: The Psychohistorical Approach*, Berkeley: University of California Press, [1969] 1985, pp. 101–35.
130 Cited in Kornberg, op. cit., p. 154.
131 T. Herzl, *From Boulanger to Dreyfus*, vol. 1, p. 100. For an English rendering see Elon, op. cit., p. 105. Schorske (op. cit., p. 154) and Boyarin ('Colonial Masquerade', p. 130) also note the importance of this observation.
132 Herzl's membership in the Albia and his duelling ordeals are thoroughly described by Elon and Kornberg (see especially Kornberg, op. cit., pp. 66–71). The autobiographical possibilities in *The New Ghetto* are interestingly raised by Kornberg, op. cit., pp. 148–52.
133 Kornberg, op. cit., p. 150.
134 Ibid., p. 152.
135 Boyarin, 'Colonial Masquerade', p. 139.
136 For an important instance of the latter see Sh. Avineri's introduction to the *Diaries*, 'From "the Cause of the Jews" to "the State of the Jews": Herzl's Path to Jewish National Consciousness', vol. 1, pp. 13–51. For a recent critical interpretation see M. A. Khalidi, 'Utopian Zionism or Zionist Proselytism: A Reading of Herzl's *Altneuland*', *Journal of Palestine Studies*, 30/4 (Summer 2001), pp. 55–68.
137 E. M. Forster, *A Passage to India*, New York: Harcourt, Brace and Co., 1924, p. 193.
138 E. W. Said, *Culture and Imperialism*, New York: Vintage Books, 1993, pp. 80–97.
139 F. Jameson, 'The Politics of Utopia', and P. Anderson, 'The River of Time', both in *New Left Review*, 25 (January–February 2004), pp. 35–54, and 26 (March–April 2004), pp. 67–77 respectively.
140 Anderson, op. cit., p. 67.
141 Ibid., pp. 68–9.
142 Herzl, *Diaries*, vol. 2, pp. 139 and 468, and vol. 3, pp. 14, 295, 296 and 354.
143 Cited in M. A. Khalidi, op. cit., p. 59.
144 L. M. C. van der Hoeven Leonhard, 'Shlomo and David in Palestine, 1907', in W. Khalidi (ed.), *From Haven to Conquest: Readings in Zionism and the Palestine Problem until 1948*, Beirut: The Institute for Palestine Studies, 1971, pp. 115–25 (citation p. 119; first appeared in Dutch in 1950), and M. A. Khalidi, op. cit., pp. 61–3. It should be added that Herzl hastily sent copies of his book to European rulers and dignitaries, including the German Kaiser and the Ottoman sultan.
145 M. A. Khalidi, op. cit., pp. 62–3.
146 It is probably not coincidental that M. A. Khalidi's attention and mine was drawn to the same reference: Sh. Avineri, *The Making of Modern Zionism: Intellectual Origins of the Jewish State*, London: Weidenfeld & Nicolson: 1981, p. 99. The same argument is expressed in Avineri, 'From "the Cause of the Jews"'.
147 M. A. Khalidi, op. cit., p. 58.
148 Van der Hoeven Leonhard, op. cit., pp. 118–19.
149 W. Khalidi, 'The Jewish-Ottoman Land Company: Herzl's Blueprint for the

Colonization of Palestine', *Journal of Palestine Studies*, 22/2 (Winter 1993), pp. 30–47.

150 Ibid., pp. 30–1.

151 Ibid., pp. 44–5.

152 T. Herzl, *Old-New Land*, trans. L. Levensohn, New York: Bloch, 1941, pp. 141–55.

153 Ibid., p. 143.

154 Ibid., pp. 145 and 146. I possess copies of the complete card catalogue of Herzl's library located at the central Zionist Archive and the Herzl Museum, both in Jerusalem. I am deeply grateful to Dror Ze'evi for helping me obtain these copies.

155 Ibid., pp. 148–51.

156 Ibid., p. 148. The monograph is G. J. Holyoake, *The History of the Rochdale Pioneers*, London: Swan Sonnenschein, [1892] 1900.

157 Herzl, *Old-New Land*, p. 170.

158 Ibid., pp. 192–232. I intend to return to this passage and examine it in comparison to its equivalents in other literary works of utopia such as Hertzka's *Freiland*.

159 Herzl, *Old–New Land*, p. 191. The Seder is presented in pp. 185–91.

# 2

# The Zionist Colonization of Palestine in the Comparative Context of Settler Colonialism

'A crusade is a war to recover the Holy Land from the paynim.'

'Which Holy Land?'

'Why, *the* Holy Land – there ain't but one.'

'What do *we* want of it?'

'Why, can't you understand? It's in the hands of the paynim, and it's our duty to take it away from them.'

'How did we come to let them git hold of it?'

'We didn't come to let them git hold of it. They always had it.'

'Why, Tom, then it must belong to them, don't it?'

'Why, of course it does. Who said it didn't?'

I studied over it, but couldn't seem to git at the right of it, no way. I says:

'It's too many for me, Tom Sawyer. If I had a farm and it was mine, and another person wanted it, would it be right for him to–'

'Oh, shucks! You don't know enough to come in when it rains, Huck Finn. It ain't a farm, it's entirely different. You see, it's like this. They own the land, just the mere land, and that's all they *do* own; but it was our folks, our Jews and Christians, that made it holy, and so they haven't any business to be there defiling it. It's a shame, and we ought not to stand it a minute. We ought to march against them and take it away from them.'

'Why, it does seem to me it's the most mixed up thing I ever see! Now, if I had a farm and another person–'

'Don't I tell you it hasn't got anything to do with farming? Farming

is business, just common low-down business: that's all it is, it's all you can say for it; but this is higher, this is religious, and totally different.'
'Religious to go and take the land away from the people that owns it?'
'Certainly; it's always been considered so.'
(Mark Twain, *Tom Sawyer Abroad*, 1894[1])

They [Arabs surrounding the camp in Palestine] reminded me much of Indians, did these people. They had but little clothing, but such as they had was fanciful in character and fantastic in its arrangement. Any little absurd gewgaw or gimcrack they had they disposed in such a way as to attract attention most readily. They sat in silence, and with tireless patience watched our every motion with that vile, uncomplaining impoliteness which is so truly Indian, and which makes a white man so nervous and uncomfortable and savage that he wants to exterminate the whole tribe.
(Mark Twain, *Innocents Abroad*, 1872[2])

The new Jews were no more familiar to me [than the old kind], perhaps less. They were just the opposite, but I never saw them; they were not to be seen in Jerusalem. They were far away. They breed in the kibbutzim, in the Palmach, in the Negev and Galilee. Always elsewhere. They were tough and blond and tender and powerful and uncomplicated. They toiled over the land all day and in the evening, made wild love to the kibbutz girls, and then later at night picked up their submachine guns, and dashed out to smash the hostile red Indians or Arabs, before calling it a day.
(Amos Oz, 'Imagining the Other: 1', 1993[3])

'We bring you civilization,' said the stranger.
'We're the masters of time
come to inherit this land of yours.
March in Indian file so we can tally you
on the face of the lake, corpse by corpse.
Keep marching, so the Gospels may thrive!
We want God all to ourselves
because the best Indians are dead Indians
in the eyes of our Lord.'
(Mahmoud Darwish, 'Speech of the Red Indian', 1992[4])

## What is the Hebrew University?

By his own admission, David Myers begins in a mischievous way an essay that issued from a conference on the founding of the Hebrew University in Jerusalem in 1924–5. In it, Myers gives a brief synopsis of a foundation story that might sound like the Hebrew University's but is actually that of the American University of Beirut. Clarifying the exercise, Myers comments: 'I believe it is fair to say that both universities were mired in a tangled web of relations symptomatic of colonialism.'[5] Given the loaded significance of the *c* word, Myers further clarifies what he means – and as importantly, what he doesn't mean – by colonialism. And what he does mean is a sort of colonial relations between the Jewish European and (less so) American benefactors and governors of the university as a metropole that tried to make its preferences and sensibilities prevail, and the 'Palestine-based Jews' who were actually creating the university as the colonized. He also explicitly states: 'my concern here is not the nature of the relations between Jewish settlers and Arab inhabitants in Mandatory Palestine'.[6]

Myers's exercise constitutes a convenient foyer through which to enter the edifice of the Zionist Israeli project in Palestine and to unfold its history within the comparative context of settler nationalism or colonialism. He chooses not to concern himself with the interaction between the Jewish settlers and Arab natives, but if we do precisely that, then the comparison of the two universities reveals an acute difference between what could be termed the two master types of colonialism, namely, metropole colonialism and settler colonialism (there are finer sub-divisions that I will return to later). The American University of Beirut was founded and managed by missionaries who did not seek to create a national home for themselves in Lebanon and Syria, and the purpose of the institution they established – however colonially condescending that purpose might be – was to educate the indigenous people. The Hebrew University was established by settlers who sought to colonize Palestine and make it their national patrimony, and the purpose of the institution they founded was to educate the community of settlers present and future, and implicitly to exclude from it the indigenous Palestinian Arabs.

The point here is not to suggest a value-hierarchy whereby metropole colonialism is somehow better than settler colonialism (even though I do think that, from the perspective of the colonized, whereas the former is bad news, the latter is *real* bad news). Rather, it is to take advantage of Myers's mischievous exercise, which elegantly sidesteps the heart of the matter, to begin discussing Zionism's comparability to other cases of settler nationalism as the main way of properly understanding it. To anticipate the taxonomy and terminology that will concern us shortly, the Hebrew

University was from its inception a pure settlement colony, in a structural rather than strictly literal sense. This structural essence overrode the intentions and politics of its individual founders, such as the university's American Jewish president J. L. Magnes. Together with Hannah Arendt, as we saw in Chapter One, he was one of the staunchest advocates of a binational state in Palestine, and persisted in pursuing this position till the period leading up to the 1948 war. Yet the university he helped to build and develop came to resemble in principle the kibbutzim and the underlying organization of labour Zionism, the Histadrut: institutions that addressed different needs in the formation of a pure settlement colony, which with time would yield a settlers' nation-state. This state – exclusively of and for the settlers and their diaspora 'hinterland' – perpetuated, in its self-fashioning, in the laws it promulgated and in the institutional practices it developed, its formative origins as a pure settlement colony.

The purpose of this chapter is threefold. First, it presents the burgeoning field of study that may be termed comparative settler colonialism and, concomitantly, the phenomenon of settler colonialism from 1500 (and more so from the 1580s) onward. Second, it explains why and how comparative settler colonialism (or nationalism) is the most appropriate framework for understanding Zionist colonization of Palestine, the establishment of the state of Israel, and the history and nature of that state. Third, to use somewhat loosely Marxist terminology, most of the works in the field of comparative settler colonialism focus on the material base (i.e., land, labour, demography and certain institutions). I will show not only in this chapter but throughout the book that the comparative settler approach works also for the superstructure (ideology, scholarly knowledge, modern literature and the Bible). In other words, I will show that the Zionist Israeli superstructure, even though it has its distinguishing features, is nonetheless typical of a settler society and comparable to those of other settler societies.

I conclude with a close reading of a fascinating text penned by a contemporary, Chaim Arlosoroff, who was a prominent politician endowed with remarkable scholarly prowess. In its own fashion, Arlosoroff's essay expressed the awareness of its author that his was a white settler context, and that the best way to grasp it was its comparison to other white settler situations.

## The Comparative Study of Settler Societies

Scholarly awareness of settler colonialism as a distinct phenomenon is relatively recent. By distinct it is meant that settler colonialism is distinguishable from metropole colonialism; and that the various cases of settler colonialism from 1500 on – and more substantially from the 1580s on –

have enough in common to form a viable comparative field. It is of course a moral imperative not to lose sight of the fact that the indigenous peoples, from the Native Americans and the Irish through the Africans and Asians to the Palestinians, who have been variously exterminated, enslaved and dispossessed for the past five centuries, did not need scholarly awareness to become cognizant of this horrific feature of modern history. I intend to chart a lineage of the comparative study of settler societies, which is by no means exhaustive and which is germane to the subject of the book. The clear and self-proclaimed chain of transmission comprises D. K. Fieldhouse (global), George M. Fredrickson (the US and South Africa) and Gershon Shafir (Palestine/Israel). To this neat lineage are added David Prochaska (Algeria) and Patrick Wolfe (Australia, the US and Brazil). I end with a recent attempt by Caroline Elkins and Susan Pedersen to conceptualize specifically twentieth-century settler colonialism.[7]

The achievements of the comparative study of settler colonialism have been at once scholarly and political. Many settler projects gave birth to powerful nation-states, which asserted their hegemonic narratives nationally and internationally. The comparative field not only acutely refutes these narratives through evidence and interpretation; it also creates a language that amounts to a transformative alternative to the way in which these settler societies narrate themselves in their own words. Three fundamentals of hegemonic settler narratives are thus undermined: the uniqueness of each settler nation; the privileging of the intentions and consciousness of settlers as sovereign subjects; and the – putatively inconsequential to the form and contours of settler societies – presence of natives.

To take uniqueness first, the idea here is not to level the field but to show how the comparability of its various cases amounts to this – settler colonialism – being a global process rather than a haphazard array of discrete historical phenomena. This is akin to what Benedict Anderson calls, in another – intimately related – context, the modularity of nation-alism.[8] The comparative studies of settler nations undercut the claim to uniqueness not because they find all settler nations identical; in fact many of these comparisons result in underscoring historical specificity as much as similarity. What they do, however, is to offer a language that, like the popular joke about the giraffe, identifies a white settler trajectory when it sees one and renders it reminiscent of other trajectories. This is true not only for explicitly comparative studies (Fredrickson and Wolfe), but also for those that are solely concerned with one case (Prochaska and Shafir).

The writers on comparative settler colonialism mentioned here are neither oblivious to the intentions of the white settlers nor do they suggest that intentions do not matter. In his masterful book on the United States and South Africa Fredrickson attributes much explanatory importance to the fact that the impulse behind the creation of the Cape Colony in the mid seventeenth century by the Dutch East India Company was to establish a secure trading post en route to the Indian Ocean; whereas the intention in establishing the English colonies in Ireland at the end of the sixteenth century, and in what would become Virginia and New England in the early seventeenth century, was to create pure settlements, and remove the local population.[9] The point of the comparative analysis of these societies is therefore not to ignore the colonizers' intentions. However, the persistently structural and predominantly material (which does not necessarily mean materialist) investigation overwrites intentions and, crucially, concludes by emphasizing results.

This sort of examination could, for example, substantially change the way many look at the ethnic cleansing perpetrated during the 1948 war in Palestine. Much of the debate on the war revolves around a rather obsessive concern with whether or not there was an Israeli master plan to cleanse Palestine from Arab presence, that is, around what the settlers' intention was. From an Israeli perspective, the absence of such intention implies moral rectitude. It might be asked, however, whether the structural logic embedded in the type of settler nationalism which the notion of a Jewish nation-state implies explains the cleansing; it also might be asked whether cleansing-as-result (the only thing that matters to the indigenous Palestinians) is not, empirically and ethically, as important as cleansing-as-intention (or absence thereof).

The third fundamental, whether or not the presence of indigenous people is consequential to how settler societies were shaped, is possibly the most elusive, and the one that exposes the exclusionary, or segregationist, nature of white liberalism, and perhaps multiculturalism as well. The more liberal versions of hegemonic settler narratives may admit that along the otherwise glorious path to creating a nation bad things were done to the indigenous people; they may even condemn these 'bad things' and deem them unacceptable. At the same time these narratives deny the possibility that the removal and dispossession of indigenous peoples and the enslavement of others is an *intrinsic* part of what settler nations are – indeed the most pivotal constituent of what they are – rather than an *extrinsic* aberration or corruption of something essentially good. My point is not whether settler nations are good or bad, but the extent to which the act of exclusion in reality is congruous with the hegemonic rendering of that reality. The exclusionary fundamental that inheres in these white hegemonic narratives lies not in the sovereign settlers' denial of the wrong they have done to those whom they have disinherited or enslaved (though such denials are protested all too often), but in their denial that the inter-action with the dispossessed is the history of who the settlers collectively are. In short, what is denied is the extent to which the non-white world has been an intrinsic part of what is construed as European or Western history.

The comparative study of settler societies is not at all a subaltern studies project. It does not seek to salvage and reassert the voices of the dispossessed victims of settler colonialism, nor does it adhere to a post-colonial method-ology or register. In fact, most of these works' chief subject matter is the settlers themselves, rather than either the metropoles or the indigenous peoples. But this subject matter is described in terms of its constant inter-action with the peoples who were dispossessed and removed or used for labour. There cannot by definition be in this type of analysis a history of the institutions and ideologies of the settler societies that is not simulta-neously a history of the settler–native relations. The history of white supremacy throughout Fredrickson's *oeuvre* is not a trajectory within the larger American or South African histories; in a very consequential way the history of white supremacy *is* the history of these settler societies. Similarly, there cannot in Fredrickson's work be a history of private prop-erty (as the subject of legal studies and political theory) in early modern England that is not at the same time a history of land-looting first in Ireland and then east of the Appalachians. Analogously – and I will be returning to this in greater detail throughout this book – there cannot be a history of the cooperative settlements and settlement theories (one trajec-tory in the hegemonic Israeli narrative) that is separable from another strand in the same narrative, namely, 'the Arab Problem'; for what shaped the cooperative settlements and made some theories more pertinent and applicable than others was precisely what the Zionists called the Arab problem, or the consequential existence of indigenous people who, from a settler vantage point, were a problem. Arabs (and, for the most part, Mizrahi Jews too) are completely absent from kibbutzim, not just from post-1967 settlements in the Occupied Territories. This is the single most important fact for the history of the foundation of the kibbutzim, as well as for what they constitute.

Typically the studies I have mentioned above analyse their cases on the basis of five thematic clusters. The first of these can be called envi-ronmental and geopolitical. Characteristic issues are the potential or actual wealth of a given territory (size, natural resources, amount of arable land and so on), its topographical layout (for example, the ratio of commercially impassable mountain ridges to navigable and arterial rivers and lakes). The second cluster is essentially demographic. It comprises such themes as the existence of population surplus in the settlers' countries of origin (e.g., the British Isles in the late sixteenth and seventeenth centuries), and the changing demographic balance between settlers and indigenous people. The third cluster is central and usually receives much attention: land (i.e., the struggle to possess it), labour, their interplay and the extent to which they explain, most crucially, race relations and policies. The fourth is indeed race, which is the apex of the intellectual endeavours of Wolfe and Fredrickson (not surprisingly, given the cases they study and the settler states in which they live and work, Australia and the US respectively), and which is much less pronounced in Shafir's and Prochaska's work. It might be of interest to note that there is something positively distinct about the explanations of race and racism which are offered by the field of comparative settler colonialism. They undo the circularity of strictly cultural analyses, which remain limited to representation and discourse but have little to say on how race has come to matter so much. Explanations emanating from the field of comparative settler colonialism, in contrast, do not a priori accept that race has some ontological presence which requires no account. By adding a material dimension to the discussion – for example, the relations between labour formation and racist ideology – these explanations offer a more comprehensive and nuanced account of race.

The fifth and final cluster consists of issues that pertain to the political history of the triangle that is so fateful for colonialism in general but for settler colonialism in particular: the indigenous people–settlers–metropole triangle. There are numerous permutations of the relations among the components of this triangle that in turn yield various questions. I find two of these questions particularly stimulating: one is whether or not the settlers are successful, at a critical juncture, in ridding themselves of the metropole and in establishing a settler nation-state; and the other is whether or not resistance by the colonized people is successful in driving a wedge between the metropole and the settlers. For example, it may be possible to account for differences in processes of decolonization by the prior success – or failure – of settlers to establish their own state; the difference between Zimbabwe and Algeria springs to mind. There are also diachronic examples: until 1948, as settlers under the metropole's rule, the Zionists were able to obtain roughly 7 per cent of Palestine's land. The settler state, to which the 1948 war had given birth, not only managed to conquer 78 per cent of Palestine and remove much of its indigenous population but also to bring under its fold more than 90 per cent of the land by the late 1950s.

To complete this brief presentation of the language of comparative settler colonialism, the thematic clusters outlined above should be supplemented with the four basic types of colonies. These four types were identified by Fieldhouse, but additional insight may be gained by looking at how Fredrickson treats them. His aim is twofold: to explain the relation of colonialism to race and how race works by juxtaposing Weber's notion of status with Marx's class; and to create a comparative framework which is underpinned by the interdependence of the historian and the sociologist.[10] The four types of colonies Fieldhouse identified are occupation, mixed settlement, plantation and pure settlement. Fredrickson observes that Fieldhouse used these types 'for taxonomic rather than analytical purposes . . . [in order] to describe the dominant tendency in actual situations'.[11] Taking a palpably Weberian direction, Fredrickson states: 'I will employ them [types of colonies] as ideal types for which there were some relatively pure examples. This approach permits analysis of the peculiar American and South African cases as deviant versions or hybrids of the basic types, rather than simply varieties of them.'[12] I think that, at the same time as using Fieldhouse's categories to furnish a comparative interpretation of the US and South African cases, Fredrickson, true to his purpose, was adding a sociological dimension to Fieldhouse's more conventionally historical study.

In my view the basic distinction is between the first type, occupation colony, and the other three; the former is what I earlier termed metropole colonialism, which did not involve settlers in a meaningful way and in which the colonizers 'could profit most handily by skimming a surplus "off the top" without systematically destroying traditional cultures, modes of production, or forms of local governance'.[13] The other three types have in common the fact of being settlement colonies, in which there existed either the permanent or the long-lasting presence of European settlers. 'And these settlers had some expectation of transplanting "civilization" (basic aspects of the way of life that they had left behind in their countries of origin) to the new environment.'[14] What distinguishes these three types of settler colonies from one another are the different interplays among the five clusters (all or some) outlined above. Leaving aside for the moment the mixed and plantation types of colony, the pure settlement was, according to Fredrickson, a colony 'in which European settlers exterminated or pushed aside the indigenous people, developed an economy based on white labor, and were thus able in the long run to regain the sense of cultural or ethnic homogeneity identified with a European conception of nationality.'[15]

This classificatory scheme underlies what in Islamic cultural tradition is called *silsila* (chain of transmission) of the field just charted: Fredrickson explicitly draws on and develops Fieldhouse's taxonomy, and Shafir in his turn explicitly draws and elaborates on both. Wolfe does not place himself as clearly within this lineage (though he cites Fredrickson), but his argument is patently of the same mould. Prochaska is in a sense the odd one out. In laying out the theoretical foundations of his study he is ensconced in Francophone literature. The result is that he correctly insists on the distinction emphasized here between metropole and settler colonialism, and sets out to rectify the utter neglect of the latter in the case of French Algeria;[16] he also introduces an interesting innovation in the shape of colonial urbanism and, in particular, the settler colonial city.[17] Yet he either ignores or is oblivious to the works of Fieldhouse, Fredrickson and Shafir, at least some of which, as his own book was published in 1990, were available at the time he was writing and would have offered insights on the phenomenon of settler colonialism in general.

Patrick Wolfe occupies a special place, I think, among commentators on settler colonialism for two main reasons: his comparative range, and the way he insists upon the discreteness of *settler* colonialism. Wolfe's comparative work is stimulating because of the tension that inheres in it between his specialized field, Australia, and the ambitious global reach of his comparative analysis. The Australian sensibility is present in the questions Wolfe asks and the themes that draw his attention, as well as in the fact that he not infrequently consciously uses settler colonialism and the pure settlement colony interchangeably. At the same time, his comparative ventures are attentive to historical differences, and the Australian perspective does not overwhelm his observations. Wolfe's comparative prowess is particularly evident in two important articles. In the first he shows how various forms of racism and racializing have been shaped in settler situations by land and labour, thereby offering – not unlike Fredrickson – a way out of circularly cultural explanations of race. This is typical of Wolfe's approach: although no small part of his work focuses on the superstructure, he never forgets the base. In the other article he offers a bold consideration of whether settler colonialism is perforce genocidal.[18]

Wolfe is neither the first nor the only scholar of settler colonialism to underscore the crucial features that set it apart from metropole colonialism. But the originality and insight of Wolfe's work on this issue lie in his appreciative critique of critics of colonialism like Amil Cabral and Frantz Fanon, and later ones like Gayatri Spivak. 'For all the homage paid to heterogeneity and difference', Wolfe observes, 'the bulk of "post"-colonial theorizing is disabled by an oddly monolithic, and surprisingly unexamined, notion of colonialism.'[19] One of the sources for this monolithic view of colonialism, he argues,

consists in the historical accident (or is it?) that the native founders
of the postcolonial canon came from franchise or dependent – as
opposed to settler or creole – colonies. This gave these guerrilla
theoreticians the advantage of speaking to an oppressed majority on
the supply of whose labour a colonizing minority was vulnerably
dependent . . . But what if the colonizers are not dependent on
native labour? – indeed, what if the natives themselves have been
reduced to a small minority whose survival can hardly be seen to
furnish the colonizing society with more than a remission from ideological
embarrassment?[20]

Wolfe, then, attributes decisive explanatory significance to the fact that
'[i]n contrast to the colonial formation that Cabral or Fanon confronted,
settler colonies were not primarily established to extract surplus value from
indigenous labour. Rather, they are premised on displacing indigenes from
(or *re*placing them on) the land'.[21] This creates a situation in which 'it is
difficult to speak of an articulation between colonizer and native since
the determinate articulation is not to a society but directly to the land, a
precondition of social organization'.[22] The bottom line is a formulation
that Wolfe reiterates on several occasions, one understandably cited by
other scholars of settler colonialism. 'Settler colonies were (are) premised
on the elimination of the native societies. The split tensing reflects a determinate feature of settler colonization. The colonizers come to stay –
*invasion is a structure not an event* [emphasis added].'[23]

There is, finally, the recent conceptualization of settler colonialism
in the twentieth century, accompanied by an array of case studies, by
Elkins and Pedersen. Their contribution is not merely temporal, that is,
it is not limited to identifying the characteristics that are particular to
the twentieth century. They also insist on accurately and subtly distinguishing settler colonialism from other settler-related phenomena, most
notably settler projects that were not clearly supported by a metropole
and settler states. Elkins and Pedersen further begin to formulate a
typology of settler colonialism which is a vector of two factors: the level
of settler incorporation into the governance of colonized territories, and
the institutionalization of settler privilege.[24] The most significant argument
set out by Elkins and Pedersen is their observation that what their edited
volume brings to the fore is 'the continued centrality of settler projects
to the histories of nations and empires in the twentieth century'.[25] They
rightly allude to Patrick Wolfe's work on Australia, and heed his insistence
on the deep and enduring consequences of colonization.[26]

## The Comparative Study of White Settler Societies:
## The Zionist Colonization of Palestine

Having selectively reviewed the comparative study of settler colonialism, I now propose to focus in on the study of the Zionist colonization of Palestine. I do so through the work of two scholars: Shafir, who has already been mentioned, and Zachary Lockman, who has written on the relations of Arab and Jewish workers in Palestine in the first half of the twentieth century.[27] There have been other attempts to view Zionism's colonization of Palestine as well as the establishment and nature of the state of Israel as colonialism, the best known among which is Maxime Rodinson's.[28] Using the term 'diluted colonialism', Ilan Pappé has offered an interesting comparison between the early stages of Zionist colonization and the German Protestant missionary activity in West Africa, especially that of the Basel Mission.[29] I focus on the studies of Shafir and Lockman not only because they are most germane to this book's concerns, but also because – while clearly political – they are thoroughly documented and their argumentation is fashioned in a way that is unencumbered by polemic. Each in his way, Lockman and Shafir reject the three fundamentals of the hegemonic Israeli narrative, and proceed to put forth sustained alternatives.

To recap, three fundamentals of hegemonic settler narratives were discussed above: the uniqueness of each settler nation; the exclusive primacy accorded to the settlers' subjectivity; and the denial of the fact that the presence of the colonized has been the single most significant factor in determining the structure and nature of the settler society. The Zionist Israeli narrative is a particular case of that general depiction. Its three fundamentals accordingly are: the alleged uniqueness of the Jewish nation in its relentless search for sovereignty in the biblically endowed homeland; the privileging of the consciousness of Zionist settlers at the expense of the colonized, and at the expense of the results of colonization by the settlers rather than their intentions; and the denial of the fact that the presence of the Palestinian Arabs on the land destined for colonization was the single most significant factor that determined the shape taken by the settlers' nation.

Shafir's work on the initial stage of Zionist colonization is one of the most fundamentally radical critiques of Zionism I am aware of, a fact masked by the work's arid register. Further, a study in historical sociology is obviously less prone to creating public hysteria of the sort aroused by the narrative histories of the 1948 war. It is also the most self-conscious attempt to reinterpret Israeli history within the framework of the comparative study of settler societies; the inspiration Shafir drew from Fredrickson in particular runs far deeper than the deployment of classificatory vocabulary. Like Patrick Wolfe, Shafir regards colonization not as a fleeting moment of formation but as a continually present and underlying structure.[30]

Here, it might be helpful to quote a summary formulation from a later work Shafir co-authored with Yoav Peled, which covers a much longer period than his monograph and is concerned with the category of citizenship:

> The most distinguishing characteristic of the Jewish Labor Movement in Palestine was that it was not a labor movement at all. Rather, it was a colonial movement in which the workers' interest remained secondary to the exigencies of settlement.
>
> Keeping this observation in mind will allow us to properly describe the movement's institutional dynamics and understand the variety of citizenship forms it fostered.[31]

The concrete articulation of the hegemonic narrative Shafir demolishes might be termed the 'dual society paradigm', which has held sway over most of the Israeli scholarship that has dealt with Zionism, as well the Israeli state, its society and culture. Although I use a more sociological expression of the paradigm, its salience crosses disciplinary and departmental lines. This paradigm is avowedly functionalist, and radiates from one of the most important sites of scholarly commitment to the ideology of labour Zionism: the Department of Sociology and Anthropology at the Hebrew University, whose pivotal figures were S. N. Eisenstadt and his students Dan Horowitz and Moshe Lissak.[32] It is no coincidence that one of Shafir's essays discussed here is a response to an ill-tempered outburst by Lissak.[33]

Like its American equivalent, the functionalist modernization theory, the dominant Israeli paradigm emphasizes the creation of value-consensus, suppressing potential as well as actual sites of conflict. Shafir's early intellectual formation is indebted to the first two truly critical Israeli sociologists, the late Yonatan Shapiro of Tel Aviv University and Baruch Kimmerling of the Hebrew University. Shafir reminisces that as a senior undergraduate he attended in 1971 the annual congress of the Israeli Sociological Society, in which S. N. Eisenstadt delivered the keynote address on 'social differentiation' in Israeli society. A question from the audience on why the Israeli Black Panthers, whose protest had exploded just a few months earlier, were conspicuously absent from Eisenstadt's analysis was an illustration of the collusion of this kind of social science with the existing order. The Israeli Black Panthers were Mizrahi working-class youth from the Jerusalem neighbourhood of Musrara, where Jewish immigrants from North Africa and the Middle East were installed in place of the Palestinians who had been expelled in the 1948 war. With perceptive political intuition, they created a popular opposition movement on both class and ethnic grounds, whose message was progressive and secular. It was crushed by the Golda Meir government and undermined by the 1973 war. Shafir would later realize that if the Black Panthers' protest, which could be construed as 'internal' (i.e., Jewish), was rejected as a conflictual situation by the powers that be, to present the Palestinian–Zionist conflict as a factor that intrinsically explains the history and structure of the Israeli state and society would make the academic establishment go berserk.[34]

The most important assumption underpinning the dual society paradigm, and correspondingly the one most thoroughly dealt with by Shafir, is the purportedly extrinsic nature of indigenous Arab society and of its conflict with the very essence of the settler nation. What I mean by dual society is the emergence of two completely separate and self-contained entities in Palestine: the Jewish Yishuv (the settler community) and the Palestinian Arab society (the indigenous community). Each developed according to its own trajectory, which is explicable in the former case by a combination of European origins, Jewish essence and internal needs in Palestine. Each trajectory is unrelated to the other, and the only meaningful relations between the two societies consisted in a struggle between two impregnable national collectives (if, that is, the national authenticity of the Palestinians is not altogether denied). It cannot be sufficiently stressed that what is denied by the settler society is not the mere presence of Arabs in Palestine, but rather the fact that their presence and resistance were consequential to the institutional dynamics and collective identity of the settler community and later nation-state. It is clearly the ultimate scholarly articulation of the empty land concept. We shall see this recurring in literature and literary criticism in Chapter Six.

Shafir begins by listing the main features that are historically specific to Zionism and to the Zionist colonization of Palestine in comparison with other frontiers of settlement and other movements of colonization, and by anticipating that the type of colonization which soon prevailed was that of the pure settlement colony.[35] He insists that while this historical specificity 'gave Zionist colonisation a particular cast', it has 'not eliminated its fundamental similarity with other pure settlement colonies'.[36] Shafir then adds a category to the system created by Fieldhouse and Fredrickson, which he calls the *ethnic* plantation colony, 'based on European control of land and the employment of local labour. The planters, in spite of their preference for local labour, also sought, inconsistently and ultimately unsuccessfully, massive European immigration. Algeria was an example of this hybrid type.'[37]

Shafir's counter-narrative is focused on the initial – and in his interpretation foundationally formative – period of Zionist settlement in Palestine. It rests on the distinction between two stages of colonization (each comprising finer distinctions that needn't concern us here) that overlap with the first two waves of Jewish immigration, known in Zionist parlance as the First Aliya (which took place between 1882 and 1903 and consisted of 20,000–30,000 immigrants) and Second Aliya (1904–14, 35,000–40,000 immigrants). During that period roughly 425,000 Palestinian Arabs lived in Palestine. The crucial moment that shaped the First Aliya came when, after early failures and supplication to the influential Rothschild banking dynasty, Baron Edmond de Rothschild, a member of the family's French branch, entered the fray. Assisted by French experts, he reorganized the First Aliya colonies on the model of French agricultural colonization in North Africa. These colonies became ethnic plantations based on vineyards, which relied on a large, seasonal, unskilled and cheap Arab labour directed by a much smaller and better-paid Jewish labour force and Jewish planters. The passage from the first to the second stage occurred around 1900, when Rothschild ended his considerable financial involvement. This meant, among other things, that land accumulation came to a temporary halt because Rothschild had disappeared and the World Zionist Organization (WZO), which Herzl had founded in 1897, was still at the phase in which it opposed land accumulation prior to having a state on the basis of an international charter.[38]

The arrival of the Second Aliya immigrants – eventually the founders of labour Zionism and the state of Israel – signalled a shift from the land being a sphere of colonization to being one of labour, and a concomitant shift from the ethnic plantation to one of pure settlement. This is an original observation by Shafir that does not always get the notice it deserves: what is perhaps the most crucial step in the process of Israeli nation-state formation out of a pure settlement colony emanated not from land as a *lieu de colonisation* but from that of labour. The shift occurred after the attempt – familiar from other settler-colonial situations – to lower the standard of living in order to compete in the labour market against the Palestinian Arab workers had failed because of the superior productivity of the latter and the reluctance to accept their employment and living conditions. In 1905 members of what was at that point one of two labour Zionist parties, Hapoel Hatzair ('The young worker'), forsook the strategy of reducing wages for the purpose of market competitiveness, launching in its place the campaign for 'conquest of labour'. Its goal was to annex all jobs in

Palestine for Jews – especially in Jewish plantations – without lowering wages. This was accompanied by the Jewish planters' drive to oust their Arab workers and hire Jewish ones in their place, for reasons of national colonization rather than purely economic considerations.[39]

As such, the struggle for 'the conquest of labour' was unsuccessful. Its pivotal importance lies in fact that it launched the appearance of the pure settlement colony as a state of mind. With the benefit of hindsight it may even be argued that pure settlement colony as a state of mind would become the only thinkable way of institution – and nation-state – building. It 'transformed the Jewish workers into militant nationalists who sought to establish a homogeneous Jewish society in which there would be no exploitation of Palestinians, nor will there be competition with Palestinians, because there would be no Palestinians'.[40] From that crucial juncture the workers' leadership reverted to its continuing colonization of land through an alliance with a changing WZO and its two colonizing agencies, the Palestine Land Development Agency (1909) and Jewish National Fund (1901). In this venture the settlers were guided by the three German Jewish master exponents of settlement: Arthur Ruppin, Otto Warburg (a member of the famous banking family) and Franz Oppenheimer. In a process that will be explored in greater detail in this chapter's conclusion, the first cooperative settlements were founded and, with the arrival of more immigrants, colonization through various forms of cooperative settlement (*kvutza*, kibbutz and moshav, all created between 1908 and 1925) gained momentum. In 1920 the final and most powerful labour institution, the Histadrut, was established. This was a multi-faceted organization that consisted of a trade union, a settlement section, a construction and industrial arm, and health, consumer and finance divisions. More than any other single institution, the Histadrut was the nation-state in the making. A common mistake, which leads to complete misunderstanding, is to see the Histadrut only as a trade union in the European mould. It is no coincidence that the position that made Ben-Gurion the uncontested leader of labour Zionism in the 1920s, and catapulted him to the leadership of the WZO and Jewish Agency in the 1930s, was that of the Histadrut's secretary general. 'The Second Aliya's revolution against the First Aliya', Shafir observes,

> did not originate from opposition to colonialism as such but out of frustration with the inability of the ethnic plantation colony to provide sufficient employment for Jewish workers, i.e., from opposition to the particular form of their predecessors' colonization. The Second Aliya's own method of settlement, and subsequently the dominant Zionist

method, was but another type of European overseas colonization: the 'pure settlement colony' also found in Australia, Northern U.S., and elsewhere. Its threefold aim was control of land, employment that ensured a European standard of living, and massive immigration . . . This form of pure settlement rested on two exclusivist pillars: on the WZO's Jewish National Fund and on the . . . Histadrut. The aims of the JNF and the Histadrut were the removal of land and labour from the market, respectively, thus closing them off to Palestinian Arabs.[41]

Lockman does not take the path of comparative settler colonialism, but the alternative he offers to the Zionist Israeli narrative and what he rejects in it bring him very close to Shafir. Lockman too discards what I have been calling the third fundamental of hegemonic settler narratives: the unwillingness to accept that what determined the nature of settler nations is first and foremost their interaction with the people whom they had colonized, rather than any civilizational or national essence.[42] The method and language Lockman develops are those of *relational* history. In the mid 1980s an interesting forum was convened at the New School for Social Research, in search of agendas for writing radical history; it revolved around the four heavyweights of British Marxism – Eric Hobsbawm, Christopher Hill, Perry Anderson and E. P. Thompson.[43] Anderson had three suggestions: to enhance the role of theory, to draw attention to the possibility of alternative outcomes on the margins of what eventually occurred in certain historical junctures, and to write relational histories.[44]

By relational history Anderson means something that is simultaneously different from comparative history (which he endorses) and non-national in its unit of analysis. He calls for a history 'that studies the incidence – reciprocal or asymmetrical – of different national or territorial units and cultures on each other', a history that 'is a reconstruction of [such units'] dynamic inter-relationships over time'.[45] Lockman's turn to relational history is inspired by Anderson's pronouncement, which he adapts to his own research.[46] Lockman studies the interaction between labour Zionism's institutions and individuals and Arab workers and their organizations in Palestine in the period 1906–48. He shows not only how these two communities interacted with and shaped each other, but also how they were constituted within the same context of late Ottoman and then Mandatory Palestine. Concerning the Jewish side of his relational study, Lockman perceptively follows the tension within labour Zionism between a commitment to a universal solidarity based on class, in which increasingly marginalized groups within that camp genuinely believed, and a national commitment to the Zionist project as a whole. By doing so he necessarily brings to the fore possibilities that might have existed as this particular history unfolded even if they did not materialize (this is Anderson's second suggestion for radical history, which Lockman does not mention).

Let me dwell slightly longer on the point of marginal (or marginalized) possibilities. They emerge in Lockman's narrative whenever some sort of joint Jewish–Arab organization or solidarity was weighed against the Zionist commitment solely to Jewish colonization by the historical protagonists themselves, especially by the railway workers in the years 1919–25.[47] He is a subtle historian, so the retrospective knowledge of failure, while noticeable, does not spoil the story's unfolding. If, however, we were to juxtapose Shafir's work to Lockman's, the conclusion would have to be that by the time the Histadrut was founded in 1920, and as it gained power, the principle of pure settlement had overwhelmingly won the day, and the groups for which class and labour solidarity across ethnic lines was paramount were very marginal. Can one in this light seriously contemplate possibilities that existed on the margins? The answer is not simple, and it is rather grim. Basically, as I think Lockman would agree, Shafir's structural explanation is correct and compounded by the benefit of historical perspective: it is palpably clear that the pure settlement structure was perpetuated and grew exponentially in scope and might, and that therefore any universalist solidarity that breached the settler/ indigene faultline did not stand a chance.

And yet I think that there is much sense in what Lockman does in both scholarly and political terms. Concerning historical writing in the narrower sense, the inclusion of possibilities that existed on the margins fashions a nuanced portrayal of the past that heeds the experience of the historical actors themselves, whether they endeavoured to make these possibilities come true or fought tooth and nail to foil them. But in the wider significance that 'doing' history has, the highlighting rather than discarding of possibilities on the margins is one of the main things we – those of us in pursuit of radical history and politics – have at our disposal. This was one of the chief points I was trying to make in the previous chapter through Bernard Lazare and the conscious pariah in general: the triumphant path of the sovereign settler is always strewn with alternatives, which, however marginal(ized), are opened up by the conscious pariah. To use Benjaminian language, in this world in which the state of emergency is the rule rather than the exception, the recovery of a collection of possibilities – unrealized, but real possibilities nonetheless – is perhaps not *all* we have, but much of it. In the repository to which radical history and politics turn for inspiration this collection of Benjaminian pearls must surely occupy a special place.

## Chaim Arlosoroff's 'Exercise' in Comparative Settler Colonialism

Shafir and Lockman are of course absolutely convincing in their critique and refutation of the dual society paradigm (and other articulations of the hegemonic narrative) as well as in the alternatives they offer. There is a sense, however, in which the dual society paradigm cannot be dismissed through scholarly refutation, simply because it has won so mightily: the dual society ideology is congruous with a material reality of which it is part and in the reproduction of which it plays a role. Many pages could be filled with reasons for this triumph. Suffice to say that since the final demise of the binational option in the 1940s there has not been a single so-called peace proposal that is not based on the logic of the dual society-cum-pure-settlement-colony. This congruity of scholarship as ideology and the material reality which is reproduced has a particular force. It stems from a frustrating paradox: the dual society paradigm fails to explain how this hegemony came into being, and yet come into being it forcefully did; there is a perverse way in which the dual society cannot be dismissed because – however much racist and colonial – it has come to prevail materially, ideologically and discursively.

While scores of pro-Zionist scholars have been at pains to suppress the fact that the Palestinian Arabs are intrinsic to the nature of the Zionist project and the settler-colonial aspect of it, a no less committed Zionist manifested awareness of precisely that which would be later denied. This was Dr Chaim Arlosoroff (1899–1933), by far the most intellectually capable politician of note within labour Zionism; it is speculated that had it not been for his untimely death he would have eclipsed Ben-Gurion (I myself doubt that Arlosoroff possessed either Ben-Gurion's knack for the organization and mobilization of power or his utter ruthlessness). Chaim Arlosoroff is best – almost only – known for his assassination in Tel Aviv on 16 June 1933; the assassins remain unidentified. He was then the maverick of Zionist politics, one of the leaders of the main labour party, Mapai, and head of the Political Department of the Jewish Agency, basically a foreign minister. At the time of his death Arlosoroff was in discussions with the Nazi leadership, which were meant to enable emigrating German Jews to salvage at least some of their wealth, provided its destination was Palestine. The revisionist agitation against the negotiations and Arlosoroff personally peaked at that time, though it has not been conclusively shown that the killers were Revisionists. A book by Ben-Gurion's biographer, Shabtai Teveth, on what had become the Arlosoroff Affair (fifty years later), accused two Revisionists and prompted Menachem Begin, then prime minister, to constitute a rather idiotic – and needless to say unsuccessful – commission of inquiry that was supposed to determine who had killed Arlosoroff.[48]

Chaim Viktor Arlosoroff was born in 1899 in Ukraine to well-off middle-class parents, who spoke both Russian and German. He studied Hebrew at home with a private tutor. The family fled to Königsberg in Germany in 1905 and during the First World War settled in Berlin. There Arlosoroff became engrossed in two worlds: German letters and culture through the Gymnasium he attended, and Zionism through Hapoel Hatzair. The latter was an anti-Marxist and for the most part non-socialist party, which was inspired by the Tolstoyan 'Religion of Labour' developed by the Second Aliya's father figure, A. D. Gordon. At the end of the War he studied economics at Berlin University. In 1919, at the age of twenty, he published his first work, *Der jüdische Volkssozialismus* ('Jewish people's socialism'), which amalgamated his intellectual and political sources of inspiration: Marx, Kropotkin (to whose work Gustav Landauer had introduced him), Russian Narodnik moods and German romanticism. In 1923 he submitted his doctoral dissertation on Marx's concept of class and class struggle, and was offered a university position by his adviser, Werner Sombart. Arlosoroff turned down the offer and in 1924 emigrated to Palestine.[49]

In 1927 Arlosoroff published a remarkable essay in Hebrew, entitled 'On the Question of Joint Organization' ('Le-she'elat ha-irgun ha-meshutaf'). It appeared in Hapoel Hatzair's daily newspaper and was included in the collection of his works published shortly after his assassination.[50] Lockman has duly noticed this text,[51] but it is significantly missing from Asher Maniv's edited selection of Arlosoroff's work and Shlomo Avineri's study of his ideational world.

The context of the essay's composition requires some clarification. The foundation of the Histadrut in 1920 as the culmination of creating a pure colony – it was explicitly created for 'Hebrew' workers rather than workers in general – in the domain of labour reduced substantially the relevance of Arab–Jewish working-class cooperation. At the same time, however, several factors temporarily prevented the total erasure of what was subsumed in contemporary discourse under the notion of 'joint organization' (*irgun meshutaf*), that is, Arabs and Jews sharing one organizational framework on the basis of class solidarity and betterment of conditions in the workplace. The first factor was the alternative labour market sustained by the colonial British state in Mandatory Palestine, especially the British-managed Palestine Railways. The second was the fact that in the early 1920s the nature of the Histadrut was still being contested by labour Zionism's shrinking leftist parties (the Socialist Workers' Party, later the Palestine Communist Party, and Poale Zion Smol – the left wing that remained from the ruins of the Marxist–Zionist Poale Zion), which insisted that the Histadrut be committed, at least to some extent, to non-ethnic workers' solidarity. By the late 1920s these oppositional parties had either dissolved or were ousted from the organization by Ben-Gurion's iron hand. Third and last was a host of related issues: the increasingly active Palestinian national movement, the attempt by the Mandatory government to establish a legislative council for all the inhabitants of Palestine, and the growing urban-based Palestinian working class.

In practical terms, the need to unionize the railway workers was what gave rise to the question of joint organization; also incorporated into the category of railway workers were the employees of the Mandatory government's postal and telegraph services.[52] The immediate interest of the Histadrut lay in the potential employment and membership that this sphere of labour offered, and in the assumption that, if negotiating the betterment of the Jewish workers' conditions was to be successful, the Arab workers could not be ignored. As secretary general, Ben-Gurion became intensely active in this evolving affair, and it was he who, in the Histadrut's council meeting of January 1922, coined the term 'joint organization' of railway workers, which gradually came to embody the complex problem of the universal commitment to workers' solidarity versus the ethnic commitment to pure settlement exclusion, that is, commitment to Zionism. Ben-Gurion's positions may ostensibly look vacillating and perhaps even contradictory, but I believe that in fact they evince coherent and consistent purposefulness.

Adopting a haughty rhetoric of a labour *mission civilisatrice*, Ben-Gurion insisted that the destinies of the Arab and Jewish workers were inextricably tied, and that it was labour Zionism's duty to educate their Arab comrades and teach them how to become self-aware and organized. His wish was to have a union of railway workers divided into *national* sections, and to have the members of the Jewish section become Histadrut members *en bloc*. Speaking in the Histadrut's name, Ben-Gurion even suggested at the railway workers' conference in 1922 that, if the Arab section took time to evolve, individual Arab workers would be allowed to join the Jewish section until there were enough of them to create their own national section. Since it had already been decided that the Jewish section within the railway workers' union would automatically become also Histadrut members, Shabtai Teveth infers that Ben-Gurion dramatically decided to allow admission of Arab workers into the Histadrut and thereby exceeded his authority concerning a most pivotal issue (lest the pure settlement principle is forgotten, the organization's full title was the General Histadrut of the *Hebrew* Workers in Eretz Yisrael).[53] It is doubtful, to put it mildly, that Ben-Gurion ever contemplated the meaningful presence of

Arab workers in the Histadrut, and in any case the result of the whole process was a resounding defeat of the attempt to create non-ethnic solidarity of settler and indigenous workers.

The Histadrut developed in two ways that made clear Ben-Gurion's true intentions. The first was the increasing intensity with which the Histadrut's leftist groups, which continued to strive for class solidarity and removal of the 'Hebrew' adjective before 'Workers' and whose main support came from the railway workers' union, were broken up and their members expelled. Without detailing his manoeuvres, this process of ejection, a purgation of the Histadrut à la pure settlement colony, makes it clear that Ben-Gurion's concern in bringing the railway workers into the Histadrut's fold did not stem from his belief in the shared destiny of all workers, Arab and Jewish, but rather from the need to prepare for an imminent showdown with the left. The organizational and numerical strength of the left resided in the railway union which, from Ben-Gurion's vantage point, was far too independent for comfort. By the ostensibly generous gesture of extending automatic Histadrut membership to railway union members, Ben-Gurion could have the leftists under his thumb, subvert the composition of the railway union council by infiltrating Histadrut loyalists, and shift crucial votes to other Histadrut forums, which he controlled and which railway union members were now obliged to obey.

The second significant aspect of the Histadrut's development was expressed in its 1924 annual conference, which came to be known in labour Zionist lore as the Ein Harod conference (taking its name from the kibbutz where it was held). The Histadrut's fault line was drawn by Shlomo Kaplansky on the left and Ben-Gurion on the right. Both were hailed veterans of the Second Aliya, but Kaplansky represented what remained of the spirit of Poale Zion, a party in which Ben-Gurion wrought havoc almost from the moment he had joined it in 1906. The bone of contention was the British proposal to establish a legislative council in Mandatory Palestine for all its inhabitants on the basis of the existing demographic configuration. Kaplansky was in favour of the proposal. He thought that if such a parliament reflected the Arab majority it would be democratically correct, that certain mechanisms could be found to hinder the possible tyranny of that majority, and that it was high time that an understanding was reached with the local national movement, however much it might be deemed 'reactionary', 'inauthentic', led by 'feudal effendis', or guided by 'obscurantist clerics'.

Ben-Gurion's rejection of Kaplansky's speech and suggestions was revealing of his fundamental political principles. He was throughout his career adamant not to allow any recognition of Palestine's Arab majority as a static state of affairs; that is, Arab demographic majority was for him a transitory phase because they could be transferred on opportune occasions (like wars) and because Jewish immigration would increase on other opportune occasions (like anti-Semitic pressure). He was concerned the legislative council would be precisely that: an institution that would reflect not only the Arab demographic majority but also the fact that the Arabs had national – not just civil – collective rights and presence in Palestine. Ben-Gurion preferred that the question of parliament vanish altogether, but since it was incumbent upon him to set out an explicit position at the conference, he proposed that the legislative council should be formed on the basis of parity between the two nations. As for the need to reach an agreement with the Arab national movement and its leadership, Ben-Gurion employed every trick in the book to avoid doing so, from a spurious white man's burden ('we' cannot reach a true understanding with the Arabs until 'we' help them become civilized and progressive, and until 'we' help transform their national movement so that it is led by workers rather than effendis and clerics), through settler-colonial superciliousness to outright cynicism and procrastination. This he did by means of what Teveth calls the 'class formula'.

Ben-Gurion's class formula, which he systematically laid out at the Ein Harod conference in the course of a 135-minute speech, insisted that 'the easy and short path' to the reactionary, exploitative and inauthentic national Arab movement, led as it was by landowning effendis and poisonous clerics, may be Kaplanky's, but not his.

Ben-Gurion's path was arduous and, most crucially, long – very long, indeed indefinitely long: cooperation with the Arab worker would take place solely within the framework of 'an inter-national workers' alliance' (inter-national meant two separate national units, not internationalist). Only when the Arab national movement is led by workers, proclaimed Ben Gurion, will such an understanding be possible. Why the need to stall? Ben-Gurion's vision of how the Zionist project would come to fruition was in essence no different from Jabotinsky's 'Iron Wall' metaphor in his 1923 article of the same name, which recognized the genuine resistance of indigenous people to the threat of external dispossession and the corresponding solution of erecting an iron wall – 'the strengthening in Palestine of a government without any kind of Arab influence'. Where Ben-Gurion differed from Jabotinsky was in his view that it was unwise openly to define the reality in Palestine as a conflict between a settler-national movement versus an indigenous one until the Yishuv became ineradicably solid.[54] The class formula was an expedient rationale for stalling, crafted as it was in a language perfectly appropriate to Ben-Gurion's institutional position as secretary general of the Histadrut. For Ben-Gurion such language was expedient; he dropped it like a hot potato as soon as he could.

Arlosoroff's 1927 essay setting out his intervention in the joint organization debate demonstrates in an original way that the leading labour Zionists had acquired a white settler consciousness: what this essay shows is that the perspective from which Arlosoroff analysed the joint organization complex and the course of action he proposed represented the perspective of a white settler who looks at other settler situations for instructive analogies. His essay reacted not only to the context just charted but also specifically to Ben-Gurion's Ein Harod speech. Arlosoroff distinguished his own analysis from the hopelessly ideology-ridden positions of his colleagues, including Ben-Gurion's, and recommended it for its scientific factuality as well as its comparative perspective. For Arlosoroff there was one, and only one, criterion by which the worthiness of joint organization ought to be judged:

> Can the joint organization nullify the competition between the expensive and modern Hebrew labour and the cheap and primitive Arab labour and [thereby] create more amenable conditions for the collective of Hebrew workers in their war for the conquest of labour . . .? The answer to this question – rather than a pre-conceived doctrine – will determine our verdict on the method of joint organization.[55]

This clear formulation vindicates, first of all, Sternhell's thesis that what labour Zionism offered in both practice and ideology was nationalist socialism, almost completely devoid of any humanistic and universalist appeal or content.[56] Arlosoroff attributed no value whatsoever to joint organization, even in its pure settlement garb of division into autonomous ethnic sections, unless it could be shown to contribute to colonization (of labour in this case), immigration (by guaranteeing wages that were commensurate at least with the more modest European economies) and settlement. Developing a detailed analysis based on substantial economic data, he argued that joint organization would not only fail to enhance the Zionist colonization of Palestine, but in certain respects would even hinder it. As far as wages were concerned, Arlosoroff questioned the assumption that joint struggle would necessarily result in an upswing in the sphere of labour generated by the Mandatory state. He maintained that there was no uniform result in such struggle, and that wages would always depend on the nature of 'an actual national economy and its objective capacity'.

While Arlosoroff agreed with Otto Bauer's observation that the joint organization and action of the German and Czech workers in their respective parts of Bohemia would be mutually beneficial,[57] he insisted that this was the wrong analogy for Palestine. The hypothetical analogy that, according to Arlosoroff, illustrated the futility of joint organization was the migration of a few tens of thousands of American or Australian workers to Poland. When these American workers unionized, they would instantly face the competition of cheaper labour from the indigenous Polish workers. 'What would we say if these American workers seriously suggested to solve the problem by uniting with the Polish workers in order [to obtain] an American wage-level? We would say that such a suggestion was to no avail.'[58] Arlosoroff's point was that inter-ethnic joint organization could work in different regions of national economies like 'the unified Austrian economic domain' that Bauer examined – but not in the type of economy represented in Mandate Palestine. In the latter case, Arlosoroff pointed out, there are two economies that are simultaneously very different yet porous to one another; these were what he called 'the native economy' (*mesheq ha-aretz*) and 'the settler economy' (*mesheq ha-hityashvut*). The former was a primitive Eastern economy whereas the latter a relatively advanced European one. And while it was true that with time the latter could transform the former, Palestine was still at the phase at which the Polish hypothetical analogy obtained.[59]

Arlosoroff then outlined what he considered to be a second problem emanating from the route to joint organization, a problem that would make joint organization not only unhelpful for the Zionist colonization of Palestine and enhanced Jewish immigration (as mentioned above, his starting point for considering the desirability of joint organization), but, worse, disadvantageous to the Hebrew worker.[60] Even if one accepted that equal and higher wages could be achieved through joint organization, he wrote, one would have to concede that such equality was nominal rather than real, by which he did *not* mean that inflation adjustment was required. Rather, what Arlosoroff meant was that the two sets of workers – indigenes and settlers – were at two different historical stages in the evolution of the working class. With few exceptions, the Arab workers did not yet constitute a fully developed working class because they had not undergone the stage of complete estrangement from their rural origin. 'The Palestinian Arab worker . . . is for the most part a peasant [*fallah*] whose farm is toiled by his family or co-villagers', Arlosoroff elaborated, 'and he migrates to the adjacent Hebrew colony [*moshava* – the First Aliya ethnic plantation] in order to work for wage. He does not have to use his labour-profit for accommodation, clothing or subsistence. He mostly accumulates his money, and having saved a certain amount he invests his money in his farm.'[61]

In stark contrast, the Hebrew worker is not only at a higher level of political awareness and has loftier social and cultural needs, but also for obvious reasons is not a part of a rural hinterland. His real wage is therefore that of the bare minimum for survival. When employment is dire, this difference of what in reality is wage-for-savings versus wage-for-survival will put the Arab worker in an insurmountably advantageous position because he will be able to absorb a reduced wage, that is, save less and still have a higher wage than prior to the joint organization, and therefore be more competitive than the Jewish worker. The result will be severely detrimental for the Hebrew workers and will sharpen national antagonism.[62] 'As Otto Bauer proved in his thorough book on the question of nationalism', Arlosoroff concluded, 'every social and economic collision among workers of a different kind becomes devoid, under such circumstances, of social and economic content and appears in its national guise. The contradiction of economic interests must then become a national war.'[63]

Clearly, then, Arlosoroff put his weight behind the complete rejection of joint organization with the Arab workers. His preferred course of action was introduced, in the latter part of the essay, through analogy, but this time actual rather than hypothetical:

> I think it is worth trying to find an equivalent to our problem in the annals of settlement of other countries, and to explain our situation by deduction. This is not easy. There is hardly an example of this [the Zionist] endeavour of a colonizing people ['am mityashev] with a European level of needs, which does not resort to enforcement measures and its purpose is to transform a country, in which there is a low level of wage . . . into a site of mass immigration and mass settlement.[64]

Arlosoroff first lists the settler-colonial examples that have no use when considering the particular question of the interaction of settler workers and native workers in the Mandate Palestine labour market. The US was not an adequate comparison, and neither were New Zealand and Australia, 'since they nipped this problem in the bud through a fervent policy of "White Australia"'.[65] He then asserts that South Africa is

> almost the only case in which there is sufficient similarity in the objective conditions and problems so as to allow us an analogy. To prevent misunderstanding in advance, it should be stressed that we know full well the different factors at work in the two countries' conditions, and that we do not wish to attempt here [to create a similar] political construction, but only to compare to one another the polar points in the two countries' economies.[66]

Arlosoroff maintains that, as in Palestine, there emerged in late nine-teenth- and early twentieth-century South Africa a labour market that consisted of a minority of white workers who were unable to compete with the vast majority of Asian and African workers and whose material expectations and needs were much higher. The gaps were especially substantial, Arlosoroff says, and much greater between the 'Anglo-Saxons' and the 'Bantu-Negroes' than between Jews and non-Jews in Palestine; the problem was therefore even more serious in South Africa than in Palestine. Eventually the solution came to be the Colour Bar laws, which were introduced as a result of the political weight of the South African labour party and trade unions. These laws excluded all the non-Europeans from the skilled, supervisory and better-paid labour, and preserved that domain for Europeans only. Arlosoroff remarks that 'it is not important whether we reject this politics . . . or justify it . . . It is important here to highlight the economic reasons and social relations that led, rightly or wrongly, to the promulgation of Colour Bar laws.'[67]

Arlosoroff's conclusion issued from the South African analogy and from an article by Lord Sidney Oliver, who combined Fabianism with colo-nialism. In that article Lord Sidney Oliver recommended an absolute separation, 'Segregation' he called it, of whites and blacks.[68] Arlosoroff asserted that in the coming decades the only way to achieve the fulfilment of Zionism would be completely to forsake any notion of joint organization (joint anything, really), and stiffen the separation into two economies, one modern, well paid and conducive to an enhanced immigration of settlers, and the other undeveloped and low paid, which would enable the settlers continuously to exclude the indigenous workers from their labour market.[69] Certain data offered by Lockman suggest that the compar-ison could be carried further. Although no Colour Bar ever existed in Palestine or was proposed as such, the WZO and the Histadrut pressured the British administration, after the economic crisis of 1925, to raise the wages of unskilled Jewish workers above those of Arabs in the public sphere of the Mandatory state. The British officials resisted this pressure, arguing that such a rise would favour Jewish over Arab labour and increase labour costs. Yet Lockman identifies a wages commission report of 1928, which discerns effectively four levels of wages for unskilled labour: rural Arab workers were paid 12–15 piastres a day, urban Arab workers 14–17 piastres, Jewish Histadrut members 28–30 piastres, and non-unionized Jewish workers 15–30 piastres.[70]

Finally, Arlosoroff not only adumbrated Arab–Jewish relations mainly in terms of a national conflict between settlers and indigenes, he explicitly said so.[71] How far he was willing to go can be gauged from a letter he wrote to Chaim Weizmann five years after the essay in question, on 30 June 1932. Arlosoroff sensed an impending international crisis that might lead to a world war. Anxious about the consequences of such a crisis for the Zionist venture, he outlined four courses of action that were open to it. The fourth, an outburst of Schmittian decisionism, was the real reason for writing the letter:

> The fourth possible conclusion is that in present circumstances it is not possible to realise Zionism without an interim period during which the Jewish minority will govern through an organized revolutionary rule; that it is not possible to obtain a Jewish majority or even a [demographic] balance of the two nations through aliya and systematic settlement, without an interim period of a nationalist [le'umanit] minority government, which will seize the state apparatus, administration and military power, in order to prevent the peril of takeover by the non-Jewish majority and a revolt against us (which we shan't be able to suppress unless the state apparatus and military power are in our hands). During this interim period a systematic policy of development, aliya and settlement will be carried out.[72]

## Conclusion: A Note on the Genealogy of Early Zionist Settlement

An account of the chain of ideas, settlement theories and settlement practices that wound up in the foundation of the cooperative settlements (kvutza, kibbutz and moshav in this chronological order from 1908 to 1925) is a fitting conclusion for this chapter. Common knowledge has it that the kibbutz originated from an astonishing socialist experimentation with an ideology the settlers (pioneers, or chalutzim) had acquired in Europe. Even someone as astutely prophetic and sober as Arendt thought that the kibbutzim were marvellous. That this rendering accords the settlers not only a central role but also hyper-agency is hardly surprising, for these settlers were members of the Second and Third Aliyas, that is, the ruling political elite of the Yishuv (from the 1920s onward), the WZO and Jewish Agency (from the 1930s on) and the state of Israel (1948–77). However, there is solid scholarship that seriously questions this story and offers a threefold correction: it tempers the settlers' hyper-agency by underscoring the pivotal role played by the German Jewish settlement experts; it shows that the decisive factors were the conditions and desire of colonization; that, even in terms of ideational flow from Europe to Palestine, what we have is ideas of colonization and race rather than socialism.

In the mid 1980s two geographers of the Hebrew University, Shalom Reichman and Shlomo Hasson, published a revealing article on the formative influence of the pre-First World War colonization project of the German Reich in the Posen (Poznan in Polish) province of the east Prussian marches, upon the early phase of the Zionist colonization effort in Palestine.[73] A sizeable chunk of the east Prussian marches, the Ostmark, had been appropriated when Poland was partitioned in the late eighteenth century. In the latter decades of the nineteenth century three of the Ostmark provinces – Eastern and Western Prussia, and Silesia – had a German majority; only the fourth, Posen, had a Polish majority of roughly 60 per cent. Posen was identified by the Germans as a centre of Polish nationalism. The purpose of the state project – the wider background of which was the crisis of German agriculture and the attendant *Landflucht* (land flight) – was to effect a demographic transformation in Posen first and foremost, and in the Ostmark more generally, by dispossessing the Polish majority of its hold on the land and settling Germans in their stead.[74]

The process began in 1886 with the Prussian Diet's promulgation of the Colonization Law, and the creation of the main instrument to implement it, namely, the Colonization Commission (Ansiedlungskommission). The Commission's chief task was to purchase large portions of land, in particular from the big German and Polish landowners, and financially facilitate the establishment of small and medium-size German colonies. A fund of 100 million marks was provided, and was regularly replenished in the next two decades.[75] 'The German method of settlement', observe Reichman and Hasson,

> was intended to produce a new space that on the one hand would check the geographical expansion of the Poles and on the other would strengthen the German presence in the area. To attain this goal the German Colonization Commission embarked on a comprehensive program that included land purchasing, planning and development, land parcelling, selling and renting land to German colonists, and provision of administrative services and guidelines for new colonists.[76]

Of crucial importance for this discussion is the Commission's attitude to labour. It subdivided the large estates it had purchased into two types of colonies. One was the farm, in which each settler received an area of 10–15 hectares, and the other was the working people's colony, where settlers employed in nearby cities were apportioned allotments of 0.5–1.5 hectares for garden produce. As for the first type of colony, the farm, '[t]he main principle underlying the choice of this size was that it would provide for the subsistence of one family without the help of hired labor.

This was intended to prevent the employment of Polish labor in areas settled by Germans'.[77] The German colonization project was ultimately unsuccessful, for, although it purchased substantial tracts of land and settled large numbers of Germans, it could not transform the Ostmark's – especially Posen's – demography nor remove the Poles. The latter, creating their own institutions, fought back effectively, and the former's immigration to the area and settlement in it was offset by emigration from it.

The German project and the Colonization Commission had a formative impact upon the Zionist project in four related ways: the impact of the German project resulted in the decisive rejection of the French model that had been introduced by the Rothschild experts; it accorded primacy to national colonization over economic profitability; it accorded primacy to (an equivalent of) the state and its bureaucracy over the market and private capitalists; and it implanted in the WZO what Shafir perceptively calls the pure settlement frame of mind.[78] The agents of this formative impact were two German Jewish settlement experts, Franz Oppenheimer (1864–1943) and, perhaps the single most important individual for the Zionist settlement in Palestine, Arthur Ruppin (1876–1943). In the background one might add the botanist Otto Warburg (1859-1938), head of the Zionist Executive Committee and chairman of the Palestine Land Development Company.

Oppenheimer was a physician who gradually discarded medicine to become a prominent professor of sociology. His thoughts on settlement formed part of the liberal socialists' (as distinguished from the social democrats') responses to the agrarian crisis in late nineteenth-century Germany. The common ideational denominator of these responses was their indebtedness to the American political economist Henry George's 1879 book *Progress and Poverty*, the thesis of which was to generate large revenue for the state by taxing the excessive land rent of idle landowners. German land reform theorists like Michael Flüscheim, who advocated the nationalization of land and establishment of colonies on collectively owned land, and Adolf Damaschke, who rejected nationalization, had been influenced by George, as had been the Austrian Theodor Hertzka, Herzl's colleague at the *Neue Freie Presse*, who in 1890 published a utopian novel entitled *Freiland*. In the novel's utopian colony in Kenya, cultivation and production would be carried out by 'self governing associations' and 'every inhabitant in Freeland [would have] an equal and inalienable claim upon the whole of the land, and upon the means of production accumulated by the community'.[79]

Like other German liberal socialists who followed Henry George, Oppenheimer was a member of the Berlin *Freiland* society and a close friend of Damschke, of whom he was nonetheless critical for diluting George's prescriptions. In addition to his ideational genealogy, Oppenheimer's theory was informed by his decade-long experience (1886–96) as a physician in a province in the Ostmark. That experience, with George and the German reformers looming large, led him to pin the blame for much of the agrarian crisis on the Junkers' monopoly over land ownership and the income derived from its rent. He prescribed a medication, which was essentially an amalgam of public landownership and cooperative settlement. Herzl successfully lured Oppenheimer into joining the WZO, and paraded him at the 1903 Sixth Congress. Even though it had been conceived for Germany's eastern frontier, Oppenheimer's programme was adopted by the WZO as a model for overseas colonization in either Africa or Palestine.[80] In 1911 this model served as the framework for the cooperative settlement of Merhavia in the Jezreel Valley; it would later become a kibbutz, of which Golda Meirson became a member in the early 1920s.

Aware of Oppenheimer's ideas, and much more thoroughly shaped by the Posen project, was Arthur Ruppin. Ruppin was born in Posen itself, though his family moved away when he was a child. A crisis in his family's finances forced Ruppin to leave school at the age of fifteen. He nonetheless managed to enrol in university, studying law in Berlin and Halle, but considered it a practical necessity, in the same way that Max Nordau and Oppenheimer viewed the study of medicine. Ruppin's real passion lay in political economy and social studies, and his hope was to become an expert for the betterment of society through public (i.e., state) service. His political leaning combined social democracy and social Darwinism. As a good German Hegelian, Ruppin firmly believed in the ultimate guidance of the state, as well as the fundamental place of the peasant and agriculture in the national edifice. In the 1900s he was increasingly drawn to Zionism and, given his immense gift for organization, soon became a prominent technocrat. In 1907 he migrated to Palestine, where in 1909 he established the Palestine Land Development Company (PLDC) and headed up the Palestine Office, in which capacities he was answerable to the PLDC chairman Warburg (a member of the famous German Jewish banking family and president of the WZO in the 1910s) in Germany.[81] Ruppin was a founding member of Brit Shalom from the 1920s but left it early on.

Before proceeding with the formative impact of the German colonization project in the Ostmark on the foundation of the cooperative settlements, it is important briefly to mention recent work on Ruppin, especially a striking article by Etan Blum.[82] Ruppin's role in the colonization of Palestine was so pivotal that he is known in Zionist Israeli lore as 'the father of Jewish settlement in the land of Israel'. In addition to settlement, which we shall see slightly later, he was also responsible for the historical alliance within Zionism between the nationalist bourgeoisie and the labour movement, and for the agreement with the Nazis on the transfer of German Jews and their capital to Mandate Palestine (the same agreement in which Arlosoroff was involved). While a leading Zionist, he was engaged in intensive scholarly research and was considered an international authority on the social scientific study (including statistics) of the Jews. At the same time, he is presented in that historiography as a 'progressive official', an external, apolitical expert. Blum challenges this view. Informed by Bourdieu, he shows that Ruppin was one of the central creators of the modern Hebrew *habitus*, and reconstructs Ruppin's *Weltanschauung* (despite considerable efforts, Ruppin never managed to master Hebrew; he himself insisted on the German term rather than its somewhat lame translation as world view, which reflected for him 'Jewish passivity').[83]

Ruppin's *Weltanschauung* was social Darwinism and its formation occurred, in the 1890s and 1900s, within a budding interdisciplinary paradigm that became known as Eugenics or Racial Hygiene (*Rassenhygiene*). One of Ruppin's mentors was a central promulgator of the new paradigm in Germany, the blond, blue-eyed biologist Ernst Haeckel, whom Ruppin described in his diary as 'the marvellous German type'. Haeckel's mission was to disseminate 'Darwinism as a *Weltanschauung*'.[84] From Ruppin's early work in the early 1900s, it is clear that he adhered to a rigid biological determinism of race, whereby 'we are connected to our predecessors not through the spiritual tradition but through the continuity of the primordial substance that exists in our body'.[85] His reflections on the superhuman (*Übermensch*) resulted in his conclusion that such a man should develop only among his physical type,[86] from which view the shift to the idea of racial purity needed just a nudge. What made Ruppin concern himself for the rest of his life with the correction and betterment of 'the Jewish race' was the anti-Semitic rejection by his beloved German nation and homeland. The poem Ruppin penned at the nadir of his realization, 'Without Homeland', conveys this rejection and swift passage to Zionism.[87]

It cannot be sufficiently emphasized that Ruppin's path was so typical of many Central European nominal Jews: not from Judaism to Zionism but the other way around. This is an important point. The unchallenged assumption that Zionism is somehow a natural and obvious emanation from Judaism is severely questioned by such Central European nominal Jews as Herzl and Ruppin. They were completely alienated from Judasim and knew very little about it. Their rejection by an increasingly anti-Semitic society made them convert to Zionism, which was an adequate substitution to the Romantic nationalism that had not wanted them. This was what defined their Jewishness. Their turn to Zionism, in other words, was never mediated by Judaism; however, the fact that they were Jews only nominally didn't matter to the anti-Semites.

Ruppin's mission was now to transform the Jewish race by renewing the purity it once knew how to preserve, and he explicitly follows Houston Stewart Chamberlain here. Chamberlain (1855-1927) was a British popularizer of philosophy and history, who at an early age became enchanted with German culture, and an admirer of Richard Wagner, whose daughter Eva he married. His ideas on Romantic pan-German nationalism as well as anti-Semitic pronouncements were read by Ruppin. One of the main tasks Ruppin set himself was the eradication of the Jews' 'commercial instinct', responsible for their excessive fondness of Mammon. On this question he adopted the thesis of the pro-Zionist economist Werner Sombart (as mentioned, Arlosoroff's adviser in the 1920s), whom he had met at Berlin University. The key to dealing with the 'commercial instinct', which Ruppin related, crucially, to the 'Semitic element', was to preserve racial purity and eschew racial mixture (Rassenvermischung).[88] This was systematized in his The Sociology of the Jews, which appeared first in German and was promptly translated by Y. H. Brenner into Hebrew in the early 1930s,[89] a period in which Ruppin also met for a conversation on race with Himmler's mentor, Professor Hans F. K. Günther.[90] Ruppin's diagnosis was that the original Jewish Volk (Urjude), which had belonged to Indo-European tribes, deteriorated because of the increasing presence of the Semitic element in its body, through intermingling with the Oriental type in particular. The Semitic component in the Jewish race gradually became dominant, extricated the Jews from nature, from their soil and their productive agricultural way of life, and infused into them the insatiable 'commercial instinct' as early as the First Temple era (i.e., before the first century CE).[91]

'The racist accusations that had threatened Ruppin within German society', Blum avers, 'regarding the Jews' materialism and excessive economic greed, he now applied, from his Hebraic (non-Semitic) perspective, to "the Semitic races": the Jews of the East and the Arabs'.[92] His plan to remove the Semitic component – or at least reduce its presence – from the Jewish Volk, since that component was dysgenic, was predicated upon identifying a human reservoir from which to effect the renewal of a purer, more Indo-Germanic, Jewish race, one whose contact with its original soil would release 'the springs of natural sensation' (Naturempfinden). That reservoir, Ruppin determined, was East European Jewry, within which non-Semitic elements were discernible. Haeckel and H. S. Chamberlain looming large in his research, Ruppin asserted that the Middle Eastern and Sephardi Jews did not exhibit the same signs of eugenic renewal that was evident in their East European race-relatives; worse, they showed signs of being in the process of biological degeneration. He never tired of categorically underscoring the superiority of the Ashkenazis over the Mizrahim and Sephardim in creativity, mathematical skills, and hygiene; and, above all, he emphasized the superiority of the Ashkenazi bio-mystic force called *Lebenszähigkeit* (roughly speaking, 'life-tenaciousness'), equipped with which the *Volk* would be able to successfully navigate through the *Daseinskampf* (war of survival). Ruppin's ultimate conclusion was that the Jewish type par excellence – the Ashkenazi Jew – was closer to the Indo-Germanic races than the Semitic ones.[93] (As already pointed out in the previous chapter, there were other bourgeois Jews and non-Jews – real like George Eliot and Gershom Scholem, and fictional like Daniel Deronda – from Western and Central Europe, to whom the East European Jews seemed most 'authentic'.)

So obsessed was Ruppin with race that, just a few days before his death in 1943 and with the Judaeocide in Europe peaking, he began to write an introduction for a study on the Jewish race, based on a taxonomy of noses. His samples were the facial features of various Zionist figures.[94]

Ruppin was not just a theoretician but also an active settler-colonial official, who was in a position to implement his research. From the outset his Palestine Office worked with much vigour to create a community of settlers that would consist of human beings of a higher type (*höherer Menschentyp*). He applied a strict process of selection to the candidates for immigration when they were still in their countries of origin. Statistics over a two-year period (1912–14) show that above 80 per cent of those who had applied for immigration were rejected by Ruppin. Even those who had been selected but contracted serious illnesses or were severely injured while in Palestine were sent back by the Palestine Office to their ports of departure. Blum observes that

> Ruppin's methods of operation were part of his comprehensive culture planning, in the framework of which he established a network of training farms and agricultural settlements, in order to facilitate a pincer movement: the control of land acquired by the Zionist movement, and the creation, through intensive selection, of 'the human matter' that would form the dominant racial component of the old-new Jewish race, a component he called 'the Maccabian Type'.[95]

Evidence for the extent to which the German colonization project in Posen and Eastern Prussia in general informed Ruppin consists both of explicit statements by him that this was the case, and structural similarities between the Prussian and Zionist colonization projects. On several occasions Ruppin stated his indebtedness to the German venture. In the PLDC foundation prospectus of 1909 he explained that 'in its work the Company will assume the methods used by the German "Land Bank", the Polish "Ziemsky Bank" [a counter-colonization bank] and the Prussian Colonization Commission, which are engaged in a colonization process in the east Prussian provinces'. The tasks and methods of the PLDC were formulated along the lines of its German Colonization Commission model right down to the sizes of farms, which were identical to their Posen equivalents: 15–25 hectares per farmer-settler, and 0.5–1.5 per settler living in a working people's colony and employed in a nearby city.[96] The PLDC Chairman Warburg was, like Ruppin, unequivocal: 'We do not propose new ways, new experiments whose nature is unknown. We assume instead the Prussian colonization method as it has been practiced in the last ten years by the Colonization Commission'.[97]

Reichman and Hasson offer a meticulous survey of the structural ways – both conceptual and actual – in which the Posen model guided Ruppin in particular and the more general thrust of the WZO settlement drive before the First World War.[98] One of the most crucial features they unwittingly uncover is, to use Shafir's term, the 'pure settlement' frame of mind of the WZO experts. I say unwittingly, because Reichman and Hasson, as well as Penslar – whose chapter on Ruppin, cited above, confirms Blum's verdict on Zionist historians' failure to address Ruppin's racist sensibilities – write from a clearly Zionist perspective. The result is rather curious. Although the material they themselves furnish, and not infrequently even their own analyses, show how both projects – Prussian and Zionist – were colonial, something happens to the model upon travelling from the Ostmark to Palestine: it ceases being colonial and mysteriously becomes something else, which is non-colonial. Shafir is only too well aware of this, and tellingly entitles his review of Penslar's study on the German settlement technocrats 'Tech for Tech's Sake'.[99]

Two principles evinced the pure settlement vision that underpinned Ruppin's colonizing approach; these in turn were congruous with the spatial concept of the German Colonization Commission. 'One', Reichman and Hasson elaborate, 'was to avoid penetration into areas densely inhabited by another national group, and the other was to form contiguous blocks of settlements'.[100] Ruppin made this patently clear in a letter to the Zionist executive, headed by Warburg: 'For systematic colonization work we need large contiguous areas, not too far from the harbours and railroads; such land can be found only among the large estate owners'.[101] It is striking in this context how Reichman and Hasson cannot – or choose not to – see that Ruppin was actually guided by the colonial notion of the pure settlement colony. They summarize:

> Given these similarities to the principles outlined by the German [Colonization] Commission, it appears that Ruppin's knowledge of the situation in Posen had a direct bearing on the policy developed in Palestine. In both areas a deliberate geographical policy was adopted to attain demographic supremacy on a regional scale. The major difference was in the degree of closure of the settlement system, that is, the degree of inclusiveness of other national groups. Contrary to the German Commission, which sought to dominate the Poles politically as well as economically, the Zionist Organization aimed at [now they quote Ruppin] 'the creation of a Jewish milieu and of a closed Jewish economy, in which producers, consumers and middlemen shall all be Jewish'.[102]

The first cooperative settlements, of the *kvutza*-type, were created at the southern tip of Lake Galilee as a result of Ruppin's initiative and with Oppenheimer's model in mind in the 1900s. The settlers were the agricultural workers of the Second Aliya, with whom Ruppin had struck an alliance. He offered to them a way out of their failure in the Conquest of Labour, which by the mid 1900s was evident, by opening up another route: the Conquest of Land, which contained the principle of pure settlement colony in the spheres of both land and labour. The esteem in which the workers held Ruppin is indicated by his burial in Degania, founded in 1908–9 just south of Lake Galilee, and considered the 'Mother of *Kvutzot* and Kibbutzim', and by the fact that the Jerusalem thoroughfare leading to the Knesset is named Arthur Ruppin Boulevard.

The input of the Second Aliya agricultural settlers into the *kvutza* was not and could not have been socialist, simply because they were not at all socialist and had little knowledge of that particular tradition. The main form of collective organization of which they were aware was the Russian *artel*, originally a medieval corporate form, which with industrialization became a loose form of labourers' association in Russian cities and was spread by the Narodniks. The introduction of socialist and even Marxist possibilities occurred only with the arrival of the Third Aliya in the period 1918–23 and the creation of the kibbutz upon an already existing foundation of cooperative settlements.[103]

Shafir confirms the argument that the kibbutz was first and foremost a colonizing tool for the formation of a settler project, and that it was based to a considerable degree on social and ethnic exclusion. He observes:

> [T]he national character of the kibbutz was its foundation and *raison d'être* and determined its composition, and in part its structure. The kibbutz became the most homogeneous body of Israeli society: it included almost exclusively Eastern European Jews, since it was unwilling to embrace Middle Eastern and North African Jews, and was constructed on the exclusion of Palestinian Arabs. I tried in this study to give these two groups their due place in the kibbutz's prehistory, since the former, having been allowed only the most limited access to the JNF's land, and the latter, no access at all, are missing from the kibbutz's history. The kibbutz was built on such land and hence became the real nucleus of Israeli state formation, despite the fact kibbutz members always constituted a distinct minority of the Jews in Palestine.[104]

I'd like finally to return to Ruppin's relations with the East European settlers of the Second Aliya. These relations were not coincidental, nor did they stem in an ad hoc fashion from circumstances Ruppin and the settlers encountered in Palestine. Rather, these relations were the product of Ruppin's ambitious project of culture planning. I have explored Ruppin's race and eugenic theory and practice; now I turn to a related source of inspiration, a discipline that also appeared in late nineteenth-century Germany, labour science (*Arbeitwissenschaft*). An anti-socialist discipline, one of its main products was a new model of labour relations named the Stumm system, after the big steel industrialist Carl Ferdinand von Stumm, which prevailed in most of Germany's large plants. The managers in this system offered to productive and obedient workers a safety net of social and economic support, in order to attract loyal workers who would form a 'labour tribe' (*Arbeiterstamm*), thereby undermining the trade unions. The Stumm system inculcated in workers the assumption that hard labour and iron discipline, which yield productivity, reflect virtuous moral dispositions. The system also predicted that this process of selection, which would weed out 'problematic' workers, would be achieved by the workers themselves.[105] Blum conjectures that Ruppin had consciously selected the Stumm system to shape his relations with the Second Aliya settlers in the training farms and agricultural settlements, in order to attain the colonization of Palestine and creation of a human nucleus for the betterment, indeed transformation, of the Jewish *Volk*.[106]

This chapter has demonstrated the suitability of the framework of comparative settler colonialism for understanding the Zionist colonization of Palestine and the formation of the state of Israel. It has done so in two main ways. One was the structural placement of the Zionist project within the existing scholarly field of comparative settler colonialism. The other way was to consider the perspective of prominent contemporaries like Arlosoroff and Ruppin. This has brought to the fore the extent to which they were cognizant of the fact that theirs was a settler venture which was comparable with others, and of what could be learned from other settler situations. Given the power and prevalence of the manner in which the Zionist Israel project tells its own story, the chapter has put forth an alternative story and the language to recount it.

# Notes

1 Cited in H. Obenzinger, *American Palestine: Melville, Twain, and the Holy Land Mania*, Princeton: Princeton University Press, 1999, pp. 252–3.

2 Ibid., p. 190.

3 R. Siegel and T. Sofer (eds), *The Writer in the Jewish Community*, Rutherford: Fairleigh University Press and London: Associated University Presses, 1993, pp. 115–16.

4 Translated by S. Boulos in M. Akash and D. Moore (eds), *Mahmoud Darwish: The Adam of Two Edens*, Jusoor and Syracuse: Syracuse University Press, 2000, p. 136.

5 D. Myers, 'A New Scholarly Colony in Jerusalem: The Early History of Jewish Studies at the Hebrew University', *Judaism*, 45 (1996), p. 143.

6 Ibid., p. 144.

7 These are the main studies discussed in this part: D. K. Fieldhouse, *The Colonial Empires: A Comparative Survey from the Eighteenth Century*, London: Weidenfeld and Nicolson, 1966; G. M. Fredrickson, *White Supremacy: A Comparative Study in American & South African History*, Oxford: Oxford University Press, 1981; idem, 'Colonialism and Racism: The United States and South Africa in Comparative Perspective', in *The Arrogance of Race*, Middletown: Wesleyan University Press, 1988, pp. 216–35; G. Shafir, *Land, Labor, and the Origins of the Israeli-Palestinian Conflict, 1882–1914*, Berkeley: The University of California Press, 1996 (updated edition); idem, 'Israeli Society: A Counterview', *Israel Studies*, 1:2 (1996), pp. 189–213; idem, 'Zionism and Colonialism: A Comparative Approach', in M. N. Barnett (ed.), *Israel in Comparative Perspective: Challenging the Conventional Wisdom*, Albany: SUNY Press, 1996, pp. 227 45; D. Prochaska, *Making Algeria French: Colonialism in Bône, 1870–1920*, Cambridge: Cambridge University Press, 1990; P. Wolfe, 'Land, Labor, and Difference. Elementary Structures of Race', *American Historical Review*, 106.3 (2001), pp. 866–905; C. Elkins and S. Pedersen (eds), *Settler Colonialism in the Twentieth Century*, New York and London: Routledge, 2005, p. 21. I exempt myself from weighing the merits and demerits of the comparative approach, which is seriously done in the literature I refer to. See especially Fredrickson, 'Colonialism', p. 216 n. 3.

8 See his *Imagined Communities*, London: Verso, 1991 (revised edition). I find the criticisms levelled at Anderson's term and analysis unconvincing.

9 Fredrickson, *White Supremacy*, pp. 3–40.

10 Fredrickson, 'Colonialism', pp. 216–18.

11 Ibid., p. 218.

12 Ibid.

13 Ibid., p. 219.

14 Ibid.

15 Ibid., pp. 220–1.

16 Prochaska, op. cit., pp. 6–7.

17 Ibid., especially pp. 21–5.

18 Wolfe, op. cit., and 'Settler Colonialism and the Elimination of the Native', *Journal of Genocide Research*, 8/4 (December 2006), pp. 387–409.

19 P. Wolfe, *Settler Colonialism and the Transformation of Anthropology: The Politics and Poetics of an Ethnographic Event*, London and New York: Cassell, 1999, p. 1.

20 Ibid.
21 Ibid.
22 Ibid., p. 2.
23 Ibid. For a condensed expression of the argument in an article see P. Wolfe's 'Should the Subaltern Dream', in S. C. Humphreys (ed.), *Cultures of Scholarship*, Ann Arbor: The University of Michigan Press, 1997, pp. 57–96. For Wolfe's critique on more recent post-colonial writing see 'Can the Muslim Speak? An Indebted Critique', *History and Theory*, 41 (October 2002), pp. 367–80.
24 My comments refer to Elkins and Pedersen's Introduction to *Settler Colonialism in the Twentieth Century*, the locus of their joint view, especially pp. 1–7.
25 Ibid., p. 1.
26 Cited ibid., p. 3.
27 For Shafir, in addition to *Land, Labour*, see 'Zionism and Colonialism: A Comparative Approach', and 'Israeli Society: A Counterview', Z. Lockman, 'Exclusion and Solidarity: Labor Zionism and Arab Workers in Palestine, 1897–1929', in G. Prakash (ed.), *After Colonialism*, Princeton: Princeton University Press, 1995, pp. 211–41; idem, *Comrades and Enemies: Arab and Jewish Workers in Palestine, 1906–1948*, Berkeley: University of California Press, 1996.
28 M. Rodinson, *Israel: A Colonial-Settler State?*, New York: Pathfinder, 1973.
29 I. Pappé, 'Zionism as Colonialism – A Comparative Perspective on Diluted Colonialism in Asia and Africa', in Y. Weitz (ed.), *Between Vision and Revision: A Hundred Years of Zionist Historiography*, Jerusalem: Salman Shazar Centre, 1997, pp. 345–65 [Hebrew].
30 For the most recent articulation see G. Shafir, 'Settler Citizenship in the Jewish Colonization of Palestine', in Elkins and Pedersen, op. cit., pp. 41–59.
31 G. Shafir and Y. Peled, *Being Israeli: The Dynamics of Multiple Citizenship*, Cambridge: Cambridge University Press, 2002, p. 37.
32 For a useful presentation of the sociological articulation of the hegemonic narrative see U. Ram, *The Changing Agenda of Israeli Sociology: Theory, Ideology and Identity*, Albany: SUNY Press, 1995, and L. J. Silberstein, *The Post-Zionism Debates*, New York and London: Routledge, 1999. Succinct and useful surveys are offered by Shafir, *Land, Labor*, pp. 1–7, and by Lockman, *Comrades*, pp. 3–8.
33 Shafir, 'A Counterview'.
34 Ibid., pp. 189–90.
35 Shafir, 'Zionism and Colonialism', pp. 230–31. This article is especially helpful because it is a succinct synopsis of *Land, Labor* coupled with additional insights gained by the author with the passage of time.
36 Ibid., p. 230.
37 Ibid.
38 Ibid., pp. 232–3.
39 Ibid.
40 Ibid., p. 234.
41 Ibid., p. 235.
42 See for instance his well-crafted critique of the dual society paradigm in *Comrades*, pp. 3–7.

43 M. C. Jacob and I. Katznelson (conveners), 'Agendas for Radical History', *Radical History Review*, 36 (September 1986), pp. 26–47.

44 Ibid., pp. 33–7.

45 Ibid., p. 36.

46 Lockman, *Comrades*, p. 8 n. 10.

47 Ibid., pp. 111–48.

48 See Sh. Teveth, *Arlosoroff's Assassination* [Hebrew], Jerusalem, 1982.

49 On Arlosoroff's life and *oeuvre* see Sh. Avineri, 'Chaim Arlosoroff: A Social and Political Thinker [Hebrew]', in A. Maniv (ed.), *Haim Arlosoroff: Nation, State and Society; Selected Essays*, Tel Aviv: Hakibbutz Hameuhad, 1984, pp. 9–31; idem, *Arlosoroff*, London: Peter Halban, 1989; Z. Sternhell, *The Founding Myths of Israel*, Princeton: Princeton University Press, by index. Sternhell's is the best study to date that does ideology critique of labour Zionism in general, and A. D. Gordon and Hapoel Hatzair in particular. It is a thoroughly authoritative *coup de grâce* to such lingering universalist socialist pretences that labour Zionism may still have.

50 Ch. Arlosoroff, 'On the Question of Joint Organization', in *Chaim Arlosoroff's Works* [Hebrew], Tel Aviv: Shtiebel, 1934, 7 vols., vol. 3, pp. 135–71. The editor of *Kitvey* dates the essay to 1926, which seems to me too early because in it Arlosoroff refers to an article by Lord Sidney Oliver of 1927 (p. 161).

51 Lockman, 'Exclusion', pp. 232–3, and *Comrades*, pp. 99–101.

52 The following passage draws on Sh. Teveth, *Ben Gurion and the Palestinian Arabs: From Peace to War* [Hebrew], Jerusalem and Tel Aviv: Schocken, 1985, pp. 92–118, and Lockman, 'Exclusion', pp. 224–36.

53 Teveth, op. cit., pp. 97–8.

54 See A. Shlaim's excellent *The Iron Wall: Israel and the Arab World*, New York and London: W. W. Norton, 2000, pp. 1–28.

55 Arlosoroff, op. cit., p. 138.

56 Sternhell, op. cit., pp. 3–47.

57 Arlosoroff, op. cit., p. 146.

58 Ibid., p. 147.

59 Ibid., pp. 147–53.

60 Ibid., pp. 155–7.

61 Ibid., p. 156.

62 Ibid., p. 157.

63 Ibid., pp. 165–6.

64 Ibid., p. 157.

65 Ibid.

66 Ibid., p. 158.

67 Ibid., pp. 160–1.

68 Ibid., pp. 161–2.

69 Ibid., pp. 162–8.

70 Lockman, *Comrades*, pp. 101–2.

71 Avineri, op. cit., pp. 60–77.

72 Maniv, op. cit., p. 169.

73 Sh. Reichman and Sh. Hasson, 'A Cross-Cultural Diffusion of Colonization: From Posen to Palestine', *Annals of the Association of American Geographers*, 74/1 (March 1984), pp. 57–70.

74 Ibid., pp. 57–60.
75 Ibid., pp. 57–8.
76 Ibid., p. 63.
77 Ibid., pp. 63–4.
78 Although the information that underpins this summary is contained in the Reichman and Hasson article, I prefer Shafir's interpretative register. See *Land, Labor*, pp. 146–86.
79 Shafir, *Land, Labor*, pp. 150–1.
80 Ibid., p. 151.
81 D. J. Penslar, *Zionism and Technocracy: The Engineering of Jewish Settlement in Palestine, 1870–1918*, Bloomington: Indiana University Press, 1991, pp. 80–111.
82 E. Blum, 'On the German Origins of Hebrew Culture: The Repression of the Nationalist Role of Arthur Ruppin – "The Father of Jewish Settlement in the Land of Israel"', *Mitaam*, 11 (2007), pp. 71–93 [Hebrew]. Amos Morris-Reich's essay takes on the question of Ruppin's scientific racism and eugenics, but clearly searches for mitigating circumstances. See his 'Arthur Ruppin's Concept of Race', *Israel Studies*, 11:3 (2006), pp. 1–30.
83 Blum, op. cit., pp. 71–4.
84 Ibid., p. 75.
85 Ibid., pp. 76–7.
86 Ibid., p. 76.
87 Ibid., p. 77.
88 Ibid., pp. 78–9.
89 The translation, as Blum notes, is obfuscating, for Brenner used biblical language that masks the German-scientific register of the original. See Blum, op. cit., p. 81.
90 On the meeting with Günther see Morris-Reich, op. cit., pp. 1–2, and Blum, op. cit., p. 90.
91 Blum, op. cit., pp. 80–1.
92 Ibid., p. 81.
93 Ibid., pp. 80–3.
94 Ibid., p. 79.
95 Ibid., p. 83.
96 Reichman and Hasson, op. cit., p. 64.
97 Ibid.
98 Ibid., pp. 64–8.
99 G. Shafir, 'Tech for Tech's Sake', *Journal of Palestine Studies*, 21/4 (Summer 1992), pp. 103–5.
100 Reichman and Hasson, op. cit., p. 66.
101 Ibid.
102 Ibid.
103 Shafir, *Land, Labor*, pp. 166, 174–5 and 184.
104 Ibid., p. 184.
105 Blum, op. cit., pp. 83–4.
106 Ibid., p. 84.

# 3

# The Foundational Myth of Zionism: Politics, Ideology and Scholarship

## A Working Definition

For largely practical reasons, the method and presentation of this chapter involves the collapse of any separation between the subject – the foundational myth itself – and the infinite variety of references to it in literary, scholarly, ideological and political texts. When dealing with an event (e.g., the 1948 war), an institution (the Histadrut) or even a concrete text (*Altneuland*), it is relatively simple to convey and grasp distinctions between the subject in and of itself and expressions that refer to it, and also between the contemporary sources and more temporally distant studies. However, the myth of a modern movement forbids such distinctions. To accord the myth existence which is distinguishable from articulations of it, be they in a novel, a political treatise or a scholarly work, would simply be obfuscating. I am well aware of pre-modern, modern and post-modern debates on the ontological and epistemological status of 'things' vis-à-vis their verbal rendering, but it is not something I wish to dwell on in the present context. What I do wish to make clear is that there is no 'negation of exile' (i.e., that Jewish existence outside a sovereign Jewish state in the land of Israel is neither normal nor fully authentic – more below) outside of poems, novels, political speeches, scholarly studies, laws and institutions that address and perpetuate the 'negation of exile', or conversely outside texts that negate the 'negation of exile' or actions that resist it.

I now turn to a definition of the three main articulations of the Zionist foundational myth as they relate to each other (they are inseparable, after all). There are of course no neutral definitions. The one I offer here has already been crafted elsewhere[1] and it is rather basic, although I will elaborate upon it in due course.[2]

The foundational myth that underlies Israeli politics and culture to this day expresses itself in three ways: the 'negation of exile' (*shelilat ha-galut*), the 'return to the land of Israel' (*ha-shiva le-Eretz Yisrael*), and the 'return to history' (*ha-shiva la-historia*). They are inextricably intertwined in the master-narrative of Zionism, the story that explains 'how we got to where we are and where we should go henceforth'. The first expression, negation of exile, establishes continuity between an ancient past, in which there existed Jewish sovereignty over the land of Israel, and a present that renews it in the resettlement of Palestine. Between the two, so this line of thought goes, lies no more than a kind of interminable interim period. Depreciation of the period of exile's value is shared by all Zionists, albeit with differing degrees of rigidity, and derives from what is in their view an uncontestable presupposition: from time immemorial, the Jews constituted a territorial nation. It follows that a non-territorial existence must be abnormal, incomplete and inauthentic. In and of itself, as a historical experience, exile is devoid of significance. Although it may have given rise to cultural achievements of moment, exile could not by definition have been a wholesome realization of the nation's *Geist*. So long as they were condemned to exile, Jews – whether as individuals or communities – could lead at best a partial and transitory existence, waiting for the redemption of 'ascent' (*aliya*) once again to the land of Israel, the only site on which the nation's destiny could be fulfilled. Within this mythical framework, exilic Jews always lived provisionally, as potential or proto-Zionists, longing to 'return' to the land of Israel.

The second expression of the foundational myth complements the first. In Zionist terminology, the recovery by the people of its home promises to deliver the *normalization* of Jewish existence; and the site designated for the re-enactment of Exodus would be the territory of the biblical story, as elaborated in the Protestant Christian culture of the eighteenth and nineteenth centuries. Zionist ideology defined this land as *empty*. This did not mean that Zionist leaders and settlers were ignorant of, or ignored, the presence of Arabs in Palestine. Israel was 'empty' in a deeper sense. For the land, too, was condemned to exile as long as there was no Jewish sovereignty over it: it lacked any meaningful or authentic history, awaiting its own redemption with the return of the Jews. The best-known Zionist slogan, 'a land without a people to a people without a land', expressed a twofold denial: that of the historical experience both of the Jews in exile, and of Palestine without Jewish sovereignty. Of course, since the land was not literally empty, its recovery required the establishment of the equivalent of a colonial hierarchy – sanctioned by biblical authority – by its historic custodians over such intruders as might remain after the return. Jewish settlers were to be accorded exclusive privileges deriving from the Pentateuch, and Palestinian Arabs treated as part of the natural environment. The Zionist settlers were collective subjects who acted, and the native Palestinians became objects acted upon.

The third articulation of the foundational myth, the 'return to history', reveals the extent to which Zionist ideology was underpinned by the emergence of Romantic nationalism and German historicism in nineteenth-century Europe. Its premise is that the natural and irreducible form of human collectivity is the nation. From the dawn of history peoples have been grouped into such units, and though they might at one time or another be undermined by internal divisions or oppressed by external forces, these units are eventually bound to find political self-expression in the shape of sovereign nation-states. The nation is the autonomous historical subject par excellence, and the state is the telos of its march towards self-fulfilment. According to this logic, so long as they were exiles, the Jews remained a community outside history, within which all European nations dwelt. Only nations that occupy the soil of their homeland, and establish political sovereignty over it, are capable of shaping their own destiny and so entering history. The return of the Jewish nation to the land of Israel, overcoming its docile passivity in exile, could alone allow it to rejoin the history of civilized peoples.

Finally, a linguistic clarification is necessary concerning the notion of the negation of exile (*shelilat ha-galut*). The problem lies in the Hebrew rather than in the English translation. In modern Hebrew discourse two words have been interchangeably used to denote the negation of exile: *galut* and *golah*. The confusion stems from the fact that Hebrew's morphology, like that of its Arabic cousin, is based upon three-letter radicals that are declined in various ways to create various forms and meanings. Sure enough, *galut* and *golah* are two nouns which are derived from the same three-letter radical (G,L,H); they therefore convey related but different meanings. Despite their proximity this semantic difference is significant, and to use these words interchangeably is consequently erroneous.

*Golah* means Diaspora, the actual circumstance in which Jews happen to reside outside of the land of Israel. *Galut* signifies something that is meaningful both literally and figuratively: it is exile as an experience, as a material circumstance, as an existential state of being, as consciousness. What Zionism negates is, fundamentally, *galut*, not *golah*. I therefore consistently translate *shelilat ha-galut* as 'negation of *exile*', resorting to 'Diaspora' only where appropriate. It is imperative to distinguish between *galut* and *golah* in order fully to grasp Zionism, both in its practice in Europe and the US and in its realization in Palestine/Israel. Zionists have always accepted the existence of a sizeable Diaspora, and have always mobilized it shamelessly and with huge success to strengthen the Israeli project. Yet Zionism perforce presupposes a hierarchy, by which existence of Jews within the land of Israel under Jewish sovereignty is the apex of collective Jewish experience, superior to the exilic experience, which is within this logic of necessity incomplete.

Take for instance a speech given by Amos Oz at Berkeley in 1988. Explicitly addressing an American Jewish audience, Oz is clearly resigned to their being in the Diaspora; he does not admonish them for this, nor does he really try to convince them to immigrate to Israel. What he does do, even though the level of the argument is quite embarrassing, is to articulate the hierarchy, whereby Jewish existence in the state of Israel is superior to Jewish existence elsewhere, which illustrates the need for linguistic accuracy. Oz first observes that there are two modes in which civilizations exist: either as a museum or as live drama. He then proceeds to tell his audience:

> Now, my point is that in all exiles, including America, Jewish culture is essentially in danger of becoming a museum where the only proposition that parents can make to their children is, Please do not assimilate . . . The other option . . . is live drama. And live drama is no rose garden, nor is it ever pure. It is a perpetual struggle; sound and fury. Sometimes even bloodshed. But Israel is the only place in the Jewish world now, where there is a live drama on a large scale at work.[3]

Having put forth a working definition of the myth, I now proceed with a more thorough discussion of it, emphasizing its negation of exile expression. The discussion starts from simple and rather crude articulations, and is brought to conclusion with a radical non-Zionist critique of the negation of exile.

## Conventional Varieties Of The Negation Of Exile

In Zionism, as in other projects of a similar nature, the authority of history replaced the authority of God. The famous Hegelian couplet defining history as both what happened in the past (*res gestae*) and the consciousness and recounting of what happened in the past (*historia rerum gestarum*) was at the heart of one of the most successful and powerful instances of settler nationalism in the twentieth century. The construction of an authoritative history, and its effective conveyance both domestically and internationally, played a significant role in the colonization of Palestine, in the dispossession of its native Palestinians, and in the establishment and development of Israel as an exclusively Jewish state.

Scholars of Zionist history identify various approaches to the negation of exile among Zionist politicians and thinkers. These, as we shall see, differ in reasoning, vehemence and rhetoric, but they share the fundamentals of the myth presented above. However, before I turn to the more intricately crafted constructions of the negation of exile, mention must be made of the more crude and popular version of the myth.

David Myers aptly identifies this crude version as the Yudke type of the negation of exile.[4] Yudke is the protagonist of a famous and widespread short story by the Hebrew writer Hayim Hazaz entitled 'Ha-Derashah' ('The Sermon'). Following its publication in 1942, this story grew in popularity and became part of the literary curriculum in Israeli schools. Yudke is a marginal and taciturn kibbutz member who, in one of the collective's assemblies, erupts and delivers a stunning speech, The Sermon. The gist of it is his uncompromising objection to, and rejection of, Jewish history. The justification is that essentially there is no Jewish history, because, while passivity, cowardice, pogroms and docility unfortunately were features of Jewish life, they do not pass for history.[5]

Another powerful articulation of this sweepingly brutal negation of exile was amply offered by the most ruthless negationist in the Zionist pantheon: David Ben-Gurion. Many of his crude and demagogic statements somehow managed to be interpreted by his admiring audiences – both political and scholarly – as deeply profound observations and moral guidelines. It is worth giving an example of the content and form of the negation of exile/return to history à la Ben-Gurion, because of the significance of their source and the breadth of their reception.

On an occasion prompted by the sixtieth anniversary of the Zionist movement's foundation (1957), Ben-Gurion engaged in a public debate with Nahum Goldman, a prominent leader of the Jewish Agency, who was disliked in Israel because of his liberal views on foreign policy and what Israelis considered as his exilic appearance and manners. The venue was the Zionist ideational gathering in Jerusalem, and the debate was provoked by what in Ben-Gurion's view was Goldman's glorification of *galut*. Ben-Gurion conceded that the way the Jews in exile, against all odds and in the face of dire circumstances, had clung to their Jewishness was admirable. 'However, the exile in which the Jews lived and still live

– is to my mind a miserable, poor, wretched, dubious experience, and it shouldn't be a source of pride, on the contrary – it should be comprehensively negated.'[6]

Ben-Gurion did not stop there, adding a literary example to remove any lingering doubt as to his standpoint:

> I do not despise Shylock for having made a livelihood of interest, he had no alternative in his place of exile, and he was morally superior to the exalted nobles who humiliated him, but I shall not turn Shylock into an ideal type and a role model to whom I shall strive to resemble. The Diaspora Jews are not Shylocks – but it is difficult to square the glorification of exilic life with the ideal that seventy years ago was given the name Zionism. And as a negationist of exile I [also] negate the glorification of exile.[7]

These remarks sealed Ben-Gurion's lifelong contribution to the construction of the negation of exile – through political as much as ideological activity – and its near-identical manifestation, the return to history. Forty years before, Ben-Gurion published an article in the American Yiddish press in reaction to the Balfour Declaration in 1917, in which he observed that:

> Since our last *national* disaster, the suppression of the Bar Kokhba revolt, we've had 'histories' of persecutions, of judicial discrimination, inquisition and pogroms; of devotion and martyrdom; of Jewish scholars and personalities, but we haven't yet had *Jewish history*; because a history of a people is only that which the people creates as one whole, as a national unit, and not what happens to individuals or groups within the people. *We have been extricated from world history*, which consists in the annals of peoples [emphasis added].[8]

No less unyielding was Ben-Gurion's single-minded commitment to the return to the land of Israel, which was formulated in an immediate comment on the Balfour Declaration, in an essay entitled 'The Realization of Zionism': 'Everything should concentrate on one focal point – the land of Israel. Zionism can now consider no other purpose, however important that might be. Anything that is not directly intended for the land of Israel is out of bounds. The Zionist slogan should henceforth be: everything for the land [of Israel] – nothing for anything else.'[9]

Yosef Gorny is absolutely correct in observing 'that there is no sharper articulation of the negation of exile and the return to history than Ben-

Gurion's'.[10] His career is evidence that mythical zeal and calculated politics are by no means mutually exclusive. We shall see later how these ideological constructions and statements were ruthlessly implicated in the realm of politics. Perhaps the most brutal statement was made after *Kristallnacht* (1938). Ben-Gurion infamously said that if he had to choose between saving all of Germany's Jewish children on the condition that they go to England, and saving only half of them but have that half sent to Palestine, he would opt for the latter.[11]

The final and most recent example of this 'vulgar' negation of exile is offered by one of the two high priests of current Hebrew literature, A. B. Yehoshua (the other being Amos Oz). In addition to his novels, Yehoshua is well known for his vehement castigation of the behaviour and nature of Jews in exile, and their unforgivable reluctance to return to their homeland prior to the emergence of Zionism. He intimates that he finds depressing the efforts of ideologues and apologists to count each and every Jew who happened to be in Palestine at one time or another, and that 'if the Jews had fought for the right to dwell in the land of Israel as they fought for the right to dwell in England, whence they had been expelled, the pathetic attempts to prove that a few Jews did dwell here would have been superfluous, [as would have been the attempts to show] that there was some Rabbi Yehuda HaLevi who was driven mad with longing and eventually came here'.[12]

Yehoshua completes the by now familiar myth, and posits the opposite state of being. If exile is abnormal, and if Jews ought to be reproached for adhering to exile so religiously for almost 2,000 years, then normality is not only regained with territoriality (in the land of Israel of course), but the two are synonymous. The title of his most famous essay on this question is emblematic: 'The Right to Be Normal' ['Bi-Zekhut ha-Normaliyut'].[13]

The curious thing about Yehoshua's observations is how they reveal his inability to examine his own presuppositions. If Jews throughout the ages did not behave as Yehoshua expects them to have behaved, that is, if they did not negate exile and return to their homeland, then something is reprehensible in their behaviour and nothing is wrong with Yehoshua's presupposed expectations. It also says a lot about the high dose of haughty authority with which his consciousness is imbued. The point in emphasizing Yehoshua's lack of reflection is that it illustrates the success with which the negation of exile has been inculcated, to the extent that it can determine what was normal and what was not among both the living (Jews who are still in the Diaspora) and the dead (Jews who for 2,000 years did not make *aliya*).

But Yehoshua is not content with the reassertion of the negation of exile through retroactively giving the exilic Jews a piece of his mind. He offers a fundamentalist, Protestant formulation of its concomitant, whereby the return of the Jews to sovereignty in the land of Israel is not just 'normalization', it is the total accomplishment of the telos of 'original Judaism'. In a documented exchange with another eminent Hebrew author, the Palestinian Israeli Anton Shammas, Yehoshua underscores the magnitude of the myth: 'For me, "Israeli" is the authentic, complete, and consummate word for the concept "Jewish." Israeliness is the total, perfect, and *original Judaism*, one that would provide answers in all areas of life [emphasis added].'[14] It should be added that Shammas posed a disturbing challenge for Jewish Israeli liberals like Yehoshua. His magnificent novel *Arabesques* (1986) was written in Hebrew. He now demanded that the state, in the Hebrew culture of which he was willing to partake, become the state of all its citizens – Jews and Palestinian Arabs – rather than one of and for the Jewish people. Yehoshua's settler-*volkisch* response left no room for uncertainty. Depressingly, after six decades of statehood this response has not changed but, on the contrary, has stiffened.

It might be noted in passing that the remarkable formulation put forth by Yehoshua – and he is after all an outstanding spokesman of the Israeli left – sheds a substantially different light on the putative religious/secular polarity that has split Israeli society, and which has been the focus of much international attention. Yehoshua's text indicates how misconstrued this polarity is in public discourse in both Israel and the West. A conflict indeed exists, but not between a secular/atheist culture and its religious adversary. Rather, one camp in this confrontation more or less adheres to the Jewish *mitzvot* (the 613 instructions of 'do' or 'do not do' that were developed in rabbinical literature on the basis of a certain way of interpreting the Torah), whereas the other camp religiously violates some *mitzvot*, especially those the violation of which annoys its foe (for example, eating pork or driving on the Sabbath). Above all, wittingly or not, the supposedly titanic clash between these two camps produces one pivotal result that is shared by the two theologies: the continued distancing of the Palestinian Israelis from citizenship, public discourse and culture, whose exclusively Jewish nature is thus perpetuated and enhanced.

The myth's successful and effective dissemination, which shaped the vocabulary and instinctive world view of so many people, and founded the well-known stereotypes of the new Jew (or Hebrew, or Sabra or Israeli) and its diametrically opposed Other, the exilic Jew, was achieved precisely in this way, through simple and crude formulae, slogans and rhetoric (*Al tihyeh Yehudi Galuti!*, 'Don't be an exilic Jew!'), rather than through painstaking debate and argument. People instinctively reached for such vocabulary and phrases when wanting to criticize peers whose behaviour was considered cowardly or evasive, and others whose physical appearance and prowess were found wanting.

## Scholarly Taxonomies

In delving deeper into the construction of the negation of exile it is worth turning to the work of Eliezer Schweid, a scholar of modern Jewish thought and culture at the Hebrew University. Schweid's 1984 essay on the interpretation and taxonomy of this question is abundantly referred to by other Zionist scholars as an accepted, even authoritative, understanding of the negation of exile. In addition Schweid, himself a Zionist, discusses the question from an intrinsic vantage point, and he would probably oppose the use of the term 'myth' to describe it.[15]

Indeed, Schweid's perspective and concerns, which he openly expresses, render his essay particularly meaningful. He begins with a brief reminder of the original context within which the negation of exile was conceived: Zionism's desire to distinguish itself from other solutions to 'the problem of the Jews and Judaism', and the genuine sense that *galut* might eliminate the Jewish people 'first spiritually and morally and then physically'. But then, he continues, 'I shamelessly confess that the motivation for this reconsideration of the idea of the negation of exile is not scientific, but stems from sensitivity to a current educational problem'.[16]

This 'educational problem' and its remedy are the key to Schweid's purpose. He regrets that the negation of exile as a primary assumption that guided the national Israeli education system was somehow, without an official or explicit decision, forsaken. There is, he correctly observes, no Zionism without the negation of exile. Consistent with his ideological commitment, Schweid states that there can be no identification of the younger generation with the state of Israel (note the crucial absence: there is no concern for how the youth of the Palestinian–Israeli town of Umm al-Fahm, for instance, would identify with the state that is putatively theirs too; this absence is precisely what makes Schweid's perspective Zionist[17]). Schweid then explains that the omission of such a Zionist *sine qua non* is the regrettable result of several factors. What needs to be done according to Schweid is reconciliation with the Diaspora in order to elicit support for Israel, and rectification of the loss by Israelis of the organic bond with Jewish tradition and continuity. Be this as it may, the negation of exile has in Schweid's view been severely undermined, and this is tantamount to an alarming erosion of the younger generation's 'Zionist conviction' (*ha-shikhnua ha-Tzioni*).[18]

Schweid seeks to convince his readers that 'there is an alternative to both the ideology that negates a positive attitude to Jewish heritage in the name of the negation of exile, and the ideology that negates the negation of exile in the name of reaffirming the heritage'. To achieve this Schweid attempts to highlight the varieties and subtleties of the negation of exile myth, to show that it was not as monolithic and rigid as its popular version might suggest, and thereby to effect its crucial reintroduction into the national education in a fashion that is more pertinent to the current realities of Israelis (i.e., the 1980s).[19]

Schweid discerns two types of the negation of exile myth among Zionist intellectuals in the formative period of, roughly, 1880–1940. The first type is generally characterized by the extreme repudiation of exilic life in both form and content. Schweid mentions most of the intellectuals during this time who adopted this version of the myth, but chooses to focus on two in particular: the writer Y. H. Brenner, and the first appointee, in 1949, to the position of professor of Bible studies at the Hebrew University, Yehezkel Kaufmann. Schweid's focus is sensible. Brenner was a highly gifted writer. Even after he had been killed in an Arab attack in 1921, his writings continued to wield much influence on the educational ideology of the Zionist Israeli labour movement, and were avidly read by the members of the Second Aliya; it is fair to say that his work played a major role in shaping the cultural horizons of the political elite that ran the Zionist Israeli show from the 1930s up to 1977. Kaufmann is especially significant because his work is still one of the most systematic and ambitious attempts to lend scholarly credence to the negation of exile from an intrinsically Zionist perspective. We shall return to Kaufmann in Chapter Seven, which deals with the place of the Old Testament in Zionist Israeli ideology.

Schweid perceptively highlights the features of the negation of exile that are unique to Brenner, and on which Second Aliya figures like Ben-Gurion and Berl Katznelson, as well as subsequent generations of labour Zionists, drew. These were Brenner's construction of the aesthetics and ethics of exile (or lack thereof), and his anti-intellectualism and anti-ideology. His portrayal of the Jewish township and neighbourhood in the East European Pale of Settlement depicts this environment as ugly, neglected, and utterly lacking aesthetic sensitivity. This, in Brenner's depiction, is true of public and private buildings, streets, and the clothing and physique of human beings. The sociological description of the exilic Jews in Eastern Europe, the protagonists of much of his work, is congruous with that of their environment and outward appearance: for Brenner, their moral and human countenance is as aesthetically repulsive as their material lives.[20]

For Brenner, ideological argument and intellectualism were synonymous with the exilic, and his rejection of them was highly influential in the shaping of the Zionist Israeli education system. In Brenner's discourse this abhorrence of intellectual activity is embodied literally and figuratively in what was called *pilpul Talmudi*, the tendency for sterile and hair-splitting debate over minute points of legal religious literature of commentary as practised in the *yeshiva*. Brenner was fundamentally rejecting no less than rabbinical Judaism itself, and its cumulative creation, the Jewish *Halakhah*, as the ultimate quintessence of *galut*. Brenner's literature negates exile not by means of a coherently sociological or historical exposition, but through rhetorical and aesthetic force, which renders *galut* an existential abomination, a life not worthy of living. The trope that underlies this is neither uniquely nor originally Brennerian, but his inculcation of it seems to have been most effective: *batlanut*, which in current Hebrew means laziness, but also suggests a disposition emblematic of exile and of exilic behaviour. More comprehensively, it denoted idleness, uselessness, unproductive being, futility, and inadequate cognitive orientation in the world of productive action.[21]

Yehezkel Kaufmann was the most influential and authoritative scholar of the Bible and of the formation of the Jewish religion in Israel. As professor of Bible studies at Hebrew University, his profile benefited considerably from Ben-Gurion's 'Bible project', to the ideological significance of which I will return in Chapters Six and Seven. Ben-Gurion held highly publicized gatherings at his residence to discuss the Bible with leading scholars, foremost among whom was Kaufmann. Although he openly disagreed with Kaufmann on certain matters, Ben Gurion rarely missed an opportunity to bestow accolades upon his scholarly prowess, and he invariably emphasized Kaufmann's heroic rescue of Biblical Studies from centuries of Gentile and rabbinical abuse, and his ensuring their safe return 'home'.[22]

Among Kaufmann's writings two books stand out, and although for current purposes we reject the conventional distinction between scholarly and political–ideological texts, it should be noted that, formally speaking, one is the former and the other the latter. In his eight-volume *Toldot ha-Emunah ha-Yisraelit* ('History of the Jewish belief')[23] Kaufmann took on, unsuccessfully as it transpired, the entire scholarly body of modern Biblical Studies. The crux of his circular argument was that the formation of pure monotheism and of the Israeli nation had been a simultaneous occurrence on Mount Sinai, for which the main evidence he adduced was the biblical account itself. It is significant that despite (or perhaps because of) the fact that his argument and approach were deemed questionable, to say the least, by the international scholarly community Kaufmann was commissioned by the Israeli editors of *The Biblical Encyclopaedia* to write the core entry on 'Jewish Religion'.[24]

The other book, *Golah ve-Nekhar* ('Exile and foreignness'),[25] was more explicitly ideological, and constitutes one of the most ambitious attempts to render plausible the myth of the negation of exile, as the book's subtitle suggests: 'A historical-sociological study on the question of the Jewish people from antiquity to the present'. Views differ as to the significance and meaning of Kaufmann's undertaking. Schweid, for example, shares Kaufmann's ideological commitment to Zionism, and therefore does not question his underlying assumptions. Boas Evron, on the other hand, shares neither Kaufmann's commitment nor his assumptions; indeed, he finds both objectionable, and consequently deconstructs Kaufmann's argument.[26]

Schweid is aware of Kaufmann's predilection for Zionism, and stresses that his compendious work 'is not just the fruit of a scientist's curiosity, but also the embodiment of a Zionist Jewish world view'.[27] Kaufmann's thesis commences with a fundamental sociological rule, to which he accords universal validity: dispersed nations that had lost their independence and territorial hold could not survive for more than a generation or two, because material interests are stronger than adherence to cultural heritage and historical memory. The imminent result was invariably assimilation. Then comes the *problématique*: if such is the nature of this universally applicable rule, how did the Jews in exile survive as a nation? And if the Jews are the exception that proves the rule, a secular explanation is required in order that they can return to the natural course of history shared by all secular European nations.

The basis of Kaufmann's ideological exposition is the universality of the Jewish religion. Vehemently rejecting previous explanations for the unassimilated survival of the Jewish nation, he asserts that the sociological function of religion alone accounts for it. Historically, Kaufmann observes, exilic Jews assimilated rapidly into their host societies, something that had been possible in relatively pluralistic pagan cultures, but this process came to a halt under the Christian and Muslim civilizations, precisely because they sought to inherit Judaism. From that point on, Jews obstinately resisted assimilation into their host societies, isolating themselves instead, and were consequently met with resentment and hostility. According to this explanation Jews, though immanently unresisting to national assimilation, demarcated the limits of this process through the self-imposition of religious lifestyles within their communities. This impossible ideological meandering is exacerbated by Schweid's attempt to present and interpret it as a coherent argument: '[What we have is] an assimilated nation from the national-earthly perspective, but [one that] retains national particularity from the religious perspective.'[28]

Although this construct was jointly erected by two proudly territorial Jews – Kaufmann and Schweid – it is most probable that Brenner would have deemed it yet another exilic manifestation of Talmudic *pilpul*.

Yet, if this universal Jewish monotheism managed to preserve the national *Geist* of the Jewish collective, then why does exile have to be negated? According to Kaufmann, there are two reasons: one has to do with a certain historical observation, the other stems from condescendingly moral pontificating. Kaufmann was adamant that the process of Jewish emancipation in Europe had failed, and that this failure had left most Jews between a rock and a hard place. On the one hand the walls of the Ghetto had irreparably collapsed, and they could see the Promised Land – full assimilation into European national societies – but on the other hand they were refused admission into it. This predicament, which is more or less what Herzl and Lazare had observed much earlier and presented as the trope of the New Ghetto, was according to Kaufmann one of 'absolute foreignness', intolerable and existentially perilous. The only solution, in his view, was for the Jews to return to their homeland, develop their national culture on the basis of their original language (Kaufmann loathed the Jewish 'jargons', Ladino and Yiddish), and come to resemble all other European nations.

But it is on the issue of the morality of exile that Kaufmann's and Brenner's negation of exile converge. Kaufmann's devotion to the study of Judaism's origins, and the esteem in which he held the universal monotheistic message, should not mask his abhorrence of exile, especially in its modern guise. For Kaufmann *galut* was tantamount to the violation of human dignity, and whoever was willing to pay that price and assimilate 'is not worthy even of pity. He is worthy of contempt and disgrace.'[29]

## The Canaanite Critique

Boas Evron's *A National Reckoning*[30] is not only a deconstruction of Kaufmann's argument, but the first and most ambitious nationalist[31] attempt by an Israeli systematically to refute Zionism as an ideology, a vision of history, and a framework for the state of Israel. Remarkably, this thoughtful book went almost unnoticed in Israel, and did not give rise to the debates it could and should have stimulated, something that shows how deeply Zionism is ingrained in the consciousness of Jewish Israelis. Only recently, with the advent of critical scholarship on Zionism, have the insights contained in this work begun to receive the recognition they deserve.[32]

Evron was born in Jerusalem in 1927, educated in the Herzliya Gymnasium in Tel Aviv, and then at the Hebrew and Tel Aviv universities. He was on the editorial board of the daily *Haaretz* (1956–64) and then that of *Yediot Aharonot* (from 1964 until the 1990s). His weekend essays in the latter became a regular and quality feature in the Israeli press.

I will explain why Evron's deconstruction of Kaufmann's *Exile and Foreignness* is significant for the former's attempt profoundly to challenge Zionism.[33] Unlike Schweid, whose thought is constrained by the same ideology and myths as Kaufmann's, Evron questions Kaufmann's a priori assumption. This assumption is the one which underpins the foundational myth, namely, that the Jews had constituted a territorial nation since time immemorial, and that therefore exile is an abnormal state of affairs; return to the homeland is a matter of destiny. The source of the problem, according to Evron, is to be found in Kaufmann's elucidation of the nation's formative moment, which he put forth in *History of the Jewish Belief* and which was rejected by the international community of Bible studies.

Kaufmann argued that the formation of the monotheist religion as an idea, and the alliance that united the Israelite tribes, were fused together on Mount Sinai, and that this fusion culminated in the formation of the Jewish nation. Rejecting the prevailing scholarly view, he insisted that the creation of the nation and of the idea of monotheism had been simultaneous and inextricably intertwined. Although it will concern us in great detail in Chapter Seven, it might be helpful to note here that the historical veracity of the biblical narrative for 'events' that occurred before the tenth century BCE is, to put it mildly, questionable, and even after the tenth century it is not without need for external evidence. Kaufmann, in other words, was seeking a secular explanation, and basing it on the Mount Sinai spectacle, which by secular criteria of proof had never occurred.

In presenting such an argument, Kaufmann was unable to avoid slipping into crude idealism (for which he castigated others), wherein the idea of primeval monotheism was there, quite independent of religious practice and institutions, but had to be held in suspense for a very long time until it thus materialized. Put differently, Kaufmann fails to place the idea of monotheism within any kind of context.[34] A possible hint that Kaufmann might have felt ill at ease with this rather nonsensical notion, but proceeded unhindered nonetheless, is the fact that he presented the book as the history of belief (*emunah*) rather than of religion (*dat*).

Laying out meticulously the contradictions and inconsistencies that stem from this false assumption, Evron concludes that when all these are put to one side, it can be evidently seen that Judaism is an exilic phenomenon, that the only thing that distinguishes Jews from non-Jews is the religious culture, and that 'the Jewish people *does not possess national territorial dispositions* [emphasis in the original]'.[35]

There is an interesting tension in Evron's critique of the negation of exile myth as *the* foundation of Zionist historical consciousness. He systematically shows that exile is not an abnormal form of Jewish existence, in so far as territoriality is not normal. On the contrary, he emphasizes the extent to which, historically, exile became immanently Jewish. He further rejects the Zionist master-narrative by constantly resorting to historicity and contingency, and in doing so shows that modern anti-Semitism and Jewish nationalism can only be understood as temporal and spatial phenomena. He demonstrates that Jewish nationalism and nationhood in all its forms – Zionism was only one of several – can only be grasped as part of nineteenth-century Central and especially East European history, not as an articulation of an immanent nationhood that is 2,500 years old.

Nevertheless, the secular Zionist aesthetic, and the moral disdain for the diasporic realities in which the Jews lived (especially in the Pale of Settlement), seem to be deeply ingrained in Evron's consciousness. And since the stereotypical representation of these realities, the realities against which the Zionists rebelled, *is* the aesthetic and moral negation of exile, Evron to some degree partakes in the pivotal myth he very plausibly shatters. This tension – of intellectually deconstructing Zionism and arguing that it is obsolete, while at the same time intuitively and emotionally feeling Zionism's aversion to exile – is the key to understanding Evron's political standpoint: Evron's critique of Zionism and alternative political agenda are conceived from what may be termed a post-Canaanite perspective.[36]

To unpack this somewhat, Canaanism (*Kena'aniyut*) is a pejorative term coined most probably by the poet Avraham Shlonsky and applied to a cultural–political movement that appeared in pre-state Palestine in the 1940s and faded early the following decade. Although politically and organizationally it was never a serious challenge to Zionism, Canaanism remained a viable cultural ambiance that has not entirely vanished. Although the movement's self-designated mission was the revival of the Hebrew nation, its derogatory name stuck.[37]

The Canaanite phenomenon was the result of a series of meetings in Paris in the late 1930s between the linguist Adiyah Horon and the poet Yonatan Ratosh.[38] The cultural ideology to which these meetings gave birth had two components: it translated political, literary and scientific moods that were current in 1930s Europe into the language of politics and culture in Zionist Palestine; and it unearthed a deep critique of Zionism. Canaanism emerged out of Zionism's womb – out of its right-wing Jabotinsky School more precisely – and sought to bring Zionism to its logical end by propagating an irrevocable divorce from Judaism. It might be seen as the ultimately rapturous version of the negation of exile.

The Canaanite *littérateurs* mapped the lore of European organic nationalism, most notably of the Italian, German and Russian types, onto a fundamentalist and primordial pre-monotheistic repository. They vehemently rejected the rabbinical literature of commentary. Ratosh's 'The Inaugural Essay' of 1944 stated that '[a] Hebrew cannot be a Jew, and a Jew cannot be a Hebrew'. It erected an insurmountable barrier between the Jews in the Diaspora, whose being was that of 'a religious sect', and the born-again territorial Hebrew nation. The nation that 'the Committee for the Consolidation of the Hebrew Youth', the organization founded by Ratosh in the early 1940s to further the cause of Hebrew nationalism, sought to rejuvenate was a nation that comprised the Hebrew-speaking (in various dialects) peoples of the ancient *Eretz Kedem*, Land of the East. This territory, which included today's Syria, Lebanon, Jordan, and Israel/Palestine, gave birth to the Hebrew nation, which was, like its neighbours, pagan, and created a glorious Hebrew culture. It was destroyed by later conquerors and its cultural heritage distorted and ostracized by monotheism and rabbinical commentary. The nucleus of the nation, the Hebrew settlers in Palestine, would spread throughout the Land of Kedem and, by conquest and force, would purge from that land Arabic (the language) and Islam (the religion), which are as alien to the region as Judaism. The reinvigorated nation would then complete its destiny by establishing the Hebrew state. This state would strictly separate itself from any church, instil the Hebrew language and culture as a foundation shared by all citizens, and sever any ties with Judaism and the Jewish people.[39] This political programme may seem ludicrous, and the ideology reflects the nationalist and linguistic theories of its contextual inception in Europe of the 1930s, but the cultural accents and instincts of Canaanism lingered on after its organizational demise in the early 1950s. It might be even argued that the mood, rhetoric and aesthetics of Hebrew culture in the

1940s and 1950s were Canaanite. For instance, many names prevalent in Israeli society can be said to reflect a Canaanite cultural sensibility (a notable example would be the female name `Anat – a Canaanite goddess of fertility). Evron perceptively remarks that when Bialik, the national poet whose world was suffused with traditional Jewish culture, wrote the legend 'King David in the Cave', he was actually reworking into a mythical Hebrew context the ancient German folktale of Friedrich Barbarossa and his knights in the depth of a Bavarian cave.[40]

Evron was for a time a follower of Canaanism. Having become a dissenting voice to the left of Zionism, he rejected wholeheartedly the lunatic aspect of Canaanite politics as well as its ties with the messianic Jewish fanaticism of the settlers in the Occupied Territories after 1967. It was also obvious to him that a Hebrew identity could not be severed from Judaism, and that the Arabic language and Islam were deeply ingrained in the culture of all the inhabitants of the Middle East, including Christians and Jews. He does, however, accept, *mutatis mutandis*, the Canaanite critique of the Zionist master-narrative, and its attendant political conclusion: that whatever has emerged in Palestine/Israel as a result of the Zionist colonization is a territorial nation that is not and cannot be Jewish but Israeli. For Evron the history of exile is the history of a religious caste or a pariah group in the Weberian sense, not one of a latent nation. As a result of a particular historical contingency a new nation has emerged – but that is all.

The effort Evron invests in refuting the portion of the Zionist narrative that deals with ancient history is quite remarkable. Aided by this Canaanite perspective, he embarks on a thorough survey of all the available scholarship, and dedicates roughly a quarter of the Hebrew edition of his book, a section entitled 'The Triumph of Halakhah and Decline of the Nation', to his argument that Halakhic Judaism and the territorial Israelite/Jewish nation were, as early as those centuries, mutually exclusive options rather than, as Zionism would have it, two expressions of the same national essence. It is interesting to note that in this respect Evron's mode of thought is itself part of the discourse of nationalism. He evidently assumes that in order to undermine a nationalist historical narrative one must not only highlight its contradictions and inconsistencies, but also refute it empirically. To be consciously crude, I would suggest that Evron assumes that there were or could be nations at that period, the ancient Israelites for instance, but their existence must be empirically established, as if the assumption that nations existed at all in these centuries was not highly problematic. In fairness, when writing the original Hebrew version (1986), Evron could not be expected to avail himself of the emerging critical literature on nationalism that has since transformed our understanding of this phenomenon. In the later English edition (1995) he became cognizant of this literature and brought it to bear on his materials.

Having undertaken this impressive intellectual enterprise, Evron puts forth his political agenda, whose crux is no less than a call for the de-Judaization and de-Zionization of the state of Israel. It comprises the principle of a fundamental separation between state and church – any church – and the transformation of the state into one for and of its citizens, members of the Israeli nation, rather than one that is for and of the Jewish people. There is actually nothing radical or dramatic in the demand that a modern state be simply a normal territorial nation-state. In the realities of Zionist Israel, however, such a proposal is tantamount to heresy.

There is also a historical irony at play here. In order to demolish the negation of exile and put forth a universal programme of citizenship and collective identity, one that is inclusive rather than exclusive, one unavoidably finds oneself adopting, even if partially and reservedly, a Canaanite vantage point – Canaanism was a fervently nationalist mood of the 1930s and 1940s. It matters little in this respect whether the universal agenda is supported by a Boas Evron or an Anton Shammas.[41]

## The Limit of the Conventional View of the Foundational Myth

In 2003 a lengthy and highly significant essay was published in *Alpayim* ('Two thousand'), the flagship-journal of Israeli liberals. Anita Shapira, whose status as the Princess of Zionism has already been noted, penned an insightful attempt to historicize the foundational myth (not a term she employs, of course) in its negation-of-exile guise.[42] Shapira's essay evinces the continuing – even if changing – importance of the myth in current political debate, which in a way contradicts her verdict that it is by now irrelevant. Most crucially, her pronouncement illustrates the inability and unwillingness of Zionist thinkers, even at this late juncture, to relate to the myth critically and to come to terms with its intellectual depth and political implications. In his review of this *Alpayim* issue, Yossi Yona observes: 'Shapira's apologetic project halts at the border, behind which putatively nothing exists; the emptiness to which the Zionist enterprise's spokespeople displace groups [Palestinians and Mizrahis] with which they either do not even bother, or are unwilling, to negotiate.'[43] I shall now turn to Shapira's essay, and then use her text as a preface to a radical critique of the negation of exile inspired by Walter Benjamin.

Shapira correctly identifies the centrality of the negation of exile in current political debates, and its deployment by non- and anti-Zionist critics 'as if we were amidst a face off between the land of Israel and the Diaspora'.[44] Shapira focuses on the changes in attitudes towards the negation of exile after the foundation of the state of Israel in 1948. In essence, her argument is that 'since the 1960s, and more so since the 1970s, there occurred in Israeli society a slow but persistent withdrawal from the concept of "the negation of exile", winding up in its becoming an anachronism'.[45] To underscore the historicity of the negation of exile, Shapira opts for a generational narrative. She identifies three generations: the fathers, that is, the European-born Zionists (*dor ha-avot*); the generation of those who were born in Mandatory Palestine and, when in their twenties, fought in the 1948 war (*dor ba-aretz*); and those who matured or were born into an already existing state (*dor ha-medina*).

The passage from the first to the second generation is illustrative of the gap between the creators and inculcators of an ideology on the one hand, and on the other the 'guinea pigs' on whom that ideology was tested. Shapira perceptibly identifies this gap and her rendering of it is one of several climactic moments in her wonderful Hebrew prose. The fathers' generation negated and denigrated exile, in ways that not infrequently were strewn with anti-Semitic vocabulary; at the same time, however, they were part of the East European townships and their rebellion and virulent onslaught against them was suffused with pain and ambivalence: this world was not an abstraction, but one they had known and experienced. The most notable expression of this ambivalence, of abhorrence and pain (and occasionally even sympathy) inextricably intertwined vis-à-vis life in the East European Jewish township, was Brenner's literature mentioned earlier. As for the first actual products of the negation of exile, here is an assessment from the 1930s by one of the mythical pioneers, the Second Aliya's Shlomo Lavi:

> We forsook the excessive spirituality which we had deemed exile's legacy. Our forefathers in exile were mostly concerned with the soul, whereas we, who are liberating ourselves from the yoke of exile, shall mostly be concerned with the body, with the ability to act, with physical uprightness, with courage. All this, it would seem, we have accomplished. We have accomplished [the creation of] a generation of roughnecks [*hisagnu dor shel shkatzim*]. And having accomplished that, we take stock and marvel: are these [i.e., the Palestine-born offspring of the Second Aliya 'founding fathers'] the ones we yearned for? . . . [What our

generation lacks is] a little thought on their position in the world, their position in Judaism, on our past and future, and in general a little self-reflection and deep sensation.[46]

Shapira's take on the changing attitude to the negation of exile is perceptive. She locates the change in the first decade of the state's existence (the 1950s), but with the crucial observation that 'changes of consciousness are diagnosed in most cases only in retrospect, once they had ripened and their direction became clear'.[47] In this way, phenomena that ostensibly suggest the flourishing of a nativist, archaeological Israeliness (e.g., the appearance of the Canaanite journal *Aleph* or Yigael Yadin's excavations in the Upper Galilee and Judaea desert) were in fact 'the light of the star that is no more', expressions of a hegemonic culture (labour Zionism's Israeliness) that is about to be severely undermined.[48] What changed was the Promised Land's demographic: the arrival of the Arab Jews and the Holocaust survivors. If for the sake of argument we momentarily ignore the Palestinian Arabs, this process transformed a society of settler–natives with European origins into one of immigrants. The latter possessed neither the mood nor the inclination for archaeological Israeliness. Reiterating Uri Avneri's observation, Amos Kenan retrospectively reflected in 1977: 'The people that was in 1948 – is no more [he was not of course referring to the Palestinian *Nakba*]. There is here another people. Actually there is no people here. There is here a sort of riff-raff.'[49] Side by side with a rhetoric that betrays the arrogance of the native settler vis-à-vis the exilic countenance of the immigrants, Kenan's and Avneri's remarks display their cognizance of the vanishing of a more or less homogeneous white settler society, united by an organic nativist culture. Their remarks lament that society and culture, whose last vestige, Ariel Sharon (who politically adjusted best to the demographic change), is expiring as these lines are written.

Then came the Eichmann trial, which completely transformed the attitude to historical Judaism and the Jewish tradition as well as to the Diaspora. Shapira meticulously explains how in the process both the negation of exile of the fathers' generation and the shape it took in the offspring's generation were substantially reversed, becoming what Shapira calls an anachronism.[50] The process, it should be clarified, was twofold: expressions that were construed as exilic became less abhorred; the content of collective identity became more Jewish and less archaeological-Israeli. Notwithstanding the potential danger of an aggressive integral nationalism that the success of a nativist Canaanite type of Israeliness might have yielded, its failure and the eventual prevalence of fundamentalist ethno-religious Jewishness can be seen as a missed opportunity for the forming of an Israeli republicanism, which might have been inclusive of Jews and Palestinian Arabs. One cannot of course be certain that a secular republic would have been the result, but – retrospectively – the risk seems to have been worth taking.

Shapira's essay is a thorough and eloquently crafted demonstration of the historicity and variety of the Zionist myth in the twentieth century. At the same time, however, it betrays the significant political and intellectual constraints of a Zionist Israeli commentary on the foundational myth. Two underlying limitations stand out. The first stems from a narrow understanding of what the negation of exile actually constitutes: only pronouncements that reject exile in a forthright way, that make pejorative statements about exilic Jews, and that forge a narrative which sidesteps the period of exile altogether – in other words, the straightforwardly crude version – are considered instances of the negation of exile. The result is the incapacity to ponder the deepest, and ideologically most coherent and ambitious, articulation of the negation of exile: the project of integrating the period of exile – rather than rejecting or sidestepping it – into a territorial narrative, which was developed from the mid 1920s onwards by the scholars who founded the Institute for Jewish Studies at the Hebrew University (the project of the Jerusalem scholars is the focus of Chapters Four and Five). The second underlying limitation is, as was explained in Chapter Two, typical of settler nations: the refusal or inability to examine the myth also in relation to the indigenous people of the land; it is as if this myth was consequential only for Jews, or as though the land were empty before their arrival.

Shapira is consistently reluctant to engage seriously with the intellectual and political critique of the negation of exile. In one example, observing that the negation of exile has become a slogan for radical critics ('negationists', as she calls them) of Zionism, she notes how

Amnon Raz-Krakotzkin has attacked the principle of 'the negation of exile' because according to his understanding it led to the founding of the state of Israel – an aggressive, malicious, devoid-of-human-sensitivity entity, which stands in contrast to the being of the exilic Jew. The existence of Jews in exile has been presented by Raz-Krakotzkin as the natural way of life for Jews, which Zionism undermined.[51]

What is strikingly prototypical here is not merely the vehement disagreement with the kind of position put forth by Raz-Krakotzkin. It is rather the fact that Shapira herself correctly presents the resurfacing of the debate over the negation of exile as ideological and political, not just scholarly. However, instead of seriously taking on Raz-Krakotzkin's radical Benjaminian critique of the Zionist myth and Israeli culture and politics, she resorts to a reductively dismissive 'summary' of his argument, which is really an attempt to caricature it. Moreover, the actual reference makes one suspicious of whether Shapira read the entire text and of the degree to which her reading was earnest, for Raz-Krakotzkin's massive essay appeared in two parts (1993 and 1994) and she mentions only the first.[52]

## 'There is no God, but He Promised us the Land':[53] A Benjaminian Critique

You received letters from the West, and here they rang from the East? Over there the township diminishes daily, over here the Arab village declines daily? Steps of camels rang? Ding-dong. Did you hear? Can't hear? How come Jews' ears don't hear? Have you ever come to know the Arabs? Our *Shoah* we have lamented, theirs we haven't? There's war now? Such a handsome generation.

And why do you write? Write for the sake of writing?

No more.[54]

This powerful citation of the non-conformist and oppositional poet Avot Yeshurun, with his unique and strange yet politically potent poetic language (a melange of liturgical and modern Hebrew, colloquial Palestinian Arabic, Aramaic and Yiddish), opens Raz-Krakotzkin's 'Exile within Sovereignty: A Critique of "the Negation of Exile" in Israeli Culture', a massive essay that constitutes one of the most original pronouncements on Zionism and Israel by a native Israeli Jew in Hebrew. It should be emphasized that by negation of exile Raz-Krakotzkin refers to the foundation of Zionist ideology in the same critical sense as the working definition supplied at the beginning of this chapter, and that for him, too, the other two articulations of the foundational myth – the return to the land of Israel and the return to history – are different expressions of the same thing.

Raz-Krakotzkin's essay sprang from his 1996 doctoral thesis at Tel Aviv University, under the direction of the late Amos Funkenstein, on 'The Nationalist Representation of Exile: Zionist Historiography and the Jews of the Middle Ages'. Although Raz-Krakotzkin reads widely and eclectically, the impact of three scholars is especially discernible in his political and intellectual world: Walter Benjamin; his teacher Amos

Funkenstein (with whom he is not always in agreement); and Carlo Ginzburg, with his simultaneous commitment to exacting erudition and scholarship, and to the moral–political distinction between oppressors and oppressed.[55]

One of the most pertinent contexts within which Raz-Krakotzkin's text should be seen is the creation of the journal *Teoria Uvikoret* ('Theory and criticism'), which, founded in 1991, is published by the Van Leer Institute in Jerusalem. Since its inception it has been a pivotal locus for the radical critique of Zionism and the state of Israel. Laurence Silberstein has effectively documented the founding of the journal, and the story is worth retelling briefly.[56] In October 1987 Adi Ophir (philosophy, Tel Aviv University) and Hanan Hever (Hebrew literature, then at the Hebrew University) founded a protest group called the Twenty First Year, referring to the 21st 'birthday' of the Israeli occupation of the West Bank and Gaza Strip. As their founding declaration implied, they were disappointed with the existing peace movement:

> The presence of the occupation is total. Our struggle against the occupation must therefore also be total. We shall resolutely refuse to collaborate with the system of occupation in all of its manifestations. Refusal is the only morally and politically sound form of participation in Israeli society during the occupation. Refusal is . . . a source of hope for our moral integrity as Israelis.[57]

Shortly afterwards the first Palestinian Intifada erupted, and in June 1988 Ophir, refusing to do reserve military service in the occupied territories, was sent to prison. He wrote to the minister of defence, Yitzhak Rabin, that he viewed the Intifada as 'a fight for freedom, whose only aim is release from Israeli rule', and stated that he was not being asked to defend his country 'but to participate in the enslavement of another people'.[58] In 1989 Ophir and Hever, together with other members of the Twenty First Year, gathered in Qalqilya to oppose the demolition of the house of a Palestinian family whose son had been defined as a 'suspected terrorist'. They refused the army's order to leave, and twenty-seven of them were incarcerated for seven days. These experiences motivated Ophir, Hever and their colleagues to look for ways to disseminate their radical critique of the Israeli state, society and culture. By this time they were despairing of the bulk of the academy, which, like its counterparts elsewhere, was (and remains) state-obliging and in collusion with power. Ophir and Hever's early attempts at critically political work had encountered 'indifference, expressions of contempt, or explicit opposition', and they now sought to create a site for 'a kind of radical academy'. The end result was the endeavour to establish *Theory and Criticism*, as a relatively independent (the Van Leer Institute is open-minded but does not share the journal's radical positions), and simultaneously political and scholarly, journal. At the journal's inception, its underlying purpose was 'to histori-cize' the entire repository 'of the foundational categories and the key concepts of Israeli discourse (Zionist, pioneering, nation, state, religion) and the accepted descriptions of the recognised lines of division (Jew/Gentile; secular/religious; Eastern/Western . . . and so on)'.[59] The first editor and driving force of the journal in its first decade was Ophir; he was succeeded in 2000 by the sociologist Yehuda Shenhav, also of Tel Aviv University.

Raz-Krakotzkin's 'Exile within Sovereignty' is part of this taking on of 'the foundational categories and key concepts of Israeli discourse', and the author himself played an important role in launching and shaping *Theory and Criticism*. A typical Raz-Krakotzkin mélange of inextricably intertwined moral, political and scholarly traits, 'Exile within Sovereignty' is an attempt to read Benjamin's 'Theses on the Philosophy of History' onto Zionist ideology and Israeli politics and culture. Faithful to his source of inspiration, Raz-Krakotzkin is interested not in the reconstruc-tion of either the Jewish past in exile or the Israeli present, but in salvaging suppressed voices and notions from the past in order to change the histor-ical consciousness and politics of the present. Furthermore, by redeploying exile, in the sense with which he endows it, against the myth that negates it (the negation of exile), what Raz-Krakotzkin aims to salvage is not just the memory and perspective of the suppressed exilic Jew of the past but, crucially, the memory and perspective of the dispossessed and excluded Palestinian of the present.[60] Here, it is worth recalling an observation made in Chapter Two, whereby one of the fundamental characteristics of settler nations is that their consciousness forbids recognition of the dispossession and presence of indigenous people as intrinsically pivotal to the identity of these nations. Raz-Krakotzkin's insistence on the ineluctable presence and remembrance of the dispossessed Palestinians vis-à-vis any collective definition of Israeli Jews is such a radically subversive challenge, so much so that it is perhaps not surprising that Shapira opts for dismissal.

As if anticipating Shapira's verdict a decade later, Raz-Krakotzkin is aware that with the development of an autonomous Israeli culture within a territorial state, and the labelling of the merry days of Oslo a post-Zionist reality, the evocation of Zionist ideology and the negation of exile in particular may be dismissed as irrelevant and anachronistic, certainly a superfluous debate. Seemingly taking a leaf out of Gramsci's understanding of hegemony, he observes that those who think Zionism and its foundational myth have only a historical relevance fail to notice that

> the conclusion that there is no need to discuss the foundations of Zionist ideology strengthens its ideological underlying assumptions, and makes it possible to ignore the central role that the myth of the negation of exile continues to play in shaping the political and cultural discourse in Israel. Moreover, precisely when the myth as a whole is not the focus of debates which are deemed archaic and irrelevant, its [the myth's] functioning becomes simpler and it is accepted as objective and self-evident [*muvan me'elav*].[61]

Raz-Krakotzkin foregrounds the tension – indeed the contradiction – between the nationalist context of the negation of exile and the theological context of the notion of exile as a state of existence in the actual world. He is well aware that the spatial and temporal varieties cannot be reduced to one definition or essence, but that '[i]f it is possible at all to talk about any component which is common to all the historical expressions of Judaism and which makes it distinct, then it [this component] lies in the definition of existence as a reality of *galut* [at least until the late eighteenth century for Central and Western Europe]'.[62] This, it should be noted, is especially true for rabbinical Judaism. Qualifiers notwithstanding, Raz-Krakotzkin insists that '[the *galut* concept] is not *one* of the foundations of Jewish existence – it is the central foundation of its definition'.[63] In his view, the place of the land of Israel in rabbinical thought and writing is certainly significant,[64] but this does not mean accepting the Zionist reduction of *galut* consciousness to merely the non-realization of territorial aspirations or to a transitory state of being (without denying the components of return and rehabilitation in certain manifestations of utopian messianism). Moreover, the yearning for the promised land of Israel inherent in existential *galut* was neither expressed in colonial terms of ownership, nor was it accompanied by a nostalgic evocation of an ancient past.[65] The other important trait of the consciousness of *galut* was its dialogical relations with Christianity. What *galut* meant in that sense was the rejection of Christian doctrine whereby reality was an era of grace, from which only the obstinate Jews were excluded, and the insistence that the circumstance of the Jews is emblematic of the world: an unredeemed world, which is itself in *galut*. In certain medieval pronouncements, even divinity itself was in exile.[66] This latter point will assume special poignancy when we discuss the foundational myth as a return to history in the next two chapters.

Turning to the national context, Raz-Krakotzkin unearths the relationship — a relationship Zionist scholars are either oblivious to or choose to disregard — between the modern myth and pre-modern *galut*, a relationship that is in a way emblematic of the one between Zionism and Judaism in general. He asserts: 'The implication of the fact that the concept of *galut*, which carries a deep and important theological load [and] is what defines Judaism as a historical phenomenon, is that "the negation of exile" means the negation of "Judaism"; the Zionism that presumes monopoly over Jewish history is in actual fact its negation.'[67] As observed earlier, Raz-Krakotzkin too knows that Zionism has always been resigned to Jewish existence in the *golah* (Diaspora), but has insisted on the territory/*galut* hierarchy, whereby such existence was at least inferior to that in the land of Israel, if not inauthentic and illegitimate. Moreover, Jewish existence outside the boundaries of Zionist ideology was also relegated to inferior status. There is a sense in which the negation of exile is not confined to Zionism, and the rejection of *galut* was an important foundation of modern Western Judaism in general from Moses Mendelssohn on.[68] The uniqueness of Zionism is of course that it entailed a project of colonization and settlement.

But for Raz-Krakotzkin the tension is not just between the historical *galut* and its modern negation. Always political, and wishing to offer an alternative stance, he turns to the present:

> The central place of concept of exile throws light on the special difficulty that inheres in the attempt at Jewish self-definition in the terminology of modern nationalism. The exile concept makes it clear that it is impossible to treat historical Judaism as . . . an autonomous system, outside the cultural context within which it exists and of which it is part. *Galut* is the basis of the Jews' self-definition vis-à-vis the society. . . in which they existed: they were part of the place — but were in exile *within it*. This means that in order to be in exile at a certain place (that is, in order to be Jewish at a certain place), the Jew must first of all be grasped as part of the [general] framework, for only thus can his self-definition become clear. In other words, identifying a situation as '*galut*' took place in the past and can take place in the present only on the basis of allusion to the terminological language of the dominant culture and as a critical stance towards that culture.[69]

As with other pronouncements critical of the negation of exile myth, the relevance of Canaanism resurfaces in Raz-Krakotzkin's essay, and helps to elucidate the alternative he proposes. He is aware that his view of Jewish history and concomitant critique of Zionism are akin, though not in register, to the Canaanite one. He also concurs in the understanding of Canaanism as a correct demand that Zionism pursue its own myth to the logical end, that is, sever the ties of the settler nation it created with Judaism. The divergence that follows between Raz-Krakotzkin's views and those of the Canaanites is crucial and interesting:

> Where the Canaanites seek, on the basis of in principle a similar analysis of Jewish history, to effect a complete severing of the new Hebrew culture from Judaism, what guides me is, contrarily, the desire to renew important dimensions of repelled Judaism, and do this by bringing back the concept of *galut* to the heart of the ideological discourse, as a key concept for shaping afresh the historical reality. In other words, in a culture for which territoriality is the underlying position, the embodiment of historical view, I seek to turn precisely to a conceptual set that is immanently a-territorial, and to construct from it a comprehensive moral–cultural perspective.[70]

Raz-Krakotzkin's position, then, is one of presence within sovereignty, within a territorial nation-state, but at the same time one of distance from and opposition to sovereignty through the invocation of exile. To develop further his critical alternative, the position of feeling in exile within sovereignty, Raz-Krakotzkin turns to Benjamin's *Theses on the Philosophy of History*.[71] There are, first, some obvious features of the *Theses* that inform Raz-Krakotzkin's readings of Zionism and Israel/Palestine: the turn to the past in order to act in the present; the rejection of linear progress and the positivist historiography of the victors; and the act of remembrance of the oppressed in order to make their memory politically present. Although he does not refer to Michael Löwy's study on the elective affinity between Jewish messianism and revolutionary utopian thought he found in the Weimar era,[72] Raz-Krakotzkin is, like Löwy, attracted by Benjamin's combination of terminology borrowed from Judaism (messianism, redemption) and progressive Marxism, though with important reservations.

Raz-Krakotzkin is aware that other Jewish writers, Arendt among them, have resorted to the notion of *galut* in a modern context in order to define forms of Jewish secular politics and to defy the Zionist Israeli claim of cultural and historical monopoly; he considers his own work

an addition to that edifice. What is distinctly original about Raz-
Krakotzkin's deployment of *galut* within this progressive secular Jewish
tradition is that it evolved within the Zionist Israeli sovereign reality
defined by the negation of *galut*, and his invocation of *galut* is a reaction
to the oppressive prevalence of that sovereign reality.[73] The distancing
of Lazare, Benjamin and Arendt from their society was, in a sense, done
for them; in stark contrast, Raz-Krakotzkin is by default part and parcel
of the privileged, oppressing society from which he has to distance
himself. There are in particular two aspects of Raz-Krakotzkin's reading
of Benjamin and understanding of *galut* that link it in an interesting
way to the genealogy of the conscious pariah charted earlier in this
book. He observes that despite Benjamin's reservation about classical
Marxism's view of history's progress towards its emancipatory resolution
he could not resist the need to offer at least an image of redemption
(especially in Thesis 3). From Benjamin's allusions to redemption Raz-
Krakotzkin infers that for Benjamin the desire for redemption (*ge'ulah*)
*is* redemption. Raz-Krakotzkin takes his inference a step further, and
argues that Benjamin is really proposing a twofold equation: the desire
for redemption *is* redemption; the desire for redemption, which *is*
redemption, *is* also *galut*.

I believe that the equation Raz-Krakotzkin brings to the fore, which
culminates in the deployment of the notion of *galut* in a particular way,
squarely places him within the genealogy of the conscious pariah and
makes him so reminiscent of Bernard Lazare. What these two share is
the centrality of the sense of absence for political action, and the
inextricability of the universal and the particular for a political position
worthy of upholding:

> Indeed, the concept of *galut* signifies an essence which is absent or
> missing . . . *Galut* signifies the absence, the cognizance of the present
> being imperfect, the consciousness of the blemished world. In empha-
> sising the blemished present the notion of *galut* posits a completely
> different stance from the modern-positivist approach, of which Zionist
> ideology is an expression, and thus illuminates the special meaning of
> remembrance. The yearning for redemption is founded upon the
> consciousness of *galut*, and thereby requires the turn towards the culture's
> oppressed, accompanied by an attempt to undermine the memory of
> the rulers. The desire for redemption is thus an activity that takes place
> within reality and by according value to the vantage point of the
> oppressed, a vantage point through which alone a moral position may
> develop. Therefore, only the definition of reality as *galut* points to the

moral values that are supposed to direct political action. This is the locus in Benjamin's thought in which the full coming together of Marxism and Jewish theology is created.[74]

This recalls Lazare's envisaged passage to becoming a conscious pariah.[75] Lazare objected to the Zionist claim that, because emancipation was synonymous with assimilation, nationalism and emancipation were mutually exclusive. On the contrary, asserted Lazare, emancipation was a prerequisite for the Jews to gain national awareness. For Lazare it was emancipation that fashioned a conscious pariah out of the Jew-as-pariah. He did not think, however, that emancipation was the final destination. Emancipation is crucial for Lazare because to some extent it frees the pariah while at the same time inculcating in him the political conscious-ness of absence and incompleteness, of what is denied and what ought to be achieved. This, I propose, links precisely Benjamin's unredeemed world, in which the yearning for redemption is redemption, with Raz-Krakotzkin's *galut,* in which reality will remain blemished until remem-brance makes the present world's oppressed and down-trodden ineluctable.

For both thinkers the universal and the particular are inextricably entwined. It must be stressed, however, that Raz-Krakotzkin's resort to, and reinterpretation of, this important Jewish concept, though certainly done with a clearly universal dimension, are at the same time chiefly directed towards the totality and oppression of a sovereign Jewish state that defines itself as exclusively Jewish as well as of and for the Jewish people, and towards its victims within the same territory. 'A position inspired by Benjamin's Theses', he says,

> does not use the memory of the oppression [of Jews] as a source for legitimizing the present, but as a basis for criticizing the history of the victors which denies the wrongdoing, the victim's memory A Jewish history of this sort is not a nationalist history of the Jews, but history written from the Jews' angle, and thereby becomes a 'universal history'. The memory of the oppressed that it preserves is not a memory of wretchedness, of 'lachrymoseness' [Salo Baron's term], but of identifi-cation that is fed by the determined aspiration . . . to remove the oppression that characterizes the present.[76]

The climax towards which the essay strives is the hopeful connection of *galut* with binationalism. Here Raz-Krakotzkin is concerned not with the notion of a binational state, even though he supports it, but with the insistence that *galut* as consciousness within a territorially oppressive reality is a prerequisite for decolonization and recognition of the binational nature of the country's history and geography. 'The sense with which *galut* is endowed here', he maintains,

> makes possible a definition of Jewish identity undergirded by the potential contained in the binationality of the country [Palestine/Israel] . . . Remembrance is simultaneously directed to the denied Jewish past and to the denied Palestinian past. The Jew who, with a sense of identification and responsibility, turns towards the consciousness of the defeated Palestinians reclaims the principles that are immanent in the theological conceiving of *galut*, and opens up to them.[77]

It is appropriate to conclude with Raz-Krakotzkin's invocation of the late Emile Habibi, the Palestinian-Israeli writer and politician, who, in his novel *Ekhtayeh* (1985 Arabic, 1988 Hebrew), called for the recognition of 'the freedom of longing for the country from within the country'. 'This', Raz-Krakotzkin observes, 'can be a starting point for all the inhabitants of the land, a basis for their partnership, a basis for their separate consciousness.'[78]

Finally, it should be noted that one of the most important ways to counter the foundational myth remains the furnishing of alternative histories, one of the finest examples of which is Joel Beinin's thoroughly documented and highly conscious reconstruction of the modern history of Egyptian Jewry.[79] Beinin's study joins Egyptian Jewry on the eve of modernity, follows the process of their dispersion from Egypt, and then unfolds the various histories of the different communities in their new destinations. Beinin not only takes on the substantial task of extricating the diverse Egyptian Jewish experience from the hold of both Zionist Israeli and modern Egyptian narratives; he also takes on Zionism in particular at a more fundamental level, as the book's subtitle evinces: 'Culture, politics, and *the formation of a modern Diaspora*'. For Beinin, in other words, what makes the Egyptian Jewish communities, including the one in Israel, a modern Diaspora is their removal from Egypt, not Zion. Although the Introduction amply manifests his theoretical subtlety and how he grapples with the problem of linear historical representations of subaltern groups, Beinin's innovative and politically consequential perspective comes to the fore most forcefully in the way he actually 'does' history in the rest of the book.

This chapter mapped the Zionist foundational myth conceptually and historically. First a working definition of the myth's three expressions (negation of exile, return to the land of Israel and return to history) was presented. This was followed by a discussion on what I called the crude version of the negation of exile. Then the taxonomy of the negation of exile by two Zionist Israeli scholars was commented upon: Schweid's conceptual survey, and Shapira's diachronic, or generational, one. Two non-Zionist radical critiques of the myth by Israeli Jews were then elaborated: Evron's neo-Canaanite and Raz-Krakotzkin's Benjaminian. Finally, Beinin's work was pointed out as an outstanding example of the importance of challenging the Zionist Israeli hegemonic myth through historical reconstruction, through the furnishing of alternative historical narratives.

## Notes

1 See G. Piterberg, 'Erasures', *New Left Review*, 10 (July–August 2001), pp. 31–47.

2 These definitions are assisted by: B. Evron, *National Reckoning* [Hebrew], Tel Aviv: Dvir, 1988; D. Myers, *Re-Inventing the Jewish Past*, New York: Oxford University Press, 1995; G. Piterberg, 'Domestic Orientalism: The Representation of "Oriental" Jews in Zionist/Israeli Historiography', *British Journal of Middle Eastern Studies*, 23 (1996), pp. 125–45; A. Raz-Krakotzkin, 'Exile within Sovereignty: Towards a Critique of the "Negation of Exile" in Israeli Culture [Hebrew]', 2 parts, *Theory and Criticism*, 4 (1993) and 5 (1994), pp. 23–56 and 113–32 respectively; L. Silberstein, *The Post-Zionism Debates*, New York: Routledge, 1999; Y. Barnai, *Trends in the Study of Eretz Yisrael, 634–1881*, Jerusalem: Magnes, 1995.

3 A. Oz, 'Imagining the Other (1)', in R. Siegel and T. Sofer (eds), *The Writer in the Jewish Community*, Rutherford: Fairleigh University Press and London: Associated University Presses, 1993, p. 119.

4 D. Myers, 'Was There a "Jerusalem School"?', *Studies in Contemporary Jewry*, 10 (1994), p. 68.

5 H. Hazaz, 'Ha-Derashah [The Sermon]', *Luach Haaretz*, September 1942.

6 The citation is from Y. Gorni, 'Negation of Galut and the Return to History', in S. N. Eisenstadt and M. Lissak (eds), *Zionism and the Return to History: A Reappraisal* [Hebrew], Jerusalem: Yad Ben Zvi, 1999, p. 355.

7 Ibid., p. 356.

8 Ibid.

9 The citation is from Sh. Ratzabi, 'The Controversy of Exile Denial in the Thirties [Hebrew]', *Zionism*, 18 (1994), p. 319.

10 Gorny, op. cit., p. 356.

11 See P. Anderson, 'Scurrying to Bethlehem', *New Left Review*, 10 (July–August 2001), p. 13 n. 10.

12 The citation is from Evron, op. cit., p. 129. The translation into English is mine.

13 Tel Aviv: Schocken, 1980.

14 The citation is from Silberstein, op. cit., p. 140. It originally appears in the English edition of David Grossman's *Sleeping on the Wire* (1993).

15 E. Schweid, 'Two Approaches to the Idea of the Negation of Exile in Zionist Ideology [Hebrew]', *Zionism*, 9 (1984), pp. 21–44.

16 Ibid., p. 21.

17 This acutely suppressed question interestingly resurfaced, with regard to Anton Shammas and the late Emile Habibi, in Silberstein, op. cit., pp. 127–65.

18 Schweid, op. cit., pp. 22–3.

19 Ibid., pp. 23–4.

20 Ibid., pp. 24–6.

21 See also Evron, op. cit., pp. 303–5. We shall return to Evron's critique of Zionism in an orderly fashion later in this chapter.

22 D. Ben-Gurion, *Biblical Reflections* [Hebrew], Tel Aviv: Am Oved, 1969, and *Ben-Gurion Looks at the Bible*, trans. J. Kolatch, New York: Jonathan David Publishers, 1972.

23 Tel Aviv: Devir, 1947–56. Translated and abridged by M. Greenberg as *The Religion of Israel: From Its Beginnings to the Babylonian Exile*, Chicago: University of Chicago Press, 1960.

24 See Evron, op. cit., p. 37.

25 Tel Aviv: Devir, 1929–30.

26 Evron, op. cit., pp. 115–28.

27 Schweid, op. cit., p. 28.

28 Ibid., p. 29.

29 Ibid., pp. 31–3.

30 Evron, op. cit. We refer to the original, and fuller, Hebrew edition. For the English translation see *Jewish State or Israeli Nation?*, Bloomington: Indiana University Press, 1995.

31 I stress 'nationalist' to make it absolutely clear that I am well aware of Matzpen ('Compass'), a movement that also offered a radical and coherent anti-Zionist critique, but from a Marxist-Internationalist vantage point that rejected nationalism altogether.

32 For a notable example of a recognition see Silberstein, op. cit., pp. 69–84.

33 See again Evron, op. cit., pp. 115–27.

34 Ibid., p. 117.

35 Ibid., p. 126.

36 Ibid., pp. 69–71.

37 On the Canaanite movement see Y. Shavit, *From Hebrew to Canaanite* [Hebrew], Jerusalem: Domino, 1984, and, in English, *The New Hebrew Nation*, London: Frank Cass, 1987; a critical review of the Hebrew version by Evron in the literary supplement of *Yediot Aharonot*, 2 March 1984; J. Diamond, *Homeland or Holyland? The 'Canaanite' Critique of Israel*, Bloomington: Indiana University Press, 1986; and Evron, op. cit., pp. 351–73.

38 For Ratosh see Y. Porath, *The Life of Uriel Shelah (Yonathan Ratosh)*, Tel Aviv: Zmora, 1989.

39 See especially Evron, op. cit., pp. 355–6.

40 Ibid., p. 352.

41 On the voices of Shammas and Emile Habibi see Silberstein, op. cit., pp. 127–65.

42 A. Shapira, 'Where Has "the Negation of Exile" Gone? [Hebrew]', *Alpayim – A Multidisciplinary Publication for Contemporary Thought and Literature*, 25 (2003), pp. 9–55 .

43 Yossi Yona, 'A Dead-End Being [Hebrew]', *Haaretz Book Supplement*, 22 December 2003.

44 Shapira, op. cit., p. 9.

45 Ibid., pp. 9–10.

46 Ibid., p. 15.

47 Ibid., p. 25.

48 Ibid., p. 23.

49 Ibid., p. 24.

50 See ibid., pp. 23–54.

51 Ibid., p. 9.

52 For a full reference of Raz-Krakotzkin's article see n. 2 above. Shapira's reference is in Shapira, 'The Negation of Exile', p. 9, n. 4.

53 This is the title of a recent article (in Hebrew) in *Mitaam*, 3 (2005), in which Raz-Krakotzkin unveils the oxymoronic nature of Israeli secularism.

54 Raz-Krakotzkin, 'Exile within Sovereignty', part 1, p. 23.

55 A. Raz-Krakotzkin, 'History, Historical Consciousness and Interpretation: Amos Funkenstein, 1937–1995', *Zion*, 61:1 (1996), pp. 113–20, and 'Carlo Ginzburg with Amnon Raz-Krakotzkin: If Not I Against Myself, Who Will Come out Against Me?', *Zemanim*, 49 (1993), pp. 4–16 (both in Hebrew).

56 Silberstein op. cit., pp. 166–9. Silberstein also offers a helpful – though in my view not always sufficiently discerning – summary of Raz-Krakotzkin's position on pp. 177–83.

57 Ibid., p. 168.

58 Ibid.

59 All citations in this paragraph are from ibid., pp. 168–9.

60 See Raz-Krakotzkin, 'Exile within Sovereignty', part 1, pp. 23–7 and 36–9, and part 2, pp. 113–18.

61 Ibid., part 1, p. 26.

62 Ibid., p. 27.

63 Ibid.

64 See the allusion to it, ibid., pp. 50–1.

65 Ibid., p. 28.

66 Ibid., pp. 28–9.

67 Ibid., p. 29.

68 Ibid., pp. 29–30.

69 Ibid., pp. 30–1.

70 Ibid., p. 34.

71 Ibid., pp. 36–9.

72 See above, Chapter One, p. 5 and 14.

73 Raz-Krakotzkin, 'Exile within Sovereignty', part 1, p. 35.

74 Ibid., pp. 38–9. Significantly, Raz-Krakotzkin explicitly objects to the common view that these two sources of inspiration in Benjamin's *oeuvre*, Marxism and certain aspects of Jewish thought, were incompatible or even contradictory. He insists that they are complementary.

75 See above, Chapter One, p. 11–12.

76 Raz-Krakotzkin, 'Exile within Sovereignty', part 1, p. 42.

77 Ibid., p. 49.

78 Ibid., p. 52.

79 J. Beinin, *The Dispersion of Egyptian Jewry: Culture, Politics, and the Formation of Modern Diaspora*, Berkeley: The University of California Press, 1998.

4

# Myth and History on Mount Scopus

## The Institute for Jewish Studies:
### Jerusalem and the Negation of Exile

In 1924, a year before the official opening ceremony of the Hebrew University on Jerusalem's Mount Scopus, its Institute of Jewish Studies was established. Its Hebrew name, Ha-Makhon le-Mada`ei ha-Yahadut (literally, 'Institute for the science of Judaism'), conveys more faithfully its indebtedness, despite much rebelliousness and criticism, to the nineteenth-century German Jewish phenomenon, Wissenschaft des Judentum or 'science of Judaism'.[1] The debate over the term 'Jerusalem School' revolves around the question of whether or not there is a uniformly authoritative academic doctrine that has radiated from the Institute of Jewish Studies. This debate is of course meaningful in itself, but it also serves as an instance that effectively foregrounds the difference between the intrinsically Zionist understanding of the foundational myth, and that which is conceived from a position that, while not necessarily explicitly anti-Zionist, is certainly extrinsic. This debate is located where politics, ideology and scholarship intersect.

I am less interested here in the extent to which the first generation of the Jerusalem scholars, and their numerous disciples, form a coherent and uniform school, or whether their diversity of approach and subject matter militates against such a categorization.[2] What I do find telling is the correlation between the position of scholars vis-à-vis Zionism (intrinsic or extrinsic) on the one hand, and how they understand the pronouncements of the Jerusalem scholars on the period of exile, on the other. Intrinsically Zionist scholars find in the Jerusalem scholars' *oeuvre* an alternative to the negation of exile; the scholars who are extrinsic to Zionism consider the very same corpus the most ambitious attempt to lend scientific credence to the negation of exile/return to the land of Israel/return to history in the shape of a coherently organic historical narrative. This observation can be demonstrated by comparing the work on this theme by two scholars: David Myers and Amnon Raz-Krakotzkin. Their important studies have much in common, in subject matter as well as interpretation, and this should be borne in mind lest the gulf between them, which I highlight in what follows, look too yawning. Myers's work combines an institutional reconstruction with intellectual analysis, whereas Raz-Krakotzkin's is more exclusively an intellectual deconstruction and more overtly political.[3]

The scholars who founded and developed the Institute of Jewish Studies in its first decade shaped the Israeli Zionist landscape of professional historiography through their research, teaching and other activities. The influential trio in this process comprised Ben-Zion Dinur (Dinaburg, prior to the name being Hebraized to Dinur, 1884–1973), Itzhak-Fritz Baer (1888–1980) and Gershom-Gerhard Scholem (1897–1982). Unsurprisingly these three figures form the focus of subsequent academic work on the Institute for Jewish Studies (Raz-Krakotzkin also examines one of Baer's outstanding students, H. H. Ben-Sasson). Here I shall concentrate on the work of Baer and Dinur; the next chapter will be dedicated to Scholem, whose genius presents an irresistible challenge.

Both Myers's and Raz-Krakotzkin's takes on nationalism and nationalist historiography are critical. The title of Myers's book, *Re-Inventing the Jewish Past*, suffices to illustrate his distance from the project of his protagonists, though not his lack of sympathy. However, they interpret differently the meaning, scope and depth of the 'negation of exile' concept. One salient difference concerns the question of the indigenous Palestinians' presence in, or absence from, the analysis of the myth. For Raz-Krakotzkin, even though the negation of exile is ostensibly an internal Jewish matter, not bringing the Palestinians into the frame, failing to understand that this is not just a nationalist myth but a settler-nationalist one, is tantamount to collusion with the myth. Although the Palestinians and their individual and collective rights are by no means absent from Myers's politics and ethics, they are absent from his discussion of the negation of exile, which he sees as a purely internal matter of Jewish history. It is no coincidence that his comparative forays are to a Central European case, the Czech national movement; while this comparison yields some insights, it sheds no light on the fact that this was not just a nation in general, but a settler nation.[4]

Another difference between Myers and Raz-Krakotzkin lies in their views of that tricky interim period, namely, the period of exile (from the first century CE to the 1880s), and it goes to the heart of the myth's meaning. The period presents a problem for historians because its infinite temporal and spatial permutations resist representation in a uniform nationalist narrative. For Myers, although his actual analysis bears resemblance to Raz-Krakotzkin's, the negation of exile is synonymous with the crude version thereof, presented in Chapter Three above.[5] In other words, he seems to deem as the negation of exile only the attempts to ignore, sidestep or consign to oblivion the period of exile, and create in its place a territorial master-narrative that proceeds from late antiquity straight to Zionism. From this perspective the Jerusalem scholars not only rejected the negation of exile but even offered an alternative, for not only did they not ignore or sidestep the period of exile, but so much of what they did was invested in that period and they did so much to illuminate it. All those within the Zionist orbit – including Anita Shapira and Myers, who occupies something of a peripheral position – share this understanding of the negation of exile. Raz-Krakotzkin similarly thinks that the Jerusalem scholars' medieval historiography yielded an explicit critique 'of the radical (and dominant) Zionist position on the negation of exile'. He does not stop there, however:

> But precisely the critique contained in the historiography of 'the Middle Ages' contributed to the perfection of Zionist ideology; contrary to the radical position that utterly negated exilic Jewish history and described it as worthless, the [Jerusalem] historians asserted that 'the Middle Ages' too express Jewish nationalism, and that there is an organic unity and continuity among all expressions of the Jewish past, irrespective of time or cultural context. The purpose [of the Jerusalem school] was to underline the continuity of a consciousness of Jewish sovereignty, and thereby to ignore the perspective of Jews from various generations when they alluded to *galut*.[6]

Moreover, Raz-Krakotzkin is acutely aware of Benjamin's observation that modernity's time is empty and homogeneous. Though not explicitly mentioned by him, this observation seems to be in the back of Raz-Krakotzkin's mind when he avers that this uniform narrative representation 'negates the perception of time it is supposed to describe, namely "exilic time"'.[7]

According to Raz-Krakotzkin, what the Jerusalem scholars did, by integrating exile into a territorial narrative, was to give Zionism the most systematic consolidation for the negation of exile concept, and also for the account that leads back in time, in a teleological fashion, to the land of Israel. A scholarly narrative was crystallizing around these formerly redundant exilic centuries, in the Hebrew University. Despite significant elements of diversity and even acrimony, the research of the Jerusalem scholars was underlain by a shared commitment to Zionism. And it must be recognized that overwriting the experiences of Jews in exile by retrospectively 'territorializing' these experiences and fitting them into an organic nationalist narrative is a deeper and ideologically more coherent and consistent articulation of the negation of exile than the quantum leap from King David to David Ben-Gurion.[8]

### Yitzhak-Fritz Baer and Ben-Zion Dinur (Dinaburg)

Fritz Baer was born in 1888 in Halberstadt, Germany.[9] After graduating from the Halberstadt Gymnasium in 1908, Baer matriculated at Berlin University, and concentrated in his first year on classical and medieval history as well as on philology. But it was his transfer in the subsequent semester to Freiburg that had a formative impact upon him, even though he later enrolled in Halle, and then again in Berlin. The two teachers who influenced him so much in Freiburg were Heinrich Finke and Friedrich Meineke. Just before Baer's arrival in Freiburg, Finke had published the first two volumes of his massive edition of the correspondence of the thirteenth-century King James II of Aragon, *Acta Aragonensia*, with a third volume to follow in 1922. Baer was one of a growing group of disciples whose research output revolved around Finke's interests and documentation. The first fruit of Baer's research was the publication in 1913 of his doctoral dissertation on the history of the Jews in Aragon in the thirteenth and fourteenth centuries. Although later in his career Baer would write on the Second Temple period, he was first and foremost a medievalist of Spanish Jewry, and one very much in Finke's mould.

The next stage in Baer's unfolding career followed his service in the German artillery corps in the First World War. In 1919 he was invited to be a permanent historical researcher in the newly established Akademie für die Wissenschaft des Judentum (Academy of Jewish Studies) in Berlin. There, Baer received inspiration and guidance from the academy's celebrated founder, Eugen Täubler. Täubler had censured previous manifestations of Jewish scholarship for being excessively literary and insufficiently contextual. He encouraged his researchers not only to adhere to the historical discipline, but also to do so with the extensive repository of archival documentation he himself was beginning to develop. To facilitate this, Täubler founded in 1905–6 the Gesamtarchiv der deutschen Juden (Comprehensive archive of German Jewry), whose director he became, and persuaded Baer to examine the previously unresearched protocols of the Jewish council of the principality of Cleve in the period 1690-1806.

After the publication of his Cleve monograph Baer returned to medieval Jewish Spain – significantly, only where the Reconquista had been successful, that is, the Christian parts of the Iberian Peninsula – to continue the research that Finke's repository and inspiration had opened up. The product of his thorough research in Spain and Germany was a volume that appeared in two parts (1929 from the Academy Press, and 1936 from Schocken): *Die Juden im christlichen Spanien*. By the end of the 1920s several formative traits were discernible in Baer's scholarly outlook: an interest and belief in the pivotal place of the *kehilah* (community) in diasporic Jewish life; the fundamental importance for Jewish history of archival documentation encompassing all domains of life, and including both 'internal' and 'external' sources; and the need to grapple with the organic immanence and continuity in Jewish history on the one hand, and the diversity and contingency wrought by 'external' contexts on the other. Baer was confident that the 'era of apologetics is over for the Jewish historian', and that the silhouette of his predecessors' world, 'the obsolete spirit of Enlightenment', could be removed.[10]

The Hebrew University's founding president Judah Magnes had been trying to woo Baer to Jerusalem since 1928; he was finally successful. Baer was appointed as professor of medieval Jewish history in the Institute of Jewish Studies, and delivered his inaugural lecture at the beginning of the winter semester of 1930. In 1936, after a depressing and alarming three-year sojourn in Germany, Baer published a short volume called *Galut* ('Exile'), under his Hebrew name of Yitzhak for the first time.[11] Crucially, he was joined in 1936 by Ben-Zion Dinur, hired to teach modern Jewish history. It is hardly possible to overstate the significance of the encounter between the two for the convergence of politics, ideology and scholarship. Myers crafts the personal side of their relationship perceptively and neatly:

> Two more diverse personalities could hardly have been invented. The product of a decorous German Orthodox background, Baer was a stern and reserved man, whose demeanor suited his vocation as an exacting archival historian . . . Dinaburg [Dinur], by contrast, had an effusive and engaging personality that was nurtured in the dynamic Jewish, and Hasidic, ambience of his native Russia. Unlike Baer, who favored the solitude of the monastic researcher, Dinaburg was a popular and populist teacher.[12]

Dinur was born in 1884 in the small Ukrainian town of Horol.[13] His family was by then Hasidic, and its lineage was one of a line of rabbis going back to the seventeenth century. Dinur's early education was formally religious, but he became increasingly immersed in the culture of the *Haskalah* (the so-called Jewish Enlightenment in Europe), learning Hebrew and showing an insatiable interest in Jewish history. He also became an active Zionist. As if anticipating his self-assigned mission, Dinur fashioned himself as the Zionist historian par excellence in the first two decades of the twentieth century. In 1900 he left Horol for Vilna, where he embarked on a gruelling preparation for a gymnasium equivalency diploma, which would pave the way to a Russian university. Although in the long run the hard work would not be in vain, Dinur failed his diploma and moved to Berlin in 1911 to study, as Baer would slightly later, with Täubler. With the latter's training and gradual leaning to ancient history, Dinur now moved to Bern University, where he joined a contingent of Eastern European Jewish students, and embarked on his PhD dissertation, 'Administration and Self-Administration in Palestine from Septimius Severus to Diocletian'. Then the First World War broke out and Dinur had to leave Switzerland and his uncompleted dissertation. His return to the Ukraine coincided with the 1917 revolution; having reportedly deposited his dissertation in Petrograd, he never saw it again. In 1921 he sailed from Odessa to Palestine.

Dinur's path to the Hebrew University was not easily paved. This was not only because of the inevitable squabbles in academic institutions, but also because his scholarly credentials could not be smoothly harmonized with the Germanic standards of the Hebrew University, especially given that the University's intended appointment was in modern Jewish history (Dinur's expertise clearly lay more in the ancient period). Baer, however, threw his considerable weight behind the appointment, and his persistence won the day. In 1936 Dinur began to teach, albeit initially on a part-time basis. He became a full professor only in 1948, at the age of sixty-four. Dinur was also 'assigned' a stereotypical role. It has already been noted that East European Jews represented a sort of primordial authenticity for the Jewish bourgeoisie of Western and Central Europe.[14] This is how his German Jewish colleagues in Jerusalem, including the likes of Scholem, Hugo Bergmann and Ernst-Akiva Simon, saw Dinur. Another German colleague, Moshe Schwabe, even wrote to Dinur that he was 'the prototypical Eastern Jew, permeated with Jewish culture, possessor of a treasure of Jewish values'.[15]

Of no less importance than his academic career was Dinur's political vocation, and indeed Dinur achieved more success in the latter. From the moment he set foot in Palestine, Dinur had been involved in all sorts of literary and teaching associations, and became an active member of Mapai, the main labour party, and the hegemonic party of the World Zionist Organization and the state of Israel from the early 1930s to 1977.

He was a member of the first Knesset (Israeli parliament) in 1949, and went on to be Minister of Education and Culture (1951–5), and founding member and then President (1956–9) of Yad Vashem, the Holocaust Martyrs' and Heroes' Remembrance Authority. Tellingly, as Uri Ram notes, it was when appointed minister that he Hebraized his name, from Dinaburg to Dinur. This was a demand imposed by Ben-Gurion on all holders of official state positions 'as a symbol of the mental return to the ancient Hebrew past'.[16]

In 1953 Dinur played a pivotal role in the promulgation and implementation of three laws: the Law of State Education, the Law of Holocaust Remembrance – Yad Vashem – and the law that gave birth to the Academy for the Hebrew Language. Many of the laws promulgated in the 1950s can be collectively seen as, among other things, a formalization of the Zionist foundational myth. Particularly worth emphasizing is that Dinur constructed the triangular foundation for the myth's inculcation through the state education curriculum in the shape of three compulsory fields: Bible, *Moledet* (Motherland) and Jewish history. As Ram pithily puts it, '[t]he historian was given by State Founder David Ben Gurion a rare opportunity to inscribe the historical narrative he had formerly composed in the official history textbooks of the State of Israel'.[17]

There is no better precis of Ben Zion Dinur's undertaking as both politician and nationalist historian par excellence than his own retrospective reflection:

> Four thousand years of [Jewish] history are very powerful if they live in the [people's] hearts; they are worthless if they are only recorded in books. If we want to be the inheritors of *Am Israel* [the Jewish People], we have to inculcate these four thousand years of history in the heart of each and every individual. The task is hard. I did my utmost to accomplish it.[18]

## The Zionist Historian in Zion

One of the first projects on which Baer and Dinur worked together on the latter's appointment in 1936 was the launch of a new series of the flagship journal *Zion*, which had been published since 1925. The decision to start afresh was taken in order to signal not so much a new direction but *the* direction of historical studies at the Hebrew University. It was clearly something for which Fritz Baer needed Ben-Zion Dinur at his side. The new series was introduced by a manifesto co-authored by Baer and Dinur. Entitled 'Megamatenu' ('Our purpose', literally 'Where we are heading'), it introduced the first issue of *Zion*'s new series. It is a text widely referred to and cited by scholars including Myers and Raz-Krakotzkin. Whereas all agree that the essay evinced a nationalist-historical consciousness, only Raz-Krakotzkin and I myself seem to think that the said essay compressed the twofold – perhaps dialectical – move of the Jerusalem medievalists. On the one hand, these Jerusalem scholars managed to integrate the history of exile into a territorial narrative by dehistoricizing and essentializing it, thereby supplying the historiographic foundation of a modern nation as a self-contained, impregnable whole floating in an empty, homogeneous (i.e., modern) time. On the other hand, this integration constitutes the most fundamental and systematic articulation of the negation of exile, for the cultural, social and political – that is, historical – context of the various Jewish communities is radically displaced. The exilic times and places themselves do not really matter; what matters is the manner in which diasporic Jewish communities are shown to preserve and manifest the nation's essence.

There are two key passages in 'Our purpose' that, first, leave little room for uncertainty and, secondly, have subsequently been buttressed by a massive historiography:

Jewish history is tantamount to the annals of the Jewish nation [ha-ummah ha-Yisra'elit], [annals] which never ceased and whose importance diminished at no period. Jewish history is held together by a homogeneous unity that encompasses all periods and places, all of which reflect on one another.[19]

And:

As for the situation of the Jews in the Diaspora in different periods, we do not think that the main thing should be the discussion and research of the particular conditions in each and every country [i.e., the 'host countries'], but that we should aspire to consider and clarify the themes according to the conditions shared by Yisrael ba-Golah [the Jewish People in the Diaspora] in each and every generation.[20]

In the context of this ideological manifesto, let us now delve a bit deeper into the individual oeuvres of Baer and Dinur, and, especially, how they related to the German Jewish scholars of the nineteenth century. The Jerusalem scholars' approach to their intellectual progenitors, I shall argue, is not just a scholarly disagreement or a generational rebellion: it is also a most interesting expression of their fundamental negation of exile. There are four discrete strands (some of which are shared by other historians) to Baer's involvement in Zionist history: the rejection of the world of his predecessors, the Wissenschaft des Judentum scholars, who were the embodiment of the fusion of Aufklärung (the German Enlightenment) and Jewish emancipation; the replacement of this *wissenschaftliche* sensibility with Zionist romanticism; the insistence on the organic unity of the Jewish nation; and the conviction that pietism has always carried the underlying essence of Judaism. It might be interesting to intersperse my own commentary with the insights of one of Baer's outstanding and revering, yet severely critical, students, Efraim Shmueli. He dedicated to Baer his important monograph on the Iberian Jewish notable, Don Isaac Abravanel, but was nonetheless unabashed in his refutation of many of his mentor's arguments as well as Dinur's.[21]

In Baer's historiography, the concepts of Jewish history and the Jewish nation were inextricably, organically entwined. Examples of this inextricability abound, and Shmueli perceptively foregrounds one of the most striking (before proceeding to reject it). It is arresting not only because of its formulation, but also because of its placement at the opening statement of Baer's central work, his study of the Jews in late medieval Christian Spain: 'Jewish history, from its earliest beginnings to our own day, constitutes an organic whole. Each successive stage in its development reveals more fully the nature of the unique force guiding it, a force whose initial vitality is universally recognized and whose future course arouses interest. Let this observation be the key to our study.'[22]

In a later book of 1955, which was less monographic and sought to position *The Jewish People Among the Nations*, Baer made a similarly forceful statement, but with a crucial addition:

> Every episode in the long history of our nation contains the secret of all periods, both preceding and following. In the end there will remain of the ancients' metaphysical-historical structure a few large columns, which the early pietists sunk into the soil of the Land of Israel, and these are implanted in the heart of every man, and will mark the future Israel's [in the sense of the Jewish People's] place among the nations.[23]

Mention of the pietists takes us to the next fundamental of Baer's historical edifice, for his presupposition that the Jewish history and Jewish nation were organically coherent across time and place went hand in hand with a Romantic rejection of rationalism and the Enlightenment. This rejection found salient expression in what Shmueli aptly calls 'the Ashkenization of Sephardi history'[24] and, more generally, in Baer's firm belief that pietism was Judaism's essence. Baer was hostile to the Iberian Jewish elite. He thought they had strayed from the pietistic core of Judaism, and were alienated from the masses because of their ostentatiously decadent lifestyle; indeed, the extent to which they had become prone to assimilation was perilous for the perpetuation of the Jewish nation. This precarious situation was providentially reversed by the arrival in the Iberian Peninsula of the Ashkenazi pietist spirit and leadership, and by the transfer of Judaism's centre from Sepharad to Ashkenaz. Along the way Baer created a series of dichotomies, most notably between elite philosophical rationalism and the pious religion of the common folk. Myers correctly comments: 'In Baer's scheme, whole classes of Jews – Hellenized Alexandrians, Spanish "Averroists," or modern German *Aufklärer* – were excluded from the narrow realm of virtuous historical activity.'[25]

For Baer the pietistic essence of Judaism was formatively created in the first couple of centuries CE by a few generations of ascetic scholars, and this continued to underlie the nation's existence in all its geographical diversity. As Shmueli puts it, Baer saw Judaism's essence thus framed as 'the measure against which the forbidden and the permitted are defined'.[26] Baer gave his essentialism a succinct formulation in 1938, in a vehemently scathing review of Salo Baron's voluminous masterpiece, *A Social and Religious History of the Jews* (1937):

> The battle against enlightenment, which begins in Spain with Judah ha-Levi and gathers momentum under the influence of the Kabbala, and in the movement of German Pietism, is an anti-rationalist, anti-secular, anti-capitalist movement, similar to the movement of the prophets, the Pharisees and the Tannaim [scholars of the Mishnah]. It transforms the people into a religious proletariat.[27]

There is a sense in which the life-endeavour of the Jerusalem scholars can be seen as their dual relation of rebellion and continuity with their *wissenschaftliche* forefathers. This was, as we shall see, famously the case with Scholem. Baer's rebellion was sometimes implicit: his objection to the excessively textual approach and literary emphasis of the nineteenth-century scholarship, something he inherited from Täubler, echoed in his own work in the accentuation of social themes, as well as in the use of archival documents.[28] But he also explicitly censured the nineteenth-century scholars for their adherence to the Enlightenment and for their concomitant failure to drink from the fountain of romanticism. In 1938 he wrote a short, often neglected, programmatic essay 'On the State of Our Historical Studies', in which he made patently clear what in his view was incomplete in his predecessors' historiography.[29] I believe that the significance of this text has thus far gone unrecognized: it is nothing less than a profound and forceful expression of the negation of exile.

Baer begins by positing the following question: why is it that the main task of Jewish studies in the past century – the transference and application of 'the modern historical thinking method to the subject matter of Jewish history' – has not yet been accomplished.[30] The main explanation for this, he argues, is palpable: the Jewish nation had diverged from the path of the classical world and its legacy to European civilization. In exile, until the eighteenth century, 'the historical approach' was suppressed by 'the religious method'. The result was that whereas modern historical thought developed organically among European nations ('with the natural life of these peoples'), 'with us, the Jews, these methods of historical research were received suddenly and abruptly [*pit'om uvli hakdamah*]'.[31] With haughty authority, Baer asserts: 'For this reason Mendelssohn had to request his friend Christian Dohm to write the book on rectifying the civil situation of the Jews [C. von Dohm, *Über die bürgerliche Verbesserung der Juden*, 1781], not only for tactical considerations, but because the Jew lacked the historical and political knowledge required to discuss the matter.'[32]

Then Baer moves to the main – though by no means the only – nineteenth-century German Jewish historian with whom all subsequent scholars have had to contend: Heinrich Graetz (1817–91), who in effect founded Jewish history as a 'properly' national field. Graetz was a prolific writer, and his main work was his eleven-volume *Geschichte der Juden* ('History of the Jews'), written between 1853 and 1875. Baer entreats his Zionist Hebrew readers to appreciate the enormity of Graetz's largely unsurpassed achievement; although his admiration is genuine, one also senses the unuttered reservation. The blow follows the praise. The first three volumes of *History of the Jews* are fine, according to Baer (the third volume reaches the end of the period of the Second Temple). 'Confusion is revealed mainly in the fourth volume, dedicated to the Talmud period.'[33] For Baer, the underlying problem is that Graetz's work

> interprets Judaism's internal development as for the most part a sort of collection of anecdotes that lose under his pen their original force and vitality, and become an arid story that he extracts from the sources on the evolution of the *Halakhah*. His critique [of legal Jewish sources] is formal-extrinsic, [rather than] that fertile critique of the gaze that penetrates into the secret of the birth and growth of creative cultural beings, and which divulges the secret to the mind's eye of the reader with the artistry of a great painter.[34]

Later Baer calls the Romantic spade a spade:

> Graetz's weakness had deeper roots . . . Occasionally some historical instinct erupts and surfaces in his mind like a burning and illuminating flame. But the foundations of his knowledge are not in the world of historical thought. In recent times some among us have talked about Ranke's influence upon Graetz and even dared to compare the two historians. The truth of the matter is that Graetz, like all his Jewish followers and critics, was alienated from views that emanated from romanticism, from people like Niebuhr, Ranke and others . . . In Graetz's book [*History of the Jews*] no real contact whatsoever can be detected with the great vision that was developed in the historical science in Germany at the time. How yawning the gap between him [Graetz], and the said great [Romantic] historians who preceded him.[35]

Baer is quick to clarify that

> [i]t is not to belittle Graetz's stature to emphasize this absolute contrast between him and those great historians. Graetz did not go to learn from the creators of the historical science in Germany, either from their mouths or from their books. He absorbed from their spirit and method only what he could find in [the works of] the Christian theologians and the philologists of the Oriental sciences. Like most of his colleagues in Jewish Studies, the entire essence of his soul was rationalist according to the philosophical heritage of the Middle Ages [Baer presumably had Maimonides in mind] and in tandem with the formulation of the eighteenth century.[36]

Baer tries to illustrate more precisely the Romantic spirit that, he contends, is absent from Jewish historiography: the German Romantic historiography that so vividly grasps the inner moral energy of the nation and the vitality of its creative force, and frames the things that cannot be reduced to abstractions, but the sensation of which 'can be aroused in the beholder's heart'. He does so by citing Ranke and one of his own mentors at Freiburg, Meinecke (from his 1936 *Die Entstehung des Historismus*, 'The development of historicism'). He calls the latter 'one of the last of the great history teachers'.[37] To recall a point made above,[38] Baer's indefatigable search for a German Romantic rendering of Jewish history is reminiscent of Herzl's indefatigable literary search for the acceptance of the Jews by Prussian Junkers in *Das neue Ghetto* and *Altneuland*.

But why should Baer's judgment of Graetz and his nineteenth-century predecessors be a fundamental expression of the negation of exile? Why did Baer think that Graetz could not drink from the fountain of Romantic historiography – which for Baer simply *was* modern historiography – and that Mendelssohn needed Dohm to write for him a book that entailed knowledge of history and politics? Why, in Baer's view, was Graetz incapable of grasping and depicting the Jewish nation's creative vitality and organic unfolding, why couldn't he 'sense' the nation? Surely Baer did not think that Graetz was intellectually incapable of comprehending the historical discipline, or that he was insufficiently rooted in German culture to be familiar with Romantic historicism. The reason is so deeply seated in Baer's mind that it is almost unselfconscious: Graetz and his contemporaries were all in exile, not an organic part of the nation on whose soil they dwelt. For Bear, in order to sense (intuitively) and grasp (cerebrally) the history of the nation, the historian must dwell in its midst and the nation must be sovereign on its soil. Graetz and his *wissenschaftliche* colleagues could not perforce write authentic history because their position and experience was not authentic: it was *exilic*. Expressing the myth in its return-to-history guise, Baer states: 'It must be further understood that a historical perspective is born and grows in nations through a political, self-aware, purposeful and common way of life.'[39]

The culmination of Baer's argument is his attempt to endow the Zionist historian with a privileged position, both absolutely and relative to his exilic predecessors. He first clarifies that '[o]ur history is the process of the development of a great force', and then emphatically declares:

We who are aware of ourselves as part, and as messengers, of this magnificent and confounding force, cannot ignore such a [historical] consciousness. The Zionist perspective, from which we approach historical research, does not aim to distort things for certain purposes, as was the case with the perspectives of previous generations; rather, it forces [the beholder] to see things as they are. We know that we have received the difficult heritage of a complicated historical development, and we see it as our duty to understand the circumstances of this development in all its variegated windings, so that we come out of the entanglement of the previous generations. And in actual fact this historical realism is really poised to manifest the magnitude of the said historical force. After all it is not the task of historical criticism to identify contradictions in the tradition . . . but rather through historical criticism one penetrates the secret of being of historical phenomena, which are a sort of personae that develop according to their own special laws that truly emanate from the depth of their soul.[40]

Baer's remarkable statement is the project of the Jerusalem scholars in a nutshell. It contains a twofold negation of exile: of the Jews in exile through the incorporation of their experienced histories into an organically coherent territorial narrative; and of the consciousness of nineteenth-century German Jewish historians because they wrote from an exilic perspective. The question of objectivity, especially pertinent to the latter expression of the myth, is a vexed point that will resurface in conjunction with Scholem's work. There is a misunderstanding in the charge of some critics that the Jerusalem scholars claimed objectivity in the literal sense, as if they were parochial or intellectual simpletons. What Baer claimed to possess was objectivity, authority and authenticity in the Romantic sense. The Jerusalem scholars wrote 'correct' history because they were Zionists and because they wrote it in Jerusalem; because for them the telos of Jewish history not only climaxes in the territorial present, but this present is also embodied in the Zionist historian in Jerusalem and his mission. Ultimately, as Raz-Krakotzkin concurs, that is why Zionist histor-ical consciousness is the consciousness of the victor, regardless of it being excessively lachrymose by overstating and exploiting persecutions, and that is why a Benjaminian critique of it is so apt to salvage the negated voice of exile, Jewish and Palestinian.

Although Dinur was a lesser scholar than Baer, he offered a similar negation of the previous generation of Jewish historians. He did so in what constitutes his discrete imprint on the Jerusalem project of creating a Zionist historiography: the work of *kinus* (literally, 'gathering'): the historical genre of compilation of edited texts and documents, whose purpose was to create a self-evident national repository. The significance of this kind of work was impressed upon Dinur by two different traditions. One was the centrality of compilation to German national historiography, beginning with the massive *Monumenta Germaniae Historica* of 1826.[41] The other was Chaim Nahman Bialik, the most eminent Hebrew literary figure of his time, later to be crowned the Hebrew national poet. Dinur had met Bialik twice in Odessa, first in 1911, and then just before Dinur's immigration to Palestine in 1921. These meetings were remarkable not only for the fact that Bialik had impressed upon Dinur the importance of *kinus* for the national cause, but also for the way in which Dinur's understanding of *kinus* bespeaks the triumphant aura of Zionism, and how early this triumphant confidence appeared. For both Bialik and Dinur the time was ripe for the genre of compilation to come to the fore in Jewish historiography because it witnessed the dusk of one epoch and the dawn of another – hence Dinur's observation in 1938 that the work of compilation would be 'the cultural-literary expression of the victory of a new world-view', and that '[t]he starting point of all work of collection in our generation is Zionist ideology'.[42]

The subject matter of Dinur's major work, entitled *Yisrael ba-Golah* ('The Jewish people in the Diaspora'), was the very same material that Baer and Dinur's manifesto 'Our Purpose' identified for integration into an organic narrative. The project of compilation was more ambitious than the result, which comprises a lengthy introduction followed by a much less impressive corpus of texts and documents than promised. The main volume was first published in 1926, and an expanded second edition appeared in 1958; Baer wrote a preface for the 1969 English edition entitled 'Ben Zion Dinur: The Jewish Historian'.[43] For our purpose, the most significant part of the work is its lengthy opening essay, in which Dinur sets out his historiographic manifesto. The two important components of the introduction Dinur wrote were his fresh periodization of Jewish history and his commentary on earlier and contemporaneous Jewish historians in Europe.

Dinur begged to differ from the conventional periodization of exile, considered to have begun some time in the first two centuries CE, and presaged by two events: the destruction of the Second Temple by the Romans in the first century CE, and the suppression of the Bar-Kokhba revolt in the second century CE. Significantly, Dinur pushed forward the beginning of the exilic era, of 'Israel in the Diaspora', to the Arab-Muslim conquest of Palestine from 636 CE onwards. What makes this periodization interesting is, of course, its justification. Dinur is well aware that Jewish dispersion in the Mediterranean predated the Arab-Muslim conquest, that there were numerous Jewish communities outside of Palestine in the Western and Eastern (Byzantine) Roman Empire, and that the majority of 'the Jewish nation' had already been residing outside of its 'national home'. He then explains that, despite all this, two criteria persuaded him significantly to postdate the beginning of the period of exile: 'first, the difference between the mere existence of scattered Jewish communities in foreign lands and the actual "Israel in Diaspora"; and, secondly, the special character of "Israel in Diaspora"'.[44] In other words, what mattered to Dinur was not the plain fact that Jews were dispersed and living throughout the region, and not even the loss of political sovereignty as such, but the point at which, in his perception, they became a nation in exile, and at the same lost grip over their homeland.[45]

Dinur gives a perfect and succinct formulation of the way in which two of the myth's expressions – negation of exile and return to the land of Israel – complement each other, that is, the way in which both the nation and the homeland are in simultaneous exile. The process of the homeland's going into exile was, according to Dinur,

> a social and colonizing process . . . in which the principal factors were, first, the continuous penetration of nomad desert tribes into Palestine and their amalgamation with the non-Jewish (Syro-Aramaean) elements of the population; and secondly, the domination of the country's agriculture by the new conquerors and the expropriation of Jewish lands for their benefit.[46]

This was a 'long struggle' that had commenced long before the seventh century, but 'the decisive event . . . was the Arab conquest of Palestine, with the resulting expropriation of Jewish lands by the conquerors and the emergence of a new national majority in the country. This, therefore, is the right moment to choose as the starting-point of the era of "Israel in the Diaspora".'[47]

Dinur constructs a rather simple schema, within which he parades his predecessors in order to pass judgment on them. First, five fundamental points that are the precondition for a correct conceptualization of Jewish history are clarified. Then the *oeuvre* of five outstanding Jewish historians is not so much discussed as evaluated in terms of their relative success in accordance with Dinur's five fundamentals. The historians, of German or East European Jewish origins, on whom Dinur focuses are Isaac Mordecai Jost (1793–1860), the aforementioned Heinrich Graetz (1817–91), Abraham Geiger (1810–74), Simon Dubnow (1860–1941), and the teacher with whom both Baer and Dinur had studied, Eugen Täubler (1879–1953). In the final stage of his introduction Dinur puts forth the correct way in which the five fundamentals of writing 'correct' Jewish history ought to be addressed, reiterates where the surveyed historians went wrong and, most importantly, concludes that this was a collective failure.[48] Dinur's schematic review of his predecessors – it is almost as if he were marking their papers – is a forcefully simplistic rendering of the organic nation's unfolding march 'back' to Zion. The narrative is manifestly historiographical, but also latently historical – by which I mean that it not only judges the previous generation of historians, but also guides the nation's historical consciousness and historical writing 'back' to Zionism. And this march of the historical spirit is observed from atop Mount Scopus by the Zionist historian (both Dinur specifically and the Zionist historian in general) to whom the march leads and in whom it culminates.

Dinur's schema has already been satisfactorily examined.[49] But two points should be made in this discussion of Dinur's distinct contribution to the Jerusalem scholars' role in the furtherance of Zionist ideology. Dinur's guideline for writing 'correct' Jewish history in effect demarcates the boundaries of the Zionist historical discourse by stressing the organic unity of the nation in exile, the fact that the nation's history in exile was uniformly shaped by its internal essence rather than external circumstances, and – with a degree of zealousness and contrivance that is unique to Dinur – the symbolic and actual centrality of the land of Israel to the continuous existence of the Jews in exile as a nation.[50] The first point, then, is the extent to which Dinur is troubled by the emphasis laid by his teacher, Täubler, upon the spatial and temporal circumstances of each diasporic community rather than on some internally organic unity. Dinur is especially disturbed by the fact that the position of his mentor on the subject of organic unity is so far behind other Jewish historians who had written before Täubler. Dinur inserts a lengthy quotation of Täubler, which is alarming to the Zionist historian simply because it encapsulates the consciousness of exile. Moreover, the Zionist historian's anxiety is compounded by the fact that this consciousness is now expressed not in rabbinical terminology, but in the idiom of modern historiography. Täubler says:

> The fluctuating vicissitudes in the integration of the Jews into the German body politic were determined by the legal, economic and cultural conditions of the German people. These conditions were, in turn, very influential in bringing about the 'inner change' in the national element in Judaism; and it is by their light that we must examine the influence exercised by the Jewish element in the population on the spiritual and social development of the German people . . . Moreover 'the internal history of the Jews' (their communal life, their reciprocal relations, the development of their religion, literature and customs) are not merely *subjected* to the continuous influence of the alien environment, but are actually *conditioned* by it: the legal system, economy, and general culture of the surrounding nations must be reckoned with as factors governing the development of the inner life of the Jews [emphasis in the original].[51]

It is difficult to overstate the significance of Täubler's assertion and, correspondingly, of Dinur's anxious response. Täubler was not depicting an idyllic picture of exile nor was he condoning assimilation or endorsing an organic German nationalism in lieu of a Jewish one. Rather, he was in his own way reiterating the consciousness of *galut* as a state of being in which Jews had many histories, in which they were shaped by their 'host' societies and in turn shaped these societies. If there is historical continuity, according to the kind of historical thinking Täubler represents, it is actually exilic. There is a sense in which Täubler's position can be seen as a development, cloaked in modernity's garb, of the constituting rabbinical injunction (in Aramaic) of *Dina d'malkhuta dina* ('The law of the land is the law'). Typical of laconic rabbinical language, in strictly legal terms this injunction instructs Jews that they must obey and live by the law of the political entity under whose suzerainty they dwell – including, incidentally, in the land of Israel itself. Less literally, the injunction could also signify the Jewishness of being in exile, of exile as a way of life and form of consciousness.

However much Dinur would wish to be deferential, he winds up unforgiving, lest he undermine the thrust of his own Zionist credo. Täubler does explain the historical trajectory of each community, Dinur concedes, but 'he does not do the same for the processes that unite the different parts of the nation into a single entity . . . Nor is that the only defect in his method. In another place, when analyzing the permanent processes of Jewish history . . . he is mainly concerned with the definition of these processes as such [economic, public and cultural], and he does not explain the extent of their organic interconnection.'[52] In concluding his discussion of Täubler, the last of the historians he evaluates, Dinur, like Baer in his own evaluation of Jewish historiography, reiterates the extent to which, despite some progress, 'fundamental historiographical questions' have not yet been satisfactorily addressed. One of the most important among them is 'the very nature of the unity which binds the scattered parts of the nation together into a single, historically significant entity'.[53]

The second point I will make about Dinur's schema concerns the concept concomitant to the organic nation in exile, that of the land of Israel in exile. The last of the five fundamentals by which Dinur tested the correctness of Jewish historiography was 'The place of the Land of Israel in the life of the exiled nation'.[54] Dinur summarizes the evaluations of the Jewish historians in Europe by stating: 'And the last of our questions, that about the part played by the Land of Israel in the history of the Diaspora, has, truth be told, hardly been dealt with at all.'[55] He is indeed right in his observation for, in different ways and to varying degrees of comprehensiveness, none of the historians he examines thought that the land of Israel played an important role in the histories of *Yisrael ba-Golah*. As is well known, the rabbinical nineteenth-century scholar Abraham Geiger was normatively positive about the evident loss of attachment to the land – a sort of 'good riddance' – thinking that Judaism benefited from not being bogged down by territoriality.

Dinur issues an assertive, forthright corrective to what he views as this unacceptably exilic marginalization of the Promised Land:

> Even during the period of the Diaspora, the Land of Israel and its Jewish population still played a part of *general importance* in the history of the nation. This was not only because the deep imprint of the past, which continued to live in the heart of the nation, and the yearnings for redemption, which fortified its spirit in times of oppression and persecution, were all inseparably connected to Palestine, the holiness of which persisted. The special importance of the Land of Israel in the period of the Diaspora was also the consequence of the historical and material uniqueness of the Yishuv, and of its distinct character among the Jewish collectives in their dispersion. This uniqueness of the Yishuv resulted from three basic facts: its historical continuity, its essence and its Jewish wholeness.[56]

There could not have been a more fitting conclusion to the triumphant march of the nation and its raconteurs 'back' to Zion than the paragraph with which Dinur brings *Yisrael ba-Golah* to a closure:

> To sum up: the political rebirth of Israel is the very essence of Jewish history. She absorbed into herself the experiences and activities of generations, the covenant of generations. She renewed the covenant with the land out of a longing, through the creation of a new community, to develop the Covenant of Man into an Eternal Covenant.[57]

## Conclusion: The Negation of Exile at Yad Vashem

Because there is no Originator, the nation's biography can not be written evangelically, 'down time', through a long procreative line of begettings. The only alternative is to fashion it 'up time' – towards Peking Man, Java Man, King Arthur, wherever the lamp of archaeology casts its fitful gleam. This fashioning, however, is marked by deaths, which, in a curious inversion of conventional genealogy, starts from an originary present. World War II begets World War I; out of Sedan comes Austerlitz; the ancestor of the Warsaw uprising is the state of Israel.

(Benedict Anderson, *Imagined Communities*, 1991, p. 205)

In April 2001 Yad Vashem and the Hebrew University organized a conference to mark the fortieth anniversary of the Eichmann trial, with a keynote opening address by Anita Shapira. The text of the address was subsequently published by Yad Vashem with an English title, *Hannah Arendt and Haim Gouri: Two Perceptions of the Eichmann Trial*, which does not convey its ideological depth as well as the original Hebrew title (*Devarim she-ro'im mi-kan lo ro'im mi-sham*). A more literal translation of the latter is 'The Eichmann trial: things that are seen from here are not seen from there'.[58] This text, which fluctuates between the striking and the preposterous, powerfully illustrates the depth of the myth's absorption by the generations of Zionist Israeli scholars who had been brought up, directly or otherwise, on the work of the Jerusalem founding fathers. Shapira amply – and perhaps unwittingly – manifests their unwillingness to confront the possibility that the negation of exile might be something much deeper and more serious than simply ignoring, sidestepping or bad-mouthing exilic Judaism. Further, she seems unaware that her presumption that being in a Jewish nation-state in the Promised Land is the authentic position from which to unfold Jewish history and to sense Jewish experience – to say nothing of the Shoah specifically – is itself an articulation of the negation of exile. It is in this context that the Hebrew title is so revealing: as we shall now see, for Shapira being 'here' (Gouri's Palestine/Israel) facilitated proximity to the Jewish experience while being 'there' (Arendt's Europe) created distance and alienation from it; for Shapira, moreover, the 'here' and 'there' vis-à-vis the Shoah was somehow self-evident rather than ideologically contrived. It is the degree to which all this is ingrained in Shapira's consciousness that evinces the hegemonic depth of Zionist ideology: its foundational myth seems to be ontologically already there.

Shapira invokes Gouri and Arendt as representing 'two models of different forms of reaction to the same event [the Eichmann trial]', before turning to examine 'how their insights influenced the public discourse, short and long term'.[59] The dichotomy Shapira draws is quite simple. Gouri is the new Jew incarnate. Born in Tel Aviv in 1923, he was educated in the agricultural boarding school Kadurie, close to Mount Tabor, an institution he shared with Yigal Allon and Yitzhak Rabin. After the Second World War Gouri was sent to Europe, where he stayed during 1947–8 and came in contact with Holocaust survivors, whom he trained and indoctrinated in Hungary and Czechoslovakia. Gouri fought in the Palmach, the elite unit of the Haganah and the backbone of the Israeli army in the 1948 war, and later joined the Mapam labour party, which was mounting a challenge to the dominant Mapai. He was the poet most identified with the first 1948 generation, known in Hebrew as *Dor Tashah*. Two of his poems, 'Bab el-Wad' (literally 'The valley's gate': the poem is titled after the Arab name of the uphill route leading into Jerusalem from the direction of Tel Aviv and commemorates the convoys that tried to reach the Jews besieged there) and 'Ha-Re'ut' ('Camaraderie'), became songs that for Israelis encapsulated the 1948 war, and have acquired quasi national anthem status.

For Shapira, Arendt was an elite European intellectual who in spite of all that transpired was proud of her position within high German culture and letters. During the Eichmann trial the only characters she deemed her equals were the judges, whose German language and demeanour she pronounced impeccable; on the other hand she despised the prosecutor, Gideon Hausner, who 'altogether seemed to the Heidelberg-educated German as if he had just come out from Galicia and still hadn't shed the features of that province, which presumes to be German'.[60] Arendt, Shapira continues,

arrived [at the trial] resolved not to be drawn into the sea of sentimentality that would rage around her: she would stay cold and alienated, seeking a just trial for one person in the accused booth, resisting any attempt to extend the trial beyond the man and his acts. She came as a researcher who seeks to examine the personality of the mass murderer or 'the murderer behind the desk' . . . and to report on Eichmann's conscience, as she said. And indeed, she met all her expectations and also found all she had expected to find.[61]

Gouri, on the other hand, had to overcome his limited historical knowledge, linguistic range and Sabra bias against the stereotyped exilic Jew:

Despite his 'Palestinocentrism', he came to the trial with a sense of partnership in a historical moment, as well as with a strong sense of belonging to the collective that brings Eichmann to justice. From the first moment he distinguished between 'ours' and 'his'. This is the trial of the Jewish people versus Eichmann – and he belongs to the Jewish people. What eventually drove each approach was the different purpose: Arendt came to examine Eichmann and figure out the nature of the Israeli legal system, whereas Gouri came without a defined purpose – curious, a bit wary of what he might learn in the trial, ready for difficult things, but not beyond that. She [Arendt] came fixated in her views and positions, and consequently found what she had looked for. He came with the preconceived notions of the common Israeli – but came out different from how he had come in.[62]

For Shapira, Gouri's metamorphosis during the trial was personal and anticipatory of the Israeli collective's more gradual transformation. She pinpoints the Eichmann trial as the moment when Arendt's and Gouri's attitudes diverge in their differing rejections of the accusation that the Jews had gone like lambs to the slaughter. Arendt committed what is for Zionist Israeli scholars, from Scholem to Shapira, *the* cardinal sin: she had a universalist perspective, to which we shall return shortly. 'Gouri's reference, on the other hand, was confined to the Jewish people. For this people he now showed an empathy and understanding that he had not possessed before the trial . . . The acquittal of the Jewish masses from the accusation of "lamb to the slaughter" transferred the burden of guilt from the [Jewish] people "there" to the [Jewish] people "here".'[63] Thus Gouri's 'return' to the Jewish people anticipated a process that undermined the Canaanite grasp over the consciousness of his generation, and '[t]he Eichmann trial launched the long and meandering trek of Israeliness back to the Jewish people'.[64] Here, Shapira's contribution to Zionist ideology is her extending of the scope of the notion of return and making it more figurative – and buttressing, despite trials and tribulations along the way, the eventual triumph of the nation's organic unity.

Arendt's sin of universalism, which had already incurred Scholem's wrath, continued to arouse Shapira's poisonous ire three decades later:

> Throughout the 260 pages of her book [*Eichmann in Jerusalem*], not once did Arendt accuse herself or her friends, who had fled burning Europe to Manhattan's safe haven, for not having acted to save Jews. In her response to Gershom Scholem's criticism, who berated her for lack of love for the Jewish people, Arendt stated that she had never loved any 'collective', be it a nation or class, but only people close to her. Therein, it would seem, lies the explanation for the absence of guilt with her. Gouri's guilt stemmed from his consciousness of identifying with a national collective, which is responsible for its various tribes. The closer the exterminated Jews become, so too becomes closer to us the guilt over their death. In contrast, Arendt waged a battle against the tribal perception of 'the whole world is against us'.[65]

It gets worse. Shapira then resorts to a 1963 *New Yorker* essay by Norman Podhoretz on the 'Perversity of Brilliance', in which he contrasts two ways of telling a national tragedy: James Baldwin's report on the Muslim African Americans and Arendt's on the Eichmann trial. Podhoretz's distinction between Baldwin's emotional and empathetic tone and Arendt's detached and ambivalent register could be applied to add insight, Shapira continues, to the contrast between Gouri's and Arendt's accounts of the Eichmann trial. In stark contrast to Arendt, 'Gouri adopted Baldwin's strategy: self-involvement, address to emotion, black is black and white is white. He remains within the confines of moral clarity and national identification'.[66] Shapira charges Arendt with trying to 'understand' Nazism and the Judaeocide from a universalist position: that is, by attempting to comprehend the depths to which a human society – any society – can sink and how humanity might avoid doing so again; with having 'positioned herself in opposition to the political-ideological-national system';[67] and with having advanced a critique of the Israeli state that made an observer like Boas Evron recall in 2000 that 'this book [*Eichmann in Jerusalem*] came to me as a fresh wind of sobriety and sensibility amidst the hysterical storm blown all around by the propaganda agencies of the Ben-Gurion regime'.[68] Shapira also charges Arendt with moral ambivalence, hence her statement that Gouri remained within the confines of moral clarity. The preposterous charge that Arendt's ethical position blurred the clear distinction between perpetrators and victims is made in a parochial fit of post-modernism-bashing, which has become one of the all-too-predictable rallying calls most favoured by Zionist ideologues. Here is Shapira's version:

> Beyond the negating-critical position of the political system was the moral ambivalence. The moral ambivalence is what makes Arendt today the focus of interest of the post-modernists. Nothing is really the way it looks: there is no truth and false, victim and murderer, guilty and innocent, there are no hierarchies of values; everything is located in the realm of the moral mists.[69]

Shapira's text reiterates the Zionist myth and ideology in several ways. I find two articulations of it especially striking. One is the contrast between 'here' and 'there' (hence the emphasis I put earlier on the original Hebrew title of her address). Hannah Arendt, one of the most outstanding individuals of the world destroyed by the Nazis, who fled to Paris literally from under the noses of the Gestapo, and from Paris (where she helped Jewish youth escape to Palestine) to New York in the wake of the Nazi invasion of France, is from 'there'. She was incapable, in Shapira's absurd judgment, of sensing the Jewish experience because she was from 'there', as if 'there' was not where the Holocaust had occurred, and as if the world that had collapsed 'there' was not Arendt's much more than Gouri's. Granted, Arendt did commit one of the many 'sins' for which Shapira sanctimoniously reprimands her: she fled the Nazi threat that was closing in on her, and had the temerity to live in New York among her degenerate universalist Manhattanite friends. The presupposition that 'here' is the location where one genuinely, authentically and authoritatively bonds with the Jewish experience in exile is precisely that deep form of the negation of exile of which Shapira is not cognizant and the one she apparently is incapable of grasping.

The other striking articulation of the Zionist myth – and one characteristic of Zionist thought more generally – is the abhorrence of universalism. We shall encounter the enormity of this abhorrence in the next chapter in conjunction with Scholem's world view. For reasons of space, I will not relate here the many ways in which Shapira adumbrates Gouri's superiority to Arendt because of his commitment and adherence to the national collective to which he belongs, and so on and so forth ad infinitum and ad nauseam. It is perhaps more interesting to point out the underlying contradiction that eludes Shapira: the moral rectitude that she praises Gouri for upholding, and which she berates Arendt and 'the post-modernists' for straying from, is actually universal rather than specifically Jewish or Zionist Israeli. It is, among other things, the result of trying to look at the Shoah in universal terms, the result of the Nuremberg trials that transcended the sovereignty of the laws of the nation-state and subjected the actions of its members to universal notions of morality, law and 'general humanity', a notion which Scholem dreaded and thought to exist only in the imagination of aloof exilic Jews like Arendt. This denial of the universalist position in general, and as the valid exilic experience of some – and the emphasis should be on 'some' – Jews in particular, is not only a mark of reactionary particularist politics but also another expression of the negation of exile.

A final comment on the relationship between Shapira's text and its context: Jerusalem, Palestine and Israel in 2001, when the lecture was delivered, and 2002, when the text was published. Shapira's apparent obliviousness to the current context – the fact that it engenders no reflection in a text that is, after all, written by a prominent member of the Israeli peace camp – is quite depressing. For instance, the rather tacky embrace of Israeliness and the Jewish people which Shapira celebrates is not tempered by the thought that this is yet another manifestation of Jewish exclusion of the Palestinian citizens of Israel, who may never have a real stake in the state unless a more universalist concept of community and citizenship replaces the current organic volkism. The fact that, just six months before the lecture's delivery, thirteen Israeli Palestinians were murdered by the police in a demonstration prompted no stock-taking, only the buttressing of civil exclusion and ethno-religious inclusion. The same is true, more

generally, of the fact that remembrance of the Shoah year after year –
with the occupation another year older, more horrific, more oppressive,
more criminal – is never a cause for a hard, universalist, look at the mirror,
simply an opportunity for yet more particularist, self-righteous collective
reaffirmation.

Nearly simultaneously with the publication of the written text of
Shapira's lecture in 2002, the denizens of the refugee camp in Jenin were
digging the rubble with their hands in search of survivors and corpses.
Could they have been present in Shapira's mind as a concomitant to her
diatribe against Arendt's humanist universalism?

## Notes

1 The best study to date is D. Myers, *Re-Inventing the Jewish Past: European Jewish Intellectuals and the Zionist Return to History*, New York and Oxford: Oxford University Press, 1995, especially pp. 38–74, where the institutional history is thoroughly documented and eloquently presented.

2 This was part of the challenges to hegemonic scholarship in the 1990s (and reactions to them), which were mentioned earlier in relation to *Theory and Criticism*. These challenges went beyond the issues raised by the works on the 1948 war and were not limited to the conventional definition of the Arab–Israeli conflict. For notable examples see two special issues of important journals: *Studies in Contemporary Jewry: An Annual*, 10 (1994), entitled *Reshaping the Past: Jewish History and the Historians*, ed. J. Frankel; and *History & Memory: Studies in the Representation of the Past*, 7/1 (Spring/Summer 1995), entitled *Israeli Historiography Revisited*, ed. G. Ne'eman Arad. Both journals are in English.

3 For Raz-Krakotzkin I use 'Exile within Sovereignty: Towards a Critique of the "Negation of Exile" in Israeli Culture [Hebrew]', 2 parts, *Theory and Criticism*, 4 (1993) and 5 (1994), pp. 23–56 and 113–32 respectively , whereas for Myers, in addition to *Re-Inventing*, I also allude to 'Was There a "Jerusalem School"? An Inquiry into the First Generation of Historical Researchers at The Hebrew University', *Studies in Contemporary Jewry: An Annual*, 10 (1994), pp. 66–92.

4 In his discussion of Baer's historiography: Myers, *Re-Inventing*, p. 118.

5 For an interesting commentary on the relations between 'The Sermon' and the budding Canaanism see D. Laor, 'From "The Sermon" to "Letter to the Hebrew Youth": Comments on the Concept of "the Negation of Diaspora" [Hebrew]', *Alpayim*, 21 (2002), pp. 171–86.

6 Raz-Krakotzkin, op. cit., p. 41.

7 Ibid., p. 42.

8 I should make it explicitly clear that the convergence of Raz-Krakotzkin's and my own views on this crucial matter is not incidental, and that we developed them in close interaction at the Van Leer Institute in Jerusalem in the 1990s. In addition to G. Piterberg, 'Domestic Orientalism: The Representation of "Oriental" Jews in Zionist/Israeli Historiography', *British Journal of Middle Eastern Studies*, 23 (1996), pp. 125–45, see also 'The Nation and Its Raconteurs: Orientalism and Nationalist Historiography [Hebrew]', *Theory and Criticism*, 6 (Spring 1995), pp. 81–105.

9 The biographical sketch of Baer draws on Myers, *Re-Inventing*, pp. 112–27.

10 Citation from ibid., p. 116.

11 Ibid., p. 119.

12 Ibid., p. 130.

13 The biographical sketch of Dinur draws on Myers, *Re-Inventing*, pp. 131–40; D. Myers, 'History as Ideology: The Case of Ben-Zion Dinur, Zionist Historian Par Excellence', *Modern Judaism*, 8 (May 1988), pp. 167–93; and U. Ram, 'Zionist Historiography and the Invention of Modern Jewish Nationhood: The Case of Ben-Zion Dinur', *History & Memory*, 7/1 (Spring/Summer 1995), pp. 91–125.

14 See Chapter One, p. 17.

15 Myers, *Re-Inventing*, p. 131.

16 Ram, 'Zionist Historigraphy', p. 109.
17 Ibid., p. 106. See also pp. 95–7 and 109–14.
18 Cited in Piterberg, 'Domestic Orientalism', p. 132.
19 Y. Baer and Ben-Zion Dinur, 'Our Purpose', *Zion*, 1 (1936), p. 1 (Hebrew, my translation).
20 Ibid., pp. 2–3.
21 E. Shmueli, 'The Jerusalem School of Jewish History (A Critical Evaluation)', *Proceedings of the Academy for Jewish Research*, 53 (1986), pp. 147–78.
22 Ibid., p. 166.
23 Ibid., p. 167.
24 Ibid., p. 169. It is on this theme that Shmueli's critique of his teacher is most adamant and devastating.
25 Myers, *Re-Inventing*, p. 126.
26 Shmueli, op. cit., p. 173.
27 Ibid.
28 Myers, *Re-Inventing*, p. 114.
29 Y. Baer, 'On the State of Our Historical Studies [Hebrew]', in *Studies and Essays in the History of the Jewish People*, 2 vols, Jerusalem: The Israel Historical Society, 1977, vol. 1, pp. 11–19. Originally *The Magnes Book*, Jerusalem: Magnes, 1938, pp. 31–8. I use the pagination of the former publication, which is more readily available.
30 Ibid., p. 11.
31 Ibid
32 Ibid., p. 12.
33 Ibid., p. 13.
34 Ibid., p. 14.
35 Ibid., p. 15.
36 Ibid.
37 Ibid., p. 16.
38 See Chapter One, pp. 31–4.
39 Ibid. See above, pp. 11–12, for the definition of this form of the myth.
40 Ibid.
41 Myers, *Re-Inventing*, p. 130.
42 Ibid., pp. 134 and 141 respectively.
43 I mainly consulted the 1958 expanded edition (*Yisrael ba-Golah*, Jerusalem: Mossad Bialik), but I use the English translation (*Israel and the Diaspora*, Philadelphia: The Jewish Publication Society of America, 1969) for citations unless the specific translation is deemed unsatisfactory. It should be noted that the title of the English translation is unfortunate, for by replacing the Hebrew '*in* the Diaspora' with '*and* the Diaspora' the congruity of the book's title and content is lost.
44 Dinur, *Israel and the Diaspora*, p. 3.
45 Ibid., pp. 4–5.
46 Ibid., p. 5.
47 Ibid., p. 6.
48 Ibid., pp. 14–63.
49 By Myers, Ram, Raz-Krakotzkin and Shmueli, all of whom were cited numerous times above.

50 Dinur, *Israel and the Diaspora*, pp. 14–16 (the five fundamentals) and 47–63 (the correct way to address the five fundamentals).
51 Ibid., p. 45.
52 Ibid., p. 46.
53 Ibid., pp. 46–7.
54 Ibid., p. 16.
55 Ibid., p. 47.
56 My translation of Dinur, *Yisrael ba-Golah*, p. 36. I find the English rendering (1969, p. 58) unsatisfactory.
57 Dinur, *Israel and the Diaspora*, p. 186.
58 A. Shapira, *Hannah Arendt and Haim Gouri: Two Perceptions of the Eichmann Trial*, Jerusalem: Yad Vashem, 2002.
59 Ibid., p. 12.
60 Ibid., p. 10.
61 Ibid., p. 11.
62 Ibid., pp. 10–11.
63 Ibid., p. 17.
64 Ibid., p. 27.
65 Ibid., pp. 17–18.
66 Ibid., pp. 22–3.
67 Ibid., p. 22.
68 Ibid.
69 Ibid.

5

# Gerhard–Gershom Scholem's
# Return to History

As the letter to Scholem of September 16, 1924, makes plain . . .
Benjamin saw in Marxism, and indeed in the human involvement and
praxis of communism, a counter to that sombre, introspective bias in
himself which he called 'mein Nihilismus'.
(George Steiner, 'Walter Benjamin: Towards a Philosophy of Language',
*The Times Literary Supplement*, 22 August 1968)

Of the Jerusalem scholars, Gershom Scholem (1897–1982) was the one
whose life and work most clearly expressed the Zionist foundational myth
in its return-to-history guise. In a way he viewed his own life – his
irreparable rupture with his father; the uncompromising rejection of
bourgeois *Deutschjudentum*; the emigration to Palestine; and his unwavering
devotion to Jewish studies in Jerusalem – as a return to history. In this
respect, it is useful to recall some revealing comments Scholem made
towards the end of his life, in a conversation with the Israeli novelist
Ehud Ben-Ezer.[1] In a sense, the project of the Jerusalem scholars discussed
here finds distilled expression in that conversation, perhaps most poignantly
in Scholem's hostility to George Steiner, to whom we shall return at the
end of this chapter.

Much of the conversation was informed by Ben-Ezer's anxiety about
the ethical and intellectual consequences of the Zionist project and life
in Israel. When asked about the price of Zionism (for Jews, that is –
needless to say that it occurs to neither interlocutor that Palestinians also
pay a price), Scholem erupts in a tirade:

You ask about the price of Zionism, and the question is not *the price of Zionism but the price of exile*. Views of people like George Steiner were already heard sixty and seventy years ago . . . I don't have an argument with George Steiner. He is trying to live outside of history. We in Israel, in contrast, are living with responsibility and within history . . . If presently the spell of the Jewish intellectuals in the Diaspora is cast upon you [Ben-Ezer], I say – please go there. Live five years among them. And see the price of *galut* they pay. Whoever feels constrained in Israel, let him go to New York or Cambridge and find out if he feels as wonderfully there as George Steiner does. Complaints of intellectuals who do not wish to identify with any national body? I heard precisely that sixty years ago . . . We [the Zionists] counter-argued and retorted [against the Jews who professed a humanistic-universalist position in Germany]: 'What is the great global thing in which you believe and of which you speak? After all no Gentile speaks this way. Only you. There is no general humanity. It exists only in your imagination' . . . I have no bone to pick with a Jewish intellectual who gives precedence to his personal spiritual problems over the problem of historical *responsibility* . . . If Steiner does not wish to share with us the responsibility for the state – then he is right. Let him be an exilic Jew. Perhaps one day he will be beaten on the head and he will then discover that he *really* does not belong there, and that his alienation is not just an impressive and fashionable intellectual posture but also a very bitter historical reality, for which the full price must be paid . . . I find it difficult to comprehend what is bothering you [Ben-Ezer]. Why is there in your question a degree of effacement before the Jewish intellectual in the Diaspora? What prevents you from leading a wholesome life? [Emphases in the original.][2]

Scholem was born in 1897 in Berlin into a family that had settled in the city at the beginning of the nineteenth century.[3] His father, Arthur, a well-to-do printer, was almost completely assimilated. The family hardly observed any Jewish holidays and celebrated Christmas as a national holiday. Gershom was the youngest of four sons, only one of whom – Erich, the second oldest – followed his father's socio-political position of a bourgeois liberal seeking assimilation. The eldest son, Reinhold, became a member of the radical right Deutsche Volkspartei, and the third, Werner, became a Reichstag deputy for the German Communist Party during the Weimar era. Gershom, meanwhile, was rebellious by nature, and as a teenager harboured a growing contempt for the assimilated German Jewish bourgeoisie, his father first and foremost. In the early 1910s he became increasingly fascinated by Jewish culture from a Zionist standpoint. He joined the Zionist youth club in Berlin Jung Juda before the First World War, almost instantly became its leader and radicalized it in a manner unrivalled in Central Europe.

Zionist youth organizations in the early 1910s were the Jewish version of Wandervogel. The most prominent among them, the Blau-Weiss, was formed in 1912 in response to the anti-Semitic tendencies of the German Wandervogel. Scholem downplayed the clubs' typical obsession with nature and hiking, and proposed that Zionists should instead immerse themselves in the study of Judaism and Hebrew in preparation for immigration to Palestine. Also, particularly in disagreement with Martin Buber, he gave public voice to his opposition to the First World War from a Zionist, rather than a universalist, point of view, insisting that it was the Germans' war, not the Jews'. Illustrative of the way in which Scholem's turn to Zionism and alienation from his family were interlaced, he retrospectively recalled, was his withdrawal in 1911 from the family Christmas celebration when his mother gave him a picture of Herzl as a Christmas present.[4]

The familial rupture became physical and material in 1917. Some two years earlier Scholem had published a letter against the war in a Zionist newspaper, which resulted in his expulsion from the Berlin Gymnasium in which he studied. Later, he would fake mental illness to dodge conscription. Now, after a heated exchange with his father, in which Gerhard had supported his brother Werner's participation in an anti war demonstration while still in uniform, Arthur Scholem sent a registered letter to his son Gerhard instructing him to leave home instantly. Scholem moved into Pension Struck, where East European Jews arriving in Berlin would dwell. The fascination of secular West European Jews with their East European brethren has been pointed out on several occasions in this study. In this manner, Scholem too was 'authenticated' by association with Pension Struck's East European denizens. Most notably, he befriended Zalman Rubashov, who would become Israel's first minister of education and third president; and the Galician writer Shmuel Yosef Agnon, who would become a Nobel laureate, and with whom Scholem would meet almost daily in Jerusalem, and would share the literary patronage of Salman Schocken. Scholem's recollection of meeting Agnon is both personal and formulaic: 'I found in him a new and altogether original incarnation of the Jewish spirit and of Jewish tradition . . . and what attracted him to me was my passionate devotion to the sources and the seriousness with which I studied Hebrew.'[5]

The study of Hebrew leads us to Scholem's academic formation, a process that evinces the extent of his astounding intellectual prowess. Scholem was an autodidact. He studied Hebrew and Jewish law and theology with orthodox teachers, soon reaching such a level of erudition that they had nothing more to teach him; however, suspicious as he was of anything that remotely seemed to emanate from Deutschjudentum, Scholem avoided the German institutions of modern Jewish studies. Instead, his insatiable interest in the Kabbalah led him to found a new field of study, Jewish mysticism. Following his 1915 expulsion from the Gymnasium, Scholem studied mathematics and philosophy in Berlin. In 1918, having successfully dodged military service and after a few months of study in Jena, Scholem went to Switzerland where he spent a year attending a few courses in Bern. Importantly, he passed his time there with Walter Benjamin, consolidating a friendship that had begun in 1915 in a public event in Berlin, at which Scholem had heard Benjamin speak. They spent that year immersed in lengthy conversations. It was this interaction with Benjamin, and the extent to which both rejected Buber's views (to whom Benjamin was also personally averse), which resulted in Scholem's irrevocable turn to the Kabbalah, and later to Jewish messianism.

As David Biale has noticed, Scholem's path produced two discernible expressions. First, Scholem, as passionate a bibliophile as Benjamin, had amassed a collection of over 600 Kabbalistic manuscripts by the time he immigrated to Jerusalem in 1923. Second was his choice of university for a doctoral degree on his return to Germany from Switzerland in 1919: although at first he considered continuing mathematics and philosophy at Göttingen, he ended up going to Munich, which had the best Kabbalah collection in Germany. There, he took a degree in Semitics with the Assyriologist Fritz Hommel, writing a dissertation on an important Kabbalistic text, *Sefer ha-Bahir*. As helpful as Hommel may have been, he surely could offer no specialized guidance given his expertise, which must mean that Scholem contended with the philology and history of that difficult text alone.[6] When Scholem arrived in Jerusalem in 1923, neither the Institute of Jewish Studies nor the Hebrew University existed, and he worked as librarian in the budding Mount Scopus library. Soon, however, he would become a professor of Jewish mysticism at the Hebrew University, where he would spend the rest of his career.

Scholem's dedication of his life to Jewish mysticism has a more deep-seated drive than a brief biography can disclose. This question will be grappled with more thoroughly later, but it is worth mentioning here a fascinating account Scholem gave of his decision in a textual gift to Salman Schocken on his sixtieth birthday in 1937, which he entitled 'A Candid

Word about the True Motives of My Kabbalistic Studies'. Biale published this remarkable letter in his study of Scholem, though he makes no observation about the ego that assumed that a treatise about himself would be a special gift for somebody else's sixtieth birthday.[7] No less telling, I think, is a retrospective reflection by Scholem on his studies, less than a decade before his death. This reflection shares with Baer and Dinur the Romantic suspicion of the ability of the cerebral, normative facets of Judaism to have been adequate sources of energy and vitality for its survival in the past and, crucially, for its continued survival in the present. This Romantic suspicion invariably led to a search for a source of vitality that emanated from the realm of the irrational and the non-legal:

> I was interested in the question: Does *Halakhic*[8] Judaism have enough potency to survive? Is *Halakhah* really possible without a mystical foundation? Does it have enough vitality of its own to survive for two thousand years without degenerating? I appreciated *Halakhah* without identifying with its imperatives . . . This question was tied up with my dreams about the Kabbalah, through the notion that it might be the Kabbalah that explains the survival of the consolidated force of the *Halakhic* Judaism.[9]

The note just quoted occasions a further comment on the possible relations between Scholem's project and that of Carl Schmitt's *Political Theology* of 1922. Schmitt has become more widely read in recent years, and has stimulated writers who do not necessarily share his, to borrow Perry Anderson's phrase, 'intransigent right' politics.[10] However, it is little known that Schmitt informed numerous German Jewish intellectuals in the 1920s and 1930s, many of whom similarly did not share his political position. It is nevertheless recognized that Walter Benjamin was inspired by Schmitt, in particular when writing his essay on the German tragic drama and in his 'Theses on the Philosophy of History' (we shall return to the latter at the end of the chapter).[11] Scholem was well aware of Benjamin's fascination with Schmitt and may have become interested in his *Political Theology* through his friend.

While studying at the Hebrew University in the early 1990s Christoph Schmidt, a scholar of modern German studies, developed an original argument on the possible connection between Scholem's scholarly project and Carl Schmitt:

> Although Leo Strauss and Walter Benjamin reacted directly to Carl Schmitt's provocation, the conjunction of Carl Schmitt and Gershom Scholem must appear strange at first sight. However, in the context of

the epistemology of culture of those years – namely, the rediscovery of the heretic as a cultural hero who represents the critique of enlightened liberal culture – Scholem's reinvention of the Kabbalistic tradition can be interpreted as a specific strategy of political theology. Schmitt's decisionist political theology calls for the suspension of the Weimar constitution, in order to protect the state against its enemies; Scholem's Sabbatean hero Jacob Frank is the theological decisionist who calls for the suspension of halakhic law in order to protect the Jewish people from their enemies. Schmitt turns to an authoritarian politics that legitimizes fascist dictatorship; Scholem's rediscovery of the heretic-hero appears to be the condition for escaping from Schmitt's politics.[12]

In what follows I draw on Christoph Schmidt's argument in proposing that Scholem's *oeuvre* was nothing less than a Zionist theology. Schmidt comments, but does not elaborate, that what made this a political theology was the fact that Scholem's narrative of Jewish history from the sixteenth century onwards leads in a dialectical manner to Zionism. My proposition develops this comment and explains why the dialectical march of Scholem's project to Zionism is precisely what makes it a political theology in the Carl Schmittean sense.

Before proceeding with the interpretation of Scholem's life work as Zionist theology, his main subject matter must be very briefly presented for the reader's reference. In the 1650s Sabbatai Sevi, the son of a commercial agent from Izmir, an Ottoman port-city in south-western Anatolia, and a group of his followers were busily trying to prepare Jewish communities in the eastern Mediterranean for the imminent arrival of the messianic era. In 1665, endorsed by his movement's chief ideologue, Nathan of Gaza, Sabbatai Sevi proclaimed himself Messiah. In 1666 he was arrested by the Ottoman authorities and persuaded by them to convert to Islam. However short-lived, Sabbatai Sevi's proselytizing and the movement bearing his name – Sabbatianism – spread far beyond the Ottoman eastern Mediterranean and sent shock waves throughout the Jewish world. Sabbatianism was succeeded by two sects in the following centuries: the Frankists in Central and Eastern Europe, and the Dönmes in today's Greece and Turkey. Especially in Scholem's schema, Sabbatianism was informed by a certain development in the Kabbalah, the major form of Jewish mysticism. As such the Kabbalah is not inherently messianic. According to Scholem, however, the teachings of Rabbi Isaac Luria in the city of Safed in northern Palestine in the sixteenth century 'messianized' the Kabbalah. Sabbatianism, in Scholem's thesis, was underpinned by the Lurianic version of the Kabbalah.

## Scholem's History of Jewish Mysticism
## as 'Mythology of Prolepsis'

In the seminal essay in which he wrought havoc with the tradition of history of ideas, Quentin Skinner organized his critique along three 'mythologies' which that field of study had in the author's view ended up producing: the mythology of doctrine, the mythology of coherence, and the mythology of prolepsis.[13] Skinner's mythology of prolepsis is, as I shall show, a particularly apposite lens through which to view Scholem's complex project. An attempt to write history of ideas may turn into a mythology of prolepsis, Skinner observes, when

> in considering what significance the argument of some classic text might be said to have for us . . . no place is left for what the author himself meant to say. The characteristic result of this confusion is a type of discussion which might be labelled the mythology of prolepsis. Such confusions arise most readily, of course, when the historian is more interested – as he may legitimately be – in the retrospective significance of a given historical work or action than in its meaning for the agent himself.[14]

Crucially Skinner later adduces a synoptic comment: 'The surest symptom, in short, of this mythology of prolepsis is that the discussions which it governs are open to the crudest type of criticism that can be levelled against any teleological form of explanation: *the action has to await the future to await its meaning* [emphasis added].'[15]

Formally, Scholem's *oeuvre* is amenable to being viewed through Skinner's notion because of the historical field within which it belongs. Biale astutely warns that Scholem's rejection – one of many – of the *Geistesgeschichte* (loosely translatable as the history of ideational essences) written by nineteenth-century historians like Graetz should not lead us to think that Scholem himself wrote a social history of mass movements, like another Jewish historian, Simon Dubnow. What Scholem rejected was the particular essence which these nineteenth-century historians had emphasized, namely rationalism and philosophy, since he insisted that both philosophy and rationalism were incommensurate with the nation's *Geist*. The social relevance he claimed for his subject matter notwithstanding, 'Scholem's history of Jewish mysticism is itself *Geistesgeschichte*: the history of the theological doctrines and speculations of a small intelligentsia'.[16] The mythology of prolepsis is an apt description of Scholem's historiography, but not because it was a crude teleology, nor because the historian was deaf to the contextual voices of his past protagonists. Scholem's scholarly stature was too gigantic for such trivial oversights. The discovery of the *full* meaning of the Lurianic Kabbalah and its dissemination from Safed, of the Messianism and apostasy of Sabbatai Sevi, of Sabbatianism and its later manifestation as Frankism, and of the *Haskalah* (these terms will be explained later), had to await for Scholem to place himself in the authoritative and authentic position from which he could reveal the full magnitude of that meaning: it had to await Scholem's becoming Zionist, his return to history and return to Zion. That is why Skinner's observation that '[t]he action has to await the future to await its meaning' is so applicable to Scholem's project.

To develop this point somewhat, Scholem's genius and the strength of his personality created Jewish mysticism as a modern secular field of study, and mysticism as a phenomenon to be unravelled historically and on the basis of meticulous philological research of its textual corpus. Embodied in this creation was Scholem's (and the Jerusalem scholars' in general, each with his distinct sensibility) complex relationship with the Wissenschaft des Judentum generation, which he himself retrospectively – and as Myers perceptively remarks, not without bitterness – summed up in an oft-cited phrase: 'We had come to rebel, and ended up continuing [*Banu limrod ve-nimtzenu mamshikhim*]'.[17] This rebellion was against the rejection by the previous generation – Graetz most notably – of mysticism in general and the Kabbalah in particular as unworthy superstition, and the concomitant obsession of that generation with philosophical rationalism; in a sense this rejection may be said to have continued the suppression of mysticism (especially the anxiety about messianism) by both normative rabbinical Judaism and the rationalists. Furiously objecting to this, Scholem saw it as emblematic of the apologetic mindset of Jewish scholarship, one that underpinned the self-deception of emancipation and assimilation. In Scholem's eyes these predecessors were the past's 'erudite liquidators', and one of the necessary steps in the creation of Zionist non-apologetic scholarship was to counter the 'destruction' of Judaism's irrational undercurrents with a dialectic move of 'the destruction of the destruction [*hisul ha-hisul*]'.[18] At the same time, however, Scholem remained explicitly and unflinchingly committed to the scientific primacy of any study of Judaism, in which sense he and his colleagues indeed ended up continuing.

The literature on Scholem's life and work is immense, and much of it, including this book and the studies by Biale and Myers mentioned above, is concerned with modern Jewish thought, in particular Zionism. To counterbalance that focus, I would like to offer a sketch of Scholem's historiography with the aid of his possibly most important critic, Moshe Idel of the Hebrew University. Idel's viewpoint is original for three reasons: he is a scholar of the Kabbalah and mysticism rather than of Zionism or modern Jewish history; his critique has emerged from within Scholem's mansion peopled by his disciples, the Hebrew University; he is a scholar of religion, who, in contrast with Scholem, is not at all convinced that history is the best scholarly discipline to understand Scholem's subject matter. It is noteworthy that the pertinent text by Idel appeared in Hebrew in *History and Criticism* (following an earlier version in French), and that Idel himself was on the journal's editorial council, even though his political stance is not always in agreement with that of the radical core that founded it.[19]

Idel pays tribute to Scholem's major achievement: the placement of the study of mysticism at the core of the debate on Jewish history and religion. Idel identifies two assumptions upon which Scholem's edifice is founded: first, that historical events engendered important changes in the nature of the Kabbalah; and second, the assumption that the dissemination of the altered Kabbalah engendered the pivotal change that occurred in Jewish history (i.e., the replacement of normative rabbinical and philosophical rationalist Judaism first by an explosion of messianism, then by the Enlightenment and secularism, and finally by Zionism).[20] Idel is perceptive in associating these assumptions, but he could perhaps have foregrounded more explicitly the tension that inheres in their connection. The second assumption's goal was to show that the ascendancy of secular modernity and Zionism was organically immanent in Judaism, to attribute this ascendancy to the inner dynamic of Jewish history rather than to such 'external' phenomena as the Enlightenment and the French Revolution. But the desire to historicize the manifestations of Jewish mysticism, the Kabbalah first and foremost, which is expressed in the first assumption, merely ascribes crucial explanatory force to one 'external' event (the Jewish expulsion from Spain in 1492) in lieu of others (Enlightenment and French Revolution).

Although Scholem never offered a formal periodization of Jewish history, Idel constructs one from Scholem's historical and phenomenological works, and charts a useful schema that amounts to a narrative of the relations between the Kabbalah and Jewish mysticism on the one hand, and Jewish messianism on the other.[21] In the first stage of Scholem's narrative of Jewish mysticism, 1180 to 1492 CE, the Kabbalah was indifferent to messianic drives, such as powerful apocalyptic yearnings and belief that the Messiah's arrival was imminent. The second stage, from the 1492 expulsion from Spain until the mid eighteenth century, witnessed the synthesis of messianism and Kabbalistic thought. Two phases of this period are especially important here. The first extended between 1570 and 1660, when Rabbi Isaac Luria immigrated to Safed in northern Palestine and developed together with his disciples a version of the Kabbalah that was saturated with brewing messianic energy, a messianic explosion waiting to occur. Although not mentioned by Idel, I think that the function of the Introduction to Scholem's magisterial study of Sabbatai Sevi and the Sabbatian movement is to propel the process forward by presenting the 'messianization' of the Lurianic Kabbalah.[22] Then, from the 1660s to around 1750, the Sabbatian and later Frankist movements created radical messianic forms that were inspired by the Lurianic Kabbalah, whose dissemination from the third decade of the seventeenth century onwards was unprecedented. Messianism ceased being at that point (the 1660s) simply an esoteric Kabbalistic framework or a mystical ideology, and was transformed into a mass movement that rocked the foundations of the Jewish centres in the Mediterranean, and in Central and Eastern Europe. In the third stage of Scholem's narrative, from roughly 1750 onwards, Hasidism in Poland sought to quell the messianic eruption, wary of the catastrophe of apostasy and conversion brought on by the Sabbatian and Frankist movements. Scholem identified in Hasidism a new form of eschatology that had not existed before in Judaism, namely, personal redemption. The gist of the change was the passage from the messianically laden Lurianic Kabbalah to a concept of piety that was completely devoid of messianic meaning.

Idel stops here, but it should be stressed that Scholem's schema continues beyond Hasidism. The abyss that was created by the messianic fervour of the Sabbatians and the nihilist cul-de-sac of the Frankists was somewhat rectified by Hasidism's caution, which offered the spiritual meditative type of redemption as a replacement for the issue-forcing redemption upon which the messianic movement had insisted. In Scholem's Hegelian dialectic, the messianic and nihilistic movements were the thesis, Hasidism's cautious and apolitical redemption was the antithesis, and Zionism is the synthesis. Zionism, in Scholem's dialectical narrative, is a mass movement whose redemptive drive expresses itself in responsible political action, in a return to history and an extrication from exile, but without the tendencies of the messianic and nihilistic explosions of the seventeenth and eighteenth centuries, which dangerously threatened to destroy the nation through unbelief and apostasy.

To digress momentarily, it is worth noting that Idel's multi-layered critique goes to the heart of Scholem's theses. Analysing Scholem's periodization, Idel maintains that seeing the expulsion [from Spain in 1492] as a central factor in the reorganisation of the Kabbalah is, at the very least, a big exaggeration, which ignores both the messianic aspects of important Kabbalistic texts that were composed before the expulsion and the indifference to messianism displayed by [other] important Kabbalistic texts that were written after the expulsion.[23]

Thus, for instance, the influential thirteenth-century Spanish Kabbalist Avraham Abulafia proclaimed himself Messiah and unearthed original thoughts on the nature of Jewish messianism.[24] Idel then questions the organic bond that Scholem identified from the late sixteenth century onwards between the experience of the mystic and the symbolic system he created, and the nation's history. It is necessary briefly to pause here, because of the importance of this point for understanding Scholem's project. Although Idel seems unaware of this, I think that the bond which Scholem identified and to which Idel objects is basically Scholem's instinctive projection of the position and experience of the Romantic national historian (i.e., his own) onto the mystic of the early modern era. For Scholem, his own return to Zion and return to history, as well his project of making manifest the vitality that was latent in Judaism's mystic and messianic repository, embodied the nation's history and the *Geist*. Similarly, the experience of the mystic and his project of making manifest the explosive force latent in the biblical myth (suppressed by rabbinical legalism and philosophical rationalism) embodied in his time the nation's history and *Geist*. This is, I believe, the full extent of the organic bond with which Idel feels ill at ease.

It is also necessary to add that Scholem understood mysticism as a symbolic reinterpretation of myth, which is contained in the biblical text but was emasculated by rabbinical Judaism for fear of its non-rational and non-legal force as well as its anthropomorphisms. Scholem's concept of the symbol followed Benjamin's distinction between allegory and symbol In an allegorical system 'the arm of God' represents a philosophical concept, whereas in the mystic's system of meaning 'the arm of God' symbolizes the actual arm of God – not corresponding to a human arm – in a higher sphere of reality.[25]

What Idel questions, then, is this almost physical way in which, in Scholem's work, the mystical experience conveyed by the mystic in his language of symbols signifies the collective history of the nation. One of the citations he supplies is aptly illustrative not only in content but also in the extent to which it is emblematic of the robustness of Scholem's thought:

As that chunk of historical reality which was apportioned to the Jews in the whirlwind of exile became narrower and more impoverished, as its cruelty and horrors multiplied, so was enhanced the transparency as well as the precision of the symbolic nature of this reality, and so increasingly shined the glow [zohar, which is also the title of Kabbalah's ur-text, Sefer ha-Zohar] of the messianic hope that would explode and transform it.[26]

Idel argues that the mystic's way of articulating his experience after the 1492 expulsion was shaped more by the language of previous Kabbalistic texts than by a correlation between his personal experience and the nation's collective experience, and that messianic expectations do not relate in a simple way to 'actual' or 'external' history. Importantly from a political perspective, Idel seriously doubts Scholem's assertion that the pivot of the Lurianic Kabbalah's symbolic system was the exile–redemption (galut-ge'ulah) tension or dyad, and that the gist of this symbolic system was messianic tension.[27]

In his concluding remarks, 'A Few Methodological Questions', Idel observes that the study of Jewish mysticism by Scholem and his disciples 'is based on the assumption that the external history shapes the evolution of Jewish mysticism, and the latter in its turn is understood as a sort of pre–programme for Jewish history. In my opinion, these two assumptions have not been proven in the research conducted thus far on these topics.'[28] Idel's methodological reservation is also concerned with substance and, implicitly, with politics. 'Instead of treating Jewish mysticism as literature that belongs in the sphere of the imaginaire, examining its varied strategies to organize knowledge and information through cognitive research . . . the research agenda was dominated by the historical approach.' It created, Idel continues, a monocausal historical explanation: 'as if the expulsion from Spain alone suffices to explain the messianic turn of the Kabbalah, especially the Lurianic one; and as if the Lurianic Kabbalah alone suffices to explain Sabbatianism as a messianic movement, and Sabbatianism in its turn offers the key to understanding Hasidism as well as other religious changes in Judaism in the modern era'.[29] Idel further avers that, by adhering to 'a certain kind of history that is interlaced with philology', the study of Jewish mysticism as dictated by Scholem saturated Jewish mysticism and its symbols with 'national historical experiences', which impeded the 'phenomenological under-standing' of the Kabbalah. Scholem himself, Idel says, conceded in 1961 that this 'antiquarian, historical–literary' method could put Jewish studies on a problematic path, which leads to the assumption that Judaism has a historical – rather than religious – destiny.[30]

## Redemption Through Sin

I would now like to take a closer look at two remarkable texts by Scholem, which illustrate how a Zionist theology emerged from his research. The first, 'Redemption through Sin', appeared in 1937 but was written two years earlier, roughly contemporaneously with the letter discussed above, for Schocken's sixtieth birthday.[31] It was a significant summation of two decades of research and reflection on mysticism and messianism – noteworthy given that Scholem was not yet forty – and a rehearsal of the two-volume monograph on Sabbatai Sevi and the movement bearing his name that would appear two decades later. Much later, in 1970, Scholem returned to what he called the abyss that the mystic-messianic explosion had created, in the shape of an irresistible study of 'A Frankist's Career', the second text to be discussed here.[32]

The English title 'Redemption through Sin' is not an incorrect rendering of the original, and it is understandable why the translator came up with it. The Hebrew, 'Mitzvah ha-ba'ah ba-`averah', is not however successfully conveyed by the English, whose meaning is too spiritual and Christian, and insufficiently rabbinical and legalistic. *Mitzvah* is a commandment, of which there are 613 in the Halakha, whereas redemption in Hebrew is *ge'ulah*, a term that doesn't appear in the title; `*averah* means transgression, while sin is *het*' Concluding his explanation of how the paradox of Sabbatai Sevi as an apostate Messiah was resolved (i.e., the paradox of Sabbatai Sevi converting to Islam more or less simultaneously with being revealed as Messiah), Scholem himself intimates that '[i]t was at this point that a radically new content was bestowed upon the old rabbinic concept of *mitzvah ha-ba'ah ba-averah*, literally, "a commandment which is fulfilled by means of transgression"';[33] he goes on to explain that the 'rabbinic concept' was used by two rabbis in the late 1660s to define the behaviour of the Sabbatians in the wake of the Messiah's apostasy.[34]

The Hebrew title is a significant instance of Scholem's propensity for dialectic pirouettes. This massive essay was the first pronouncement of his fundamental thesis, presented above through Idel's critical lens, which repeatedly emphasized the 'explosion' of rabbinical Judaism from within. And Scholem chose to crown the exposition of this grand explosion and reinvigoration of Judaism with a rabbinical title that alluded both to what had been exploded (authoritative rabbinical stability) and to the explosion itself (messianic Sabbatianism, accompanied as it was by 'transgression'). This brilliant encapsulation of the text by its title is missed in the English rendering.

In the essay, Scholem promptly announces the superiority of the Zionist position in Zion, as the only location from which Jewish history can be unfolded authentically and objectively:

It has come increasingly to be realized that a true understanding of the rise of Sabbatianism will never be possible as long as scholars continue to appraise it by inappropriate standards, whether these be the conventional beliefs of their age or the values of traditional Judaism itself. Today indeed one rarely encounters the baseless assumptions of 'charlatanry' and 'imposture' which occupy so prominent a place in earlier historical literature on the subject. On the contrary: in these times of Jewish national rebirth it is only natural that the deep though ultimately tragic yearning for national redemption to which the initial stages of Sabbatianism gave expression should meet with greater comprehension than in the past.[35]

This basic presupposition is never a matter for demonstration through evidence, but is simply stated and reiterated as a given. It is no coincidence that the epigraph of Scholem's two-volume study of Sabbatai Sevi is a citation of Wilhelm Dilthey (1833–1911), arguably one of the most important thinkers who developed German Romantic hermeneutics in the nineteenth century.[36] Scholem clearly subscribes to the hermeneutic act of recreating the psychological and historical protagonists' experiences from their own standpoint, an empathic process meant – or presuming – to understand the protagonists' contexts and intended meaning better than the protagonists themselves. This hermeneutics drew on the assumption that spatially and temporally the interpreter had a preferential position relative to the object of interpretation. One of the more vigorous reiterations by Scholem of his own preferential position underscores the hermeneutic combination of the Romantic interpreter's superior perspective coupled with the intrinsic recreation of the historical experience:

> Undeniably, the difficulties in the face of this [the uncovering of Sabbatianism's positive vitality underneath its nihilism, sexual excesses and so forth] are great, and it is not to be wondered at that Jewish historians until now have not had the inner freedom to attempt the task. In our own times we owe much to the experience of Zionism for enabling us to detect in Sabbatianism's throes those gropings toward a healthier national existence which must have seemed like an undiluted nightmare to the peaceable Jewish bourgeois of the nineteenth century . . . To be sure, as Jewish historians we have clearly advanced beyond the vantage point of our predecessors, having learned to insist, and rightly so, that Jewish history is a process that can only be understood when viewed from *within* [emphasis in the original].[37]

The extent to which the view 'from within' was pivotal for Scholem cannot be overstated. It made possible not only the 'correct' understanding of Sabbatai Sevi as Messiah, his apostasy and, most crucially, the consequences of both the messiahship and apostasy for his believers, but also the cognizance of the organic immanence of the whole process, of its unfolding having been an intrinsically Jewish dialectic:

> Sabbatianism must be regarded not only as a single continuous development which retained its identity in the eyes of its adherents regardless of whether they themselves remained Jews, but also, paradoxical though it may seem, as a specifically Jewish phenomenon to the end. I shall endeavor to show that the nihilism of the Sabbatian and Frankist movements, with its doctrine (so profoundly shocking to the Jewish conception of things) that the violation of the Torah could become its true fulfilment [*bitulah shel torah zehu kiyyumah*], was a dialectical outgrowth of the belief in the Messiahship of Sabbatai Zevi, and that this nihilism, in turn, helped pave the way for the *Haskalah* [so-called Jewish Enlightenment] and the reform movement of the nineteenth century, once its religious impulse was exhausted.[38]

In Scholem's thesis, the precise point at which, in his powerful rhetoric, the abyss of nihilistic Sabbatianism was opened, the explosion occurred or the conflagration spread, was the paradox of the apostasy of the Messiah Sabbatai Sevi. Based in Salonica, he was recognized and declared Messiah in 1665 by the foremost theoretician of his movement, the prophet Nathan of Gaza, and other Kabbalists such as Abraham Cardozo, who together with Nathan created the post-apostasy Sabbatian doctrine and was one of the most effective proselytizers of the movement. Then, however, the Ottoman administration, alerted by the rabbinical leadership in the empire to Sabbatai's burgeoning influence, grew concerned about this phenomenon. In 1666 the Messiah was promptly taken to Edirne (Adrianople) where he was presented with two options: conversion to Islam or death. He chose the former on 16 September 1666. The believers were now confronted with a paradox: if the authenticity of the Messiah had been beyond doubt, if he had revealed himself to the people and redemption was imminent, 'why', asks Scholem, 'had he forsaken them and his religion, and why had the historical and political deliverance from bondage [note how Zionism's prolepsis rhetorically appears] which was to have naturally accompanied the cosmic process of *tikkun* [restitution] been delayed?'[39]

Before proceeding with the way in which the paradox of an apostate Messiah was resolved according to Scholem, a comment on the historical understanding of Sabbatianism ought to be made. The deficiency that inheres not only in Scholem's approach but in that of Jewish studies in general is the following: in their march to create an autonomous national Jewish subject they are oblivious to the non-Jewish context within which phenomena like Sabbatianism occurred. In this case hardly any attention is paid to the Ottoman context, except for the fact that the Ottoman administration forced Sabbatai Sevi to convert at the rabbinical judges' (*dayyanim*) behest, and no Ottoman sources are consulted. Studies by two Ottoman historians, Madeline Zilfi and Jane Hathaway, expose the incompleteness of the intrinsically Jewish approach to the histories of the Jews.[40] What their studies show is that throughout the seventeenth century Ottoman cities were saturated with Islamic mystical activity practised and disseminated by Sufi orders and lodges. This was encountered by the rigorous anti-mystical, puritan movement of Muslim preachers known as the Kadizadelis. The appearance of Sabbatianism in the 1660s coincided with the heyday of the Kadizadelis, patronized as they were by the powerful dynasty of Ottoman grand viziers, the Köprülüs. It was the former (not only the Jewish *dayyanim*) who, in their zealous war against manifestations of mysticism in the Ottoman realm, pushed the administration dominated by the latter to force the issue with Sabbatai Sevi and suppress his followers. This very brief intervention makes clear how much the Ottoman context matters for fully comprehending Sabbatianism, to say nothing of the ways in which Islamic-Ottoman mystical features – e.g., the crucial distinction between the exoteric (*zahir*) and the esoteric (*batin*) – echo in Sabbatian doctrine and Jewish mysticism in general.

The resolution of the paradox of the apostate Messiah was crucial. Formulated according to Scholem as a new doctrine expressed in Kabbalistic discourse by Nathan of Gaza and Abraham Cardozo, this resolution began by propounding the underlying logic that the details of how redemption would occur were unknown, and would become manifest only as the redemption unfolded; at the same time, however, everything that occurred as redemption was unfolding, according to the circular logic of envisaging redemption, had already been alluded to in the Scriptures. Scholem remarks that this logic was referred back to no less eminent an authority than Maimonides, to whom, incidentally, he resentfully alludes on other occasions as one of the chief representatives of rationalist philosophy.[41] Scholem does not mention which text of Maimonides's Nathan and Cardozo drew on, but I suspect that it might have been *Mishneh Torah*, the code of Jewish law written in the late twelfth century that is regarded as his magnum opus. The opening statement of that work sets the tone: 'All the commandments that were given to Moses on Sinai were given in their interpretation [*Kol ha-mitzvot she-nitnu lo le-Moshe mi-Sinai be-ferushan nitnu*]'. Nathan and Cardozo would not have been the only readers who took this to mean that all interpretations inhere in the text.

From this underlying logic the doctrinal resolution of the paradox of the apostate Messiah proceeds to explain that since Adam's primordial sin the last divine sparks of holiness and good (*nitzotzot*) had been trapped within the realm of 'the hylic [a term emanating from gnostic theology] forces of evil whose hold in the world is especially strong among the Gentiles [*kelipot*]', the realm that lay past the gates of impurity. Redemption cannot be complete until the *nitzotzot* were salvaged from the grasp of the *kelipot* and restored to their source, prior to the primordial sin. Evil would perforce collapse when that had been achieved, for it is sustained solely by the divine sparks captured in its midst. The enormity of this task is such that only the Redeemer may accomplish it. As it entails crossing the gates of impurity and delving into the domain of the *kelipot*, the Messiah must perform 'alien acts' (*ma'asim zarim*), 'of which his apostasy is the most startling'.[42] It is within the context articulated by this attempt to resolve the paradox – almost the oxymoron – of the apostate Messiah, that sayings such as 'the violation of the Torah is its fulfilment' (*bittulah shel torah zehu kiyyumah*) or 'a commandment which is fulfilled by means of a transgression' (*mitzvah ha-ba'ah ba-averah*) ought to be comprehended.

The nature of the Sabbatian doctrine in the wake of the Messiah's apostasy is perhaps the only point in Scholem's *oeuvre* where he tries to establish a contact between the expulsion from Spain and a messianic eruption that is historically concrete rather than being just stated metaphysically. As I will argue, this is politically very significant, but first let us examine Scholem's statement itself:

> Underlying the novelty of Sabbatian thought more than anything else was the deeply paradoxical religious sensibility of the Marranos and their descendants, who constituted a large portion of Sephardic Jewry. Had it not been for the unique psychology of these reconverts to Judaism, the new theology would never have found the fertile ground to flourish in that it did. Regardless of what the actual backgrounds of its first disseminators may have been, the Sabbatian doctrine of the Messiah was perfectly tailored to the needs of the Marranic mentality.[43]

The Marranos were Iberian Jews who had converted to Catholicism and then reconverted to Judaism. They may have done so in response to direct threats from the Inquisition, in response to a general sense of persecution, or simply because it was beneficial to do so. Some continued to adhere to Judaism secret while others became genuine Catholics. The word *marrano* is most probably a Portuguese and Spanish corruption of the Arabic *muharram* or *mahram*, something that is forbidden. The word then acquired in both Iberian idioms the meaning of 'filthy' or 'swine', and sometimes also pork, which is of course forbidden in Judaism. Abraham Cardozo, who was of Marrano origin, stated: 'It is ordained that the King Messiah don the garments of a Marrano and so go unrecognized by his fellow Jews. In a word, it is ordained that he become a Marrano like me'.[44] The more yawning the chasm between the inner experience of the believers and the outer reality, Scholem asserts, the more Marranic Sabbatianism became. The Sabbatians' intuitive sensation was that the outwardly professed belief could not by definition be true belief; in order to be genuine, belief must be concealed and publicly denied. 'For this reason every Jew is obliged to become a Marrano'.[45]

Deploring the Jewish historians for whom these expressions of trans-formation were no more than 'inanities', Scholem identifies in the doctrinal resolution of the apostate Messiah paradox nothing short of a new theology: 'From bits and pieces of Scripture, from scattered paradoxes and sayings in the writings of the Kabbalah, from all the remotest corners of Jewish religious literature, an unprecedented theology of Judaism was brought into being'.[46] It is impossible to overstate the extent to which Scholem saw in this 'unprecedented theology of Judaism' and the mood that surrounded it a fundamental transformation, and concomitantly the extent to which this argument constituted his Zionist theology. All the compo-nents of this theology can be found in the dialogue between Scholem and his Sabbatian protagonists: the destruction of rabbinical Judaism; the negation of exile; the revival of a non-rabbinical religious belief; the insistence on the organic inclusiveness of the Jewish nation/Jewish history even – perhaps especially – in the face of something as liminal as Marranism and apostasy.

The non-rabbinical 'religion' that the Sabbatian doctrine revived, 'albeit in a transvalued form' and in a way that was 'totally unexpected', was second-century Gnosticism. At the risk of digressing, I think it is worthwhile briefly to look at Scholem's thesis that the Sabbatian doctrine was basically a reinterpretation of Gnosticism, for it reveals the revivalist depth of his own ideology. According to Scholem, Sabbatian thinkers 'stumbled upon' the gnostic spiritual world via their reading of the Bible in search of 'the mystery of the Godhead [*Elohut* in Hebrew]' which 'exilic Judaism had allowed to perish'.[47] The Gnostics had distinguished the good but hidden God, the Supreme Being or the First Cause, whom the elect people should serve, from a Demiurge or creator of the physical universe, who was identified as the law-giving God of the Bible, the Jewish God. The law-giving God's superior authority was rejected by the Gnostics, and He was reviled by them. Abraham Cardozo was the one who recovered and reinterpreted the gnostic myth for the Sabbatians. What he did was, in a sense, to invert the gnostic concept by arguing that the First Cause should be cast aside, for His authority has already been acknowledged by the intellect of the philosophers of all creeds. It is the Creator God, the God of Israel, who is the appropriate object of religious worship. The problem is, to quote Scholem paraphrasing Cardozo, that

> [i]n the confusion and demoralization brought on by the exile this mystery . . . was forgotten and the Jewish People was mistakenly led to identify the impersonal First Cause with the personal God of the Bible, a spiritual disaster for which Saadia Gaon, Maimonides, and the other philosophers will yet be held accountable . . . Here we have a typically Gnostic scheme, only inverted: the good God is no longer the *deus absconditus*, who has now become the deity of the philosophers for whom there is no room in religion proper, but rather the god of Israel who created the world and presented it with his Torah.[18]

The 'renewed' bond between an ancient myth (the gnostic) and the ur-text (the Hebrew Bible), without the distorting mediation of rabbinical commentary or philosophical literature, and implicitly the 'renewed' bond between the ancient myth and the land of Israel, seems to have injected with elan not only Judaism but also Scholem. From that point his negation of exile argument flows unrestrained, as does his adulation of the Sabbatian revolutionaries. The depth of Scholem's yearning for an ancient myth that would renew, reinvigorate and transform is manifest in the force of his rhetoric, in the Zionist excitement with which he negates exile and rabbinical Judaism, and in the almost visible spark in his eyes when he senses a 'return' to the source – mythical, textual and territorial. Emphasizing the Sabbatians' fondness of paradoxes that 'reveal a dialectical daring that cannot but be respected', Scholem moves to underscore the authenticity of their Jewishness:

> Here we are given our deepest glimpse yet into the souls of these revolutionaries who regarded themselves as loyal Jews while at the same time completely overturning the traditional religious categories of Judaism. I am not of course speaking of a feeling of 'loyalty' to the Jewish religion as it was defined by rabbinical authority. For many, if

not most, Sabbatians the Judaism of the rabbis, which they identified with the Judaism of exile, had come to assume an entirely dubious character. Even when they continued to live under its jurisdiction it was not out of any sense of commitment; no doubt it had been suited to its time, but in the light of the soul-shaking truth of the redemption that time had passed.[49]

Having then presented Cardozo's reinterpretation of the gnostic position, Scholem sheds such fragments of inhibition as may still linger:

> What yearnings for regeneration of faith and what disdainful negation of exile! Like true spiritual revolutionaries, with an unfeigned enthusiasm which even today cannot fail to impress the reader of Cardozo's books, the 'believers' unflinchingly proclaimed their belief that all during exile the Jewish people had worshipped a powerless divinity and had clung to a way of life that was fundamentally in need of reform . . . Determined to avoid a full-scale revolution within the heart of Jewry, the rabbinical traditionalists and their supporters did all they could to drive the 'believers' beyond the pale. And yet in spite of all this, one can hardly deny that a great deal that is authentically Jewish was embodied in these paradoxical individuals too, in their desire to start afresh and in their realization of the fact that negating the exile meant negating its religious and institutional forms as well and returning to the original fountainheads of the Jewish faith. This last practice – a tendency to rely on matters of belief upon the Bible and the *Aggadah* [non-legal literature] – grew to be particularly strong among the nihilists in the movement. Here too, faith in paradox reigned supreme: the stranger the *Aggadah*, the more offensive to reason and common sense, the more likely it was to be seized upon as a symbol of that 'mystery of faith' which naturally tended to conceal itself in the most frightful and fanciful tales.[50]

Scholem identifies four forms taken by 'organized Sabbatian nihilism' from 1683 (the year of the Dönmes' conversion to Islam) onwards:[51]

(1) The Dönmes, 'who chose "voluntary Marranism" in the form of Islam' (1683, Salonika and then other Ottoman cities).
(2) 'Believers' who outwardly continued to adhere to rabbinical Judaism but inwardly adopted a non-rabbinical understanding of the Torah. They existed first in Palestine and the Balkans, and from the eighteenth century also in northern and Eastern Europe.

(3) The Frankists who 'Marranized themselves' by converting to Catholicism (1759, Poland).
(4) The Frankists in Bohemia, Moravia, Hungary and Romania, who remained Jewish.

I will now turn to the third form, the Frankists who 'self-Marranized', in order to bring Scholem's narrative to its temporal conclusion – European modernity before Zionism – and then to examine his 'mythology of prolepsis' or scholarly-ideological construct.

The son of a rabbi, Jacob Frank was born in Podolia (then Poland, now a region of Ukraine) in 1726. His travels as a merchant in the Ottoman Empire in the 1740s brought him in contact with the Sabbatians, and on his return to Poland in 1755 he founded the Frankists, as an offshoot of Sabbatianism. In 1759 the Frankists underwent a spectacular mass baptism at Lvov, Poland, in the presence of members of the Polish nobility. But the Catholic church brought charges of heresy against Frank, possibly prompted by the strangeness of his teaching, which resulted in his imprisonment in 1760. On emerging from prison thirteen years later, Frank assumed the role of Messiah. Selecting twelve apostles, he settled at Brünn, Moravia (now Brno, Czech Republic), where he gained the patronage Maria Theresa, Archduchess of Austria, who employed him as an apologist of Christianity to the Jews. After 1786 Frank moved to the small German town of Offenbach, where he spent the rest of his life in luxury, thanks to the donations of his followers. After his death, leadership of the sect passed to his daughter Eve Frank, but the movement was soon absorbed into the Catholic church.

Scholem thinks that Frank 'was in all his actions a truly corrupt and degenerate individual'.[52] He is, however, unwilling to stop there, because

> in spite of all this . . . we are confronted in his person with the extraordinary spectacle of a powerful and tyrannical soul living in the middle of the eighteenth century and yet immersed in a mythological world of its own making. Out of the ideas of Sabbatianism, a movement in which he was apparently raised and educated, Frank was able to weave a complete myth of religious nihilism.[53]

The most notable feature of Frank's religious myth was its striking antinomian drive. 'The Law of Moses' was utterly rejected as 'injurious and useless', the main obstacle to the re-emergence of 'the Good God'. Thirty years after his conversion to Catholicism Frank stated: 'This much I tell you: Christ . . . said that he had come to redeem the world from the hands of the devil, but I have come to redeem it from all the laws and customs that have ever existed. It is my task to annihilate all this so that the Good God can reveal himself.'[54] In Scholem's schema of unfolding *Geists*, Frankism led to the *Haskalah*, the so-called Jewish Enlightenment, but because of its unyielding antinomian drive Frankism wouldn't halt there. Scholem concludes 'Redemption through Sin' by noting that the French Revolution imbued with special meaning 'Frankist subversion of the old morality and religion . . . and perhaps not only in the abstract, for we know that Frank's nephews, whether as "believers" or out of some other motive, were active in high revolutionary circles in Paris and Strasbourg'.[55]

One of Jacob Frank's nephews, whom Scholem had mentioned anonymously in 1937 in 'Redemption through Sin', became the subject of his reconstruction of a quintessential Frankist life three decades later in 'A Frankist's Career: Moshe Dobruska and His Metamorphoses'.[56] Dobruska was born in 1753 in Brünn, Moravia (now Brno), where Jacob Frank would settle in the 1760s. His father held the monopoly over sales of tobacco in the Austro-Hungarian Empire under Maria Theresa, and his mother, Scheindel Hirschl, was Jacob Frank's cousin (hence the description of Moshe and his brother Emmanuel as his nephews). Hirschl was the foremost patron of the Sabbatians in Moravia, her rabbinical detractors referring to her as 'the whore of Brünn'. Dobruska's education comprised rabbinical learning, Sabbatian Kabbalah, German letters, Latin and several European vernaculars. In 1773 he married Elke, the adopted daughter of one of the wealthiest leaders of Prague's Jewish community, Joachim Edler von Popper.

Scholem makes his point in his unfolding of Dobruska's life. Like most of his siblings, Dobruska converted to Catholicism in 1775 and became Franz Thomas Scheinfeld; his wife Elke became Wilhelmina. He moved to Vienna where he served the Habsburgs and from 1781 to 1784 was an active member in one of the 'Asiatic' Freemason fraternities. It was a mystically inclined fraternity, which supported Judaeo-Christian interaction and which was engaged in the reading of Kabbalistic texts. In the wake of the French Revolution Dobruska/Scheinfeld began to lean leftward in both his explicit political pronouncements and the literary circles in which he moved. He was especially attracted to the Jacobin revolutionaries. In the early 1790s he left Vienna for Strasbourg, where he now became Sigmund Frey, later adding Junius, after the Roman Junius Brutus, one of the leading conspirators in the assassination of Julius Caesar. On arriving in Paris with Wilhelmina and his brother and sister, Dobruska/Scheinfeld/Frey's Jacobinic tendencies intensified, and he never left home 'without wearing the carmagnole' – though the suspicion that he was a counter-revolutionary Habsburg agent never died away. His younger sister married the prominent Jacobin François Chabot. The Dobruska/Frey brothers together participated in the August 1792 onslaught on the king's Tuileries Palace, and even earned a citation from the revolutionary authorities. On 5 April 1794 Danton, Chabot and others were executed; among them, condemned to death for treason, were the brothers Frey.

Scholem concludes his account of Dobruska's life poetically:

> Thus ended the overt and covert, surprising and tumultuous career of Moshe Dobruska – Franz Thomas von Scheinfeld – Junius Frey . . . Partially a Jew and partially an assimilated convert; partially a Kabbalist and man of the concealed and partially a man of enlightenment; partially a Jacobin and partially a spy – everything partially, but a true and complete Frankist.[57]

Let us now return to Abraham Cardozo, the Marrano formulator of the gnostic Sabbatian doctrine that, according to Scholem, resolved for the 'believers' the paradox of the apostate Messiah. In the late 1660s Cardozo was leading a comfortable life in Tripoli in Ottoman North Africa. A physician, he had been sent there by his patron, the Duke of Tuscany, to treat the Ottoman governor Osman Pasha, and was looked after by the local grandee Receb Bey. When the Jewish judges (*dayyanim*) of Sabbatai Sevi's home town of Izmir (Smyrna) convened to discuss the apostate Messiah, they solicited testimonies from several persons, and Cardozo too offered one. His testimony, *Iggrot le-dayyanei Izmir* ('Epistles to the judges of Izmir'), was dated (to 1669) and published by Scholem.[58] However, in the *Epistles* Cardozo alludes to the messianic era in a way that Scholem omits to mention in 'Redemption through Sin'. Cardozo explains to the judges that his messianic belief by no means stemmed from 'my being in exile, for I experience no exile'[59]

Cardozo explicitly objected to the notion that the Messiah would bring the Jews back to the land of Israel. As David Halperin senses, '[h]is own image of the Messianic era is a strangely prescient foreshadowing of the Jewish political emancipation of the eighteenth and nineteenth centuries'.[60] Cardozo shared his own vision with the judges: 'When the Redeemer comes, the Jews will still be living among the Gentiles even after their salvation is accomplished. But they will not be dead men, as they had been previously. Through their redemption they will experience happiness, enjoy dignity and honor'.[61]

If we momentarily remain within the logic of what I called, via Skinner,

Scholem's mythology of prolepsis, it should be evident that Dobruska and Cardozo as important precursors of things to come seriously challenge the direction of this logic. What they and other figures show is that being a Zionist historian in Zion is not necessarily advantageous to understanding Cardozo and Dobruska better. In fact being an authoritative Zionist historian in Zion, if anything, utterly distorts both what the historical experiences of Cardozo and Dobruska could mean within their own context, and – should one wish to toy with prolepsis – what they could mean as precursors within Scholem's grand historical schema that dialectically went from the Lurianic Kabbalah to Zionism. My contention is that the Marrano Cardozo, who did not feel he was in exile in the negationist sense, and the Frankist-Jacobin Dobruska, whose turn to Jacobinism was, according to Scholem, quintessentially Frankist, in fact resist Scholem's Zionist theology at the levels of both proper history and prolepsis. And perhaps the perspective that is more adequate for an empathetic understanding of these two figures is that of the non-Zionist, so much reviled by Scholem. It might be, in other words, that the position of 'general humanity' whose existence Scholem so adamantly denied, except in the imagination of hallucinatory exilic Jews, as he told Ehud Ben-Ezer in the conversation quoted at the beginning of the chapter, is actually more appropriate for an empathetic interpretation of Cardozo and Dobruska.

## The Fight Over Walter Benjamin

I will conclude this chapter with an intervention in the debate over the significance of Benjamin's fragmented *oeuvre* and his legacy. I want to respond to an argument put forward by David Biale on the affinity between Scholem's and Benjamin's methods and philosophies of history. Biale's study of Scholem, which I have already referred to on several occasions, is possibly the most accepted and cited overall interpretation of the content and meaning of his project in the English-speaking scholarly community. Biale finds affinity between what he terms Scholem's counter-history, and Benjamin's radical stance against triumphant positivist historicism as elucidated in the 'Theses on the Philosophy of History' and his famous call to 'brush history against the grain'. He is aware of Scholem's aversion to Marxism and dialectical materialism, as well as of his unwillingness to accept Benjamin's unorthodox adherence to both. Biale avers that 'Scholem's close friendship with Benjamin suggests the plausibility of considering their philosophies of history together'.[62] The motto Biale chose for the book as a whole is, moreover, Benjamin's call just mentioned.

I find this argument objectionable intellectually, politically and ethically. I would argue that although Scholem indeed sought to use Benjamin's critique of historicism, and was in a way influenced by it, he completely distorted it for his own ends. I think, moreover, that the political and ethical world views that guided Benjamin and Scholem and to which they were committed – unorthodox Marxist humanism (strewn with Jewish messianism and romanticism) and Zionism, respectively – were and have remained not only incompatible, but also mutually exclusive.

What the 'Theses' express, in other words, is not a historical method in the narrowly academic sense but an ethical and political drive to redeem humanity's oppressed, the very same 'general humanity' Scholem imagined to exist only in the imagination of some feeble Weimar Jews; the very same 'general humanity' the mere mention of which made Scholem lose his temper. Michael Löwy, in his Talmudic interpretation of the 'Theses',[63] is well aware of the three sources that comprise Benjamin's thought: German romanticism, Jewish messianism, and Marxism. Yet when placing the 'Theses' within a tradition he is unequivocal: 'Walter Benjamin's "Theses 'On the Concept of History'" (1940) constitutes one of the most important philosophical and political texts of the twentieth century. In revolutionary thought, it is perhaps the most significant document since Marx's "Theses on Feuerbach".'[64] I shall register my firm objection to Scholem's misuse of Benjamin by alluding to two original critics: first the Moravian-born Israeli Barukh Kurzweil, and then, befitting the chapter's closure, an individual with whom it began: George Steiner.

Possibly the most vehement Israeli critic of Scholem and the Jerusalem scholars, Barukh Kurzweil made a particularly enlightening pronouncement on Benjamin's legacy and its appropriation. Kurzweil was a thoroughly cultured literary critic. Born in 1907, he emigrated from Moravia to Palestine in 1939, and found work as a high-school teacher in Haifa. In 1955 he was recruited by the national-religious Bar-Ilan University to teach Hebrew literature. Yet Kurzweil conducted a critical campaign aimed at the community of Jewish studies at the Hebrew University, and in particular at Scholem. He held the latter in high esteem and regarded him a worthy adversary because of his intellectual prowess; however, he considered the majority of Scholem's colleagues lightweights, busily engaged in academic tourism. This can be seen in his vicious judgment on one of Scholem's younger associates: 'Jacob Katz interests me only as a symptom on the margins of the general picture. I mentioned him incidentally and my main concern [is] G. Scholem, for in him I see an exceptional but dangerous intellectual talent, while Katz did a decent and nice job as long as he was content with writing history text-books for schools.'[65] Kurzweil was doubtless hurt by the lack of recognition of his work and by never being offered a position at the Hebrew University, and his iconoclastic life came to a sad end with his suicide in 1972. His systematic critique of Scholem appeared in the late 1950s and the 1960s in *Haaretz* and other journals. It has received scholarly attention, although the part of it which deals with the relevance of Benjamin has been largely passed over.[66]

To understand properly Kurzweil's take on Benjamin, it is necessary to present the gist of his overall view of Scholem's project.[67] What must be made clear first is that Kurzweil's wrath was incurred by the authority that Scholem and the Jerusalem scholars had, in his view, usurped: they claimed the right to speak for and revitalize Judaism, secure its perpetuity. He did not deny their right to study Judaism, even when he disagreed with their methods and conclusions, but he furiously and adamantly objected to the golden calf of science becoming the custodian of something – Judaism – that was after all a matter of religious belief. This is a point which Kurzweil reiterated throughout his work, and which is most directly made in the title he gave to the second part of his book that gathered his main essays on Scholem and the Jerusalem scholars: 'Dovreha ha-medumim shel ha-Yahadut' ('Judaism's false spokesmen').[68] Kurzweil held Scholem's project in high esteem and admired its enormous contribution to the study of Judaism, but he was very wary of Judaism's fate being entrusted to a non-believing religious anarchist with an irresistible genius and charisma like Scholem. And he was cagey about, as he put it, 'the obsession of the neo-mythic stupor [*ha-dibbuq shel ha-shikkaron ha-neomiti*]'.[69] Citing again Scholem's famous statement, 'we had come to rebel and ended up continuing', Kurzweil adds: 'And what is it that we are continuing? Judaism's burial procession.'[70]

Four intimately related points in Kurzweil's criticism are crucially pertinent to his view on the Benjamin/Scholem complex. These are: the immanence of secularism and modernity within Judaism; the presumption of scientific objectivity; the absolute authority accorded to philological history; and the allegedly superior position and scholarship of Scholem and his Jerusalem colleagues vis-à-vis the nineteenth-century Wissenschaft in Germany.

Kurzweil rejected categorically and comprehensively Scholem's narrative of immanence that led from the altered, 'messianized', Kabbalah, through Sabbatianism to secularism and Jewish nationalism. For him all modern phenomena, including those that could be identified as Jewish, owed their emergence to the Enlightenment and the French Revolution.[71] In Kurzweil's view, Judaism was a religion first and foremost, and essentially an exilic and rabbinical entity; he therefore had no stake in an organically immanent narrative, linear or dialectic.[72]

Next, adopting Nietzsche's (and as we shall see, Benjamin's) position on the crisis of historicism, Kurzweil sets out to attack Scholem's claim of scientific objectivity and its concomitant, the claim of authoritatively superior authenticity over the nineteenth-century German Jewish scholars. Referring to one of the pillars of nineteenth-century *Wissenschaft*, Eduard Gans, Kurzweil underscores the continuity between Gans and Scholem:

> The difference between Scholem and Gans and his friends is not in substance but in appearance, and from the point of view of religious Judaism the difference is not all that large. Both Scholem and Gans begin from a [similar] assumption: halakhic Judaism is a stumbling block on the way to normalization. Granted, Gans's method is more rationalist, whereas Scholem blasts Judaism through Jewish mysticism, which was, for him, not a foundation and fountain for belief, but an anarchistic vehicle through which rabbinical Judaism could be destroyed from within . . . Scholem is the first great Jewish scholar who with an ingenious instinct chose the supposed mystic pose, more precisely: the pose of nihilistic mysticism or mystical nihilism, in order to throw stones from it at the Judaism of the 'a-normal' Jewish existence, at the Judaism of the rabbinical Halakha. The anarchist's target [is] the Judaism of the Halakha; his weapon, the mystical texts. There is no more conclusive evidence for the absurdity of our time than the fact that precisely Scholem is today – Judaism's spokesman![73]

Although this is not the thrust of the present discussion, I should highlight (as I keep doing throughout the book) the extent to which the Kurzweil/Scholem debate was Judaeocentric, the extent to which it ignored the Palestinian Arabs. Kurzweil is not incorrect in underscoring the continuity between Gans's and Scholem's attitudes to Halakhic Judaism, but he is utterly oblivious to the acuteness of one difference: Gans's aim was full integration into German society, whereas Scholem's was 'return' to the land of Israel. From a Palestinian perspective, this difference is what matters most. Kurzweil then addresses Scholem's categorical assertion that the Wissenschaft scholars could not produce a 'pure objective science' by definition, because they served a non-scientific purpose, namely, emancipation and assimilation, and because their stance was perforce apologetic. Kurzweil agrees that scientific objectivity was unattainable – he had Nietzschean doubts about objectivity as such – but not only by that particular scholarly community:

With Scholem the deviation from false objectivity does nothing more than substitute secular nationalism for apologetics. That is to say: there [in the nineteenth-century Wissenschaft] the apologetics is for integration into a secular–Christian society and state; here [the scholarship of Scholem and his Jerusalem colleagues] we are dealing with a historical–philosophical validation of a secular nationalism of the future [Kurzweil is referring specifically to Scholem's 1937 'Redemption through Sin'] Zionist state.[74]

Perhaps it is a deeply ingrained, ineradicably modernist prejudice that causes one to be astounded by the extent to which Kurzweil, an explicitly self-confessed religious Jew in Franz Rosenzweig's sense,[75] intellectually and ethically admired and emotionally liked Walter Benjamin; and concomitantly, the ferociousness with which he insisted on the wrongfulness of Scholem's attempt to claim Benjamin. Kurzweil points out the ever-present tension, indeed contradiction, in Jewish studies between 'Enlightened and Romantic trends', and contends that within this tension 'is ensconced the deep contrast of Scholem's way and that of his friend Walter Benjamin'.[76] He then utterly refutes Scholem's appropriation of Benjamin:

> Scholem's interpretation of W. Benjamin's attitude to the land of Israel and to Judaism is *most subjective* and his attempt to 'Judaize' Benjamin originates in Scholem's efforts to interpret Benjamin as if he were G. Scholem. Anyone who knows Benjamin's writings as I do, his works on Goethe and the German tragedy play, must see that in Benjamin's spiritual world Judaism had only marginal significance, and therefore all of Scholem's observations – also regarding Benjamin's place in German [culture] criticism – are stamped with subjective excess and do not come close to being an objective discussion. Benjamin was unwilling to partake in Scholem's escape to historicism, Romantic Zionism, mysticism and philology. The problems of society guided his way and Marxist dialectics was his beacon – albeit not in the orthodox sense – which is what distinguishes between him and his friend Brecht. But the Zionist venture . . . was suspicious in his eyes as a bourgeois experiment of which one ought to be wary. Even to French culture Benjamin was closer than to Judaism.[77]

Kurzweil's intimate knowledge of German culture and letters, a world he shared with Benjamin and Scholem (but not with institutional Hebrew literary criticism as a whole), allowed him to present a precisely argued analysis of Scholem's use of Benjamin. He correctly deduced that underlying Scholem's turn to Jung in the latter part of his career, as well as his self-conscious seclusion behind the walls of 'pure science' and 'immaculate philological fidelity', was despair of both Judaism – including its mystical side – and Zionism.[78] This was inevitable, Kurzweil thought, because 'Without a binding relation to normative religion, every mysticism leads to demonic anarchism . . . Kabbalah without Talmud, a theory of the occult without practical commandments, wind up in pan-demonism'.[79] Posing the question of how this occurred specifically with Scholem, Kurzweil observes:

> The key to understanding [this] lies in Walter Benjamin's 'Theses on the Philosophy of History'. Scholem depends on Benjamin's assumptions but he deserted them by giving them an arbitrary interpretation. Therefore Benjamin's humanistic, messianic–secular–Marxist trajectory was transformed by Scholem's touch into the demonic, which is the most dangerous adversary of the humanistic.[80]

Kurzweil develops this explanation by positing the following equation: '[h]istorical materialism/historicism = Jewish mysticism/classical rabbinical Judaism'. He elaborates: 'This equation is the solution for the riddle [of Scholem's arbitrary use of Bejamin]. Scholem transferred to rabbinical Judaism Benjamin's critique of historicism. His idea of exploding classical, rabbinical Judaism's continuum through the foundations of Kabbalah and mysticism is the transfer of Benjamin's idea of exploding the historical continuum through historical materialism'.[81] Before the final stage of this precise explanation as to how Scholem misused the 'Theses', Kurzweil pauses to emphasize the nature of Scholem's dance with the mythic consciousness rekindled within the Kabbalah. He joins Scholem in rejecting the view that Jewish monotheism severed its ties with the mythic; Kurzweil even joins Scholem in seeing the occasional reinvigorating and stimulating impact mythic stir may have had. Resorting again to Franz Rosenzweig, however, he shows that Scholem's mystical and mythic path led to an unrestrained self-indulgent absorption in individual fulfilment, something to which Rosenzweig objected as 'the worship of the Self [Das Selbst]'. This attraction of Scholem to protagonists obsessed with gratification of the Self, and correspondingly averse to social concerns, Kurzweil continues, throws 'new light on the spiritual ties between Benjamin and Scholem'.[82]

Like Benjamin (first and foremost) and Scholem, Kurzweil kept returning to Paul Klee's painting *Angelus Novus*. Among the many ways in which it inspired Benjamin, Klee's painting gave visual form to the organizing principle of the 'Theses'. Kurzweil observes that '[i]n the image of the horror-spectacle of Klee's "*Angelus Novus*" the angel of history was revealed to both Benjamin and Scholem . . . Twice however Scholem strayed from Benjamin's interpretation of the horror-spectacle'.[83] I believe that the first such deviation identified by Kurzweil reaffirms the significance of the Herzl/Lazare bifurcation as an *Ansatzpunkt* that was developed in Chapter One.[84] The appearance of the bifurcation here is the point at which the universalist path, so dreaded and reviled by Zionist writers from Baer and Scholem to Anita Shapira, and the particularist one diverge. In the storm that irresistibly propels the angel into the future Benjamin sees in his mind's eye the force that shatters, 'in the name of human society, the illusion of the continuum of the empty and homogeneous time, which is historicism's artificial construction'.[85] And this, according to Kurzweil, gives rise to an ethical–political vision that is fundamentally incompatible with Scholem's:

> It is patently evident that *Angelus Novus*'s horror-spectacle has with Benjamin a constructive purpose. Shattering historical contiguity, the turn to the present and future is anti-individualistic, humanistic, in favour of the unprivileged, the oppressed. The anti-bourgeois explosion is in favour of the exploited, suffering class. It serves a moral purpose and realises a secular, generally human messianism. It certainly is not a narrow messianic-nationalist ideology, and hence the storm in the history's angel's wings does not push him into the whirlwind of the demonic, the one that overwhelms history's angel only if he is absorbed in his Self, in the individualism that eclipses the image of Man, whose site of fulfilment is society alone. Thus with Benjamin the horror-spectacle of *Angelus Novus* is not history's final station, but secular messianism in the spirit of historical materialism.[86]

And then, Kurzweil continues, with regard to Scholem more explicitly:

> The shattering of historical contiguity is dwarfed in Scholem's view, by the shattering of Jewish history, the negation of classical Judaism, of rabbinism. And for what [purpose] this shattering? For the Self, for individualistic anarchism. With Scholem *Angelus Novus* paves the way for the rule of demonism and nihilism. The [various] phenomena of Judaism become piles of rubble. A heap of destruction and single catastrophe rise at the angel's feet. He does not turn to the future. For there is no belief in his heart.[87]

Scholem's second deviation from Benjamin is concerned with history itself as a scholarly undertaking. As Kurzweil notes, Benjamin was suspicious of and, if it was devoid of ethical–political purpose, uninterested in it:

[Scholem's] [h]istorical research serves, as it were, only itself. It is not only that history's angel was shifted from its imposing, generally human, observation point to the narrow frame of a national-Romantic movement – Zionism. Ultimately, after Scholem denies the unavoidable bias of his studies, he refers to himself as a pure science man, as an objective historian, to whom nothing matters but philological fidelity. Jewish studies' angel of history was transformed from the announcer of the horror-spectacle into the official and most respectable representative of Judaism in the whole wide world. The storm does not blow from paradise and it does not clasp the wings of history's angel, but the wings of the airplanes that bring to all corners of the globe the message of Judaism from the mouth of the learned traveller, which is the message of the living dead, the merry message of accounts of the clothes of the naked king. *Ex oriente lux nihili*.[88]

Pointing to other pronouncements of dissatisfaction with Scholem's misuse of Benjamin, Kurzweil referred to two essays, both of which appeared in 1968. One was penned by Arendt. The other was described by Kurzweil as a 'great article', but he did not identify the author. I have done so: he was none other than George Steiner, the target of Scholem's fulmination in his conversation with Ben-Ezer. On the occasion of the publication (1966) of Benjamin's letters, edited and annotated by Adorno and Scholem, Steiner offers an intervention in the debate over the true meaning of Benjamin's life and work. Steiner discerningly saw through much of the pious discourse, and foregrounded the extent to which this debate was as much about the claimants to Benjamin's intellectual legacy as about his actual work.[89]

The two main camps in the debate were the orthodox Marxists on the one hand, and Adorno and Scholem on the other, with Arendt awkwardly placed in the middle, though clearly distanced from Scholem. The orthodox Marxists were adamant that 'American-financed sociology [Adorno and Horkheimer's] and Jewish mysticism [Scholem's] have no right to claim Walter Benjamin'.[90] Adorno was always unhappy, to put it mildly, with Benjamin's turn to Marxism, and famously expressed this discontent in his 1938 rebuff of a draft of Benjamin's interpretation of Baudelaire, which was a crucial intellectual and especially material setback for Benjamin. Steiner has an interesting insight on this refutation that would alas take us too far afield here.[91] Scholem of course spared no effort – during Benjamin's lifetime and after his death – to say and show that Marxism was not only alien and unnatural to Benjamin's interests and intellectual countenance, but that Benjamin's accepting it was tantamount to self-betrayal. Adorno and Scholem appointed themselves as the executors of Benjamin's spiritual will, and their 1966 edition of his letters is not unproblematic, most notably in the case of a 'version' of Benjamin's reply to Adorno's 1938 refutation that is suspiciously different from the original draft held in Potsdam's Deutschen Zentral Archiv.

In his 1968 essay Steiner tries to avoid taking sides in the debate over Benjamin's legacy, but it is clear throughout that he more than appreciates how pivotal Marxism was to Benjamin, however unorthodox the version of it he developed. This is evident in his reference, cited at the beginning of this chapter, to Benjamin's letter, as well as in Benjamin's interaction with Marxist friends and comrades in the KPD (the German Communist Party). Most notably, it is evident in a wonderfully sensitive passage on Benjamin and Brecht, which wittingly or not is a rebuttal of the repeated attempts by Adorno and Scholem to imply or explicitly say that Brecht bullied Benjamin into Marxism.[92] Making his own remark look incidental, Steiner nonetheless questions, if not the motives, then the behaviour of Adorno and Scholem:

> Is it worth insisting on certain truths, i.e., that Scholem and Adorno – however pure their motives, however disinterested their editorial labour to which, after all, much of Benjamin's achievement and presence owes its survival – tend to patronize their unfortunate, dead friend, that the growth of his stature in relation to *theirs* poses psychological traps? Or that a man writing letters to friends far away, to backers whose emotional and material support he urgently requires, may omit from a finished version acerbities or provocations he will put in a rough draft?[93]

Cautious not to pass to the side of what he calls 'the Potsdam contingent' and mindful of Judaism's presence in certain ways in his work, Steiner ultimately rejects Scholem's negation of exile via Benjamin and insists on his right to hold on to the position that he and Benjamin share, and that Scholem so vehemently denies to them. This is evocative of Arendt's remark about Rahel Varnhagen, that she 'had remained a Jew and pariah. Only because she clung to both conditions did she find a place in the history of European humanity.'[94] I would like to end with Steiner's, and through him Benjamin's, insistence:

> Of course Gershom Scholem is right when he affirms that Benjamin was deeply interested in Jewish history, and thought often and seriously of emigrating to Israel [it is striking that Steiner should refer to Mandatory Palestine as Israel] . . . Of course it is true that Benjamin did not share

any ready Zionism, that he felt emotionally and intellectually rooted in classic and West European humanism . . . To the very last, and when he must have known it was too late, Benjamin felt that emigration to either Jerusalem or New York signified an abandonment of irreplaceable values. There is nothing sinister about this ambivalence . . . There is scarcely a feeling, thinking European Jew in this century who has not at some time, in complete sincerity, regarded emigration to Israel as the only sane course; yet who has, even in extremity, found himself trapped in his own needs of spirit, in his own unwillingness to exchange the legacy of Spinoza, Heine and Freud for that of Herzl.[95]

# Notes

1 G. Scholem, 'Zionism – A Dialectic of Continuity and Rebellion [conversation with Ehud Ben-Ezer]', in Avraham Shapira (ed.), *Continuity and Rebellion: Gershom Scholem in Speech and Dialogue* [Hebrew], Tel Aviv: Am Oved, 1994.

2 Ibid., pp. 25, 26, 27 and 29.

3 This brief biographical summary draws on D. Biale, *Gershom Scholem: Kabbalah and Counter-History*, Cambridge, Mass.: Harvard University Press, 1979, pp. 52–79, and D. Myers, *Re-Inventing the Jewish Past: European Jewish Intellectuals and the Zionist Return to History*, New York and Oxford: Oxford University Press, 1995, pp. 151–77.

4 The Christmas 1911 incident is related by Biale, op. cit., p. 53.

5 Myers, op. cit., p. 155. Biale discusses what he aptly titles 'Scholem and the Cult of the Ostjuden' on pp. 69–72.

6 Biale, op. cit., pp. 72–3.

7 Ibid., pp. 74–6 (English translation) and 215–17 (German original).

8 Halakha is the Jewish legal framework.

9 Biale, op. cit., p. 77.

10 P. Anderson, 'The Intransigent Right: Michael Oakeshott, Leo Strauss, Carl Schmitt, Friedrich von Hayek', in *Spectrum*, London and New York: Verso, 2005, pp. 3–29. For more on Schmitt see G. Balakrishnan, *The Enemy: An Intellectual Portrait of Carl Schmitt*, London: Verso, 2000, and M. Lilla, *The Reckless Mind: Intellectuals in Politics*, New York: New York Review of Books, 2001, pp. 47–77.

11 See Lilla, op. cit., pp. 93–4.

12 Christoph Schmidt, 'The Political Theology of Gershom Scholem [Hebrew]', *Theory and Criticism*, 6 (Spring 1995), pp. 149–61; citation from the English abstract on p. 187. Schmidt was also the scientific editor of, and wrote the introduction for, the Hebrew translation of *Politische Theologie* (Tel Aviv: Resling, 2005).

13 Q. Skinner, 'Meaning and Understanding in the History of Ideas', *History and Theory*, 8 (1969), pp. 3–53. I quote from the reproduction in J. Tully (ed.), *Meaning and Context: Quentin Skinner and His Critics*, Cambridge: Polity Press, 1988.

14 Ibid., p. 44.

15 Ibid., p. 45.

16 Biale, op. cit., p. 127.

17 Myers, op. cit., p. 176.

18 Ibid., 160.

19 M. Idel, 'The History of the Kabbalah and the History of the Jews [Hebrew]', *History and Criticism*, 6 (Spring 1995), pp. 137–49. The non-Hebrew reader may consult the essay's early version in French: 'Mystique juive et histoire juive', *Annales, Histoire, Sciences Sociales*, 49 (1994), pp. 1223–40.

20 Ibid., p. 138.

21 Ibid., pp. 138–40. For another attempt to identify Scholem's implicit periodization see Biale, op. cit., pp. 120–1.

22 Reference to G. Scholem, *Sabbatai Sevi: The Mystical Messiah*, Princeton: Princeton University Press, 1973.

23 Idel, op. cit. [Hebrew], p. 140.

24 Ibid.
25 Biale, op. cit., pp. 123–4.
26 Idel, op. cit. [Hebrew], p. 141. The comment of the Hebrew word used by Scholem for 'glow' is mine.
27 Ibid., pp. 142–4.
28 Ibid., p. 145.
29 Ibid., p. 146.
30 Ibid., pp. 146–7.
31 G. Scholem, 'Mitzvah ha-ba'ah ba-`averah', *Knesset*, 2 (1937), pp. 347–92. Translated into English by H. Halkin as 'Redemption through Sin', in *The Messianic Idea in Judaism*, London: George Allen & Unwin, 1971, pp. 78–141. For the essay having been written in 1935 see asterisk note on p. 85 of the English translation, to which all references are made unless otherwise stated.
32 G. Scholem, 'A Frankist's Career: Moshe Dobruska and His Metamorphoses', in *Studies and Texts Concerning the History of Sabbatianism and Its Metamorphoses*, Jerusalem: Bialik Institute, 1974, pp. 141–219 [Hebrew]. Originally appeared in *Zion*, 35 (1970), pp. 127–81.
33 Scholem, 'Redemption', p. 99.
34 See the asterisk note to 'Mitzvah' in Scholem, *Studies and Texts*, p. 9.
35 Scholem, 'Redemption', p. 78.
36 The quote is: 'Paradox is a characteristic of truth. What *communis opinio* has of truth is surely no more than an elementary deposit of generalizing partial understanding, related to truth even as sulphurous fumes are to lightning.' Whereas in the Hebrew original (Tel Aviv: Am Oved, 1957) it is attributed simply to Dilthey (without even the Wilhelm), in the English translation (Princeton University Press, 1973) the attribution is 'From the correspondence of Count Paul Yorck von Wartenburg and Wilhelm Dilthey'.
37 Scholem, 'Redemption', pp. 84–5.
38 Ibid., p. 84.
39 Ibid., p. 94.
40 M. Zilfi, *The Politics of Piety*, Minneapolis and Chicago: Bibliotheca Islamica, 1988, and J. Hathaway, 'The Grand Vizier and the False Messiah', *Journal of the American Oriental Society*, 117:4 (October–December 1997), pp. 665–71.
41 Scholem, 'Redemption', p. 94.
42 Ibid., pp. 94–5.
43 Ibid., p. 95.
44 Ibid.
45 Ibid., pp. 110–11.
46 Ibid., pp. 96–7.
47 Ibid., p. 104.
48 Ibid., pp. 105–6.
49 Ibid., pp. 103–4.
50 Ibid., p. 106.
51 Ibid., pp. 114–15.
52 Ibid., p. 126.
53 Ibid., pp. 127–8.
54 Ibid., p. 130.
55 Ibid., p. 137.

56 See n. 32 above.
57 Scholem, 'Redemption', p. 209.
58 In *Studies and Texts*. The date is identified on pp. 298–303.
59 D. J. Halperin, Introduction to *Abraham Miguel Cardozo: Selected Writings*, trans. and intro. D. J. Halperin, New York: Paulist Press, 2001, p. 48.
60 Ibid.
61 Ibid., p. 49.
62 Biale, op. cit., p. 197. The argument on the affinity is on pp. 196–8.
63 See above, Chapter One, p. 26.
64 M. Löwy, *Fire Alarm: Reading Walter Benjamin's 'On the Concept of History'*, London and New York: Verso, 2005, p. 4.
65 B. Kurzweil, 'Reflections of an Hallucinatory Reader', in *In the Struggle over Judaism's Values* [Hebrew], Jerusalem and Tel Aviv: Schocken, 1969, p. 153 (originally appeared in 1965).
66 See for example Biale, op. cit., pp. 95–7; D. Myers, 'The Scholem–Kurzweil Debate and Modern Jewish Historiography', *Modern Judaism*, 6 (1986), pp. 261–86, and *Re-Inventing*, pp. 172–4.
67 My presentation is gleaned from B. Kurzweil, *Our New Literature – Continuity or Revolution?*, Jerusalem and Tel Aviv: Schocken, 1965, pp. 11–146, and the following essays in *In the Struggle*: 'Comments on Gershom Scholem's Sabbatai Sevi', pp. 99–135, 'Dissatisfaction with History and Jewish Studies', pp. 135–50, 'On the Limits of History's Authority', pp. 167–83, and 'On Jewish Studies' Benefit and Damage', pp. 184–240.
68 The second part of *In the Struggle*.
69 Kurzweil, *Our New Literature*, p. 91.
70 Kurzweil, *In the Struggle*, p. 195.
71 See especially Kurzweil, *Our New Literature*, pp. 78–86.
72 See especially the section on 'The Pluralism of A-normalcy as the Foundation of Jewish Existence', in *In the Struggle*, pp. 206–13.
73 Kurzweil, *In the Struggle*, pp. 210 and 211.
74 Ibid., p. 223.
75 Ibid., p. 212.
76 Ibid., p. 200.
77 Ibid., pp. 201–2.
78 Ibid., p. 226.
79 Ibid.
80 Ibid.
81 Ibid., p. 227.
82 Ibid., p. 229.
83 Ibid., p. 230.
84 See above, pp. 2–3.
85 Kurzweil, *In the Struggle*, p. 230.
86 Ibid., pp. 230–1.
87 Ibid., p. 232.
88 Ibid.
89 G. Steiner, 'Walter Benjamin: Towards a Philosophy of Language', *The Times Literary Supplement*, 14 (22 August 1968). I quote from *T.L.S: Essays and Reviews from The Times Literary Supplement, 1968*, Oxford: Oxford University Press, 1969, pp. 193–204.

90 Ibid., p. 198.
91 See ibid., pp. 197 and 202.
92 Ibid., pp. 200–2.
93 Ibid., p. 203.
94 See above, Chapter One, p. 25.
95 Steiner, op. cit., pp. 198–9.

# 6

# The Bible, the Nakba and Hebrew Literature

In the wake of the War of Independence small groups of young poets sporadically appeared in Israel . . . To the catastrophe of the Jewish People in Europe they were hearing witnesses; and to the disaster of Palestine's Arabs they were seeing witnesses. Neither had any echo in their poems. Their fathers, who had pioneered in the early twenties, told them, as the Shoah had come, what had happened to the Jews there, in Europe. But they hid and didn't tell nor made them [the young poets] cognizant of what had happened here, in front of their own eyes, to the Arabs. None of that elicited a single intervention in their poems. Just yesterday the Arabs would bring to their homes the *mishmish*, and on the morrow – *mafish*. They were, and are no more.

All this extracted not one question from them, in their poems.
(Avot Yeshurun, a draft from his private papers, published in *Mitaam*, 9 (March 2007), p. 6)

Irresponsibility. This whole idea of a Jewish neighbourhood to the side of Arab Jaffa, during the day one lives off the other and in the evening one disengages from the other, the enlightened, clean and civilised will be here and the retarded and filthy native, who has caused the desolation of the land, will be there. On top of Jews (father calls them 'our brethren') against Muslims (father calls them Muhammadans), immigrants against inhabitants, on top of advanced against backward, Europeans against Asians – as if it were possible that just like that they would get along peacefully, without a wall

between them, and without an iron gate between them, and without arms for the day of reckoning, how come?
(S. Yizhar, *Mikdamot* ['Preliminaries'], 1992)

How can we protest their strong hatred of us? For eight years now they have been dwelling in refugee camps in Gaza, and in front of their eyes we are transforming into a patrimony the land and villages on which they and their ancestors dwelt . . . Our life's choice – to be prepared and armed, strong and tough, lest our fist would lose grip of the sword and our life would cease.
(From Moshe Dayan's eulogy of Roi Rotenberg from Kibbutz Nahal-Oz, 1 May 1956)

Here is a place that has left its place and is not.
(S. Yizhar, 'Sippur she-lo Hitchil' ['A story that has not begun'], in *Sippurey Mishor* ['Stories of the plain'], 1963)

In this chapter I show how the Zionist methods of settlement, land appropriation and labour exclusion, discussed elsewhere, combined with the realms of culture, literary imagination and consciousness. As I have been exploring in the course of this book, the framework of settler colonialism is adequate for understanding Zionism and the state of Israel not only at the material level, but also at the discursive and ideological ones. Here, I look in particular at Ben-Gurion's reading and use of the Old Testament, and in doing so take a fresh look at his well-publicized 'Bible project' of the 1950s. I ask whether Ben-Gurion's instinctive attitude to the Old Testament was in any obvious sense Jewish, or whether it might rather be understood as 'Protestant' and in this sense comparable with the attitudes of other settler societies. Here I treat the project as a whole – what Anita Shapira aptly terms 'Bibliomania' – as a pivotal foundation of Ben-Gurion's settler nation-state building, and as a route leading to the observations I shall make on the Nakba, on the first two decades of statehood, on Hebrew literature and settler literary imagination, and on what it is that constitutes settler consciousness. In the next and final chapter I shell concentrate on Ben-Gurion's biblical exegeses.

The term 'Bible' requires a clarifying remark. In English it stands for both the Old and New Testaments. 'Old' (pre-Christian) and 'New' obviously reiterate, in a misleadingly innocuous way, the Christian theological view. In Hebrew the Old Testament is known by an acronym,

*TaNaKH*, which comprises the letters TNK. Each letter signifies one of the three clusters of books of which the Old Testament consists: T stands for Torah, that is, the Law or Pentateuch; N stands for *Nebi'im*, or Prophets, both Minor and Major; K stands for *Ketubbim*, or Writings. Unless clearly stated otherwise, by Bible I mean the Hebrew Bible or Old Testament.

I should also point out that occasionally in the course of this chapter the reader will encounter quotations on which no commentary is offered, from Oz Shelach's 2003 remarkable novel, *Picnic Grounds: A Novel in Fragments*. Shelach was born in 1968 in West Jerusalem, and served in the military radio station as reporter and editor during the first Intifada. He left Israel for the US in 1998 and became non-Zionist. *Picnic Grounds* is his first novel, and one he wrote in English rather than Hebrew because, among other reasons, the latter 'has a built-in ideology that I am not comfortable with'.[1] Oz Shelach is the grandson of the poet Uriel Shelach, better known by his pen name Yonatan Ratosh, the founder of the previously discussed Hebrew Youth movement in the early 1940s, a phenomenon pejoratively called 'Canaanism' by its detractors.[2]

## Scholarly Pronouncements

Earlier in this study I considered Anita Shapira's series of essays on central issues relating to Zionism and Israel, such as the negation of exile and the Holocaust. Shapira has also written on the place of the Bible in Israeli collective identity and on its use in the process of nation-formation. Her pronouncement comprises a substantial essay on Ben-Gurion and the Bible, and a collection of texts on the Bible by various notable Zionist and Israeli figures, accompanied by a lengthy introduction by Shapira herself.[3] To recall, Shapira is significant at two intimately related levels: as a pre-eminent scholar of Zionist and Israeli history, the intrinsic position from which her scholarship is conceived makes her also a foremost Zionist Israeli thinker. I view her texts correspondingly: as insights into the use of the Bible; and as the reiteration and elaboration of Zionist Israeli ideology. The latter, I argue, are not just expressions of a nationalist ideology, but of a nationalist *settler* ideology.

In the introduction to the collection of texts and documents (*The Bible and Israeli Identity*), Shapira observes that one of the main things setting Zionism apart from other manifestations of secular Jewish nationalism in the late nineteenth century was the place of the Bible within its ideology. Such movements as the Autonomists or the Bundists rejected the Bible as a religious text that was incompatible with their sensibilities (she uses the adjective 'progressive' in quotation marks in relation to these movements, presumably to indicate that the attribution of this disposition to the Autonomists and Bundists is not a view she shares). 'Zionism, in contrast, took the Bible to its heart as the story of the formation of a nation, the annals of its glory in ancient times on its land, and the great spiritual creation which it had produced on it, and which it gave to the whole world. Before the Jews had a country, they had forged a country in their imagination that was the destiny of their desire'.[4] Her basic argument is that '[f]or almost a century the Bible was the foremost identity shaping text for the Jewish society that was being formed in the land of Israel'.[5]

Shapira recognizes, on the one hand, that the resort to the Bible in this particular fashion is not self-evident but constructed within a certain context that is essentially modern. Every national movement, she avers, needs

> a golden age in which the nation was created and its dispositions shaped, a primordial moment . . . The Bible accorded the tender Jewish nationalism the mythic-historical foundation for conceiving the consciousness of the nation's singularity in its bond to the land of the forefathers. In an almost obvious way it [the Bible] served as proof of the 'naturalness' of the Zionist solution for the Jewish problem.[6]

On the other hand, Shapira makes the Jews' turn to the Bible appear self-explanatory, something I shall later question. Relying on the notable Labour leader and Second Aliya's founding father Berl Katznelson, whose hefty biography she wrote, Shapira deduces that 'when the Jewish national movement appeared, the Bible was available as a source of legitimacy and genealogy. Thus the passage from the cultural following of the Bible as part of the cultural renaissance of the Haskalah [the so-called Jewish Enlightenment] to its acceptance as the cornerstone of the new Hebrew culture as well as of the emerging national awareness occurred, almost unnoticed, at the end of the nineteenth century'.[7]

Since the 1970s, Shapira observes, there has been a substantial decline in the exalted status of the Bible in Hebrew culture. She attributes this decline to the Bible's ideological appropriation by the nationalist-religious right and the movement of settlement in the Occupied Territories after 1967. This development brought about the alienation from the Bible of the socio-political circles that express what she calls humanist Zionism. The Bible assumed something of its previous centrality in Hebrew culture in the wake of the findings of the new Israeli archaeologists in the late 1980s and the 1990s (something to which I will return in the next chapter). In this context Shapira rightly notes that the refutation by these archaeologists of the Bible's validity as a historical source for the events to which it refers has rekindled attention to its national importance.[8] In the end, however, she ascribes to the decline in the Bible's prominence the same arguments that she uses in the context of the negation of exile, that is, the waning of archaeological Israeliness and the concomitant ascendancy of Jewishness, concluding that:

> The face-off between the extreme religious-nationalist views of Israeli identity and the extreme secular-Canaanite views is indicative of the long strides Israeli identity has made since the beginning of the [twentieth] century. The appropriation of the Bible by these two extremes brought upon the decline of its standing among the central groups in Israeli culture. The Bible's place in Israeli identity has been largely seized by the Shoah, as a source of identification with the Jewish people, with contemporary Jewish history and with the lessons of Jewish martyrdom. Instead of going to archaeological diggings, [Israeli] youth are now going on 'roots-finding expeditions' to Poland . . . Among those secular circles for whom the Bible was a cornerstone of the new Hebrew culture, a sense of absence and loss has persisted: is there a way to restore the Bible to the centre of Hebrew culture?[9]

Shapira's view of Ben-Gurion is clear-cut. At the outset his interest in the Bible or in Jewish history was limited at best, and he did not even share the fascination of his Second Aliya peers with the book; his rhetoric was devoid of biblical themes.

Ben-Gurion's ideological interventions consisted of virulent comments suffused with anti-Semitic overtones, and the familiar settler-colonial argument whereby the labour the Zionist settlers invested in the colonized land, and the way they bettered it, legitimize their claims to ownership.[10]

According to Shapira, the fundamental change in Ben-Gurion's attitude to the Bible had begun to occur in the late 1930s, and came to full fruition during the first decade of statehood, the 1950s. Ben-Gurion's awareness of the need for a historical foundation of the bond between nation and homeland was initially awakened by the explicit possibility of a Jewish state in the wake of the 1937 Peel Commission. Shapira quite perceptively bears in mind that Ben-Gurion was the ultimate political animal, and is therefore correct in emphasizing that in his testimony before the Peel Commission he coined the phrase 'the [British] Mandate is not our Bible, but rather the Bible is our mandate [to the land]'.[11] Then, in 1944, the prominent Labour Zionist leader Berl Katznelson died, and the division of labour between him and Ben-Gurion came to an end (Rabin once intimated that his father had told him that his generation's reaction to things had been conditioned by what Katznelson would say and what Ben-Gurion would do): the latter began to feel an obligation to fill the void that his ally's death had left in the sphere of ideological production.[12]

The change in Ben-Gurion's attitude to the Bible was complete by the time the 1948 war had been decided and the state came into being. It went hand in hand with the pivotal role he envisaged for the army in the process of nation-formation — especially in the integration of the immigrants from the Middle East and North Africa into veteran Zionist Israeli society — and in forging a national ethos. 'A hundred thousand Jews fighting for the freedom of their people — this is the greatest human opus of our time, which will inspire literature and art for generations to come', he said at a gathering of writers and artists.[13] Shapira interestingly conjectures that, within the higher echelons of the army itself, Ben-Gurion's ideological project, in which the Bible figured prominently, was meant to combat the seemingly irresistible lure of Communism and the Soviet Union for the high-ranking officers whose political orbit was the Marxist–Zionist Mapam party, and whose leader, Yaacov Chazan, coined the term 'the second motherland' for the USSR. Ben-Gurion's unyielding war against this orientation had begun with the dismantling of the Palmach, many of whose commanders came from kibbutzim affiliated with Mapam, admired the Red Army and looked up to Soviet Russia for guidance. He now continued with the purging of these officers, who had led the army in the 1948 war.[14] To Shapira's analysis should be added the fact that Ben-Gurion pacified Mapam by apportioning to its kibbutzim a share in the plunder of Palestinian land by the state during the 1950s.

The content of Ben-Gurion's approach to the Bible (which I shall examine more fully in the next chapter) was characterized, first of all, by a direct engagement with it, that is to say, by pushing aside the rich literature of commentary and law (the Talmud), which was the product of exile. Then there was what really attracted him to the Bible as distinguished from that which he used as propagandistic embellishment: the latter were sections of the book that are conventionally construed as universally moral messages, which Ben-Gurion deployed when he wished to promote such slogans as 'chosen people' and 'light unto the nations'.

Shapira is clear about that of which he was genuinely fond:

> His real interest in the Bible lay in concrete, worldly instances, such as the Jewish settlement in the land of Israel, Exodus, the great conquerors Joshua, David, Uzziah, the return to Zion under Cyrus and Darius. The historical facet of the Bible, which was meant to serve as conclusive evidence for the ancientness of Jews in the land, as distinguished from the reflective-philosophical facet, was foremost in his mind. Thus, already in 1949 he endorsed Jewish archaeology, 'all the conquests of which actualize our past and realize our historical continuity on the land'.[15]

As time went by Ben-Gurion's obsession with the Bible overwhelmingly informed his outlook. He rejected all other ideological options, including 'old' Zionist texts and views, as irrelevant to Israeli immigrants from Middle Eastern countries, as well as to the generation born into the state. Only the Bible mattered, and with it the archaeology that supposedly confirmed it and congealed the bond between the nation and its motherland.[16] As we have seen, Shapira argues that all the attempts to forge a biblical-archaeological, almost Canaanite, 'Israeliness' failed as soon as the society ceased being comprised exclusively of the early Zionist settlers and their offspring. Here too she concludes: 'Not the mythical past but the recent history was the source of their [the masses'] way of relating to the state. The Bible was important, but the bond [of the Israeli Jews] to the Jewish people emerged as more important'.[17]

### The Bible and Settler Consciousness, Past and Present

Shapira's texts rest upon a presupposition that makes them at the same time a scholarly contribution to the place of the Bible in Zionist Israeli history and culture, and a contribution to Zionist Israeli ideology. The presupposition that informs her work is that the resort to the Bible by Zionism and the state of Israel is Jewish in a natural and obvious way, and no demonstration of how exactly it is so is felt to be necessary. As a result, three related points are obscured: first, the 'return' to the Old Testament in this particular fashion is not organically or immanently Jewish, but Protestant, and has a history that is indebted to the Reformation; secondly, other settler societies (and colonial ventures more generally) have resorted to the Bible in comparable ways and for comparable purposes; and thirdly, the resort to the Bible is not just part of a national project, but part of a national-colonial, or national-settler, project, for in the putative land of Israel there existed not only fauna and flora, valleys, ravines and mountains, but also Arabs.

I will address this third observation here, and deal with the first two in the following chapter. Earlier, in Chapter Two, I presented the field of comparative settler colonialism and identified the fundamentals of hegemonic settler narratives, the ways in which settler nations narrate themselves. One such way is the assumption that the presence of indigenous people on the land that was transformed into a national patrimony through conquest and dispossession was inconsequential for the collective identity of the settler nation, for the contours of its history and the shape of its institutions. It must again be stressed that what is denied is not the mere presence of, or the conflict with, the indigenous people. Rather, what is denied and ignored is the fact that the presence of the indigenous people and the conflict-ridden history of the land that they and the settlers 'share' have any bearing whatever upon what the settler nation actually is: from a settler perspective 'who we are' is one thing; 'what we do to others' is quite another. I reiterate that this is one of the most salient – yet not infrequently unidentified – manifestations of the exclusionary or segregationist disposition embedded in white liberalism.

Shapira is cognizant of the Palestinian presence and of the 1948 Nakba. Few scholars on her side of the political spectrum are willing to engage in serious debate with the 1948 historians and other critical scholars. Her own observations often evince a critical distance, as indicated by her examination of the Bible as a source of national mythology and narrative. The point at which Shapira's approach becomes emblematic of liberal settlers is her inability, or refusal, to see that the place of the Bible in collective Israeli identity and the need to address the presence of natives upon the biblical land are two inseparable aspects of the same colonial history. It is, in other words, what might be termed the compartmentalization of the sacred and the profane that is so illustrative of this consciousness and imagination. The profane is the appropriate realm for discussing such things as the conflict, the treatment of the Palestinians, the attitudes to 'the Arab problem', and the image of the Other. The sacred is the temple where, among other things, 'we' discuss 'our' identity and 'our' obsession with 'our' Bible. That the infatuation with the Bible as a central – if contested – ingredient of Israeli identity, and the presence of natives of whose claims and presence the land must be emptied, actually might collapse into one history is inconceivable. And it is inconceivable precisely because of the depth to which this compartmentalization runs, because of the extent to which the ontological gap between 'who we are' (intrinsically, according to this discourse) and 'what we do' (extrinsically, according to the same discourse) is presupposed to be unbridgeable. However, the only facet of Jewish Israeli identity that is not fragmented is the agreement upon the purity and exclusivity of the state as Jewish, or at least as an unassailable Jewish majority; put differently, the only facet of Jewish Israeli identity that is not fragmented is the agreement upon the *sine qua non* principle of distancing the Palestinians from the collective and, where possible, from the land.

Some examples from Shapira's texts serve to illustrate this crucial point. One cluster of such examples concerns the way in which the pillars of the Second Aliya appropriated – or, in Zionist parlance, returned to – the homeland through the lens of the Bible. Thus, for instance,

> The turning point [of the shift from the *Haskalah*'s Bible to Zionism's Bible] lay in the passage from the Diaspora to the land of Israel: what in the Diaspora was an impressive, yearning text, which acts on the imagination, became in the land of Israel a link that attached the people to the country. The Bible's landscape ceased being the fruit of a writer's imagination . . . It became a concrete landscape, with which are associated toponyms, events and people. Mountains and hills, valleys and rivers, suddenly became a living actuality. The Second Aliya people 'discovered' the Bible's landscape.[18]

Or, in another instance:

> The Bible was for them [the Second Aliya settlers] a mediator between the country they had imagined and the country they encountered upon arrival. It helped the youngsters overcome the feeling of foreignness and acquire the feeling of home. Not infrequently they used to wander the width of the country, and identify places, and fauna and flora, according to the Bible. Beyond that, however, the Bible so to speak bridged hundreds of years and instilled the sense of direct continuity between the nation's patriarchs and their grandchildren and grand-grandchildren, who are trying to return and strike root in it [the homeland].[19]

It would be difficult to think of more emblematic, almost tangible, manifestations of settler imagination and consciousness. For Shapira the passages just cited are expressions of the formation of merely national territoriality, in which process the Bible was a pivotal tool in acquiring and concretizing the patrimony. This is precisely why she is not only a keen commentator on that process, but also a genuine product of it. What she is unable to see is that, while her Second Aliya protagonists were seeing the biblical flora and fauna, conquerors and kings, hills and valleys, they were at the same time *not* seeing Palestine. There could hardly be a better illustration of the settler construct of the empty land, the construct that cleanses the mind's eye of the indigenous people's presence. Furthermore, while Shapira realizes that the 'return' and direct appeal to the Bible is another form of the negation of exile (in its crude version, rather than the one created by the Jerusalem scholars),[20] she fails to notice that it is simultaneously the negation of Palestine. It is not only the experienced histories of the Jews outside the land of Israel that are being negated, but also the experienced histories of the land of Israel/Palestine as long as there is no sovereign Jewish possession of it. Thus, in the settler's resort to the Bible, the temporal return to the formative era of the nation on its soil, converges with the spatial return to reclaim the nation's ancestral soil.

Shapira's compartmentalization of 'the Palestinian problem', which is one thing, and the place of the Bible in 'our identity', which is quite another, reaches a climax with her discussion of the transition from the Second Aliya and the Mandatory period to the 1948 war and the 1950s. The specific allusions to that period exhibit the triumphant celebration of 1948 as Independence and the utter suppression of 1948 as Nakba, as if the two were not inextricably intertwined, as if the two were not one. After noting that as late as the mid 1940s the Bible barely figured in Ben-Gurion's world, she observes:

It seems that the War of Independence was for Ben-Gurion a watershed also in this respect: the encounter with the country's expanse, with sites whose toponyms are interlaced with the Bible's stories, sharpened Ben-Gurion's awareness of the Bible. The process of the country's conquest invoked associations with a mythological past. The Book of Joshua suddenly became actual: 'None of the Bible interpreters, Jews or Gentiles, in the middle ages or in our time, could have interpreted Joshua's chapters as did the adventures of the Israel Defence Forces last year [1948]', Ben-Gurion declared . . . Immediately after the war Ben-Gurion began to unearth the idea that the Bible's internalization, its understanding, unmediated reading, are given only to a people that possesses sovereignty over its country . . . Therefore, Ben-Gurion held that those who are uncircumcised and even Jews who do not know the Book's language or are not planted in the homeland's soil are incapable of understanding the Bible: 'Only a people that dwells in its homeland . . . will [be able to] read with a widely open eye and intuitive understanding the Book of Books, which was created in the very same country by the same people. Only a generation that renewed its independence in the immemorial homeland would grasp the spirit and soul of its predecessors, who had acted, fought, conquered, created, laboured, suffered, reflected, sung, loved, and prophesied within the boundaries of that homeland'.[21]

Shapira glosses over the fact that what 'sharpened Ben-Gurion's Bible awareness' in the wake of the 1948 war was not – indeed could not have been – only his encounter with biblical geography, but also the ethnic cleansing that had emptied the sacred geography of its indigenous inhabitants. How is it possible not to see that the 'sharpened Bible awareness', the settlement of Israeli youth and immigrants from Middle Eastern countries upon the razed Palestinian villages, the need Ben-Gurion felt to inculcate in both youth and immigrants a Bible-based national identity, the Bible-like renaming of dozens of settlements in the cleansed geography, the planting of vast expanses of pine forests (so that Palestine would look a bit more European and the pine trees would irrevocably suffocate the previous vegetation)[22] that covered for evermore the ruins of levelled Palestinian villages, are all one inextricable history? How many times should Ben-Gurion have reiterated the importance of the Book of Joshua in the 1950s – indeed reiterated his obsession with the Book of Joshua – before the inseparability of the Bible's place in 'who we are' and the cleansing 'we' perpetrated becomes apparent?

### One Afternoon

A professor of History from Bayit Va-Gan took his family for a picnic near Giv`at Shaul, formerly known as Deir Yassin. It was not too cold to be in the shade and not too warm to build a fire, so the professor passed on to his son camping skills he had acquired in the army. They arranged three square stones in a U, to block the wind, leaving access on the fourth side. They stacked broken branches on top of dry pine needles. He let his son put a match to it. Listening carefully, they heard a faint low hum from the curves of the winding highway, hidden from view by the trees. The professor did not talk of the village, origin of the stones. He did not talk of the village school, now a psychiatric hospital, on the other side of the hill. He imagined that he and his family were having a picnic, unrelated to the village, enjoying its grounds outside history.

(Oz Shelach, *Picnic Grounds*)

In a sense more striking are Shapira's allusions to the 1948 generation (*Dor Tashah*), also referred to as the Palmach generation: those who were born in Palestine, fought in the 1948 war, and within that discourse 'delivered' the state. She laments their alienation from the Bible after 1967, as a result of its appropriation by the religious right. For Shapira this represents the alienation from the Bible of a whole social stratum she calls humanist Zionism. She sets out the standpoint of this social grouping as follows:

> The romanticism of the land of the Bible was associated in the imag-
> ination of . . . the natives and disciples of the Land of Israel, the 1948
> generation, with the country's virginal image before the War of Inde-
> pendence: the cactus bushes, water wells, stone houses embedded in
> a mountain's slope, gown-wearing figures who as it were belonged
> to the days of the patriarchs, camel convoys, tents, and other images
> that were actually associated with the Arab Eretz-Israeli landscape,
> which they saw as a reflection of the patriarchs' way of life in the
> land of Canaan. Lo and behold, in all places reached by Israeli progress
> the cactus bushes and water wells have disappeared. In lieu of dirt
> paths concrete roads have been spread, and in lieu of camels moving
> at a leisurely pace cars are zooming by. In lieu of the stone houses
> that are one with the landscape, white houses with red tiled roofs tear
> up the harmony. Israeli modernization has made the marks of the
> biblical past disappear. Not by coincidence Amos Kenan, a writer of
> the 1948 generation and one of 'the Canaanites', cried out: 'the state
> killed the homeland for me'. Thus then, the renewed encounter with
> the land of the Bible after 1967 was one that gave birth to foreignness
> and did not rekindle the sense of mastery [*tehushat ha-adnut*] over the
> country, which was an integral part of the mental texture of the 1948
> generation.[23]

The passage is remarkable in many ways, not least because Shapira represents faithfully and eloquently the voices of the 1948 generation and the peace camp of the past three decades; the point is that for the most part she reproduces these voices rather than examining them critically. Thus goes unnoticed in Shapira's account the fact that the construction of Arab Palestine as a remnant of the Bible's patriarchs' era, through which 'the sense of mastery over the country' is obtained, is a typical settler – and more generally colonial – mechanism for emptying the designated home-land of its indigenous people as well as its history. Most crucially, what was earlier termed 'compartmentalization' by Shapira and the socio-political class she represents, now becomes almost schizophrenia. It might be recalled that those who cleansed Arab Palestine, who razed the rural landscape that included the stone houses so at one with it, the cactus bushes and water wells, are precisely those who have been lamenting the disappearance of Bible-like Palestine: the 1948 generation. However, the former catalogue of destruction, if not altogether denied, tends to be subsumed into the 'what we had to do to survive' narrative; the latter comes more generally under the heading of the 'Bible and our identity' narrative. As in Euclidian geometry, these two putatively separate narratives run parallel to one another, and never meet.

### Surprise

In the Yizr'ael Valley, formerly known as Marj Ibn-'Amer, where the inhabitants of almost two-thirds of the indigenous villages were allowed to keep their houses, though not their land, our friend, whose family was also allowed to stay in their house, told us how, as a youth, he used to go out and search for the sandal Jesus is said to have dropped in mid-leap from Nazareth to Mount Tabor. Our friend then took us to the nearby Museum of Bedouin Heritage, where a black goat-hair tent, a wooden plow, and various artifacts dating from the 1960s and 1970s are exhibited to illustrate for us, we surmised, how our ancient shepherd ancestors had lived. We thought it strange that there was no camel in the exhibit. Our friend was surprised to discover his old classmate from the regional high school seated inside the tent, pounding coffee beans with a traditional pestle and mortar. 'What are you doing here,' he asked, and his friend replied, 'I am the Sheikh on duty.'

(Oz Shelach, *Picnic Grounds*)

## 'The Spandau Never Conferred any Rights':[24]
## Literature and the End of 'Biblical' Arab Palestine

In developing my own argument I now move to something Shapira could and should have reminded herself of, namely S. Yizhar's 'The Story of Khirbat Hiz'ah', on the composition and reception of which she wrote a substantive essay.[25] (Nevertheless, this is precisely the point on settler consciousness and imagination I keep reiterating: the Zionist separation of the two themes – Bible and identity on the one hand, and the removal of the indigenes on the other – owes more to instinctive compartmentalization than to a research strategy.) However, in that essay Shapira came as close as ever to seeing, through Yizhar's eyes as well as her own, the inseparability of the Bible and 'who we are', and the ethnic cleansing 'we perpetrated'.

S. Yizhar is the pen name of Yizhar Smilansky. Yizhar was born in 1916 into a family of early settlers in the area of Rehovot, which was in Gershon Shafir's terminology a *moshava* or ethnic plantation colony, rather than a pure settlement colony like the kibbutz or moshav.[26] This meant that he grew up seeing and being among Arabs, without necessarily idealizing this togetherness. Shapira correctly observes that, because cohabitation of Jews and Arabs – in what he thought was 'a kind of harmony of limited rivalry' – was such a formative feature in Yizhar's childhood, '[t]he destruction of the Arab village was for him the destruction of the pre-state land of Israel'.[27] He resented the arrival of the post-1948 mass immigrations as much as he lamented the 'disappearance' of the Arabs, whose presence was crucial for the 'primordial landscape [*nof qedumim*], which was reminiscent of the Bible's stories'.[28] As a highly promising young author Yizhar was recruited by Mapai to counter the writers identified with the other labour parties. He served as a member of the Knesset in the 1950s and early 1960s, and together with Dayan and Peres followed Ben-Gurion out of Mapai in 1965 to join the latter's breakaway Rafi Party.

As an illustration of how intimately small-scale the early community of Zionist settlers had been, it is worth noting Yizhar's retrospective description of himself as standing 'between two founding uncles'. The paternal one, Moshe Smilansky of the First Aliya, was in contemporary parlance on the 'right', that is, on the non-labourite side of the early Yishuv. A wealthy grove-owner, he employed both Arabs and Jews, was a member of Brit Shalom, and a consistent adherent of the binational path. The maternal uncle, Yosef Weitz of the Second Aliya, was on the 'left', that is, he belonged to Hapoel Hatzair and later to Mapai. He was also a great 'redeemer of land' from the Arabs as director of the Jewish National Fund's land department, and as an arch-cleanser in the 1948 war and during the 1950s.[29]

I believe that Yizhar, who died in 2006, remains the greatest Hebrew author among those born in Palestine/Israel whose first language was Hebrew, as distinct from those who had emigrated from Europe like Bialik, Brenner and Agnon. Yizhar's aloofness and lack of marketing acumen or motivation have resulted in his relative anonymity in the past few decades, nationally and internationally. This anonymity, however, must not be allowed to hide the vast superiority of his literary gift over that of better-known and translated writers. Yizhar's expansive landscape descriptions as well as streams of consciousness have impelled modern

Hebrew prose to unsurpassed peaks. He fought in the 1948 war and in May 1949 wrote 'The Story of Khirbat Hiz`ah', which was published the following September by Sifriyat Poalim (literally 'The workers' library'), together with another 1948 war story, 'The Prisoner', in a book entitled *Khirbat Hiz`ah*.[30]

Khirbat Hiz`ah is the name of a generic Arab village, which was conquered without offering much resistance by an Israeli force. Many of the villagers had already been hiding in the surrounding hills, knowing what might await them. Following their pre-battle orders, the detachment's soldiers enter the village, begin to blow up the houses and raze the village, and drive out its inhabitants, mostly the elderly, women and children. It might be noted that the Arabic word *khirbah*, like the Hebrew *hurbah*, means a site of ruins. In 1964 the story became part of the high school curriculum, and in the late 1970s was worked into a television play, whose screening gave rise to huge controversy. Shapira's screening of that play in her seminars and the reactions of her students prompted her to write the essay on the story and its reception.[31]

Since Khirbat Hiz`ah was not the name 'of a village in reality', Shapira is anxious about whether in Yizhar's mind this was an exceptional case, like Deir Yassin, for which 'we' (the bearers of humanist Zionism) conveniently accuse the Revisionists – or whether this might in fact be the rule. What should be noticed in her way of crafting the anxiety is the refuge sought in patriotism's surrogate, the passive voice:

> Does 'The Story of Khirbat Hiz`ah' describe a particular case, single and unique, or is it a metaphor for the entire reality that was created in the wake of the War of Independence, when the country was emptied from its Arab inhabitants, whether they had gotten out of their own volition, of fear of war, had fled in the heat of battle, or were expelled by the IDF soldiers?[32]

Even when the perpetrators are identified as the IDF soldiers, they are not the subject of the sentence. Language could not have invented a better technique to circumvent the cognizance that 'we' who lamented the disappearance of the Bible-like – that is, Arab through the settler lens – Palestine and 'we' who made it disappear were actually the same 'we'.

However, Yizhar's narrator in 'The Story of Khirbat Hiz`ah' foregrounds this sameness. The description of the village and landscape before the 'battle' erupts is serenely beautiful, precisely that landscape which would soon be missed by the 1948 generation. The final part of the story, the destruction of the village and expulsion of its inhabitants, is the most powerful. It makes patently clear the fact that Khirbat Hiz`ah is a *lieu de mémoire* for unearthing Yizhar's experience of the erasing of rural Arab Palestine, and that Shapira's anxiety about whether this is an exception or a metaphor is not something that concerned him. His narrator implicitly likens himself to the prophet Jeremiah, bemoaning and consoling another human convoy on its way to exile: 'I wondered where the echo came from. The echo of footsteps made by other exiles. Dim, distant, almost legendary, but angry, like the prophet of Anathoth,[33] rolling like distant and threatening thunder, foreboding darkness, coming from beyond, a terrifying echo. I could stand it no more'.[34]

The evocation of Jeremiah is the climax of a stream of consciousness. As if anticipating Amnon Raz-Krakotzkin's call almost half a century later to use exile not only to justify sovereignty but also to identify with the victims of that sovereignty, Yizhar indeed remembers. Looking at the humiliated Palestinians as, huddling in the Israeli lorries, they resign themselves to their world falling apart, his narrator has an epiphany:

Something suddenly became clear to me in a flash. At once I saw everything in a new, a clearer light – Exile. This is Exile. Exile is like this. This is what Exile looks like . . . I had never been in the Diaspora – I said to myself – I had never understood what it was . . . but they had spoken to me about it, told me stories about it, taught me and kept on dinning into my ears, wherever I turned, in books and newspapers, everywhere: Exile. They had played on every fibre of my being. It had come to me, it seemed, with my mother's milk. What really had we done here today?[35]

An elegiac farewell then follows:

I passed among them [Palestinians], among those who were weeping loudly, those who were grinding their teeth in silence, those who mourned their lot and the loss of their belongings, those who were objecting to their fate and those who were accepting it mutely, those who despised themselves and their shame, and those who were already planning to adapt themselves somehow, those who were weeping for fields that would soon be waste, and those who were silent because they were tired, gnawed at by hunger and fear. I longed to discover among all these people even one with a burning anger who would forge within himself such wrath that he would cry out, as if he were being strangled, to the God of ages, from the lorries that were leading them to exile.[36]

Yizhar's awareness of the cleansing's fullness is quite remarkable. In one of the story's best-known passages, the narrator's outrage is sensed by one of his comrades, Moyshe, who 'reassures' him: 'To Hirbet, what's-its-name, immigrants will be coming. Are you listening? And they'll take this land and they'll till it and everything here will be fine'.[37] Another epiphany:

> Of course, what then? Why not? Why did I not think of that at first? Our Hirbet Hiz`ah. There will be problems of housing and absorption. Hurrah, we shall build houses and absorb immigrants, and then we shall build a grocer's shop, we shall put up a school, perhaps also a synagogue. There will be political parties here. They will debate about a lot of things. They will plough fields and sow and reap and work wonders. Long live Jewish Hiz`ah! Who will dream that once there was a place called Hirbet Hiz`ah which we removed and to which we then moved in? We came, we shelled, we burned, we blew up, we pushed and we shoved and we sent into exile.[38]

### Yizhar's Inspiration

Yizhar's literary elegy of pre-1948 Palestine and his rage at its erasure have inspired a thorough and poetic equivalent in the scholarly domain by Meron Benvenisti.[39] Like Yizhar, Benvenisti did not experience until adulthood the pure settlement colonies (kibbutz and moshav). Born in 1934, he grew up in the affluent Jerusalem neighbourhood of Rehavia, and spent time in an ethnic colony, Pardess Hannah, some 25 miles south of Haifa, near the coast. In the 1970s he was deputy mayor of Jerusalem, under Teddy Kollek. The latter's Viennese charm and moderate appearance should not conceal his pivotal role in Judaizing occupied East Jerusalem, and making the lives of the city's Arab inhabitants increasingly unbearable. Benvenisti was one of the first observers to argue, from a progressive position, that the post-1967 geopolitical layout of the land created by the occupation had become irreversible, in the sense that the separation of the two communities into two ethnically homogeneous states was impossible, and perhaps also undesirable.

In retrospect, Benvenisti's book *Sacred Landscape* may be said to have begun in the expeditions throughout Mandatory Palestine on which he accompanied his father. The latter, a cartographer of note, took upon himself with zeal 'to draw a Hebrew map of the land, a renewed title deed. In his naïve or self-serving way, he genuinely believed that he was doing so peaceably, that there was enough room in the country for everybody. And he was convinced beyond any shadow of a doubt that it was his absolute right to reclaim his ancestral patrimony.'[40]

The appeal of Benvenisti's personal account lies not only in its candour, but also in the absence therein of the bleeding-heart, dilemma-ridden, crocodile-tear syndrome that one invariably encounters among Israeli liberals. In a matter-of-fact tone he notes of his father that '[t]he Arabs did not take him seriously at first, and when they realized the danger, it was too late. His map triumphed, and I, a dutiful son, was left with the heavy burden of the fruits of victory.' He then reveals the dialectical result of the father's mission: 'I often reflected on the fact that my father, by taking me on his trips and hoping to instil in me a love for our Hebrew homeland, had imprinted in my memory the very landscape he wished to replace'.[41] This latent irony – or dialectic – became manifest only after 1967, when Benvenisti began to meet the Palestinians who had been expelled in 1948. It is impossible not to notice the Yizharian state of mind, in which one laments the erasure for which one is responsible: 'Suddenly I saw before my eyes the geography of my childhood, and I had the feeling that the men talking to me were my brothers – a feeling of sharing, of affinity. I could not share their sense of loss, but I could and did share deep nostalgia mixed with pain for the lost landscape and a nagging feeling of pain, for my triumph had been their catastrophe.'[42]

Yizharian too is the complete and instinctive feeling that Palestine is not only a homeland, but a binational homeland, in its history and geography:

It wasn't my human landscape, nor was it the physical space that my people created; they were its destroyers. But the pain and the sorrow were deep and genuine, and with them arose the compelling need to commemorate the vanished landscape, both because it was a human creation and because it is my homeland, a land that never forgets any of her sons and daughters. I cannot envisage my homeland without Arabs, and perhaps my late father, who taught me to read maps and study history, was right in his naïve belief that there is enough space, physical and historical, for Jews and Arabs in their shared homeland.[43]

To put Benvenisti's study in the language of the present discussion, what he does is to illuminate, especially through cartography and toponymy, the horrific fate of the indigenous land as the settlers triumph, as the settler colony becomes a settler nation-state. As early as July 1949, Ben-Gurion assembled a small group of scholarly experts – cartographers, archaeologists and historians – and appointed them the Negev Names Committee, an initiative that drew on similar bodies in existence during the Mandatory period. The Negev and Arava (the strip of desert plateau from the Dead Sea down to the Red Sea) constituted more than half of the new state's area. The committee's mission was, to quote the official formulation, 'to assign Hebrew names to all the places – mountains, valleys, springs, roads, and so on – in the Negev region'.[44] To remove any lingering doubts over such a process, the same notion was conveyed in a typically ruthless fashion in Ben-Gurion's letter to the chair of the Negev Names Committee: 'We are obliged to remove the Arabic names for reasons of state. Just as we do not recognize the Arabs' political proprietorship of the land, so also do we not recognize their spiritual proprietorship and their names.'[45]

Upon completion of its assigned task in 1950, the committee was assigned another one, of a similar mould. Over the decade that followed it laboured hard to accomplish the 'flawless Hebrew map' (mappah 'Ivrit le-lo pegam).[46] The same Hebraization would be meted out to the Occupied Territories after 1967. As an interesting instance of settler mapping using as its starting point metropolitan colonial cartography, it may be pointed out that the basic map (of 1:125,000 scale) employed by the Negev Names Committee had been prepared by two quintessential colonial figures, Herbert Horatio Kitchener and T. E. Lawrence, just before the First World War. The Bible also connected the two cartographies: the formal reason for the British surveys, under the auspices of the Palestine Exploration Fund, was presented as the study of the land of the Bible and the reconstruction of the whereabouts of the Children of Israel in the desert.[4]

Benvenisti offers a perceptive and erudite account of the manner in which the Hebraization was carried out, especially in two sections entitled 'New, Biblical World' and 'Judaization of Hills and Valleys'.[48] The techniques and criteria varied, but it is evident that in the vast majority of cases the Hebrew names deliberately misleadingly and shrewdly convey Bible-like ancientness, but have no real geographical and/or historical relation to the sites they signify.[49] As Benvenisti is so well aware, this was made possible because the landscape was literally emptied, and became the apotheosis of settler cartographic imagination. To use his chillingly apt term, the terrain before the eyes of the map-making and name-giving committees was 'a blank slate'.[50] By the end of the 1950s the preparation of the 'flawless Hebrew map', its transformation into a 'biblical' landscape, was complete. Erased Palestine was buried not only physically under new Jewish settlements and newly planted forests, but also under a new cartographic discourse. Thus in a meeting of the governmental naming committee of 16 August 1959 the chairman, Avraham Biran, reassuringly noted: 'We have ascertained that no traces are left [again the passive voice becomes the scoundrel's refuge] of the abandoned villages. Since the locations to which the committee gave the name of "mounds" [*iyyim*] no longer exist "on the ground", their names are hereby abolished'.[51] The oneness of the Nakba and the Bible-inspired 'flawless Hebrew map' could not have been made more concrete than in the person of Yosef Weitz, Yizhar's maternal uncle mentioned earlier. After the cleansing he became 'one of the most active members of the committee'.[52]

### The Road to Jerusalem
We made the mountains evergreen – like Switzerland, we liked to say, just like the snowy-peaked mountains we liked to assemble with our children – without, naturally, the snow, or the lake (we had to constantly remind ourselves: this is not Switzerland). All along the road to Jerusalem we planted over the past. We covered slopefuls of terraces with pines. The pining hillsides, we dotted with red-tile-roofed houses, but our trees grew sick and stood bare and gray, fell one over the other, dry, and burned for three smoky summer days. An army officer whose regiment happened to have depopulated several villages along what was to become the forested road to Jerusalem, and who later became a construction contactor in the same region said, in response to the fire, that these tress had done their job, it was now property developers' time.
(Oz Shelach, *Picnic Grounds*)

The creation of the Bible-like 'flawless Hebrew map' also entailed an act of settler ingratitude towards the indigenous society, which illustrates the historical distinctness of colonialism in general, and especially of settler colonialism, from other types of invasion, conquest and settlement. The Arab-Islamic conquest of Palestine in 638 CE did not engender the erasure of existing toponymic layers. In fact, '[t]he irony was that the Jews were returning to their ancient homeland, but were able to identify the places there only because the people who had inhabited them . . . had preserved their names. Had the Arabs not adhered closely to the ancient Hebrew–Aramaic names, the Zionists would not have been capable of reproducing a Hebrew map'.[53] The map's creation also shows that the foundational myth of the negation of exile and return to the land of Israel excludes from history not only the Jews as long as they were in exile but also Palestine (with its various dwellers) as long as it was not under Jewish sovereignty:

[T]hey [Zionist settlers] rewarded the Arabs by erasing the Arabic names from the map: not only were names of biblical origin Hebraized, so was virtually every Arabic name, even if no ancient Hebrew name had preceded it. This was an act of sheer ingratitude; the destruction and eradication of all record of the 2,000 years of their absence from the land and of the civilization that had existed there in their stead, only because of their desire to make direct contact with their own ancient heritage.[54]

The Bible-like 'flawless Hebrew map' brings us back to the relations between metropole and settler colonialism. It has already been remarked that British cartography in Palestine proved very useful for the British colonial successors; however, that cartography did in fact preserve the indigenous toponymy that the latter map erased and replaced. Benvenisti offers an interesting hypothetical colonial moment:

> Herbert Horatio Kitchener, were he to rise from the dead, would surely be saddened by the loss of old names that he endured such hardships to collect. But the legendary empire builder – son of an English colonist in Ireland – would have understood the logic of the Israeli bureaucratic campaign. After all, that is precisely how the British had behaved in every region they chose to colonize – from Ireland in the seventeenth century to the plateaus of Kenya in the early years of the twentieth; in Canada, Australia, and Rhodesia. In every one of these British colonies, topographical maps were plotted, and upon them were printed official names: a mixture of English names, names chosen by colonists and soldiers, and local 'native' names, altered so as 'to be pronounceable in a civilized language'. The natives, who had been 'resettled', adapted themselves to the new map, to the point that they themselves often forgot the original names.[55]

Benvenisti's perception and imagination are constantly inspired by Yizhar's. Generally, the inspiration is the extent to which the erasure of pre-1948 Arab Palestine is clearly the creation of an incomplete homeland, a homeland that is defined more by what it is not – by absence – than by what it is. I shall shortly return to the complexities of this erasure. However, possibly the most striking observation in Benvenisti's book is the likeness he draws between Yizhar and the great Palestinian poet Mahmoud Darwish, whom he compares as two native sons of the land.[56] He concludes as follows:

> When all is said and done, as Mahmoud Darwish puts it, 'The geography within history is stronger than the history within geography.' And S. Yizhar's comment complements the thought: 'The land, in its depths,

does not forget. There, within it . . . suddenly, at different times, one can hear it growling an unforgetting silence, unable also to forget even when it has already been ploughed and has already brought forth fair, new crops. Something within it knows and does not forget, cannot forget.' Only one who knows how to listen to the unforgetting silence of this agonized land, this land 'from which we begin and to which we return' – Jews and Arabs alike – only that person is worthy of calling it homeland.[57]

## A Sobering Note à la Gramsci

In a mercilessly acute essay, which looks back at Yizhar's work of the 1950s, Yitzhak Laor questions the extent to which Yizhar was an oppositional figure:

Yizhar Smilansky was a member of Knesset representing the ruling party precisely in the years during which what had been destroyed was being buried. On the ruins of Palestine-Eretz Israel (which was both binational and more rural) grows with much cruelty a sharp Israeli statism [mamlakhtiyyut], and Yizhar is located, politically, amidst its mouthpieces (Mapai and later even Rafi) and perhaps his literary vantage point – had he not found himself as a Mapai and Rafi man – could have produced a tragic work. This sorrow, however, the Yizharian sorrow, does not become a tragic sorrow because Yizhar does not permit himself real heresy. He remains within the confines of the dominant ideology . . . and it a priori disallows any heresy, any real questioning of its values and institutions.[58]

Born in 1948, Laor has become one of the most notable Hebrew writers in the past three decades. He is a marvellous, rather Brechtian, poet, who also indefatigably keeps producing Hebrew translations of Brecht's poems. He has published novels, collected stories, and a play (*Ephraim Returns to the Army* [Hebrew], a title that plays on Yizhar's first published work of 1938, *Ephraim Returns to the Alfalfa*), which was first banned by government censors and then successfully challenged in court. Laor is possibly the most radical critic of Hebrew literature and Israeli culture, as is amply manifested in his dozens of *Haaretz* articles and in the masterful 1995 collection of essays on Hebrew literature and Hebrew literary criticism, from which the above citation was taken (the suggestive Hebrew title of which is *We Write Thee Homeland*, a pun on a line from a famous pioneer song, 'We Love Thee Homeland'). Laor's work has been translated in Europe, especially in Germany, but hardly at all into

English, even though he has written for the *Guardian, London Review of Books* and *New Left Review*.

I would argue that Laor's critical writing is meaningfully and instinctively underlain by a Gramscian understanding of hegemony and ideology. The book on Hebrew literature as a whole and the essay on Yizhar in particular are rich in theoretical insights which are brought to bear on the subject matter in a substantive way. Thus, for instance, the author's indebtedness to Benedict Anderson or Jacques Lacan is both evident and explicit. Gramsci, however, is not cited, even though Laor is steeped in the Marxist tradition in general and the Italian left's in particular. And yet one of the main themes of his scholarly and literary work is the incessant search for what he calls 'the self-evidently obvious' (*ha-muvan me-elav*): that which is so powerfully and effectively constructed and inculcated that it looks ontologically pre-existing, objectively already there. Laor seeks to expose these constructs for what they are, that is, to historicize them; and to destroy them, sometimes violently and grotesquely, in such novels as *A People, Food Fit for Kings* (1993) and *Ecce Homo* (2002). This activity is so fundamentally conditioned by Gramsci's writing on hegemony and has become Laor's modus operandi to such a degree that he does not make explicit the connection with Gramsci's work. Laor's essay on Yizhar contrasts the latter's writing on pre-1948 Palestine and its eradication, which is at the very least partly oppositional, with his almost simultaneous decision to become – the use of Gramsci's term is mine rather than Laor's – one of the organic intellectuals who rendered service to Ben-Gurion's regime.

The text of Yizhar that Laor reads is not 'The Story of Khirbat Hiz`ah' but the massive novel *Days of Ziklag*, published in 1958. It tells the story of a hill, where troops engage in a murderous battle against the Egyptian army. Ziklag itself is a location mentioned in the Bible, and is said to have been not far from Beer-Sheba. In the allocation of the land to the tribes after the Israelite conquest, Ziklag appears once as the patrimony of Judah (Joshua 15:31) and then as that of Benjamin (Joshua 19:5). Later it is reported that when David had fled from Saul's wrath to the Philistine King Achish, the latter gave him Ziklag as a base, 'wherefore Ziklag pertaineth unto the kings of Judah unto this day' (1 Samuel 27:6). As we shall see later,[59] these territorial allocations were probably invented to justify the irredentist ambitions of King Josiah in the second half of the seventh century BCE.

In a recent article, Gideon Nevo of the Ben-Gurion Research Centre at Sde Boker examines the minutely detailed realism of Yizhar's massive novel.[60] *Days of Ziklag* referred to an actual battle, which Yizhar invested an inordinate effort to research, fought to gain control of Khirbat Machaz, a hill close to the dirt road connecting Beer-Sheba and Fallujah (some 40 miles to the north-west of Beer-Sheba), and which lasted from 30 September to 7 October 1948. The confrontation occurred during a crucial period in the larger strategic face-off over control of the Negev, during which a Palmach brigade, Yiftach, was dispatched south to relieve another Palmach brigade, the Negev, which was in dire need of relief. It is worth mentioning that one of the junior officers on the Egyptian side of the see-saw battle over Khirbal Machaz was Gamal Abdul Nasser, who would later find himself besieged in what the Israelis called the Fallujah Pocket.

Yizhar's text adhered with striking fidelity to the documentary evidence he had gathered on the unfolding battle, both in terms of land-scape and military sites, and in his construction of the characters. Such were his descriptive powers that researchers have been able to identify the precise site of the battle, Khirbat Machaz, which *Days of Ziklag* never mentions, as well as the real people who took part in it but are given different names by Yizhar, almost one by one. Yizhar drew on a variety of sources: accounts composed by the battalion's intelligence officer and by the intelligence officer of the whole Yiftach Brigade; an article on the battle, published in the official IDF magazine in 1952; a pertinent chapter from the official *Palmach Book*; and the memorial for the fallen in the 1948 war from Kibbutz Beit Hashita (at the foot of the Gilboa Mountain in the eastern Jezreel Valley), many of whose members fought in the Negev and Yiftach brigades of the Palmach.[61] The 'memorial for the fallen' genre is an important commemorative text in Israeli culture, in which each individual soldier is paid tribute through photographs and notes written by his family and friends. Yizhar used it for the depiction of his characters.

For the pre-1977 Israeli governing class, *Days of Ziklag* was a formative text, and Laor announces at the outset of his essay both his appreciation of Yizhar's aesthetic achievement and his view that ultimately the text is hegemonic rather than oppositional:

> More than anything else, *Days of Ziklag* is a monument to the 1948 war . . . It has nothing but this: the desire to write the concluding epic account of that war. It contains protest against resignation to the war, and it has a rather sober grasp of the conflict . . . Yizhar's story has horrific descriptions of death, of bloodshed, of burning to death, of hysteria in battle, of fear and rage, and it has an almost cosmic love for the Negev, and touching descriptions of youth, and themes of horror

and the rule of the present tense and the love of life, but beyond all those things this piece erected a narrated memorial [*andartah mesupperet*] for the Palmach warriors of 1948.[62]

It is to them and for them and about them, the first human fruits of the Zionist pre-1948 colony, who were born in Palestine, fought and won the 1948 war, cleansed Palestine of Arabs and then lamented the disappearance of Bible-like Palestine that *Days of Ziklag* was written. In Gramsci's terms, Laor shows how Yizhar creates the hegemonic Sabra (prickly pear), who is the total sum of the characters who are 'proper' natives. In this way, the unit defending Ziklag undergoes a sort of literary purgatory, and all those who fought there but were not part of the labour Zionist Palmach elite are excluded from the tightly knit group of comrades and the book's narrative: the Mizrahis, Rahamim and Ovadia, the exilic Avrum and Jakobson, and the German Jewish artillery men.[63]

As for the nature of this hegemonic Sabra, Laor's examination could have benefited from a seminal study of the 1948 generation by one of the first critical sociologists in Israeli academia, the late Yonatan Shapiro. In his path-breaking, and alas hitherto not translated, 'Elite without Successors', Shapiro convincingly argues that the Second and Third Aliya leaders of labour Zionism and then of the Israeli state formed a genuine political elite from the 1930s to the 1970s that was hegemonic (Ben-Gurion, Katznelson and Tabenkin are the most notable figures from the Second Aliya, Levi Eshkol and Golda Meir from the Third Aliya), both materially and ideologically. As such, however, the elite also gave birth to a politically sterile generation, one that was ostracized by the authoritarian founding fathers. The 1948 generation docilely accepted the hegemonic ideology without being able to reinvigorate it, let alone rebel against it; a generation which was not at all political. This generation (Allon, Dayan and Rabin stand out) excelled in carrying out policies and tasks set by the ruling political elite. According to Shapiro, this generation's mindset was that of the bureaucratic institutions, of which the modern army is a typical example. As soon as the vestiges of the old hegemonic elite had disappeared (first Eshkol and then Golda Meir) and the revered 1948 generation of necessity had to become politically independent, rather than being appointed to positions by the old elite, it swiftly lost power to Likud; irrevocably, it also lost hegemony.[64]

There is in this respect a double eclipse: Laor makes no use of Shapiro, and Shapiro made no use of Yizhar, who not only wrote about and for the Palmach 1948 generation, but was himself – to some extent at least – part of it. As early as 1953, before *Days of Ziklag* and referring to the more oppositional war stories, the critic David Canaani noticed that 'with all the rebelliousness of Yizhar's protagonists . . . they never rise against the main thing. It [the main thing] – is beyond argument and dispute, an axiom that requires no evidence, the [Zionist] project is what marks the farthest limit to rebellion'.[65] Laor extends this observation to *Ziklag*. 'Yizhar's great talent and his limitations', he says, 'ought to be read within the confines of the ruling ideology . . . Zionism. His limitations are connected, first and foremost, to his obedient relations with this ideology. It may be that he does not like whole parts of the ideology, to put it mildly, but this entire beautiful story [*Ziklag*] is devoid of a single attempt to rebel against "the project".'[66]

By 1958, with Ben-Gurion's statist regime in full control, the very slight oppositional buds of the war period and its immediate aftermath (questions in the Knesset on the cleansing, Yizhar's war stories) were suppressed until the 1980s. As we shall see, Yizhar would visit and revisit 1948, but with his burgeoning political career under Ben-Gurion in the late 1950s the rage of 'Khirbat Hiz'ah', albeit politically sterile, gave way to the wholesome beauty and purity of the tender boys, the sacrificial youth of 1948. Here is Laor's Gramscian insight:

> If there is a location at which it is possible to observe how 'a state' thinks, if there is a location through which it is possible to examine how the state is written and how it writes its annals and its subjects' biography, and their representation even before they are born, that location must exist somewhere in the distance between 'Khirbat Hiz'ah' [1949] and *Days of Ziklag* [1958].[67]

What sort of pure Sabra boys does Yizhar forge in *Ziklag*, after they had been distinguished from the other protagonists (Mizrahim, German Jews and so forth), and after they had finished shelling, burning, blowing up, pushing and shoving and sending into exile at Khirbat Hiz'ah? Addressing the Hebrew Writers' Association in April 1958, just before the publication of *Ziklag*, Yizhar reassured his audience that out of the grim reality of the war 'occasionally originates that spring of unalloyed youth who wish to believe [*yesh umeqqer oto ma'ayyan shel zokh ne'urim ha-rotzim leha'amin*]'.[68] It is here especially that Laor's literary analysis could have been complemented by Shapiro's political sociology. The most telling point in this pathos-ridden promise is not that the pure altruistic boys would like to believe, but that what the boys would like to believe in is a void that has no substance.

One way to fill this void is to assume that the boys want to believe in whatever the current task of Ben-Gurion's *mamlakhtiyyut* happened to be. The other way is to realize that in fact its not being filled is precisely the point: the desire to believe is itself a permanent state of being that is not meant to lead to political action or even to a systematic political position. Laor perceives how politically sterile this generation is:

> The central point is that there really are no big differences among the soldiers, except for the difference between those who are 'ours' (the handsome ones, who are mobilised for the project wholeheartedly) and those who are 'not ours' (who are not handsome and also complain too much). Furthermore: since there really are no differences among the characters in relation to the one action in which they all partake, the narrator is forced to load upon them the differences in 'ideational' debates, and from this originate the famous differences between Chibby (who is wicked regarding ideas) and Benny, or Pinny. Each is characterised through something that is utterly unrelated to the action itself: Barzilay quotes from the Bible, and Benny is a Marxist and so forth. It would be superfluous to say that these differences have no significance whatever other than [within] the acts of discussion [themselves].[69]

What this means is that the Marxist world view versus quotations from the Bible, for instance, are utterly vacuous as opposing positions on anything, and they certainly do not lead to differing political action. It is just there, because the boys need something to believe in.

## The Problem of S. Yizhar's Temporality

Laor's substantial insight notwithstanding, I propose that there is nevertheless something singular about Yizhar, something which I believe Benvenisti and Laor himself also sense. Like no other Hebrew prose writer, Yizhar's sorrow over the disappearance of pre-1948 Palestine is ultimately intricate and contradictory, for it is both settler-colonial and binational; and it is colonial in a way that is not, nor can be, ethnically exclusive. Yizhar is unable to mourn his friends, the sacrificial not-yet-men boys, without inevitably mourning the erasure of rural (significantly, never urban) Arab Palestine. As a writer, Yizhar is also incapable of temporally extricating himself from pre-1948 Palestine; the war is as far as he can go. Partly, of course, Yizhar's singularity lies in his literary prowess, but it also lies in the different colonial experience that distinguished the *moshava* (ethnic plantation colony) from the kibbutz and moshav (pure settlement colonies).

Laor is aware of this when he cites Uri Shoham, a particularly irate critic of Yizhar's *oeuvre* from the kibbutz movement, who 'despite his high sensitivity for the text, is incapable, because of his ideological position, of grasping the tragic motive, which is perhaps characteristic of *moshavas'* people and their world that largely perished in '48'.[70] Explaining why Yizhar's hostility towards the collective, which made Shoham fume, could not develop into a tragic rendering of the destruction of pre-1948 rural Palestine and the death of his comrades in 1948, Laor then lists the elements that comprised this unrealized tragic potential: 'the death of the boys, the destruction of the villages, the "anarchy" of the *moshava* in contrast to the "rational organization" of the kibbutz, or the state, the demise of Palestine-Eretz Israel, [and] the growth of the new Israeli statism [*mamlakhtiyyut*]'.[71]

I would add an atemporal view of Yizhar to Laor's temporal, even developmental, interpretation. As we have seen above, Laor concentrates on the transformation of Yizhar the person and the author between 'Khirbat Hiz`ah' (1949) and *Ziklag* (1958), from a critic – however ineffectual – of the cleansing into one of the hegemony's organic intellectuals. Laor also uses Yizhar's transformation as a synecdoche for the process that Israel as a whole underwent in the 1950s. This interpretation of Yizhar is indeed compelling, but it must be complemented by an understanding of him in which there is no clear and irrevocable temporal development in his thought, but rather an unending vacillation – not unlike that of Rahel Varnhagen between parvenu and pariah in Arendt's study of her life. Yizhar's constant – and temporally debilitating – oscillation is between the lamentation of rural Arab Palestine and bitter resentment of the ideological project that made it possible, and the unwavering affection for, and attachment to, his comrades, especially those who had died in the 1948 war, most notably his maternal cousin Yehiam Weitz. Spatially, this oscillation is manifested in his remembrance of the binational landscape of the southern *moshavas* (Rehovot, Ekron and Gederah) on the one hand, and on the other his cosmic descriptions of the Negev's humbling awesomeness.

In his article, referred to above, on Yizhar's documentary reconstruction in *Ziklag* Nevo is correct in observing that critics have misunderstood what Yizhar was trying to do. In Nevo's view, Yitzhar was in a Platonic fashion aiming to achieve an asymptotic – infinitely almost there, but never quite – sense of reality through literary portrayal.[72] It was his attempt to hold on to that element of his vanished world – the world of the 1948 comrades and the Negev – and never let it go. The Yizharian hold is not necessarily motivated by fondness of the collective's embrace or of camaraderie; rather, the attempt to hold on to the experience of the 1948 comrades was simply the last grasp of that vanishing world.

Yizhar's most forceful and tangible expression of this inability to move away from and beyond this element of the now eradicated world, to the extent that his marvellous gift as raconteur inscribes in the reader's mind the feeling that Yizhar's narrator is physically bogged down by his attachment to that vanished world, is the relatively unnoticed (though not missed by Benvenisti's keen eye) 'A Story That Has Not Begun' ('Sippur she-lo Hitchil').[73] Literary critics and translators render the title as 'A story that did not begin', thereby missing the present perfect tense that the English offers but the Hebrew lacks, a tense especially appropriate for conveying the congruity of title, content and form. 'A Story That Has Not Begun' concludes Yizhar's 1963 collection *Stories of the Plain*, after which he would not write for three decades. The story never begins precisely because the narrator is bogged down. He wanders, accompanied by an interlocutor (perhaps his son, or grandson), in the landscape that is no more. Every time he attempts to begin his tale a variation of twin themes re-emerges and halts it. In place of this tale (which we never get to hear), this becomes the story. The twin themes are the death of Yizhar's older brother in a motorcycle crash with his Arab friend sitting behind him, when excessively speeding through the binational landscape of the *moshava*/Arab village; and the erased, buried and covered landscape of rural Arab Palestine.

'The Story That Has Not Begun' consists of five sub-stories. The title of the fifth, 'Another Sermon or Two and I Shall Hush', anticipates Yizhar's ensuing silence. The second, 'The Silence of the Villages', in a way picks up where 'Khirbat Hiz`ah' left off. In bringing the latter (the story and the village) to a closure, Yizhar invokes God's descent to earth in order to inspect the severity of Sodom and Gomorrah's sinfulness (Genesis 18:21):

> All around silence fell, and soon it would descend upon the final scene, and when silence would blanket everything and no man would disturb the tranquillity, and there would be a quiet murmuring beyond the silence – then God would come down to the valley to see if the deeds that were done matched the cries [*lir'ot haketza`aqatah* – the elegant economy of the Hebrew is unmatched by the English in this case] . . .[74]

In 'The Silence of the Villages' Yizhar's narrator, rather than God, comes down to the valley not so much to inspect, but desperately to hold onto, and never relinquish, 'the final scene'.

The narrator keeps lamenting to his interlocutor the landscape's disappearance as an existential state of mind, recalling with intimate knowledge and familiarity what had been, avoiding sentimentalized portrayals of what had been buried, and − with irony so biting that he himself struggles to bear it − commenting on the rationally modernized, technological reality that is his world's disinheritance. 'I am but one seeing man', he falters, 'and his heart aches too much to see. Here is a place that has left its place and is not. Neither enemies here, nor non-enemies, just a story of that which happened in past tense. Human lives, with a possible moral, for anyone who seeks it.'[75] Now, everything is

> outwardly painted anew. New names also given to all. More civilized of course, and from the Bible too. They covered and disinherited him on his way to exile, and may there be peace upon Israel. Masmiyye has become *Mashmia-Shalom* [Peace-Announcer], Qastina I don't know, perhaps *Kheshet-Te'ena* [Fig-Bow] and more probably *Ka'as veTina* [Anger-and-Resentment]. Let's not continue.[76]

The echoes of this renaming in Benvenisti's study are all too evident.

The paralysing indecision that is so emblematic of Yizhar's position − ironic distance from what has become of his vanished world, aching love for what has been erased and indignant resentment of the erasure, yet obedience to Ben-Gurion's *mamlakhtiyyut* and passionate affection for the tender sacrificial boys of 1948 − is poetically articulated by another of his narrators in a different story, 'First Sermon', in the same collection. Yizhar again makes use of the episode in Genesis that closed 'Khirbat Hiz'ah': 'I too, like many of the good ones, am walking, my eyes in my nape, looking backwards with yearnings of glee, as a sort of Lot's wife whose heart craved what had ended'.[77] The key to the meaning of the metaphor lies in the linguistic precision of the reference: not to Lot's wife herself, but to 'a sort of Lot's wife. She disobeyed God, 'rebelled', turned her head back to look at what had been Sodom and Gomorrah, and was duly punished ('But his wife looked back from behind him, and she became a pillar of salt', Genesis 19:26). The most Yizhar could summon was 'my eyes in my nape', but he could neither disobey nor rebel, just walk away − sad, critical and even resentful − and lament.

### Here Come the Gatekeepers of Humanist Zionism

Let us now see how the intelligentsia of the Israeli labour movement and peace camp, the entity Shapira and others call 'humanist Zionism', has responded to Yizhar.

### An Original
A Professor of Philosophy inhabited a large old house in Baqa`a, which had all the usual properties of large old houses in Jerusalem: stone walls, arched ceilings, an original, still-bearing walnut tree, an original underground cistern, and a well on which the garden was maintained in dry years. His reputation as a broad thinker was amplified by a proven ability to out-argue his colleagues in their own fields. For a while children were allowed to play in the garden, but in the summer of 1967 the professor followed the example of the famous millionaire S and ordered a tall stone wall to be constructed around the house and garden, to prevent the original inhabitants of the house from visiting.

(Oz Shelach, *Picnic Grounds*)

Typical of liberal intellectuals in settler nations, this intelligentsia's deeply ingrained anxiety is foregrounded in their views of Yizhar. They are concerned that he might be confusing the compartment of settler–native relations with the clearly demarcated sense of 'our identity', that he might risk collapsing cleansing and identity into one, thereby spoiling for them the reassuring warmth (or chill) of the impregnable fraternity of the settler nation. They permit Yizhar neither contradiction nor complexity, and deny him genuine sorrow for the burial of Mandatory Palestine's vaguely binational possibilities, deprive him of the right to be bitter and indignant concerning the erasure and the disappearance from the landscape of natives who are excluded from appearing on 'our' stage, if only as objects of elegiac literature. It is always and without exception about 'us', 'our' dilemmas, doubts, soul searching, struggles with nature, and so on and so forth ad nauseam. The centrality of this denial for a proper understanding of what liberal settler consciousness is all about cannot be overemphasized. Settler–indigenous relations are not merely important for comprehending Yizhar's literature; in a sense they *are* Yizhar's literature, even when he writes exclusively on the settler community, just like George Fredrickson's analogous insistence that the history of white supremacy in a sense *is* American and South African history.[78] What is fundamentally being denied and circumvented by the liberal commentators on Yizhar's writing is precisely that inextricability.

Dan Miron, formerly of the Hebrew University and now Leonard Kaye Professor of Hebrew and Comparative Literature at Columbia, is one of the two most influential scholars of Hebrew literature and a recipient of the state-awarded Israel Prize for his contribution to the subject. Miron wrote an overview of Yizhar's work, which concluded an English collection of a few of Yizhar's stories.[79] One of the main ways in which the hegemony's voice emasculates and depoliticizes Yizhar is the extrication of his work from any historically concrete context, and the concomitant presentation of its content as absolutely abstract or universal, in the sense that its temporality and spatiality are immaterial. Miron exemplifies this approach by interpreting Yizhar's *oeuvre* as an abstract and ahistorical (meaningless, I think) struggle between individuality, or the freedom of the individual, and the imposing will of the collective. In Miron's Yizhar, the most concrete reference we get is A. D. Gordon, whose heritage gives precedence to the collective body. A. D. Gordon (see Chapter Two) was the chief ideologue and father figure of the Second Aliya settlers, especially of its Hapoel Hatzair members, one of whom was Yizhar's father. For Miron there are neither Arabs nor Zionist settlers in Yizhar's work, nor any concrete landscape. And when the individual protagonist resists the collective's strictures, we never know what these are and what the resistance to them comprises. According to Miron, Yizhar's work is ultimately nothing but allegory. Some of his forced observations in this regard verge on the embarrassing, such as his comment on the text discussed above, 'A Story That Has Not Begun', in which:

> Yizhar goes almost to the point of ceremonious splendour in describing a motorcycle dash, which ends in collision with a train and death. This is the most extreme embodiment, in Yizhar's work, of the tension between human collective existence (the train) and the individual liberated in the momentum of his freedom (the motorcyclist). Here there is not a hint of possible compromise; and as to submission, we are led to understand that death, especially that which comes during a dash of freedom, is better.[80]

That the dashing motorcyclist was Yizhar's older brother, that behind him on the dashing motorcycle was his Arab friend (who doesn't exist even as an abstract figure in Miron's interpretation), that the motorcycle was speeding through the concrete landscape shared by the *moshava* and the Arab village doesn't matter at all to Miron. They are all stripped of concrete historical and political – even personal – significance, as an abstract allegory of the individual's search for freedom from the collective. Yizhar, it would seem, has ceased being Yizhar and has become an Anglo-Saxon liberal philosopher.

A Yizhar critic whose influence on Hebrew literary criticism in general outstrips Miron's was another recipient of the Israel Prize, Gershon Shaked of the Hebrew University who, like Yizhar, died in 2006. Shaked was the most prolific scholar of Hebrew literature, and determined its commonly accepted periodization (the 1948 generation of writers, the state generation and so forth) as well as the dominant methods of analysing it. He was also one of the main voices of response to the non-Zionist critiques of the 1990s. The most notable response was his somewhat hysterical essay against Laor's 1995 *Narratives with no Natives*, a text with which this chapter is in constant dialogue.[81]

In an essay on Yizhar's late autobiographical novella of 1992, *Mikdamot* ('Preliminaries'), which is situated against a period ranging from 1916 to the end of the 1920s, Shaked also resorts to an interpretation based on the individual's struggle with the imposing collective, and on the individual's guilt for being aloof from the collective, for looking at it from an extrinsic vantage point with a kind of ethnographic curiosity.[82] And although he, like Miron, ultimately dismisses the specifically historical foundation of Yizhar's literature, his way of doing so is different. Shaked does not ignore the significance for Yizhar of the colonial struggle between settlers and indigenous people (though he reduces this significance to a bare minimum); however, he empties it of any concrete consequence, indemnifies Yizhar against possible charges of being too critical of the collective, and while doing so reveals his own colonial sensibilities. Shaked addresses one of the most powerful passages in the novella, in which Yizhar wonders whether the whole settler project is not ultimately ephemeral because of its foreignness to the environment, and its aggression against the land and its indigenous dwellers and cultivators.[83] It is a truly compelling text, at once a statement on the settler-colonial situation and the modernizing project in general, and an allusion to a very concrete settler-colonial situation occurring in a particular environment in which, for instance, erased villages are named ('Today there is no Mansurah and you shall not find it').

Shaked robs the passage of its force by attributing to it, again, a purely allegorical meaning. Yizhar/the child narrator is unforgiving of civilization undoing nature, and of the settlers taking away 'the land's innocence and virginity'. This wrecks 'the dream of eternal childhood of the naïve child, in whose life eternal childhood . . . is bound with the assimilation into the completeness that exists in complete [sic] nature alone'.[84] In this interpretation, Yizhar's ostensible resentment of 'the settling Jews' is also allegorical. He is not really resentful of the destruction of an actual natural and human landscape by particular settlers with a nameable ideology. Rather, he is indignant allegorically: they represent the element that facilitated the 'swallowing up' of nature by civilization, in the struggle between nature and civilization, which is beyond or without history.

For Shaked, 'Yizhar's only drama is the drama between the settlers and the land'.[85] Later, when recalling that perhaps the land came with a rather inconvenient burden, his colonial mindset becomes manifest. 'As an adult', Shaked opines, '. . . [Yizhar] thinks that man's struggle with nature is futile and the land (and the Arab world is part of that land) would inevitably overcome those who disturb it.'[86] Shaked's fidelity to his calling as one of the project's gatekeepers does not permit him to be content with neutering Yizhar through the allegorical strategy. To remove any lingering doubts, he has to end by stating that Yizhar is a good Zionist and all the rest is secondary at best.

Thus Shaked avers that these yearnings

> for the destruction of the 'Zionist' entity and for the return of the Israeli landscape to the bosom of great mother nature come out of an extraordinary libidinal power, a power which shows that that under-current, which appears chiefly in the reflections of the narrator from the vantage point of narrative-time, is not part of the foundational layer of the novella, which is suffused and overflowing with love for Eretz Israel and love for the founding fathers.[87]

And he concludes: 'Beyond all the ideologies, chronicles and histories Yizhar celebrates in this novella the remembrance of his childhood and erects in its honour and memory – a beautiful Eretz Israel of words. Fiction overwhelmed reality here, and as in Goethe's work the *Dichtung* (fiction) is more interesting, complex and rich than the *Warheit* (reality)'.[88]

## Literature and Propaganda

Neither Miron nor Shaked, nor for that matter any other commentator, has posed any serious challenge to Amos Oz's self-righteous achievement of bringing Yizhar back into the reassuring bosom of the Bible, of 'our' collective identity – who we are, and how wonderful we must be, for we have dilemmas. Oz published his brief 1978 essay on Yizhar in the Histadrut daily, *Davar*, as an intervention in the heated debate that resulted in the education minister postponing the broadcast of the dramatization of 'Khirbat Hiz`ah' (in the late 1970s there was one, state-owned, television channel). When eventually it was aired, Oz decided that he too had the right 'to say two or three things about Khirbat Hiz`ah', and immediately proceeded to announce, that 'on this occasion perhaps something must also be said about ourselves at this time', as if all that had already been said and almost all that would be said thenceforth was about anything other than 'ourselves'.[89] This text is worth examining, for, in addition to being an outstanding example of the typical settler-nationalist drive to remove the colonial conflict with the indigenous people from the parameters of 'our identity', it also illustrates Oz's remarkable propagandist prowess, his ability to compose all his texts so that they can be drawn on as speeches to diverse audiences, from potential donors to Israeli universities, to the American chapter of Peace Now, or as conversations with guilt-ridden liberal German intellectuals.

Oz plays on the rhetoric of hysteria that dominated this debate, and which spoke of the 'mortal danger' of screening 'Khirbat Hiz`ah'. The first danger he describes is 'the welding line':

S. Yizhar's story does not deal with the Jewish–Arab conflict. In this respect the foaming-at-the-mouth [commentators] of all sorts have got it wrong. There are no Arab characters in 'Khirbat Hiz`ah', but just hovering sketches, pencil drawings, illustrative devices. The story's subject is not the Israeli–Arab conflict but, doubly unfortunate, the Israel-Israel conflict. And more precisely: a conflict between one boy-warrior of ours and his divided soul. This pure-eyed boy, exquisite product of the education for the values of Judaism, Zionism and Humanism, such a milk-and-honey soul, absorbed and inter-nalized well the stunningly beautiful values of heroism and masculinity and Maccabis and whirlwind conquerors of Canaan and Samson and Jephthah the Gileadite and Trumpeldor, and he also absorbed well the no less stunningly beautiful values, the tears of the dispossessed, the sorrow of exile, the ten righteous thanks to whom even Sodom and Gomorrah are spared, and the ethics of the prophets, and the equality of human worth etc.; from the ideational crème de la crème and from the moral vitamins.

And then, it befell upon this precious boy that in the heat of battle, in the gruelling temperatures of the operation of expelling the inhabitants of Khirbat Hiz`ah, suddenly a wedge was driven along the 'welding line' of the aforementioned value-systems . . . between Joshua son of Nun and Isaiah son of Amoz, between love of man and love of homeland, and in short: between good and good. And the soul of the precious boy in the story grew tortured and he did not know what ought to be done.[90]

Struck by a part of the passage just quoted, Laor remarks in disbelief: 'Just like that. S. Yizhar was not S. Yizhar. He was Amos Oz.'[91] The immense political importance of Amos Oz cannot be overstated. He is the most translated Hebrew author, probably the best known internationally, and his autobiographical novel *A Story of Love and Darkness* (first published in Hebrew in 2002 and in English two years later) has been hailed nationally and internationally for its literary accomplishment and political courage. In closing this chapter I would like to linger on Oz precisely because of this importance, and because of the enigmatic contrast between the acclaim he has garnered, and the quality of his writing. After all, however far we might wish to take the cliché that art is a matter of taste, it is hard to argue with Perry Anderson's succinctly apt observation, that what 'a figure like Amos Oz' offers is a 'mixture of machismo and schmaltz'.[92] Uncannily (and equally aptly), Laor entitled the pertinent chapter in his book 'The Sex Life of the Security Forces: On the Corporality of the Handsome and Military Israeli in Amos Oz'.[93]

What is transparently clear to Laor and Anderson is not at all evident to others, for example Nadine Gordimer.[94] It is not clear even to a critical scholar like Rachel Feldhay-Brenner.[95] The book Feldhay-Brenner composed on Israeli literature, in which works by both Israeli Arabs and Israeli Jews are discussed together in defiance of ethnic exclusion, is based on the premise that the proper context for its interpretation is that of a settler-colonial situation, for which she resorts to Gershon Shafir, whose work I have discussed above.[96] Feldhay-Brenner identifies the ways in which dissenting literature has been neutralized and incorporated into the canon by its gatekeepers.[97] She then breaks down the wall of ethno-cultural essentialism by creating various pairings of Israeli Arab and Jewish authors and texts, such as Yizhar's 'Khirbat Hiz`ah' and Emile Habibi's *Pessoptimist*, or A. B. Yehoshua's 'Facing the Forests' and Atallah Mansour's *In a New Light*.

Although daring and at times insightful, there is a serious tension in Feldhay-Brenner's argument between her own dissenting view of the context on the one hand, and on the other who and what she considers to be dissenting Israeli Jewish writers and texts – depoliticized and incorporated by the canon's gatekeepers. In addition to Yizhar, Feldhay-Brenner chooses as dissenting voices Oz, Yehoshua and David Grossman (the trio who had publicly endorsed the 2006 Israeli onslaught against Lebanon, only to call for its halt a few weeks later, presumably when some audiences that matter to them in the West were beginning to feel ill at ease with the wanton destruction). She is aware of some observers who persuasively demonstrate why they should not be accorded such a dissenting status, and her attempt to argue otherwise is unsuccessful. Disingenuously in my view, Feldhay-Brenner avoids openly dealing with Laor's insistence that

Oz and Yehoshua have not just been 'canonized' by the hegemonic ideology's critics but that their writing and explicit politics have always been part and parcel of that ideology. Relegating his study to an endnote, she notes that Laor's 'relentless offensive, absence of critical methodology, and repetitive argumentation detract from the credibility of his interpretation'. She is however unable to tackle – let alone refute – it.[98]

Of the three central writers mentioned by Feldhay-Brenner, Oz is the most effective contributor to the Israeli project in its labour Zionism guise, in terms of both literature and propaganda. However problematic Yehoshua's 1964 'Facing the Forests' might be as oppositional literature, Oz could have never written a text of this kind, nor could he have engaged with the plight of the Palestinians as Grossman did in his *The Yellow Wind* (1988) and *Sleeping on a Wire* (1993). Oz as a cultural and political phenomenon, and as part of what is defined above as the state generation (authors who matured into an already existing state as distinguished from the 1948 generation), offers yet another angle from which to appreciate the transformation of a colony of settlers into a settler nation-state.

There is a perfect congruity between Oz's contributions to Zionist Israeli ideology as a novelist on the one hand, and as a non-fiction writer and public speaker on the other. In his 1968 novel *My Michael*, Oz gives expression to settler-colonial fantasies and obsessions by speaking through a female narrator, Hannah Gonen. Many commentators have remarked upon Gonen's fantasy and fear of violent and orgiastic sex with the Arab twins Khalil and Aziz, who had been her childhood friends. Oz's imagination did not stop with that rather frequent trope in colonial culture. His female protagonist not only has fantasies about wild sex with orientals but, later in the novel, these fantasies are predicated upon imagining *herself* an oriental woman. And not just an oriental woman in general, but an oriental Israeli Jewish one. Laor's keen eye spots this crucial passage, which others did not – or chose not to – see:

> The poet Saul leaned over to intoxicate me with his moustache and his warm odor. Rahamim Rahamimov the handsome taxi driver came too and clasped me round the waist like a wild man . . . Hands pressed my body. Kneaded. Pounded. Probed. I laughed and screamed with all my strength. Soundlessly. The soldiers thronged and closed round me in their mottled battle dress. A furious masculine smell exuded from them in waves. I was all theirs. *I was Yvonne Azulai. Yvonne Azulai, the opposite of Hannah Gonen.* I was cold. Flooded. [Emphasis added.][99]

For the uninitiated into Israeli culture it should be clarified that Yvonne Azulai signifies a North African – Mizrahi – Jewish woman, most probably a Moroccan one. It would not be a huge interpretative leap to suggest that in order to experience the sexual fantasy described above, Hannah Gonen, the respectable white woman, must become a Moroccan slut.

The construction of native Israeli identity of the state period, in perfect contrast to the exilic Jew within Israel itself – in the same kibbutz in fact – occurs in *Perfect Peace* (1984), to my mind the best novel Oz has written, especially in his insights on the relations between the greater-than-life founding fathers and their offspring. The dichotomous pair of Yonatan Lifshitz, the handsome and heroic – and tortured, they always are – Israeli, and Azariah Gitlin, whose exilic persona is an anathema to the social texture of the kibbutz's prodigal sons, is the main site for the construction of the post-1948 Israeli. The fact that Gitlin covets Yonatan's wife, the fragile and dysfunctional Rimona, and shares her with him, evinces the extent of Oz's anxiety about the invasion of Israeliness by foreign bodies, and about the imminent disappearance of this Israeliness. In this sense Oz gives voice to and amplifies the existential concern of the social stratum that is his most faithful domestic readership.[100]

Oz's anxiety, and its political and aesthetic expression, peak in *Black Box* (1987). Ilana and her son Boaz had have been left by another prodigal Israeli, Dr Alexander Gideon, a brilliant scholar teaching in an American university. Alienated from Israel, he returns to command an armoured battalion in the 1973 war. In the meantime Ilana Gideon has become Ilana Sommo, marrying Michael, a right-wing religious Mizrahi Jew ('And you let that *thing* fuck you every night?'[101] the disgusted Boaz asks her). As in the case of Yvonne Azulai, his French first name, Michel-Henry, is constantly invoked, so the general Mizrahi rubric can again be narrowed down to North African and most probably Moroccan. In *Black Box*, Oz's anxiety has become more aggressive, for in response to Sommo Oz creates Boaz, whom his mother describes to his father thus: 'And in the meantime, like *a genetic time bomb*, Boaz is now sixteen, six foot three and still growing, a bitter, wild boy whose hatred and loneliness have invested him with astonishing physical strength [emphasis added].'[102]

The demise of Ashkenazi labour Zionist Israeliness in the 1977 elections and the eruption of the Ashkenazi–Mizrahi clash in the 1981 elections gave rise to much introspection on the losing side, typical of which were pieces that appeared in a liberal journal, *Politika*. In a thoughtful essay in that journal the perceptive literary scholar Ariel Hirschfeld examined the expression of these political and social changes in the 1980s literature of notable Israeli novelists like Oz, A. B. Yehoshua and Yehoshua Kenaz. Hirschfeld observes that in *Black Box*

> Oz continues where he left off in *Perfect Peace*, constructing a long and very horrific decadence of Ashkenaziness. It is true that Alexander in *Black Box* extrcates himself from Eretz Israel, his wife, his son and his land, and a Sephardi man, Michel-Henry Sommo, takes his place . . . However, Oz transforms Alexander's story into one of aristocratic decadence reminiscent of the last days of the Romanovs. It is difficult not to hear princely Russian echoes in terms of the only son, the successor, of Volodya Gudonsky, Alexander, and Oz endows his family with a huge fortune that is spread throughout 'labourite Eretz Israel' as kind of *latifundia*. Luckily he doesn't have peasants for sale. The exiled prince deals with 'fanaticism' in a scientific spiritual fashion . . . and examines from afar the rise of a right-wing Sephardiness, cunning as a fox, small as a mole, sexual as a billy-goat, exilic as a Jew.
>
> The pages of this book are seething with pressed, racist and domineering hatred for the Sephardi, together with admiration of his might and great fear of him. Oz is unwilling to disengage from the ancient proportions of Mother Israel's uniform portrait, and he is therefore forced to accord Ashkenaziness poetic and aristocratic, supposedly elegiac, [counter]proportions, in order to balance the mythological demonism arising from the Sephardi side. And he cannot bring up this 'Sephardi' without preparing for him, in the shape of Boaz, Alexander's son, 'a genetic time bomb' that will destroy him. Boaz, very tall, extremely muscular, duly fair-haired, fills up the pits and granaries, brings the figures of Elik and Uri [the quintessential native Sabras enshrined in the novels of Moshe Shamir of the 1948 generation] into their indubitable fascist sublimation.[103]

In the following issue of *Politika*, though they praised the rest of the text, Oz's friends A. B. Yehoshua and Yehoshua Kenaz promptly rebuked Hirschfeld for the passage on *Black Box*. They ended by noting: 'It is puzzling to us how Ariel Hirschfeld sees in the hippy, anarchic, somewhat discombobulated figure of Boaz fascist elements. Is there perhaps the new use of a conventional term?' Hirschfeld's unyielding reply reminded the two authors of choice features of Boaz's characterization and asked them not to pretend innocence. He then stated: 'The pre-Reason domain, in which *Black Box*'s plot actually occurs, in which Boaz's pre-Reason figure arises, including the apotheosis of his corporality, is the very domain in which quite ordinary fascist thinking occurs, without any correction of the term [being required].'[104] It might be added that there is something unfair, even malicious, in framing a North African religious Israeli Jew as the quintessential settler activist in one of the most dreadful settlements, Qiryat Arba near Hebron, as if the whole post-1967 settlement project was not Ashkenazi first and foremost, from Allon the Palmachnik and his friend Rabbi Moshe Levinger, through Shimon Peres and Sharon to the veteran Ashkenazi leadership of Gush Emunim, the Brooklynite cadres of settlers and the American and Australian donors and patrons.

*Black Box* is the expression of Oz's literary participation in the project to create the hegemonic Israeli of the state period, what Hirschfeld so poignantly calls the fascist sublimation of Elik and Uri. The last expression of it is Yoel, the guilt-ridden and tortured Mossad agent in *To Know a Woman* (1989), who is nonetheless as potent as both Yonatan Lifshitz and Boaz Gideon and, moreover, makes this latent potency manifest with the aid of a knowledgeable non-Jewish woman, in a demonstration of what Jerry Seinfeld has memorably termed the *shiksappeal*. How anyone can see dissent in this literature, aesthetically and/or politically, is puzzling.

Then there is Oz's subtle propagandizing. In a 2006 review essay, Laor has taken apart the widely acclaimed autobiographical novel *A Story of Love and Darkness*, insightfully explaining the ways in which this text is so appealing to the white liberal strata in Israel, Europe and the US in the age of the war on terror, and also exposing some important differences between the Hebrew and English editions, published two years apart.[105] In the section of the book that recounts the establishment of the state there is a passage that presents the 1948 war in a putatively descriptive, matter-of-fact register. This extract, with which Laor commences his essay, also caught my eye when I was reading the novel; like Laor, I was aghast at the cynical manipulation of this account by one of the Israeli peace camp's most notable spokespersons:

> All the Jewish settlements that were captured by the Arabs in the War of Independence, without exception, were razed to the ground, and their Jewish inhabitants were murdered or taken captive or escaped, but the Arab armies did not allow any of the survivors to return after the war. The Arabs implemented a more complete 'ethnic cleansing' in the territories they conquered than the Jews did: hundreds of thousands of Arabs fled or were driven out from the territory of the State of Israel in that war, but a hundred thousand remained, whereas there were no Jews at all in the West Bank or the Gaza Strip under Jordanian and Egyptian rule. Not one. The settlements were obliterated, and the synagogues and cemeteries were razed to the ground.[106]

'As the expert propagandist that he is', Laor notes, 'Amos Oz is well aware of how much more powerful "absolute ethnic cleansing" is than "partial ethnic cleansing". He therefore takes great pains to describe minutely the "extermination of the Jewish nation" in the territories behind the Green Line, without specifying numbers. It is an absolute we're talking about – a veritable genocide, one after which no traces remain of the exterminated nation'.[107] The absence of numbers for Jews is of course paralleled by numbers given for the expelled Arabs, a hundred thousand of whom stayed within Israel. The inevitable inference must be that the Jews committed something far less genocidal than the Arabs, whose deeds, framing this passage, constitute an 'absolute' atrocity. 'This of course is an old trick of salesmanship', Laor remarks. On the one side there is the removal of Kfar Darom by the Egyptian Army, and that of Gush Etzion and the Old City of Jerusalem by the Jordanian Arab Legion, on the other the Palestinians are not even specifically mentioned, simply lumped together with all the Arabs. The obvious must be stated:

> The ruin of the Palestinian people, four hundred of whose villages were laid waste, who were reduced to numerically negligent, racially discriminated against and poverty-stricken minorities in their own cities, hundreds of thousands of whom lost all they possessed, including the chance of decent human existence, this ongoing destruction, which continued while Oz wrote his book, is turned in the citation above into a not so terrible event, with many far worse than itself, our own fate for instance. Let us be clear. Oz has never employed the term 'ethnic cleansing' in relation to the conduct of the IDF in 1948. Now he does so only in order to say: if it happened, another was perpetrated that was far worse, a real one.[108]

## Conclusion: *Siah lohamim* ('Soldiers' Talk')

I would propose that Oz's career as a mobilized propagandist began after the 1967 war, when he became one of the chief editors of the book *Siah lohamim* ('Soldiers' talk'), and that this undertaking had significant impact on the type of handsome military Israeli that would figure so prominently in his novels. I develop this contention with the aid of a hitherto unpublished PhD thesis by Alon Gan of Tel Aviv University on the identity of the kibbutzim's second generation, in which an entire chapter reconstructs how *Siah lohamim* came into being. From a rather sympathetic perspective, Gan also analyses the book's text itself and, most interestingly, the editorial process. *Siah lohamim* is at once closely related to Oz; it also moves beyond him.[109]

In 1967 the kibbutzim were still grouped into different movements affiliated to the various labour parties. Three weeks after the war Dov Tzamir, the secretary of the Kevutzot and Kibbutzim Union close to Mapai, summoned to party headquarters two individuals: Avraham Shapira of Kibbutz Jezreel, founding editor since 1960 of the journal *Shdemot* ('Fields'), a prestigious literary and ideological organ, and Amos Oz, then teaching literature in Kibbutz Hulda, and already known as a rising young author following the publication of his 1965 *Where the Jackals Howl*. One of the main themes they discussed was the strange silence, coupled with perceived sadness, which typified the behaviour of soldiers from the kibbutzim since the war had ended, in stark contrast to the general civilian atmosphere of euphoria, jubilation and insatiable, cult-like consumption of war albums. The initial attempts by Oz and Shapira to make the demobilized soldiers talk were unsuccessful. This cloak of silence was shed one night in Kevutzot Geva and, following some preparatory work in other kibbutzim, the floodgates opened. What had been called 'the mute generation' or 'the silent generation' began to talk. 'We pushed the cassette player's buttons and the lava erupted', Shapira recalled.[110]

Such was the spread of the ritual of the cassette player's button being pushed and the tough prickly Sabras revealing the sensitivity and complexity of their inner selves, that by October 1967 the first edition of *Siah lohamim*, comprising 12,000 copies, was distributed in the kibbutzim for internal consumption only. Information on the book of conversations with kibbutz soldiers soon leaked to the media and became a cause célèbre. It was printed in five editions and sold 95,000 copies within Israel alone. It was promptly translated into English, Spanish, French, German, Swedish and Yiddish. Radio producers and playwrights queued to use it, as did American television networks. *Siah lohamim* became one of the most effective propaganda tools in Israeli history, creating the image of the handsome, dilemma-ridden and existentially soul-searching Israeli soldier, the horrific oxymoron of 'the purity of arms', and the unfounded notion of an exalted Jewish morality. It elicited some of the most self-righteous and self-congratulatory pronouncements from some of the most self-righteous and self-congratulatory figures. '*Siah lohamim* . . . is a sacred book and we are fortunate to have been blessed with such sons', declared Golda Meir in 1968; '*Siah lohamim* is a very big book, very big, it's a shame that no one has seen to its translation to all the languages in the world [this seems like a rhetorical gesture by Wiesel rather than a reference to actual translations] . . . an enormous testimony, truly enormous', Elie Wiesel proclaimed a year later. Eliyahu Ben Horin, director-general of the foreign office, reported on the extensive use made of the book throughout the world. Shapira received an emotional letter from Abraham Holtz in the US, in which the latter recounted how in a well-attended gathering Rabin (the then ambassador) and Wiesel had read passages from *Siah lohamim* 'in order to present the Israeli soldier's profile'.[111]

Oz and *Siah lohamim* were made for each other. His imprint is recognizable in the text as well as in the process that produced it and, in its turn, much of the text anticipates Oz's literature and public activity. In it, there are views expressed by Oz himself and others against the celebratory mood and, more importantly, against the messianic eruptions, land-greed and land-of-Israel fetishism. This caution was however apolitical, sterile and self-indulgent. At a time when the ethnic cleansing of that particular war – in the Latrun area, in the Old City of Jerusalem – was still fresh and signs of the budding occupation perceptible, Oz chose to play a central role in an involuted and self-indulgent discourse of 'us', how 'we' feel about this, that and the other, about the validity of 'our values', and how much of a dilemma 'we' are in, and so on and so forth. It is not difficult to identify in his work in *Siah lohamim* the germ of Oz's later intervention in the debate over Yizhar and the broadcast of 'Khirbat Hiz`ah'.

A typical example of Oz's *Siah lohamim* work is the preparatory circular the editors sent to potential interlocutors in the kibbutzim, which, Gan discovered, had been formulated by Oz. This circular is an anthropologist's dream come true, for it conveys so well the mood and register of this self-absorption that made *Siah lohamim* such an attractive tool to Golda Meir, Wiesel and Rabin:

> Neither a victory album nor a collection of heroic tales, but episodes of hearkening, conversation and observation: if we can express in words the silences between the words, this will be a booklet of silences . . . To be right and strong – we haven't been trained for that . . . We seek to make speak some members of 'the mute generation' which withstood the fire of this war. Not about the warriors, not in their name, but from their mouth . . . not accounts of 'what I did' but ones of 'what I went through' . . . We shall try to give idiom to our inner thoughts. We shall listen to ourselves and our comrades.[112]

The same is true of the testimonies' title. Oz had suggested calling the collection 'To the limits of silence', its title in the first internal announcements. Later the editorial group took the suggestion of Abba Kovner (a poet, leader of partisans in the Vilna area, and member of Kibbutz

Ein Hachoresh) to name the book 'Soldiers' talk', but conceded to Oz the subtitle 'Episodes of hearkening and observation'. The announcement resembled the circular Oz had written earlier, and included statements like 'The gist of the collection – episodes of observation and listening to ourselves'.[113]

Finally, we have what is revealed by Gan's meticulous research. Among other analyses, Gan compares the original transcriptions prepared from the cassettes with the published text, thereby reconstructing the editorial process. For the purpose of the present discussion I leave aside the few external interventions by the state censor and his military counterpart. What the text's editors themselves, Oz and Shapira, did comprised two interventions: one was the omission of entire conversations as if they had not occurred at all; the other was the manipulation of and tampering with statements and conversations that were included, significantly altering their meaning in the process.

The first kind of editorial intervention, omission, is striking because the omitted material yields certain similarities between some of the kibbutzniks and the post-1967 national religious settlers such as the passion for the Greater Land of Israel. By extension it illustrates a point I made earlier on the extent to which Oz's decision in *Black Box* to make the North African religious Michel-Henry Sommo his quintessential settler is self-serving and disingenuous. One wonders why in creating the character he was not inspired by the Ashkenazi settlers with whom he had interacted closely in the process of making *Siah lohamim*.

One of the omitted transcriptions was an account of an interesting conversation between the editors and the Sarig family in Kibbutz Beit Hashita, the same kibbutz whose commemorative literature Yizhar had consulted for *Days of Ziklag*. Beit Hashita belonged to the extreme nationalist Hakibbutz Hameuchad movement, which consistently opposed all the partition plans from the 1937 Peel Commission onwards, and firmly adhered to the vision of the Greater Eretz Israel. It was an important constituency for the 'secular' Greater Eretz Israel movement founded in 1969. Nahum Sarig was the legendary commander of the Negev Brigade in 1948. His son Ran fought in 1967. The editors discarded the conversation at the family's behest.[114]

Ran Sarig summarized his overriding feelings about the war as follows:

The greatest thing, for me at any rate, was that we were going to make the country complete [*holkhim lehashlim et haaretz*] . . . The feeling I had was . . . of, as it were, the completion of father's deeds 20 years ago [i.e., Nahum Sarig's in 1948]. At that time there was constant talk about the injustice [sic] – what Ben-Gurion called 'a lasting regret' [i.e., halting at what became the 1949 Armistice borders rather than conquering the whole of western Palestine]. I felt regarding this matter, that we were completing the assignment that actually should have been accomplished then [in the 1948 war]. When the newspapers had talked about 'a lasting regret' I knew what they meant.[115]

Another conversation Shapira chose to exclude was the meeting between some of the founding members of *Siah lohamim* with the students of the Merkaz Harav Yeshiva in Jerusalem, which was led by Rabbi Kook Junior and would become one of the pivotal centres of the post-1967 settlers' movement. It was held in the yeshiva itself, and some of the students with whom the conversation was conducted would become leading figures in Gush Emunim. Shapira revealed thirty years later that he had decided to omit that exchange from *Siah lohamim* because of his utter shock at 'the manifestations of messianism' that 'no human obstacle . . . certainly not a humane one, can stop'. Since Shapira did publish much of it in his journal *Shdemot*, it would seem that the fuller reason was to preserve the 'shooting and crying' image of the Israeli soldier and thereby the propaganda value of the collection. By contrast, the Merkaz Harav soldiers were uninhibited in giving voice to their messianic elation, unabashed hatred of the Arabs and trigger-happiness.[116]

Kibbutzniks like Ran Sarig and future settlers in the Occupied Territories shared the passion for land-grabbing. There was also a common ethos and rhetoric. As Gan senses, 'Concerning issues related to the war, such as the attitude to looting, the sense of fear of the soldier in war, moral dilemmas during the battle and afterwards, it is possible to delineate many resemblances between Rabbi Kook Junior's disciples and what the kibbutzniks said.'[117] Thirty years later the participants of the original conversation were convened for yet more soul-searching and visceral communing. What is striking here is the extent to which the national religious settlement movement perceived itself as continuing the trail blazed by the labour settlement movement.

Yoel Ben-Nun of the Ofra settlement, one of Oz's favourite interlocutors on the spectacle of national unity, lamented:

I have had a deep sense of a greatly missed opportunity ever since [the first meeting at Merkaz Harav], for I truly believe that the 'Shdemot' group and 'Merkaz Harav' group had, spiritually speaking, a very high potential of connectivity . . . The tremendous experience of the six-day war, 'the shock of light' as Hanan Porat [a senior settler politician and decorated army officer] called it, threw these two groups in opposite directions . . . The struggle . . . became: man versus land [*adam mul adamah*]. Instead of man and land being joined . . .'[118]

Dov Begun, who had been educated in Mishmar Hasharon (Ehud Barak's kibbutz) before becoming a settler, crafted continuity in a more confrontational manner: 'What has happened here is a historical relay. Our public has taken the baton and the kibbutz public that held the baton of pioneering . . . was unwilling to let it go and admit that its role in the relay had come to an end.'[119]

As for internal censoring, Gan has sympathy for the 'great responsibility' of the editors for the final public product, but he nonetheless minutely details their editorial alterations. All *Siah lohamim*'s editorial efforts were directed to one end: to intensify the image of the handsome, morally pure soldier, and to render the reasons for his dilemmas and bad conscience less specific, to blur them and reduce their sharp outlines as much as possible. One editorial method was to omit direct description of events, substituting in its place insinuation. A commanding officer describes in the edited text the feelings of his soldiers after they killed a Palestinian peasant in an ambush in this way: 'What perhaps added to this terrible feeling was my impression of the soldiers who were lying in ambush and who as it happened killed [that peasant]'. The original unedited transcription read: 'What perhaps added to this terrible feeling was my impression of the enormous gaiety of the soldiers who as it happened killed this *fallah* [peasant in Arabic]'.[120] Another technique of omission was the use of the ellipsis. In recounting the initial encounters with civilian population *Siah lohamim* has a soldier say that 'There was a sort of collapse [of codes of behaviour] . . . an abnormal collapse . . . really . . .' In the transcript the soldier reports: 'A collapse that bordered on true cruelty . . . I know that one corporal . . . a forty-year-old man raised his hands, and then he emptied an entire magazine into his belly . . . grenades in every house . . . burning houses just like that . . . a sort of collapse.'[121]

Another, related, editorial method was to sanitize explicit accounts of the war. In 1948 one of the settlers' chief means of effecting the ethnic cleansing was to prevent the return, at all costs, of those who had been expelled or had momentarily fled. This was repeated in 1967, especially along the Jordan River. The example here is of an order that was reportedly not heeded, but the editors' purpose was palpably to conceal the order itself. The book has a soldier tell that '[t]here was an order to prevent crossing the Jordan [back into Palestine] by means other than the bridges. I know that we carried out the order's spirit without harming people.' The original transcription: 'There was an explicit, written order: as for today, anyone who crosses the Jordan – shoot. No matter who he is, what he is, how he is and why he is. I know that my battalion did not carry out the order. Not a single bullet was shot, despite the fact that 400 and 500 and 800 refugees crossed.' The most striking example of this method is a case in the Golan Heights, in which the editors changed a soldier's report in such a way that the desire of some troopers to finish off a wounded Fatah soldier (the Fatah fighters were hated with vengeance), fighting in the Syrian army, is thwarted by others with proper moral fibre. In the original transcription, however, that soldier reports the situation but ends by saying: 'Suddenly that man who was so innocent and so quiet . . . that man took his rifle and placed it pointing to the side of that Arab's head and killed him.'[122]

Many more similar instances of editorial intervention might be cited; in this process, moreover, certain patterns emerge. One such is the removal of soldiers' testimonies in which the brutally murderous behaviour of the troops elicited explicit comparisons with the Nazis. Another is the tampering with testimonies of cleansing, in which outright falsehoods were inserted at editorial stage, and in which the editors replaced the word 'expulsion' with 'evacuation'. It also transpires that Oz was well aware of the thorough cleansing of the villages in the Latrun area. In addition to his literary and propagandist undertakings, Oz was informing the national religious settlers how much they had hurt 'our' feelings and how much 'we' have been suffering. In yet another gathering, this time in the settlement of Ofra, he reminisced about that formative meeting at Merkaz Harav. The kibbutzniks had returned from that exchange, Oz told the Ofra settlers, 'downcast and mourning'. What 'really hurt', he intimated, 'was the utter apathy towards our moral crisis. There was enormous self-doubt after the victory, about our values, our ideals, our conscience, our world view.' All that unfolded in the wake of the war, in which 'we' participated on the understanding 'that it was to defend its [Israel's] very existence', Oz concludes, 'was a shock to us, a source of suffering and moral dilemma'.[123]

## Acquisition

Self-congratulatory conversation is part of Israeli decorum, and confirming that *our beauty is in our problemacy* is common about the dinner table. 'How beautiful a language is ours', said a linguist to his companion in an Arab restaurant. 'How open and accommodating

it is' (read: we are so open and accommodating). 'We say this coffee is ya'ani 'ala kefak. 'Ala kefak, superb; ya'ani, that is to say. Arabic words, adopted by our ever-absorbent language' . . . Of course, many words remain, unadopted, with the people of this country, ya'ani Falastin. Try saying it.
(Oz Shelach, Picnic Grounds)

## Notes

1 Sarah Coleman's interview with Oz Shelach, 21 March 2003, available HTTP: http://www.worldpress.org/1012.cfm.

2 See above, pp. 107–9.

3 A. Shapira, 'Ben-Gurion and the Bible: The Creation of a Historical Narrative?', *Alpayim*, 14 (1997), pp. 207–31, and *The Bible and Israeli Identity*, Jerusalem: Magnes Press, 2006 (both texts are in Hebrew).

4 Shapira, *The Bible*, pp. 3–4.

5 Ibid., pp. 2–3.

6 Ibid., p. 3.

7 Ibid., p. 4.

8 Ibid., pp. 25–33.

9 Ibid., p. 33.

10 Shapira, 'Ben-Gurion and the Bible', pp. 207–14. The description of his interventions as anti-Semitic or settler-colonial is mine rather than Shapira's.

11 Ibid., p. 214.

12 Ibid.

13 Ibid., p. 215.

14 Ibid., p. 217.

15 Ibid., p. 221.

16 Ibid., pp. 221–31.

17 Ibid., pp. 231.

18 Shapira, *The Bible*, p. 4.

19 Ibid., p. 7.

20 Ibid., p. 6, for example.

21 Shapira, 'Ben-Gurion and the Bible', p. 220.

22 I. Pappé, 'The Green Langues and the JNF Box [Hebrew]', *Mitaam*, 4 (December 2005), pp. 89–103.

23 Shapira, *The Bible*, pp. 23–4.

24 This is a statement from S. Yizhar's 'Story of Khirbat Hiz`ah', which is at the centre of this section.

25 A. Shapira, 'Khirbat Hiz`ah – Memory and Forgetting [Hebrew]', *Alpayim*, 21 (2000), pp. 9–53.

26 See above, Chapter Two, pp. 64–7.

27 Shapira, 'Khirbat Hiz`ah', p. 14.

28 Ibid.

29 S. Yizhar, 'About Uncles and Arabs', in K. Yaron and P. Medes Flohr (eds.), *Mordecai Martin Buber in the Test of Time* [Hebrew], Jerusalem: Magnes Press, 1993, pp. 11–15. There is a rather careless English translation by S. Bowman in *Hebrew Studies*, 47 (2006), pp. 321–6.

30 Shapira, 'Khirbat Hiz`ah', pp. 12 and 18.

31 Ibid., pp. 9–10.

32 Ibid., p. 12.

33 'The words of Jeremiah the son of Hilkiah, of the priests that were in Anathoth in the land of Benjamin', Book of Jeremiah 1:1.

34 S. Yizhar, 'The Story of Hirbet Hiz'ah', partially translated by H. Levy in *Jewish Quarterly*, 1957. I cite from a collection that reproduces this translation,

entitled *Caravan: Hebrew Prose and Verse*, New York: T. Yoseloff, 1962, p. 331. My transliteration follows the standard written Arabic (and hence Khirbat rather than Levy's Hirbet).

35 *Caravan*, p. 330.
36 Ibid., pp. 330–1.
37 Ibid., p. 331.
38 Ibid., pp. 331–2.
39 M. Benvenisti, *Sacred Landscape: The Buried History of the Holy Land Since 1948*, Berkeley: The University of California Press, 2000.
40 Ibid., p. 2.
41 Ibid.
42 Ibid., p. 3.
43 Ibid., p. 9.
44 Ibid., p. 12.
45 Ibid., p. 14.
46 I take the Hebrew term from Benvenisti's article, which is more or less the book's first chapter. See 'The Hebrew Map', *Theory and Criticism*, 11 (Winter 1997), p. 22.
47 Benvenisti, *Landscape*, p. 15.
48 Ibid., pp. 20–7.
49 See for instance the table that breaks down these techniques and criteria concerning the Negev and Arava, ibid., p. 23.
50 Ibid., pp. 33–7.
51 Ibid., p. 42.
52 Ibid.
53 Ibid., p. 46.
54 Ibid., pp. 46–7.
55 Ibid., p. 23.
56 Ibid., pp. 258–9 and 340.
57 Ibid., p. 340.
58 Y. Laor, ' "We Are the 12 in the Trenches": Reading *Days of Ziklag* at the End of Three Decades', in *Narratives with no Natives: Essays on Israeli Literature* [Hebrew], Tel Aviv: Hakibbutz Hameuchad, 1995, pp. 62–3.
59 See below, Chapter Seven, pp. 269–73.
60 G. Nevo, 'The Realism of S. Yizhar's Days of Ziklag', *Hebrew Studies*, 47 (2006), pp. 299–326.
61 Laor, *Narratives*, pp. 302–8.
62 Ibid., p. 50.
63 Ibid., p. 51.
64 Y. Shapiro, *Elite without Successors: Generations of Leadership in Israeli Society* [Hebrew], Tel Aviv: Sifriat Poalim, 1984.
65 Laor, *Narratives*, p. 52.
66 Ibid., pp. 52–3.
67 Ibid., p. 140.
68 Cited ibid., p. 53.
69 Ibid., pp. 53–4.
70 Ibid., p. 59.
71 Ibid., p. 62.

72 Nevo, op. cit., pp. 316–20. For a survey of the critical literature on Yizhar in Hebrew see Ch. Nagid, 'Introduction', in idem (ed.), *S. Yizhar: A Selection of Critical Essays on His Writings* [Hebrew], Tel Aviv: Am Oved, 1972, pp. 7–38.

73 S. Yizhar, 'A Story That Has Not Begun', in *Stories of the Plain*, Tel Aviv: Zmora Bitan, 1990, pp. 83–161. First published by Hakibbutz Hameuchad, 1963.

74 S. Yizhar, 'Hirbat Hiz`ah', in *Caravan*, p. 334.

75 S. Yizhar, 'A Story That Has Not Begun', p. 121.

76 Ibid., p. 126.

77 S. Yizhar, 'First Sermon', in *Stories of the Plain*, p. 101.

78 See again G. Fredrickson, *White Supremacy: A Comparative Study in American and South African History*, Oxford: Oxford University Press, 1981.

79 D. Miron, 'S. Yizhar: Some General Observations', in S. Yizhar, *Midnight Convoy and Other Stories*, Jerusalem: Israel Universities Press, 1969, pp. 257–73.

80 Ibid., p. 267.

81 G. Shaked, 'On *We Write Thee Homeland* [Hebrew title of *Narratives with no Natives*] (1995) by Yitzhak Laor', *Alpayim*, 12 (1996), pp. 51–73.

82 G. Shaked, 'A Beautiful Eretz Israel of Words (on *Mikdamot* by S. Yizhar)', in *Literature Then, Here and Now* [Hebrew], Tel Aviv: Zmora-Bitan, 1993, pp. 181–203.

83 Ibid., pp. 196–9.

84 Ibid., p. 197.

85 Ibid., p. 196.

86 Ibid., p. 198.

87 Ibid., p. 199.

88 Ibid.

89 A. Oz, 'Khirbat Hiz`ah and Mortal Danger', in *Under This Blazing Light: Essays* [Hebrew], Tel Aviv: Sifriat Poalim, 1979, p. 157. Originally published in *Davar*, 2 February 1978. The English edition of this collection of essays contains only eighteen essays of the thirty-six in the Hebrew original. The essay on 'Khirbat Hiz`ah' was among those omitted.

90 Ibid.

91 Laor, *Narratives*, p. 151.

92 P. Anderson, 'Scurrying towards Bethlehem', *New Left Review*, 10 (July–August 2001), p. 23 n. 23.

93 Laor, *Narratives*, p. 76.

94 Among her other praises of Oz see N. Gordimer, 'Forgotten Promised Land', in *Writing and Being*, Cambridge, Mass.: Harvard University Press, 1995, pp. 94–114.

95 R. Feldhay-Brenner, *Inextricably Bonded: Israeli Arab and Jewish Writers Re-Visioning Culture*, Madison: The University of Wisconsin Press, 2003.

96 Ibid., pp. 42–4. For Shafir, see above, Chapter Two, pp. 62–5.

97 Feldhay-Brenner, *Inextricably Bonded*, Chapter Four for the Israeli Jewish dissenting voices and Chapter Five for the Israeli Arab ones.

98 Ibid., p. 101 n. 29.

99 Laor's point is in *Narratives*, p. 80. I quote from Nicholas de Lange's translation of Amos Oz, *My Michael* (New York: Harcourt, 1972), p. 174.

100 For a thorough interpretation of Oz's writing from a similar perspective see Laor, *Narratives*, pp. 76–105.

101 Nicholas de Lange's translation of Amos Oz, *Black Box*, New York: Harcourt, 1988, p. 3.

102 Ibid., p. 4.

103 A. Hirschfeld, 'One Identity Ends and Another Begins [Hebrew]', *Politika*, 33 (July 1990), pp. 48–54. The citation is from p. 52.

104 *Politika*, 34 (September 1990), p. 57.

105 Y. Laor, '*A Tale of Love and Darkness* – Propaganda, Narcissism and the West [Hebrew]', *Mitaam: A Journal for Literature and Radical Thought*, 7 (September 2006), pp. 67–91. I quote from an English translation by Revital Sela, which will hopefully appear soon. I am grateful to the author for making the translation available to me.

106 Laor, 'Propaganda', p. 67, quoting from Nicholas de Lange's translation of *A Tale of Love* (New York: Vintage Books, 2004), p. 329.

107 Ibid.

108 Ibid., p. 68.

109 A. Gan, 'The Discourse that Faded Away? The Attempts To Form a Distinctive Identity for the Kibbutzim's Second Generation [Hebrew]', PhD Thesis, Tel Aviv University, 2002. Chapter Four is solely concerned with *Siah lohamim*. I am grateful to Avi Raz for making the text available to me.

110 Ibid., pp. 84–5.

111 Ibid., pp. 87–90.

112 Ibid., p. 85.

113 Ibid., p. 87.

114 Ibid., pp. 107–8.

115 Ibid., p. 108.

116 Ibid., pp. 109–12.

117 Ibid., p. 109.

118 Ibid., p. 112.

119 Ibid.

120 Ibid., p. 116.

121 Ibid., p. 117.

122 Ibid., pp. 117–18.

123 A. Barzilai, 'The Messianic Were Taken out', *Haaretz*, June 2002, posted in *Aron's Israel Peace Weblog*.

7

# The Bible of an Autochthonous Settler:
# Ben-Gurion Reads the Book of Joshua

On Gibeon's turrets stand thou still, O Sun!
Look down, thou Moon, on dreary Ajalon!
Fix'd in high heaven the awful splendors stood,
And flam'd tremendous on the field of blood;
From dread orb ensanguin'd streams aspire,
The skies all mantling in fierce waving fire;
Amaz'd, Canäan's realms the pomp descried;
The world grew pale; the heats of nations died . . .
A sudden blaze gleam'd round the dusty gloom
And plung'd ten thousand warriors to the tomb.
For now, o'er all the fight, the heathens yield, and Israel triumphs round
    the dreadful field.
High in the van, sublime great Joshua rode,
Wing'd the dire flight, and swell'd the tide of blood . . .
Through the long day, Canäan's widows stood,
And look'd, all anxious, toward the plain of blood.
(From Timothy Dwight, *The Conquest of Canaan: A Poem in Eleven Books*,
1785, dedicated to George Washington, Commander in chief of the
American Armies, The Saviour of his Country, The Supporter of Freedom,
And the Benefactor of Mankind[1])

It was fortunate for the future of monotheism that the Israelites of the
Conquest were a wild folk, endowed with primitive energy and ruthless
will to exist, since the resulting decimation of the Canaanites prevented
the complete fusion of the two kindred folk which would almost

inevitably have depressed the Yahwistic standards to a point where recovery was impossible. Thus the Canaanites, with their orgiastic nature worship, their cult of fertility in the form of serpent symbols and sensuous nudity, and their gross mythology, were replaced by Israel, with its pastoral simplicity and purity of life, its lofty monotheism, and its severe code of ethics. In a not altogether dissimilar way, the African Canaanites, as they still called themselves, or the Carthaginians, as we call them, with the gross Phoenician mythology . . . with human sacrifices and the cult of sex, were crushed by the immensely superior Romans, whose stern code of morals and singularly elevated paganism remind us in many ways of early Israel.

(W. F. Albright, *From the Stone Age to Christianity: Monotheism and the Historical Process*, 1957[2])

With what voice will we, the Canaanites of the world, say, 'Let my people go and leave my people alone?' . . .The indigenous people of this hemisphere have endured a subjugation now a hundred years longer than the sojourn of Israel in Egypt. Is there a god, a spirit, who will hear us and stand with us in the Amazon, Osage County, and Wounded Knee? Is there a god, a spirit, able to move among the pain and anger of the Nablus, Gaza, and Soweto of 1989? Perhaps. But we, the wretched of the earth, may be well advised this time not to listen to outsiders with their promises of liberation and deliverance. We will perhaps do better to look elsewhere for our vision of justice, peace and political sanity – a vision through which we escape not only our oppressors, but our oppression as well. Maybe, for once, we will just have to listen to ourselves, leaving the gods of this continent's real strangers to do battle among themselves.

(Robert Allen Warrior, 'A Native American Perspective: Canaanites, Cowboys, and Indians'[3])

## A Pertinent Context: The Modern History of the Prefix *Re-*

Why I choose to begin with a fresh look at 'the return to history' will become clear as the present discussion unfolds. What should be anticipated now is that by the history of the prefix *Re-* I mean the discursive and political historical context, within which such words as *return* (to the Old Testament and the land of Israel most pertinently), *restoration* and *re-*establishment signified the obviousness of the Zionist colonization of Palestine and creation of a Jewish nation-state. The Zionist foundational myth, as we have seen, has manifested itself in three ways: the negation of exile, the return to the land of Israel, and the return to history (*ha-shiva la-historya*). The myth in its return-to-history guise is premised on the Romantic presupposition that the natural and irreducible form of human collectivity is the nation. In this view, from the dawn of history peoples have been grouped into such units and, though these units might at one time or another be undermined by internal divisions or oppressed by external forces, they are eventually bound to find political self-expression in the shape of sovereign nation-states. The nation is the autonomous historical subject par excellence, and the state is the telos of its march towards self-fulfilment. According to this logic, so long as they were exiles, the Jews remained a community outside history, a history within which all European nations dwelt by virtue of having sovereignty over their patrimonies. Only nations that occupy the soil of their homeland, and establish political sovereignty over it, are capable of shaping their own destiny and thus by this logic entering history. The return of the Jewish nation to the land of Israel, overcoming its docile passivity in exile, could alone enable it to rejoin the history of civilized peoples.

The importance of the return to history concept to Zionist thinkers past and present is underscored by a relatively recent volume of essays dedicated entirely to a reappraisal of Zionism as a return to history. In it Amnon Raz-Krakotzkin, whose radical critique of the negation of exile we have already encountered, pushes the debate beyond its Zionist confines by posing the question that the myth so obviously begs but which has not been hitherto asked: to exactly what history does the nation return?[4] The stated Zionist desire for sovereignty and responsibility should be respected, in Raz-Krakotzkin's view, but it leaves unexplored the full implication of the myth in its return-to-history guise, precisely because the nature of that 'history' to which the nation 'returns' remains unexplored. By identifying the specific history towards which the return is directed, he not only divulges the gist of his argument but also transforms the debate:

[T]he 'history' to which the 'return' . . . relates is the Christian West's, and it is based on a comprehensive adoption of the Western concept of history, and also the acceptance in principle of the Christian under-standing of Jewish history, especially as it was shaped in the Protestant context. Thus, paradoxically, the exit from Europe and the wish to establish a distinct Jewish entity in the East was a way of being integrated into the Christian West on the basis of complete identification with the European self-image. Concomitantly, the 'return' to history also meant the displacement of the Jews from the various 'histories' within which they had existed onto a discrete narrative.[5]

Revisiting medieval Christian–Jewish polemics, Raz-Krakotzkin maintains that it is there that the reconstruction of the modern notion of return – as the evolution of a fundamental Christian belief – should commence. The Christian view held that the exile of the Jews indeed marked their exit from history, understood by Christians as the history of redemption, because of their obstinate refusal to accept the era of Grace. History would come full circle with the *return* of the Jews to the fold – that is, with their acceptance of Christianity. The Zionist return to history, Raz-Krakotzkin avers,

> in actual fact adopts the Christian conception of the history of the Jews: it is underlain by the assumption that there is a meaningful history, out of which only the Jews exist . . . It [the Zionist return to history] is also underlain by the assumption of the possibility of redemption which the Jews join, in a joint framework with the Christian West. In terms of the religious polemics – this is patently a return to the history of redemption, which is based on accepting the ambivalent Christian attitude to Judaism.[6]

Although it would be imprudent to talk about a uniform Jewish approach to world history and exile that could be contrasted with the main Christian one, since there existed no 'church' with central authority, it is possible to point out a more or less common attitude among Jews. This common attitude did not recognize a history (of the sort to which the Zionist return is directed) of the world, from which the Jews alone were excluded because they were in exile and not politically sovereign. Moreover, contrary to the position that held the world to be in the era of Grace from which the Jews were excluded because of their obduracy, that common Jewish attitude deemed the world to be in exile after the temple's destruction and, according to some views, even divinity itself was in exile.

Raz-Krakotzkin is of course aware that modernity infused notions like history and redemption with a signification different from the various Christian meanings. Redemption would now be obtained through human progress, while Grace was replaced by Reason. Most important for the present discussion is Raz-Krakotzkin's observation that 'the revamped [i.e., Zionist] definition of Jewish identity was not built upon the secularization of Judaism but on the secularization of Christianity'.[7] The severing of collective Jewish identity from the medieval polemics of exile versus Christianity's Grace, and the attempt to construct Jewishness as an organically national and autonomous concept, unavoidably incorporated within this idea the presence of the historical consciousness that shaped Christian ambivalence towards the Jews, who witnessed, but rejected, the true message. Within Zionism in particular, this ambivalence was articulated in relation to the Jewish exilic past: on the one hand the present fulfils what was already immanent in Jewish history but could not be realized because of the circumstance of exile; on the other hand, that past is devoid of intrinsic significance, but merely manifests a partial existence upon the negation of which the present is predicated.

There is an initial, but limited, sense in which the 'nationalization' of Jewish history resembles that of the colonized, or third, world. The embracing of nationalism was for all these collectives a way to join 'history', but in order to do so they had to adhere to the very same model of historical consciousness that had excluded them from that 'history', even if the Jews were within Europe and the colonized nations without. This, however, is also the point at which any resemblance to colonized nations ends. While for the colonized world adopting 'history' was a dialectical move that led to the anti-colonial removal of Europe from its colonies, for Zionism the return to history was a settler-national impulse, which was meant to achieve a complete integration into the European story through the carving of a national patrimony in the East. As I showed in Chapter One, this is what Herzl was trying to do, in a literary way, in *Altneuland*. With Zionism we have an inversion of the famous line of the medieval Spanish Jewish poet Yehuda Halevi in medieval Spain: 'My heart is in the East while I am at the far end of the West'.

Raz-Krakotzkin highlights the resemblance between the Zionist and Protestant notions of return. For Protestants, return to the ideal and pure community of the ancient church, whose values had been corrupted by the Catholic Church, was a prerequisite for religious reform. In Zionist literature, Raz-Krakotzkin elaborates,

> the image of the ancient church was replaced by the sovereign Jewish community of the Biblical era and the period of the Second Temple, just before Christianity's appearance. This community embodied the same values that had been attributed to pre–fourth century church in the Protestant literature, and was described in equivalent terms . . . The 'return' pointed to similar values, to ideals of purity that had been lost, to the organic community of pietist-farmers [*ikkarim–hasidim*].[8]

Interestingly, Raz-Krakotzkin points out that Yitzhak-Fritz Baer (one of the pillars of the Jerusalem Jewish studies community from the 1930s on), discussed above in Chapter Four, argued that the concepts that defined the ancient Christian church were borrowed from Judaism, where they had originated. Baer's argument is not implausible, but what matters more here is that it made it possible for him to borrow Christian theological language and notably define the authentic Jewish entity as *ecclesia*. Most crucially, 'the "return" was also articulated as "return" to the Tanakh [the Hebrew Bible] and its presentation as the expression of national culture, while concomitantly divorcing it from the exilic-rabbinical culture. Rendering the Tanakh the ultimate source of authority, a downright Protestant principle, conveyed in another way the fact that defining Jewish identity as national was based on being integrated into a joint context, Judeo-Christian'.[9] It is important to clarify that Raz-Krakotzkin is less concerned with whether or not Protestant culture did directly influence Zionism – though it undoubtedly did exist – than with underscoring the theological-colonial dimension of Zionism as well as the context within which the concept of 'history' in its national – putatively secular – sense acquired its meaning.

The Protestant context of the prefix *Re-* in the sense of return to the Old Testament and return of the Jews to the Holy Land – is considerably expanded in Mayir Vereté's thorough essay on pertinent strands in evangelical restorationist English thought in the period 1790–1840.[10] Vereté's study stemmed from his long-standing interest in British attitudes towards, and policy on, Palestine, leading to the Balfour Declaration and its consequences. In the history of Protestant English infatuation with 'the Restoration of the Jews', he discerns two especially interesting phases: the first occurring from the late sixteenth century (although he doesn't comment on the coincidence of this phase with the intensifying colonization in Ireland) to 'the great Puritan ferment', which died out with the Restoration of the British monarchy; the second coming with the religious millenarian revival that took place between the 1790s and the 1840s. Vereté concedes continuities that join these two periods, but at the same time insists on a number of features that make the second period with its obsession with the Jewish Restoration distinct from the first. Pivotal among them was the 'specifically Jewish aspect' of that millenarian revival.[11]

It is of course well known that the fate of the Jews is an integral part of the prophecies on the Latter Days, but the development of millenarian thought charted by Vereté stands out in its political concreteness, for this millenarian trend saw in revolutionary France the saviour of the

Jews, and in Bonaparte's invasion of Egypt in 1798 and his campaign in Palestine a year later a signal for their possible restoration to the promised land. The millenarian literature of the early nineteenth century referred to by Vereté did not condition that return or restoration on the Jews' conversion even though the question itself was significant and amply discussed; some of that literature not only did not require conversion as a prerequisite for the process of redemption to commence, it also increasingly omitted the discussion on the conversion of the Jews altogether. 'The Jewish return', he observes, 'was therefore also becoming a theme in its own right'.[12] Like Raz-Krakotzkin, Vereté locates in the Reformation the turning point in what might be termed the history of the prefix *Re-*:

> For over a thousand years, Christian thought had not conceded the possibility of a Jewish return any recognition whatever, for the literal interpretation of the Bible had, in the Middle Ages, been generally rejected in favour of other interpretations adopted by the Fathers, especially the allegorical exegesis . . . Old Testament passages referring to the Jews returning to their homeland . . . were held to apply not to the Jews but to the Christian Church and its faithful.[13]

With Luther, Melanchthon, Calvin and Zwingli, Protestant exegesis crucially rejected the allegorical line of biblical interpretation 'for a "grammatical", "literal" approach, seeking to uncover the original, innate, plain meaning of the text. The faithful were summoned to "return to the Bible" itself as the source of true, pure Christianity . . . The idea of the Return to Zion was similarly affected.'[14] In the English context, Vereté attributes 'this new trend' to a treatise published by the biblical scholar Andrew Willett in 1590. Rejecting the Augustinian interpretation of St Paul's 'all Israel shall be saved' (meaning the new and 'true' Israel – the Christian community), Willett was adamant that the statement must have meant 'the whole nation of the Jews', and that 'Israel' must be 'taken in the litteral [sic] sense, for the nation and people of Israel'.[15]

In the early seventeenth century Sir Henry Finch, an MP and a scholar fluent in Hebrew, was influential in setting an interpretative guide for Latter Day prophecies:

> Where Israel, Judah, Tzion and Jerusalem are named [in the Bible] the Holy Ghost meaneth not the spiritual Israel, or the Church of God collected of the Gentiles or of the Jewes and Gentiles both . . . but Israel properly descended out of Jacob's loyens . . . These and such like

are not Allegories, setting forth in terrene similitudes or deliverance through Christ (whereof those were types and figures), but meant really and literally of the Jewes.[16]

Fifty years later the English Orientalist Samuel Lee, influenced by Finch's work, amplified his insistence that the Restoration prophecies had unequivocally meant 'national Israel', 'national restitution of Israel' and 'the return of Israel to their own land'. The Jews, he concluded, 'shall . . . certainly return to their ancient land [and] inherit it forever'.[17]

In the first half of the eighteenth century the literalist, anti-allegorical, discourse on the restoration of the Jews took a more scholarly turn at the hands of writers like Joseph Eyre and Thomas Burnet. Fervently speaking to 'the allegorists', Burnet made them aware that denying the eminent place of the Jews in the apocalyptic prophecies was tantamount to undermining their foundation, for '[t]here is no promise oftener repeated in the Old Testament . . . than that which concerns the preservation and future restauration [sic] of the Jews'.[18] In 1784 Edward Whitaker, whom Vereté defines as 'an Evangelical of millenarian leanings', wrote a treatise that rebuffed an allegorical sermon delivered by the Archdeacon of Worcester at Oxford. Paul's 'all Israel shall be saved', he averred, was congruous with earlier divine promises, and it was 'expressly declared that the restoration shall be national'. The restoration was literal, and it would take place 'on this globe'. The promise made to Abraham, Whitaker emphasized, 'is absolute . . . and part of the subject of this promise was the everlasting possession of that very country in which the patriarchs themselves sojourned'.[19]

These trends came to a systemic conclusion in a 1796 text that in certain ways launched the discrete discourse and mood of the nineteenth century, which was becoming politically concrete and imperially ambitious and possible.

Each year, in time-honoured fashion, the Norrisian Professor of Divinity at Cambridge University would announce a religious subject for an annual essay competition; as Vereté observes, the subject for the 1795 competition, 'The grounds contained in Scripture for expecting a future restoration of the Jews', bore 'the sign of the times'. It is noteworthy that the current Norrisian Professor, 'a rationalist and sceptic', had no strong feelings on the subject. 'That he suggested the topic for an essay, however, is a clear reflection of the climate of the [seventeen] nineties, when . . . millenarian notions were achieving popularity and the restoration of the Jews was often discussed'. The winner was Charles Jerram, a theology student with close association with Evangelical circles at Cambridge and elsewhere. He was, Vereté intimates, 'A rationalist by nature . . . but he was also drawn to the warmer religion of the Evangelicals'. His winning essay was published the following year.[20]

Arguing like his predecessors against the allegorical approach, Jerram also determined that according to God's promise 'the title of the Jews to the land of Palestine [is] inalienable', and that 'the claim of the Jews to the land of Palestine will always be reasonable and just'. Mulling over some prophecies in Hosea, Jeremiah and Ezekiel, Jerram reiterated that 'a real restoration is intended', and was confident in '[a] future restoration . . . in which the house of Israel shall be united with Judah in the . . . possession of their own land'.[21] Vereté ascribes much importance to Jerram as someone who not only summarized the discourse hitherto, but presented his subject

> not as an occasional, polemical tract, but within the context of a broad theological system. By its very nature, it could not become a popular work, but the enlightened religious public read it and drew teachings from it. Hardly anything of substance was added to the debate by later writings on the subject, and the very idea of the Jewish return to Palestine seems not to have been in dispute at least for several decades.[22]

To illustrate why I make the prefix *Re-* the emblem of the context within which I shall later place the Zionist 'return' to the Bible, it is helpful to quote Vereté's list of the typical verbs and verbal nouns used in millenarian English discourse:

> Yet another implication [of the fact that in that proposition the entire Jewish people were destined to be restored] was that the redemption would be achieved through the Jews *returning* to their ancient homeland. God would *call, recall, revoke, restore* them to himself, and they would recognize Jesus as their Messiah, thus accepting Christianity; and *repairing, returning, restoring, reducing* them to their land, God would *reestablish, restore, reinstate* them as an independent nation in their own state and confer upon them all the blessings promised by the prophets.[23]

Prudence and precision are necessary in order to understand the transition from this brewing millenarian discourse to British imperial coveting of the Holy Land and the place of the Jews and Zionism in it. Vereté demonstrates both in his meticulous corrective to what is conventionally seen as the beginning of Britain's official involvement in modern Palestine, namely, the establishment of a British Consulate in Jerusalem in September

1838.[24] It is lack of prudence and precision that led a series of scholars to infer from a single entry in the Earl of Shaftesbury's diary for 29 September 1838 that English millenarian circles and the missionaries in Palestine had pushed the British government into establishing the consulate as the first step towards realizing their aspiration. It is understandable why Shaftesbury's elation about the consulate being an important stage in restoring the Jews to the land of Israel misled Zionist historians in particular. He was probably the foremost fundamentalist figure of his time preoccupied with the restoration of the Jews to 'their ancient homeland', and was also related through marriage to Lord Palmerston, who basically shaped British foreign policy in the eastern Mediterranean and the Balkans in the 1830s. Vereté refutes this narrative, and in his laborious fashion shows that the decision was first and foremost a concrete expression of Britain's Eastern Question policy on the Ottoman front and its attempt to curb the French and Russian influence in Palestine. The influence of the millenarians and missionaries was not insignificant, but it is wrong to conclude that their pressure resulted directly in the establishment of the consulate.

In a similar vein Vereté rejects the thesis that Britain's decision to oust France from Palestine and keep it for itself in the Middle East carve-up following the First World War, and Britain's pro-Zionist policy as embodied in the Balfour Declaration, were the products of Zionist diplomatic activity and Chaim Weizmann's singular skill and standing. He insists that by far the most decisive factors were the protection and furthering of British imperial interests in the Middle East in general and Palestine in particular, and that the pro-Zionist gestures were made in order to woo American Jewry and induce it to persuade the US to join the war, and to convince France to cede Palestine to Britain. Vereté also argues that the Declaration's name notwithstanding, Balfour's role in it has been overstated.[25] He leaves no doubt as to who the chief protagonists were: 'The Catholic Conservative Mark Sykes found an enthusiastic supporter for his subtle policy in the Protestant Radical Lloyd George. Both of them were great British patriots and pronounced imperialists, with a fertile mind and, sometimes, devious ways, which a ready and smooth tongue abounding in oratory together with plenty of personal charm enabled them to conceal'.[26]

There is, however, I believe, an elusive process embedded in his own portrayal of the nineteenth century that Vereté missed. He did so partly because his close reading of the individual documents precluded a wider focus, and partly because his researches dictated an exclusive concern, for the first half of the nineteenth century, with millenarian discourse, and for the second half of that century with diplomatic subject matter. The process I am referring to is the somewhat intangible osmosis of the prefix

*Re-* from the discursive sphere of the Protestant millenarian discourse into that of a wider political sphere. This osmosis is most evident in a proposition made by Vereté himself, who was not, however, fully aware of its significance. He suggests that one of the main assumptions that guided Sykes and others was '[t]he idea of winning over world Jewry to the side of the Allies by means of a generous Zionist declaration',[27] but does not pause to ponder why such an assumption could be taken at face value, rightly or wrongly, by contemporary actors. Why, for instance, hadn't it been more obvious to assume that commitment to better the lot of the Jews wherever they were in the world would have been a more appropriate way to win over world Jewry? It is the ostensible obviousness of the former assumption, whereby one could successfully woo a Jewish community by dangling Palestine in front of its eyes, that evinced the relevance of the prefix *Re-* to imperial politics.

What had been missed by Vereté was noticed by Alexander Schölch, the late Erlangen University scholar of the modern Middle East, precisely because he examined the *Re-* discourse and the economic and political penetration of Britain into Palestine in the second half of the nineteenth century simultaneously.[28] 'Naturally', Schölch observes,

> the doctrine of the 'restoration of the Jews' did not become a general conviction for the population of Great Britain. But the authoritative assertion that Palestine was the God-given home of the Jews, to which they sooner or later would return, gained currency. In this restricted sense the idea of the 'restoration' became a commonplace bit of knowledge. Like a self-evident fact that one mentions only to confirm, it permeated the English literature on Palestine in the second half of the nineteenth century. In association with the 'Peaceful Crusade' [introduced after the Crimean War] that was being preached on the continent, appeals were even made for a crusade that would pave the way for the Jews.[29]

Surveying the various colonization projects for Palestine from the 1870s on, Schölch extends the osmosis further and makes it more explicit: 'Thus, there was an overarching continuity in thinking, extending from the conceptions of individual propagandists who promoted the restoration of the Jews in the 1840s, to the colonization enthusiasts of various derivations in the last third of the nineteenth century, and up to the Zionist conceptions of the twentieth century.'[30] The most significant instance of this osmotic continuity is Herzl's political and literary imagination. One domain in which this comes to the fore is that of the various – albeit largely unsuccessful –

colonization projects that proliferated from the 1870s on, goaded by the Ottoman bankruptcy of that decade. Charles Warren, an important figure in the Palestine Exploration Fund (the organization founded in 1865 to promote the exploration of Palestine, mostly but not exclusively through archaeology, in order to bring to the surface its biblical ancientness), suggested that the 'Holy Land' be placed under the aegis of a colonial company, the Jewish Ottoman Land Company, closely modelled on the East India Company. That company would relieve the Ottoman state of its severe fiscal difficulties, and would then facilitate the 'return' of the Jews to Palestine and the concomitant 'return' of Palestine to its rightful owners. Aware of the question as to the fate of Palestine's Arabs, his reply was, 'I ask in turn: Who Are the Arabs?'[31]

These proposals bore an uncanny resemblance to the way in which Herzl was trying to obtain the charter over Palestine from the Ottoman sultan Abdülhamid II, while the fate of the Arabs was close to that envisioned in *Altneuland*: they would for the most part simply disappear.[32] The roles allotted to the Bible and to the local Palestinian Arabs also manifest eerie affinities to Herzl's vision. In the 1880s, Lord Laurence Oliphant, one of the most ardent Zionists among the British evangelical Christians, recommended the settlement of the Hula Valley in the north-eastern Upper Galilee. He suggested a biblical model of settlement that would emulate 'the men of Dan'. That part of the Promised Land was the patrimony of the tribe of Dan according to biblical fiction, and the tribe's men had expelled the peasants residing there.[33] The actual drainage and settlement of the Hula area occurred in the 1950s and 1960s, and was celebrated as a typical Zionist Israeli achievement. This heroic enterprise was accompanied by a massive ethnic cleansing of the area. In the late 1870s C. R. Conder (a cartographer of note who, together with Kitchener, drew in 1878 a map of Palestine for the Palestine Exploration Fund), like Oliphant and others, believed that the indigenous population could be used for the settlers' benefit as 'hewers of wood and drawers of water', prior to being driven out of the area.[34] According to Herzl, 'The poor population was to be worked across the frontier *unbemerkt* [surreptitiously], after having for Jewish benefit rid the country of any existing wild animals, such as snakes. This population was to be refused all employment in the land of its birth.'[35]

The climax of the osmosis of the millenarian discourse into that of a wider cultural sphere, to the extent that 'restoring' the Jews to Palestine became a commonplace, might be literary, related to George Eliot's *Daniel Deronda* (1876). The possible similarities between Herzl's *Altneuland* (1902) and Eliot's novel have been remarked upon,[36] but I would like to make two new points in the current context: one is the significance of *Daniel Deronda* in and of itself, and the other *Daniel Deronda*'s remarkable instrumentality as a filter for Herzl's ideas in the mid 1890s, before he had written *Der Judenstaat* and *Altneuland* (*Das neue Ghetto* had been written in 1894, but was not sufficiently known and in any case lacked the theme of return).

The ways in which *Daniel Deronda* articulates the context I have charted have been powerfully presented by Edward Said, who discusses the significance of George Eliot's evangelical leaning, and places the novel together with Disraeli's *Tancred* and Moses Hess's *Rome and Jerusalem*.[37] Citing a pronouncement of Mordecai, Said adds emphasis to the statement that '[the Jews] *have wealth enough to redeem the soil from debauched and paupered conquerors*'.[38] I would add that what George Eliot and Anthony Ashley Cooper, the Earl of Shaftesbury, shared was the inability to envisage the extension of the politics of universal equality to Jews in their European societies, only their exodus to, and colonization of, Palestine.

The usefulness of *Daniel Deronda* in making sense of Herzl's ideas has not been noticed, though the associations between them are clear-cut. The earliest indication of Herzl's awareness of the novel is his diary entry of 7 June 1895: 'Ought to read *Daniel Deronda*. Teweles [Heinrich Teweles – the Czech–Austrian dramatist] speaks of it. I do not as yet know the book'.[39] A few days later, on 11 June, he reminded himself that 'I ought to read *Daniel Deronda*. Perhaps it has ideas that resemble mine. It is impossible that they are identical, for a convergence of many particular circumstances was necessary to give birth to my plan'.[40] It is not clear whether Herzl read the novel, or even portions of it, but he seemed to have been familiar at least with the gist of it. A year later, on 15 May 1897, he encouraged Leon Kellner, his co-editor of *Die Welt*, to 'write a series of articles on literary people who had propounded Zionism: Disraeli, George Eliot, Moses Hess'; these, it might be recalled, are the same texts that Said discusses as preludes to Herzl.

With this in mind I now turn to two tellingly similar Jewish responses to Herzl's ideas, crucially before their systematic and clear articulation in the shape of *Der Judenstaat* and *Altneuland*. On 23 November 1895 Herzl dined at the weekend residence of Britain's Chief Rabbi, Hermann Adler, in Finsbury Square, where he expounded his vision. After dinner Herzl elucidated his epiphany, and '[t]he Chief Rabbi remarked: this is Daniel Deronda's idea'.[41] Two days later, Herzl travelled from London to Cardiff for an eagerly awaited meeting with Colonel Albert Edward Goldsmid, a British officer from a distinguished Jewish family who had been brought up Christian, and had then 'returned' to Judaism. He was one of the leaders of Hovevei Zion's British chapter, and spent two years in the Jewish colony in Argentina on behalf of Baron Hirsch, until he gave up on the venture, insisting that only Palestine would do.

After dinner with Goldsmid, Herzl again presented his plan, after which came a 'puzzling story' – and the fact that Herzl found it puzzling suggests that his acquaintance with *Daniel Deronda* was at that point rather limited. Herzl went on:

> 'I am Daniel Deronda', he [Goldsmid] said. 'I was born a Christian. My father and mother were Jews who had been baptised. Upon finding out as a young man, in India, I decided to return to my forefathers' tribe. When I was a lieutenant I converted to Judaism. My family was stunned. My wife too was a Christian of Jewish extraction. I was shrewd with her, first we got married non-religiously in Scotland, later she had to convert to Judaism and we married in a synagogue. I am an Orthodox Jew. This did not impede me in England. My daughters Rachel and Carmel received a strict religious education, learned Hebrew in their childhood.'[42]

Later, as Herzl pressed indefatigably for the First Zionist Congress and Goldsmid's commitment was wavering, Herzl wrote him a confidential letter, dated 4 April 1897, in which he implored his interlocutor: 'You, Colonel Goldsmid, who so touched my heart when you told me in Cardiff the story of your life [the puzzlement is now gone] and opened with the words: "I am Daniel Deronda", is it possible that you will not want to attend this Jewish national assembly?'[43]

The importance of the use of *Daniel Deronda* (the novel) and Daniel Deronda (the novel's protagonist) by Rabbi Adler and Colonel Goldsmid as a way of signifying to Herzl that they had understood his plan cannot be overstated. This harks back to Raz-Krakotzkin's critical probing into the notion of the return to history as well as to the Anglo-Protestant restoration discourse charted by Vereté and Schölch, and brings them together. It shows the extent to which Zionism's various 'returns', to Palestine, to the Old Testament, to history, to normality, did not and indeed could not immanently spring from an organic Jewish history, whether in its linear or dialectical rendering. Rather, the 'returns' can, and should, be located at the intersection of Protestantism, colonialism and anti-Semitism. Otherwise, to be facetious, why was it that two Jewish men resorted to a novel by a *shiksa* to say to a third that they had understood what he was talking about?

## Bible Studies and Biblical Archaeology

In 1999 the critical Israeli archaeologist Ze'ev Herzog of Tel Aviv University published an article in *Haaretz*, in which he refuted the veracity of the most foundational part of the Old Testament's narrative. Reminiscent of the 1948 revisionist historiography a decade earlier, Herzog's article transferred the scholarly findings of critical Israeli archaeologists into the domain of wider public debate and engendered a series of stock-taking, politically charged, academic conferences. The opening of his piece was explosive:

> This is what archaeologists have learned from their excavations in the Land of Israel: the Israelites were never in Egypt, did not wander in the desert, did not conquer the land in a military campaign and did not pass it on to the 12 tribes of Israel. Perhaps even harder to swallow is the fact that the united monarchy of David and Solomon, which is described by the Bible as a regional power, was at most a small tribal kingdom. And it will come as an unpleasant shock to many that the God of Israel, Jehovah, had a female consort and that the early Israelite religion adopted monotheism only in the waning period of the monarchy and not at Mount Sinai. Most of those who are engaged in scientific work in the interlocking spheres of the Bible, archaeology and the history of the Jewish people – and who once went into the field looking for proof to corroborate the Bible story – now agree that the historic events relating to the stages of the Jewish People's emergence are radically different from what that story tells . . . The critical question of this archaeological revolution has not yet trickled down into public consciousness, but it cannot be ignored.[44]

The critical scrutiny of the Bible did not of course start with the group of Israeli archaeologists of whom Herzog is a notable representative. It goes back to the second half of the nineteenth century. The work of the German philologist Julius Wellhausen, to whom we shall return later, is commonly accepted as the beginning of modern textual criticism of the Bible. However, although they should not be privileged per se, the role played by Israeli archaeologists and Bible scholars is particularly interesting in the context of this study. It should be noted that the Israeli archaeologists have a crucial advantage over their Bible studies compatriots, in that they have controlled a large chunk of the text from 1948 to 1967, and almost all of it since 1967 (excluding Transjordan). This explains the centrality of the Israeli archaeologists in the international scholarly community, and the relative anonymity of those engaged in intrinsically textual Bible studies. There is, additionally, an ironic (or dialectical) twist in the history of Israeli archaeology. The transformation in 1948 of the settler community (the Yishuv) into a settler nation-state, and its annexation in 1967 of almost the entire land of the Bible, might seem auspicious for a decisive archaeological campaign that would underpin the appropriation of the mythical site of return. However, the results of this research have been rather subversive, even if unwittingly so. The fidelity to scientific truth of the archaeologists of Herzog's generation has refuted precisely that which was supposed to be confirmed and reasserted. To borrow a biblical analogy, it is as if the Balaam episode was inverted: he had been sent to curse and ended up blessing (Numbers 22–24), whereas the critical archaeologists keep deleting from the record events whose occurrence they were dispatched to confirm.

The debates over the Bible, how to study it, its historical validity and many other themes emanating from it have in recent years generated a rather extensive volume of academic activity, both in Israel and internationally.[45] I wish to focus on two themes, which in different ways are significant for understanding how Ben-Gurion read the Bible in general and the Book of Joshua in particular. The first is the unfolding pronouncements of Israeli archaeology on the biblical narrative of the creation of the Jewish nation, and its conquest of and settlement in the Promised Land. The second theme is what is known as the Deuteronomistic History, within which the Book of Joshua ought to be placed.

## 1 Biblical archaeology in Israel from the 1950s to the 1990s

As has been noted throughout this study, the crucial triumph of the settler community in 1948 comprised its assertion as a settler nation-state, the removal of the metropolitan colonial power and of the vast majority of the indigenous community from within the boundaries of that state, resulting in that community's near-complete destruction. In the nation-state formation, based on the army and the Bible, that ensued under Ben-Gurion's regime, archaeology played an important and multifaceted role. For nineteenth-century Western archaeology, Palestine was marginal compared to Mesopotamia and Egypt. Things began to change with Britain's growing colonial interest, American fascination with the region that, as we shall see, became pivotal from the 1920s, and of course the Israeli settler-national project after 1948.

The first stage was what in the late 1950s and early 1960s would grow into a bitter feud between two founding archaeologists of the Hebrew University: Yigael Yadin and Yohanan Aharoni. The Aharoni–Yadin feud, which developed out of their digs in the Upper Galilee in the second half of the 1950s, would be formative for nascent Israeli archaeology.[46]

Yadin was the IDF's chief of operations in the 1948 war, going on to become formal chief of staff. Although he gained celebrity status through his excavations in Masada and the Judaea desert, it was his digs in the Upper Galilee, Hazor in particular, in the second half of the 1950s that established him as the charismatic doyen of Israeli archaeology. The combination of pomposity on the one hand and utter scientific vacuity on the other made Yadin an interesting figure and, during his abortive political career in the late 1970s and early 1980s, a pitiable one. Aharoni migrated to Palestine from Germany in 1933 and was a founding member of Kibbutz Allonim, on the western edge of the Jezreel Valley. After fighting in the 1948 war, he became a professor of archaeology at the Hebrew University, later leaving for the newly founded Tel Aviv University because of his bitter feud with Yadin.

At the risk of repetition, it cannot be overemphasized that the Zionist Israeli project was not merely national but, crucially, settler-national. Correspondingly, the appropriation of the national homeland through the Bible and biblical archaeology had to be two-dimensional: it was simultaneously claimed for the Jewish nation, and implicitly denied to the indigenous foe. To be sure, the choice of the Galilee for excavations had scientific reasons. Before 1967, Israeli archaeologists were denied access to the central hill area (i.e., the West Bank) and East Jerusalem, under Jordanian sovereignty, while the littoral was, as we shall see, considered to have been under Philistine yoke in the crucial period. This left the Negev in the south and the Galilee in the north for digs that were intended to reconstruct the possession of the land by ancient Israel. There was another reason for choosing the northern site, however: the Galilee was an area where the success of the 1948 ethnic cleansing was *relatively* limited. It was no coincidence that the 1958 annual convention of the archaeological society, in which the initial Hazor findings were unearthed and Aharoni and Yadin had one of their showdowns, was held in Safed. That city, in the eastern part of the Upper Galilee, unlike other parts of the region had been thoroughly cleansed in 1948. And the convention was not just a normal academic gathering, but a well-orchestrated jamboree, which was attended by the mayor of Safed and state officials, by the public, and by the Mizrahi immigrants, whom Yadin exploited as cheap labour in the digs, supposedly to inculcate some Israeliness in them.

As with much biblical archaeology, the temporal focus of the dispute between Yadin and Aharoni was the transition from the late Bronze (also called Canaanite) to the early Iron (also called Israelite) Age, roughly the thirteenth and twelfth centuries BCE. To that period was attributed the entrance of the Israelites into Canaan, and their colonization of and settlement in it. Aharoni, inspired by Albrecht Alt, the German Protestant scholar of theology and archaeology, interpreted the Hazor findings, and those in the Galilee more broadly, as confirming the settlement narrative conveyed by the Book of Judges: a gradual and relatively peaceful process, accompanied by tolerable relations with the local Canaanite population, something akin to the Zionist strategy of 'another acre, another goat' minus the 1948 ethnic cleansing, by the end of which the Israelites had not just settled in the country, but had taken it over. Standing on the shoulders of William Foxwell Albright (about whom more shortly), Yadin would have none of it: with the recently concluded 1948 war looming large, he saw in the same findings a confirmation of the Book of Joshua, Chapters 1 to 11 of which relate how the country had been swiftly conquered by a nationally unified army of invading Israelites led by a brilliant and charismatic commander; they removed and disinherited the Canaanite peoples, allotted the land to the various tribes, and settled on it.[47]

In order to give some context to the Yadin–Aharoni dispute, it is worth turning briefly to W. F. Albright, whose striking statement on the alleged annihilation of the Canaanites is cited at the beginning of the chapter. There could hardly be a better example for the elective affinity between the consciousness of an American Protestant settler and that of his Zionist Israeli counterparts, manifested through the Bible and biblical archaeology. Albright was born to Protestant missionary parents in Chile late in the nineteenth century, and he grew up in a succession of small Methodist communities in the American Midwest, where his father was minister. Graduating from Upper Iowa University in 1912, Albright became the principal of a high school in a small German-speaking community in South Dakota. The turning point in his life came when Albright's remarkable linguistic ability manifested itself in an article on Akkadian that was published in the *Orientalische Literaturzeitung*, and that earned him a Fellowship in Semitics to write a PhD dissertation under the renowned Semitic scholar Paul Haupt at Johns Hopkins. Albright went on to become one of the most influential biblical archaeologists of the twentieth century, and the pivotal figure of what became known as the Baltimore School.[48]

Albright's *oeuvre* and world view form a remarkable combination of dedication to scholarship and settler-Protestant fundamentalism. His starting point was the unerring authority of Scripture, the underlying feature of fundamentalism.[49] Beginning in the 1920s he carried out a programme of excavations whose explicit purpose was to prove wrong the pronouncements of critical German scholarship – known as High Criticism – on the Old Testament, and restore the historical veracity of the Old Testament's main narrative, namely, how Judaeo-Christian monotheism had come into being through the Israelite sojourn in Egypt, the exit to freedom, conquest of and settlement in the Promised Land. Albright believed uncompromisingly in the moral superiority of Judaeo-Christian theology as the foundation of Western civilization, and averred that scientific archaeology should be put at the service of that spiritual purpose.[50]

Perhaps more than any other scholar, Albright can be accredited with the conception of an authoritative circular epistemology, which could not be questioned and which was hugely influential, in particular on both Aharoni and Yadin. This argument held that the biblical text truthfully represented the events and figures that it recounted, and that these events and figures really occurred and existed. Archaeology existed not to question but to confirm their veracious representation, occurrence and existence; moreover, the biblical text itself determined the questions to be posed and the terms and categories to be examined, even though as such they could not be found anywhere other than in the biblical text itself. The most notable example of this forceful tautology, which Nadia Abu El Haj robustly analyses,[51] is the way Albright assigned ethno-cultural identity to material remains, especially pottery, identifying them as 'Israelite', 'Canaanite' and so forth. Such attribution, however, did not in any way emanate intrinsically from the evidence itself − from, say, a piece of ceramic − but from the biblical text. This unchallenged presupposition shaped the scholarly discourse of both Aharoni and Yadin and their community (even if the former preferred Alt's Book of Judges version of settlement to Albright's Book of Joshua) to a degree that cannot be overstated.

Albright was also a firm believer in the two pillars of settler societies: conquest, removal and settlement; and the ethnic purity of the impregnable settler entity − in the biblical as well as in the more recent past, without denying the horrendous violence that inhered in the process. As he observed in 1957:

. . . we Americans have perhaps less right than most modern nations, in spite of our genuine humanitarianism, to sit in judgment on the Israelites of the thirteenth century B.C., since we have, intentionally or otherwise, exterminated scores of thousands of Indians in every corner of our great nation and have crowded the rest into concentration camps. The fact that this was probably inevitable does not make it more edifying to the Americans today. It is significant that after the first phase of the Israelite Conquest [i.e., Joshua's] we hear no more about 'devoting' the population of Canaanite towns, but only of driving them out or putting them to tribute. From the impartial standpoint of a philosopher of history, it often seems necessary that a people of markedly inferior type should vanish before a people of superior potentialities, since there is a point beyond which racial mixture cannot go without disaster. When such a process takes place – as at present in Australia – there is generally little that can be done by the humanitarian – though every deed of brutality and injustice is infallibly visited upon the aggressor.[52]

Albright's work also occasions a note on the two main scholarly models in biblical scholarship that were drawn upon to explain the rise of ancient Israel. These were the German 'rise of the nation-state' model, and the American 'nation of immigrants' model. Each model of explaining the birth of ancient Israel is congruous with the origins and concerns of each modern nation. The Germans in the latter part of the nineteenth century and the early decades of the twentieth looked at the ancient Israelites through the lens of Bismarck's unification and creation of a nation-state, which made them chiefly interested in the Davidic monarchy as a 'nation-state', how it had come into being, its strength and disintegration. The Americans, Albright first and foremost, were not only intent on proving wrong German scepticism of the textual coherence and historical reliability of the Old Testament, but also obsessively focused on the earlier part of the narrative, that which described conquest, disinheriting and settlement and which they thought they were re-enacting.[53]

Yadin, Aharoni and their students adhered to Albright's fundamentals, even if Aharoni went on to adopt Alt's version of the settlement narrative. On the whole they rejected complex views like those put forth by the German philological wizard Martin Noth (on whom more shortly), and operated unquestioningly upon the assumption that the biblical story was veracious, and that it was therefore perfectly sensible to call pottery or eras BCE Israelite or Canaanite – even though there was not one iota of extra-biblical evidence that supported these designations. Shulamit Geva of the Hebrew University in particular exposes the utter absence of epistemic depth and intellectual sophistication in Israeli archaeological discourse from the 1950s to the 1970s. The questions posed were merely technical, and debates took place over the most trivial and mundane issues. Even though there was much to learn from Albright on the deeper themes relating to archaeology as a discipline and form of knowledge, nothing was gained[54] except of course the adoption of his fundamentalist belief in scriptural inerrancy and political predilection for settlers' conquest.

The later generation of Israeli archaeologists, whose findings have been systematically published from the 1990s on, are not the only ones to have challenged the orthodoxy of Albright and his American and Israeli followers. Their control of the archaeological text – i.e., the territory – has been so overwhelming, more so after 1967, that it has accorded them a pivotal position in the scientific discourse. These scholars undid the Gordian knot that had tautologically tied archaeology to biblical narrative and terminology, and gradually began to operate on the assumption that archaeological evidence might acutely call the biblical narrative into question rather than inexorably confirm it. Concomitantly, the tautology whereby material evidence, from pottery to architecture, had been infused with pure ethnic essence was refuted and discarded.[55] The severance from the Bible continued apace, culminating in what Herzog identifies as the transition 'from biblical archaeology to social archaeology'.[56] The textual turning point was a volume entitled *From Nomadism to Monarchy: Archaeological and Historical Aspects of Early Israel*, edited by Israel Finkelstein and Nadav Na'aman, who together with Herzog are the most notable critical Israeli archaeologists.[57]

Admittedly the most radical of the three, Herzog charts the unfolding of this transformation as a case of what Thomas Kuhn identified as a scientific revolution.[58] He helpfully highlights the crucial junctures at which according to Kuhn's model the irrevocable crisis of the prevailing paradigm occurs, prior to the scientific shift being fully effected.[59] These junctures are the following events that the biblical narrative recounts. First, the period of the patriarchs is described anachronistically, as Benjamin Mazar (professor of biblical history and archaeology of Palestine at the Hebrew University from the early 1950s to the late 1970s; Herzog calls him 'father of biblical archaeology's Israeli branch') observed, in terms appropriate for 'the late era of the Judges and early monarchy';[60] this observation would eventually lead to questioning the notion of the patriarchs' era, indeed their existence, altogether. Second, archaeologists have found no extra-biblical evidence whatsoever for the Hebrews' slavery in, and exodus from, Egypt, or for their wandering in the desert and Mount Sinai spectacle; indeed, lack of evidence for the latter has provoked desperate scholars spuriously either to 'discover' the mountain in the northern Hijaz (the area where Mecca is located) or to identify it as Mount Karkom in the Negev.

Third, and highly significant for modern politics, the conquest of the Promised Land by the invading Israelites under Joshua, and the allotment of that land among the tribes, has been proven to be fiction. The unparalleled work done by Na'aman on this question[61] was acknowledged by Aharoni towards the end of his life, while Herzog wryly points out: 'The contradictions between the archaeological findings and the tradition of the united military conquest under Joshua's leadership have been known for decades, and to the best of my knowledge Yadin was the last archaeologist who endorsed its historical reliability.'[62] This is a faithful epitaph for Yadin the scholar: all that could be got wrong he got consistently wrong. The two main indicators informing the archaeological dismissal of the biblical conquest were the absence of large walled cities in Palestine in the Late Bronze–Early Iron Age (thirteenth–twelfth centuries BCE) and the failure of the biblical text to mention Egypt, which ruled the area until the middle of the twelfth century BCE. Herzog concludes: 'The cities of Canaan were neither mighty nor fortified nor reached the heavens. The heroism of the conquerors, few against many, and the deeds of the Almighty, who fought for his people, is a theological reconstruction devoid of factual foundation.'[63]

Fourth is the alleged grandeur of what is wrongly termed the 'united monarchy' as established by David and further aggrandized by Solomon in the tenth and ninth centuries BCE. Although we begin to enter a period in which the biblical story has some fidelity to external evidence, and the figures of David and Solomon seem to have been real, much of the story is still highly suspect. Jerusalem, for example, was clearly a small town with perhaps a modest fortified castle; it certainly was not the sumptuous capital of an empire, but the centre of a tribal principality. Moreover, there had never been a united monarchy, but from the outset two separate entities, Israel and Judah. Jerusalem's status grew after the Assyrians had destroyed Judah's northern nemesis, the Kingdom of Israel, in 722 BCE. Another significant theme relating to the same period is the beginning of monotheism. In this respect too the biblical story is questionable at best. Throughout most of the period external evidence shows that worship focused on two gods: Jehovah and his female partner Asherah. Monotheism as a concept and centralized state religion appeared at the earliest in the final phase of the Kingdom of Judah some time in the last third of the seventh century BCE, at which point the Kingdom of Israel had ceased to exist.[64]

What alternative explanation does critical archaeology offer, underlain as it has been by the paradigmatic shift from biblical to social archaeology? Here is a pithy reply by Finkelstein, one of the most notable critical archaeologists, who crucially excavated the central hill area (the south–north axis from Jerusalem to Nablus in the occupied West Bank) in the 1980s and 1990s. His conclusions vindicate my point that excavation of the territories occupied in 1967 – the heartland of the biblical story – ironically resulted in the refutation of that story rather than its confirmation:

As far as I can judge, the rise of Early Israel was not a unique event in the history of Palestine. Rather, it was one phase in long-term cyclic socio-economic and demographic processes that started in the 4th millennium BCE. The wave of settlement that took place in the highlands in the late second millennium BCE was no more than a chapter in alternating shifts along the typical Near Eastern socio-economic continuum, between sedentary and pastoral modes of subsistence. The genuine change – the ground-breaking transformation in the history of Palestine – came with the rise of the territorial-national [sic] states in the first millennium BCE. I will argue that full-blown statehood was not achieved before the 9th century BCE in Israel and the 8th century in Judah.[65]

Drawing on his own project in the Beersheba Valley and extensive use of the anthropological literature on ethnicity, Herzog insists on a corrective to Finkelstein, which is important for both the knowledge of the past and the politics of the present. Herzog's starting point is of course the downright rejection of the Albright/Yadin thesis. He also qualifies, however, the lineage that begins with Alt's 'peaceful infiltration' (adopted by Aharoni), Gottwald's 'sociological model' (which 'translates' Alt's biblical archaeology language into the idiom of the social sciences), and Finkelstein's sedentarization of nomads in the central hill area. Herzog's main qualification is that '[e]ach of these models suggests a specific [ethnic] source for the Israelites. An integrative definition of ethnicity, as well as the archaeological evidence and the biblical data, refute such an exclusive approach'. In other words, Herzog's higher awareness of the historically constructed nature of ethnicity leads him to look at the evidence differently, and to reject the identification of an exclusive Israelite ethnicity. He identifies instead a long process of fusion of several autochthonous elements in various parts of Palestine, until 'the ethnic Israelite identity . . . was comprehended by the occupants themselves and also defined as such by others'. Herzog's historicist doggedness does not stop there: 'Israelite ethnic identity . . . existed in reality only for about 100 years, from the late eleventh to the late tenth centuries BCE. It was mostly in the ideological sphere of the Old Testament and later theological literature that the Israelite identity relating to the settlement and monarchic periods obtained its glorified eternal survival'.[66]

Finally, note should be made of a group of scholars called minimalists, which consists mostly of non-Israelis, although Herzog is occasionally numbered among them. Their name refers to their ascription of minimal historical reliability to the biblical narrative. The two most notable articulators of this approach are Philip Davies and Keith Whitelam. The minimalists identify three different kinds of 'Israel'. One is Biblical Israel, an ideological construct that was created when the Old Testament, or at least a crucial part thereof, was composed, which could not have taken place before the end of the seventh century BCE, and more probably in the post-exilic era. The second is Ancient Israel, a scholarly construct that amalgmates varying combinations of the biblical story and archaeological findings. The third is Historical Israel, which is revealed by archaeological research and encompassed the inhabitants of that land in the Iron Age. The most explicit political point is made by Whitelam, who reveals how the history of all of Palestine's inhabitants has been occluded – indeed denied outright – by the overwhelming domination of the Judaeo-Christian discourse, and the extent to which this serves the Zionist Israeli cause. The problem with Whitelam's argument is its occasional lack of clarity over what is meant by Palestinian history in the Late Bronze and Early Iron Ages. It is one thing to argue that Judaeo-Christian Zionism denies the existence of all human groups that have comprised the rich texture of the land; it is quite another to suggest that Palestinian history at that period is in some obvious sense the exclusive history of the modern Arab Palestinian nation. I find the latter as absurd as the Zionist concoctions.[67]

## 2 Joshua and King Josiah: Deuteronomistic History

To complete the context within which Ben-Gurion's exegesis on the Book of Joshua ought to be understood, we must move from the way in which the biblical text relates to extrinsic evidence to the biblical text itself. The composition of the historical narrative, the veracity of which has been demolished by archaeology, is itself an interestingly complex question, as is the scholarship that has deconstructed the narrative's composition. Scholarship on the composition of the Old Testament – when it was written, by whom, and on the basis of what sources – had evolved gradually since the Reformation, but exploded from the second half of the nineteenth century on. Today, the body of work on it has reached such voluminous magnitude that even a crude summary would inevitably confuse rather than inform. I focus here on the identification of what is called Deuteronomistic History, which – variations and nuances notwithstanding – is something the scholarly community broadly agrees upon as an explanation for the composition of a coherent biblical unit that comprises seven books. This unit begins from Deuteronomy, which is severed from the Pentateuch, continues with Joshua and Judges through 1 and 2 Samuel, and ends with 1 and 2 Kings.[68]

According to 2 Kings 22–23 the temple of Jerusalem underwent repairs and renovation in the eighteenth year of King Josiah's reign (the last third of the seventh century BCE). A high priest, Hilkiah, found a scroll, which was read to the king by Shaphan, one of his courtiers. Josiah was startled by what he had heard and sent his men to seek the interpretation of the prophetess Huldah. She in effect said that the divine judgment declared in Deuteronomy would indeed befall Jerusalem, but that Josiah's adherence to Yahweh's law had earned him a peaceful end. The King followed her words, which as Thomas Römer notes are reminiscent of Jeremiah's,[69] with a religious 'reform'. He read the scroll aloud to his subjects, eliminated the priests of the deities Baal and Asherah, and destroyed their places of worship, as well as that of Yahweh in the now extinct Kingdom of Israel. He 'renewed' the covenant between the people and Yahweh, and in that spirit celebrated Passover.

Early Jewish commentators and Church Fathers identified Hilkiah's discovered scroll as the Book of Deuteronomy, and interpreted Josiah's cultic centralization and religious cleansing as confirmation of Deuteronomistic Law. On that basis Julius Wellhausen, who laid the foundations of the German High Criticism in the second half of the nineteenth century, both adduced from this evidence that a 'primitive edition' of Deuteronomy was composed during Josiah's reign, and proposed his 'pious lie' theory, according to which Deuteronomy's first edition was written to legitimize the so-called Josianic reform. In order to achieve this legitimacy, Deuteronomy was presented as Moses' concluding testament. As Römer cautions, however, these theories assume that the story recounted in 2 Kings 22–23 really happened, which is highly problematic. This passage, he says, 'is above all the "foundation myth" of the Deuteronomists, and cannot be used naively as an eye-witness report of the so-called reform'.[70] Pharaoh Neco killed Josiah in 609 BCE; Josiah had apparently become an Egyptian vassal after the decline of Assyria, but retracted his allegiance.[71]

Who then were the Deuteronomists, when did they compose their Deuteronomistic History, and what are they said to have written? For that we must first turn to the German scholar Martin Noth. Although not necessarily coming out against Wellhausen, Noth transformed the focus and method of the textual and historical study of the Old Testament. Proceeding from his Documentary Hypothesis, which was mainly concerned with the types of sources ('documents') used by the 'authors' of the Pentateuch, Wellhausen had identified continuities between the books of Deuteronomy and Joshua, and therefore deemed the Hexateuch (the first six books of the Bible – the Pentateuch and the Book of Joshua) to be more coherent than the Pentateuch. Noth did not refute these continuities or Wellhausen's method of reconstructing the 'ancient sources', but neither did he adopt it as his chief modus operandi. Following the approach concerned with the history of the transmission of the Bible with its interest in the development of large units, and his own commentary on Joshua (informed by his teacher Alt), Noth put forth a different structural proposition. Ensconced at Königsberg during the Second World War, in 1943 he published his *Deuteronomistic History* (the English translation appeared three decades later), in which he argued that the genuinely coherent textual unit in the Bible was not the Hexateuch but that comprising the books from Deuteronomy to 2 Kings. That unit, he continued, had been composed after 560 BCE at the earliest in the Babylonian exile, and its purpose was to make sense of and religiously justify exile by constructing a teleological narrative, whose beginning was the presentation of Deuteronomistic/Mosaic Law in the desert.[72]

As a foundational argument Noth's thesis has withstood the test of time, but there have been correctives, of which two in particular stand out. The first was put forward by the American scholar Frank Moore Cross in the late 1960s and early 1970s, especially in his book of 1973, *Canaanite Myth and Hebrew Epic: Essays in the History of the Religion of Israel.* Moore showed that not all the Deuteronomistic composite could have been a creation of the exilic period in Babylon, and that a substantial part of it was written during Josiah's reign. He went on to identify two redactions or editorial phases: one in the final decades of the seventh century BCE under Josiah and the other in the second half of the sixth century BCE in exile. Although his German students defended Noth's thesis, Moore's corrective prevailed in the English-speaking scholarly community.[73] A social archaeologist like Finkelstein confirms the currency gained by Moore's double-redaction thesis.[74] The second corrective is Römer's, put forward in his 2005 work cited above, *The So-Called Deuteronomistic History: A Sociological, Historical and Literary Introduction.* In this thorough and eloquent commentary on the Deuteronomistic unit, Römer makes a sustained argument for three redactions: during Josiah's reign; Babylonian (making sense of exile); and Persian. In the final, Persian phase, the Torah (Pentateuch) was formed as a coherent unit and changes were introduced to sever Deuteronomy from the Book of Joshua, in order to integrate the former better with the four books that precede it; at the same time, changes were made that elevated the stature of Moses above all the outstanding figures who followed him (in the biblical narrative), especially Joshua.[75]

The founders of this narrative, the Deuteronomists, are believed to have been high-ranking scribes in Jerusalem in the second half of the seventh century BCE, with access to a possible archive in the temple, who used official documents deposited there, at least for the period of the monarchy.[76] Finkelstein summarizes the foundation of the Deuteronomistic Historiography by these scribes under Josiah:

> This writing served as an ideological stage for his [Josiah's] actions in the realm of the cultic centralisation and his ambition of territorial expansion to the Israeli [i.e., the extinct kingdom of Israel] provinces, which the retreating Assyria had vacated. I think that this was an ideology, which might be subsumed under 'one God, one temple, one capital (Jerusalem) and one king (from the Davidic dynasty)'. It stressed the cultic concentration in Jerusalem and the eternal divine fidelity to the House of David. To the best of my understanding, it created for the first time the pan-Israelite idea. Thus the original Deuteronomistic History climaxed with the description of Josiah as the Davidic dynasty's ultimate righteous king.[77]

The final piece in the contextual jigsaw leads directly to Ben-Gurion's exegetical pronouncement. This piece is the absolutely crucial – for scholarly, political and ideological reasons – Book of Joshua. The book's structure comprises three different parts that are clearly crudely stitched together: the conquest narrative (Chapters 2–12); the distribution among the tribes of land that had been reportedly cleansed from its original inhabitants (Chapters 13–22); and speeches by Yahweh (Chapter 1) and Joshua (Chapters 23 and 24).[78] As we shall see, Joshua's speeches were the focus of Ben-Gurion's commentary. The role of the redactor or editor in the book's composition comes to the fore most conspicuously in the transition from the first (conquest) to the second (land distribution) parts. In 11:16 we are told that '[s]o Joshua took all that land', an episode which is then expanded upon; in 13:1, however, the Lord says to Joshua, 'Thou art old and stricken in years, and there remaineth yet very much land to be possessed.' Since in Palestine there was little prospect for westward expansion, the book's textual coherence comes unstitched.

There are two further points that should be made, which are critical to the understanding of the Book of Joshua, especially the substantial chunks of it that were probably composed by Josiah's Deuteronomist scribes: the Assyrian politico-cultural context, and the presence – so to speak – of Josiah in Joshua, which will be clarified shortly. Römer insightfully discusses the extent to which Deuteronomistic writing was steeped in Assyrian culture, something true not only for the Book of Joshua, but also for its underlying text, Deuteronomy itself. Römer offers two striking comparisons between the two books. He first compares the loyalty oaths forced upon vassal kings by Esarhaddon in 672 BCE, to ensure their continued allegiance to his successor Assurbanipal: 'You shall love Assurbanipal . . . king of Assyria, your lord, as yourself. You shall hearken to whatever he says and do whatever he commands, and you shall not seek any other king or any other lord against him. This treaty . . . you shall speak to your sons and grandsons, your seed and your seed's seed which shall be born in the future', with Deuteronomy 6:4–7: 'Hear, Israel: Yahweh is our God, Yahweh is One. You shall love Yahweh your God with all your heart, with all your life and with all your might . . . Keep these words that I am commanding you today on your heart and teach them to your sons.'[79]

In a similar vein, the conquest narrative in Joshua (Chapters 2–12) is basically modelled after the rich tradition of Assyrian conquest accounts. Römer's presentation on this point is particularly helpful, as he gleans the main features from the Assyrian textual corpus and convincingly shows their appearance, one by one, in Joshua.[80] To take just a couple of examples, one feature in the Assyrian accounts is that the conquest of some sites is recounted in detail whereas the conquest of other locales is summarily presented. Similarly, in Joshua the conquest of Jericho and Ai-Bethel is reported in detail while subsequent victories are much more briefly presented. Assyrian accounts highlight the voluntary submission of peoples who, having become cognizant of Assyrian might, come from afar to surrender; this is also precisely the case with the Gibeonites in Chapter 9 of Joshua. Lastly the Assyrian accounts convey the totality of victory by the description of the capture and killing of the enemy's kings. A campaign of King Sennacherib is concluded thus: 'And the mighty princes feared my battle array; they fled their abodes, and like bats [living in] cracks [caves], they flew alone to inaccessible places . . . the governors (and) nobles who had sinned I put to death; and I hung their corpses on poles around the city.' In Joshua, Chapter 10, the defeat of the alliance of the kings of the south ends with these five kings fleeing and hiding in the cave at Makkedah (verse 16). They are chased out, '[a]nd afterward Joshua smote them, and slew them, and hanged them on five trees; and they were hanging upon the trees until the evening' (verse 26). Fittingly, Römer concludes his detailed demonstration of the Assyrian conquest model's strong presence in the Book of Joshua by stating: 'It is quite possible that the so-called "conquest tradition" is nothing else than an invention by Deuteronomistic scribes.'[81]

In a thoughtful essay, Richard Nelson adds to the depiction of the late seventh-century BCE environment within which the Deuteronomist created the Book of Joshua and the figure of Joshua.[82] Nelson presents his argument in two stages. He first summarizes the scholarship that remarked upon the fact that Joshua's figure was portrayed by Deuteronomistic writers according to the conventions of describing a royal sovereign. Nelson then avers that the royal portrayal of Joshua is not just a general one, but is reciprocally referring to Josiah – reciprocally, for Nelson argues that the figure of Joshua was created 'as a sort of prototypical Josiah'.[83] Joshua's figure, in other words, was meant to legitimize and glorify Josiah by endowing the latter's deeds and ambitions with the depth that emanates from following a long and hallowed tradition: Joshua was an allegorical portrait of Josiah. Nelson identifies three parallels, in both content and literary form, between the rule of Josiah and Joshua of the Deuteronomist: obedience to Yahweh's law as specified in Deuteronomy; acting as mediator and facilitator of the covenants between Yahweh and his people; the celebration of Passover as a public feast, conducted only in the sanctuary of Yahweh's choice, in order to enhance cultic – and hence political – centralization.[84]

There are numerous examples of the way in which seeing Joshua as an allegorical portrait of Josiah adds insight to the understanding of the Deuteronomist's theology of history, to use Nelson's term. The example I would like to present would become central for modern settler societies: ethnic purity. In the Book of Joshua the construction of this principle is founded upon Deuteronomy 7:3, and it is not difficult to see what made it so germane to a settler ideology, presented as it is to a group about to invade a 'promised' territory and disinherit its indigenous people: 'Neither shalt thou make marriages with them; thy daughter thou shalt not give unto his son, nor his daughter shalt thou take unto thy son.' This injunction is then repeated after colonization was apparently accomplished, in Joshua's penultimate speech (23:12–13): 'Else if ye do in any wise go back, and cleave unto the remnants of these nations, even these that remain among you, and shall make marriages with them, and they to you . . . God will no more drive out any of these nations from before you.' In the Deuteronomistic unit this issue is also raised in the context of Solomon and Ahab. Nelson stresses the extent to which unveiling the Josiah/Joshua reciprocity sheds light on the Deuteronomist's world. Ethnic purity took on 'increased importance' because of Josiah's irredentist policy towards the territory of the former kingdom of Israel, in which the outsiders brought in by the Assyrians had a whole century to intermingle, and because of Josiah's possible use of Greek mercenaries. 'Joshua's call for ethnic purity now takes on a deeper meaning. It is as though the Deuteronomist has taken it upon himself to suggest a national policy to his hero king. As in the days of Joshua, Josiah's policy towards this issue of miscegenation can only be that of Deuteronomy 7:3.'[85]

## Ben-Gurion's Exegeses

The convergence of comments by Anita Shapira and Herzog may helpfully introduce Ben-Gurion's commentary on, particularly, the Book of Joshua. In a footnote in one of her pronouncements on the Bible's place in Israeli identity, on which I dwelt at some length in the previous chapter, Shapira observes: 'There is similarity between Protestantism and its attitude to the Scriptures and the attitude to the biblical "literalness" [*pehsat*] of the [Zionist] Jews.'[86] In the essay in which he casts the work of the critical archaeologists in the form of a Kuhnian scientific revolution,[87] Herzog concludes with some comments on the relation of this work to Israeli society, and begs to differ from the assumption that 'undermining the historicity of the Bible's stories would be understood as undermining "our historical right" [over the land of Israel]'.[88] One of the reasons for which Herzog rejects this assumption is that 'it is possible to reach political conclusions, which contrarily stress the autochthonous-ness of the Israelites, who had not arrived in it as foreign conquerors. The sense of being natives of the country prevalent among the young generation is unencumbered by the need "to justify" the existence of the state of Israel on the basis of divine promises'.[89]

So, what Shapira relegates to a seemingly incidental footnote is actually pivotal for understanding the context within which the Zionist 'return' to the Bible and, particularly, Ben-Gurion's reading of the Bible were Protestant. I should first clarify what I do *not* mean by Protestant: nothing that has anything to do with identity politics and the theme of identity in general. In other words, I am not arguing that Ben-Gurion, or for that matter the Zionist Israeli settlers, were Protestants or were fond of Protestantism in a simple, straightforward way. The point is, rather, that the modern Zionist way of referring to the Old Testament and using it is Protestant, in the sense I have explored as a history of the prefix *Re-*. This way of referring to the Old Testament has three related characteristics: the direct approach to the text, and the concomitant disregard for (and stripping away of) the layers of theological commentary that mediate between the reading individual and the foundational text; the assumption that it is the right of the individual subject to engage with the scriptures precisely because he is an individual subject; the emphasis laid upon the narrative parts of the Old Testament, under the assumption that the narrative is veracious, and that its occurrence is an authoritative legitimizing source for all sorts of returns, re-enactments, re-establishments and restorations.

For Ben-Gurion, pushing the Talmud and Mishnah to one side and addressing the Old Testament directly was a central constituent of his negation of exile, which has received ample attention in this study. And yet it is helpful to furnish a few examples of the removal of exilic Judaism in the context of Ben-Gurion's Bible project of the 1950s and early 1960s, examples that are remarkable in their fundamentalism. Some notable intellectuals and writers were censorious of Ben-Gurion's biblical messianism and dismissive attitude to exilic scholarship. One such was Nathan Rotenstreich, professor of philosophy at the Hebrew University. In a letter dated 23 March 1957, replying to Rotenstreich's reservations about his Bible-fetish, Ben-Gurion unabashedly defended his notions of 'messianic vision' and 'historical leap' as a political path worth pursuing. Explaining his idea of spatial leap (*kefitsat ha-derekh*), he moves on to temporal leap *(kefitsat ha-zeman)*. By the latter, he meant that the Zionist project in Palestine constituted a new beginning,

> which instantly congregates with the remote past, the past of Joshua son of Nun, David, Uziah, the early Hasmoneans. Of all the books that had been created in the Diaspora there is no book as close to the country's youth as the Bible. It is true that it is not a book but a collection of books; and not all these books are equally close to us. If, however, you take [all the books written in the Diaspora from first to last] – the Bible books tip the balance as far as the Israeli youth is concerned in their sparkle, 'freshness', actuality, geographical and plot-like proximity, in their breath; you will not find a single Hebrew book created after the Bible until the last fifty or thirty years, that would be as close, intimate to the youth as the Bible. The distant past has ceased being distant. The immediate past has ceased being immediate. The country's youth looks now at the Jewish People through the lens of the Jewish state and the Bible – not that of the township in Poland or of the ideology created in Vienna and Odessa and Warsaw sixty years ago. The Jewish nineteenth century is farther and more alien to the Israeli youth than the distant past of three thousand years ago.[90]

Another instance that evinces the 'Protestant' nature of Ben-Gurion's Bible project is the perspective of a critic who was aware that this project was not in any obvious or linear way Jewish. In May 1962 Ben-Gurion attended the annual convention of the Writers' Society, where he had a public debate with Haim Hazaz. It might be recalled that two decades earlier Hazaz had written 'The Sermon', a short story in which a recluse kibbutz member denounces Jewish history, saying that exile's passivity is not history.[91] Whether he had undergone a change of heart, or whether he had in fact meant to criticize the negation of exile by letting it speak for itself so forcefully, Hazaz had become a critic of what Isaiah Leibowitz had termed Ben-Gurion's *Biblioteriah* (Bible-idolatry). As the debate unfolded, Hazaz said to Ben-Gurion:

> I am not opposed to the study of the Bible, which is self-evident, but to the biblical 'cult', when the Bible becomes the exclusive foundation. The Bible is just part of Judaism, and actually the Jewish People was not too concerned with this part, nor did this part facilitate the preservation of the Jewish people . . . In itself the Bible is no more than still water that leads nowhere other than a dead-end . . . At best we shall obtain the archaeology, geography of the land of Israel, erudition. But we shan't obtain spiritual life.[92]

Ben-Gurion's obduracy was unshakeable and he concluded by reiterating:

> As for the Bible, I refute your approach entirely. You do not see why the Bible is needed here, [the reason is] that we need a Jew to know what his bond to the land is, we need to deepen his bond to the land. It is not [just] archaeology. When Yadin recounted his excavations in the Negev Mount – with what awe and gaiety were his words heard, as if Bar-Kokhba's hand was stretched to us. [Until recently] it was not known whether he was Bar-Kokhba or Bar Kuziba, and suddenly he has become a living warrior; this speaks to the heart . . . You say not to make a 'cult' of it; in my view 'cult' must be made, this is holiness, there is nothing like it . . . The Bible speaks to them [Israeli youth] from every rock. If they are in the Negev – they know that Abraham our Patriarch wandered here.[93]

Then there is the resort to the Bible which is not just Protestant but Protestant-settler, that is, the 'return' to the Bible is mobilized to wrest from its indigenous society a territory which is settled upon, and transformed into a national patrimony, in which the community of settlers retains its ethnic purity vis-à-vis the indigenes. Herzog's observation, that archaeology's thesis on the gradual fusion of the early Israelites should have been embraced by Zionist Israelis, might be posed as a question. One of the main arguments put forward by the critical archaeologists is that early Israel emerged out of a long process in which various autochthonous elements had been fused into a composite 'ethnicity' (whatever that means): would this not be a viable ideological alternative to the biblical narrative of conquest, annihilation and settlement?

The reason Herzog cannot – perhaps does not wish to – see the obvious answer is precisely because the project for which the Old Testament has been mobilized is a settler one; and it is a settler project not only in terms of the conquest of land and labour, of settlement patterns and institutions, but also in terms of historical consciousness, ideology and literary imagination. And for settler nations there is, as Albright emphasized so robustly, a twofold *sine qua non*: invasion and conquest as a foundational origin, and ethnic impregnability vis-à-vis the indigenous population. Other settler nations made comparable use of the Old Testament.[94]

Ben-Gurion's exegeses are uniquely bold in their attempt to square the circle, to make the oxymoron 'autochthonous settler' look feasible. In other words, Ben-Gurion's reading of the Book of Joshua is an exegetical attempt to endow the Hebrew nation with an autochthonous origination, but simultaneously to retain the formative foundation of conquest and ethnic purity. Although Ben-Gurion's daring biblical exegesis is not unknown to scholars, its content has not been seriously analysed. There are two exceptions, in which the exegesis is discussed, but the Protestant-settler foundation is entirely missed.[95] One of these exceptions, Michael Keren, keeps reminding the reader that Ben-Gurion's approach to the Bible, however adulatory, was nonetheless secular. By 'secular' Keren really means, without fully realizing the significance of what he is saying, non-religious and anti-rabbinical with reference to Judaism; and Protestant or secular in the sense of modernity's secularization of Christianity, as Raz-Krakotzkin postulates. To be fully, truly secular Ben-Gurion would have had to follow the Autonomists and Bundists in discarding the Bible completely as a form of superstition or mystification. But then he wouldn't have been a Zionist.

In turning now to the exegeses themselves, I will start with one of Ben-Gurion's final interpretations. On 13 May 1960 the *Jerusalem Post* reported a rather dramatic press conference, held the previous day at Tel Aviv's Press Centre, under the headline 'Ben-Gurion Gives His Version of Tale of Exodus from Egypt'.[96] The address was later reproduced in a volume collecting much of Ben-Gurion's biblical commentary.[97] Taking full advantage of the spectacle, and on the basis of internal biblical evidence and his own – mostly circumstantial and deductive – interpretation of it, Ben-Gurion announced to the nation that, in fact, only a fraction of its ancestral community had gone to Egypt, and that therefore the number which participated in the Exodus, was present on Mount Sinai, and invaded the land promised to Abraham to claim it, was much smaller than conventionally believed: closer to 600 than 600,000. 'If my hypothesis is correct', Ben-Gurion explained, 'that with the exception of Joseph's family, the Hebrew people lived in the land continuously, from the days of Abraham – then there is no doubt that the numbers of the Hebrews believing in one God, who remained in the land, was several times larger than the number of those who left Egypt and returned to the land.'[98] Furthermore, he averred, his argument clarified otherwise inexplicable phenomena in the biblical narrative:

> If the number of those who left Egypt was only 600, or even several hundred more – and in this early period this was not a small number – then we can explain their wanderings in the desert [i.e., a much smaller number could survive], their entrance into the land, and their eating from the produce of the land immediately after arriving there. They had returned to their countrymen who had always lived in the land along with several of the Canaanite nations [note how ethnic purity is preserved].[99]

The staged press conference came at the tail end of a decade of Tanakhomania, one of the central components of which was the fortnightly gathering at Ben-Gurion's prime ministerial residence to study the Bible. This too was a well-publicized affair, for which the prime minister found in the Israeli Association for Biblical Research a partner that was eager and willing to cooperate in his exegeses; these meetings formed the basis for the subsequent volume of Ben-Gurion's interpretations.[100] A few scholars, such as the Hebrew University's Talmud professor Ephraim Urbach, refused to play along, but intellectuals, in particular those institutionalized in universities, tend to bow down in the presence of power, and Israeli intellectuals are no exception.

Although Ben-Gurion used every possible gesture to defer to scholarly authority, it is clear from records of the meetings that he dominated proceedings and, as Keren is keenly aware, the subjects discussed were dictated by Ben-Gurion's preference. It is especially important to note that, as Keren has observed, '[i]n 1959 . . . all sessions were devoted to the book of Joshua – one of Ben-Gurion's favourites – and the lectures by foremost scholars concerned such topics as the conquest of Canaan, the military aspects of the conquest, and the settlement of the tribes in the country'.[101]

The 'hypothesis' Ben-Gurion presented at the 1960 press conference drew on his sustained exegeses at the fortnightly Bible group. It was an argument conceived in 1959, the year dedicated at Ben-Gurion's behest to research into Joshua and the conquest, and developed over the next four years over several sessions. This was later reproduced as essays or more literally transcribed proceedings, and consisted of four pronounce-ments, which, like most of his exegetical project, were somewhat repetitive and intertextual, to the extent that they constituted an intra-referential system with its own logic. They were, in order, 'The Ancientness of Israel in His Land', 'The Ancientness of the Hebrews', 'The Early History of the Hebrews in Canaan' and 'Chapters 23–24 in the Book of Joshua'. The first two were composed in 1959, the third was a conversation of 1962, and the fourth was delivered at the President's Residence in February 1963. This last text, clearly the most thorough and sustained exegetical effort offered by Ben-Gurion, propounded the theory that Hebrews had already existed in the land as a collective that adhered to some form of monotheism; it was this which attracted Abraham from Mesopotamia following his own monotheistic epiphany. The text is then completed by an argument for the simultaneously early centrality of Shechem/Nablus, and the revamped Exodus narrative.[102]

It is on this fourth essay, on the concluding chapters in the Book of Joshua, that I will now focus. Reading Ben-Gurion's exegesis as a whole, one strongly feels that this text, though chronologically last, was the cognitive starting point that had set in motion Ben-Gurion's entire thought-process. There was no book in the Old Testament that Ben-Gurion preferred to Joshua, nor one to which he had devoted more intellectual endeavour. In this exegesis – as in the entirety of the project – his main interlocutor was Yehezkel Kaufmann (who was discussed in Chapter Three), the first Bible professor at the Hebrew University, with whom he had many a public and documented debate.[103] Ben-Gurion lionized Kaufmann as the outstanding Bible scholar of the epoch, who had salvaged the Book of Books from the clutches of ill-wishing Gentile scholars (with the honourable exception of Albright, naturally), especially the German ones, as well as rabbinical abuse, and brought the Old Testament home. There was something embarrassing in Ben-Gurion's adulation, given both Kaufmann's international anonymity and the scholarly superiority of those whose work he vowed to refute. The tension between the ferocity with which Ben-Gurion argued against Kaufmann and the accolades he bestowed upon him makes one wonder whether these accolades were very honest.

Ben-Gurion drew on two books by Kaufmann, both of which appeared in the 1950s. The first was his eight-volume *Toldot ha-Emunah ha-Yisraelit* ('History of the Israelite belief'), published between 1947 and 1956.[104] In that book Kaufmann took on, unsuccessfully as it transpired, the entire scholarly body of modern Bible studies. The crux of his circular argument was that the formation of pure monotheism and of the Israeli nation had been a simultaneous occurrence on Mount Sinai, for which the main evidence he brought to bear was the biblical account itself. It is significant that despite (perhaps because of) the fact that the international scholarly community deemed his argument and approach questionable, to put it bluntly – they were utterly demolished by S. D. Goitein – the Israeli editors of *The Biblical Encyclopaedia* commissioned to Kaufmann the central entry 'Jewish Religion'.[105] The second volume, a by-product of the multi-volume project, was solely concerned with the Book of Joshua. Appearing in 1953 in English (from Magnes Press) and in Hebrew two years later, it was called *The Biblical Account of the Conquest of Palestine*. Why Kaufmann chose the Book of Joshua as his subject is clear in my view: the conquest and ethnic cleansing of 1948 must have made a commentary upon the Book of Joshua very timely indeed in the early 1950s. Since it is much shorter and more narrowly focused than its voluminous relative, the Joshua monograph is a tangible demonstration of the flawed circular approach that underlay the exegeses of not only Kaufmann, but also Albright, Ben-Gurion and many others. Kaufmann was well aware, as were the other Zionist scholars, of the master German philologists and of Noth's Deuteronomistic thesis. He was no match for them, however, and all he could do was rhetorically reassert the basic historical veracity of the conquest account, with certain reservations, and relate the narrative in his own words, as if this constituted bona fide evidence. What he tried to preserve and reaffirm was, once again, the twin pillars of settler consciousness: the formative conquest story, and the ethnic purity of the invading nation vis-à-vis the indigenous people.

A preliminary glance at Ben-Gurion's essay on the two final chapters (23 and 24) of Joshua evinces why this particular commentary must have been a convenient starting point for his thesis. What puzzled Ben-Gurion was how these chapters, essentially Joshua's farewell speeches, related to one another, for 'the content, structure and importance of the two chapters are essentially different'.[106] He identifies numerous significant differences between them. In Chapter 23 the location of the speech is not mentioned, only that Joshua was old, whereas in Chapter 24 there is no temporal frame but the place is given as Shechem, to which locale Ben-Gurion attributed foundational importance. In Chapter 23 Joshua addresses only the people's elders, whilst in 24 he gathers together the twelve tribes. In Chapter 23 only Joshua speaks. 'In chapter 24, there is a dialogue; Joshua speaks and the people respond; Joshua argues and the nation listens. And then Joshua assembles the tribes of Israel and calls to the elders, the leaders, the judges and officers "stand before God." Nothing like this occurs anywhere [else] in Joshua. It can be felt, immediately, that this is a unique festive scene.'[107] Most importantly according to Ben-Gurion, in Chapter 23 the clear impression gained is that Joshua was speaking to people who had witnessed and accepted the covenant with God on Mount Sinai and only needed a reminder not to transgress it, whereas in Chapter 24 Joshua actually mediated a covenant in Shechem between God and the people, and warned the latter to be aware of God's wrathful disposition. Chapter 23 implicitly assumes that the audience is cognizant of the path that has led them thus far, while 24 commences with Joshua's historical survey of national history from Abraham onwards. All this conveys the sensation that '[Joshua] seems to be speaking in these two chapters to two peoples who did not share the same religion'.[108]

Before concluding with Ben-Gurion's solution to this puzzle, it should be briefly recalled that, as far as we know, the conquest story is most probably an invention by the Deuteronomist scribes in Josiah's time, roughly six centuries after the story had allegedly taken place, followed by substantial redactions in the Babylonian and Persian periods; that it was steeped in Assyrian culture and modelled after Assyrian conquest accounts; that Joshua was a figure constructed as an ideological device that would enhance Josiah's stature and the legitimacy of his policies; and, finally, that Chapter 24 is evidently an addition from the Persian period (539–450 BCE), which was meant to relate the Book of Joshua more directly to the Torah than to the books that follow it.[109] Ben-Gurion disagreed that Chapter 24 was a late addition – a point conceded even by Kaufmann, for which he was explicitly castigated by Ben-Gurion. Ben-Gurion asserted that it was wrong to surmise, as did Kaufmann, that the rest of Joshua is coherent, chiefly because of its frequent contradictions over whether or not the whole of the land had been conquered, and whether or not all of its peoples had been disinherited. Chapter 24, Ben-Gurion insisted, was an authentic expression of the glorious conquest of the Promised Land, written towards the end of its completion.

And then he proceeded with the culmination of his exegetical endeavour. In Chapter 23 Joshua addressed the relatively few who had left Egypt:

There is no need to tell them of the early history and of the exodus from Egypt, because they participated in these experiences no less than Joshua himself. They were no longer divided into tribes, because those who went down to Egypt and those who left Egypt were united all the while by one faith, one hope; and were led by one teacher and leader – Moses son of Amram. And Joshua, in his words to them before his death – in chapter 23 – contented himself with the request that they cling, in the future, to the Lord their God as they had done 'until that day'.[110]

So who were Joshua's addressees in Chapter 24? They were those whom Ben-Gurion calls 'the autochthonous Jews' in the original Hebrew edition, or 'the native Jews' in the English edition.[111] They did belong in a tribal structure, and hence, Ben-Gurion explains, Chapter 24 begins with 'Joshua [having] assembled all of the tribes of Israel in Shechem'. They were unaware of the exodus and the covenant in Sinai, and 'though a belief in one God was their historical legacy', their contact with 'idol-worshippers' required reminder and purgatory. They needed to be told of the nation's historical narrative, although Ben-Gurion does not explain why these autochthonous Jews needed to be told about the patriarchs any more than the 'Egyptian' Jews, given that the reported whereabouts of the patriarchs had been the land of Canaan, where they dwelt. The covenant with the autochthonous nationals was not something that had already been made and needed a reminder (which was the case with the 'Egyptian' Jews), but was being made for the first time, according to Ben-Gurion. That is also why, Ben-Gurion explains, Joshua had to summarize in Chapter 24 the nation's history. Joshua inscribed the covenant he mediated between God and autochthonous Jews, took a big stone, and erected it as a witness of the covenant under an oak tree in Shechem – the very same oak tree, Ben-Gurion stipulates, that was mentioned at the time of Abraham and then Jacob.[112] Joshua 24 in Shechem had been, Ben-Gurion passionately insisted in the face of rebuffs by Kaufmann and others, 'a new Mount Sinai revelation'.[113]

Finally, Ben-Gurion neither challenged nor tried to qualify the exodus, desert-covenant and conquest narrative; furthermore, he did not question the central importance of that part of the narrative for the nation's origins. As has already been explained, these narratives were glossed over in order to preserve the purity of the settler foundation myth, which remains unspoiled by the 'discovery' that the Jewish nation had at the same time been autochthonous, or indigenous. In addition to this being a settler exegesis, Ben-Gurion's insistence on the indigenous nature of the Jewish nation stems, in my view, from his visceral and vehement negation of exile. As he repeatedly stressed, he could not fathom a historical circumstance in which any nation, least of all his own, could be born outside the soil of its homeland and survive the consequences. Victimizer of Yiddish and Ladino that he was, Ben-Gurion refused to accept that a proper national language could be preserved in exile, let alone be created there. Like another messianic Zionist, Gershom Scholem, Ben–Gurion drew his ultimate authority to interpret the Old Testament from the mere realization of the foundational Zionist myth: negation of exile, return to the land, and return to history. In April 1959, brushing aside rabbinical commentary, he said to the scholars who congregated in his adopted kibbutz in the Negev, Sde Boker:

> Conquest, settlement, tribe, nation – I doubt if a scattered and dispersed people without a land and without independence is capable of knowing the true significance and full meaning of these words. They did not participate in conquests and did not know what is involved in conquest. And the same holds true for settlement. Only with the rebirth of Israel in our generation did these vague concepts take on flesh and we have become aware of their content and essence. Now that we are aware, we must delve anew into the stories of the Bible.[114]

# Notes

1 See B. Templer, 'The Political Sacralization of Imperial Genocide: Contextualizing Timothy Dwight's *The Conquest of Canaan*', *Postcolonial Studies*, 9/4 (2006), pp. 358–91.

2 Cited in K. W. Whitelam, *The Invention of Ancient Israel: The Silencing of Palestinian History*, London and New York: Routledge, 1996, pp. 83–4.

3 In RS. Sugirtharajah (ed.), *Voices from the Margin: Interpreting the Bible in the Third World*, Maryknoll: Orbis Books, 1995 (new edition), pp. 277–85. The citation is from pp. 284–5.

4 A. Raz-Krakotzkin, 'The Return to the History of Redemption, or: What Is the "History" to which the "Return" Takes Place in the Term "the Return to History"', in S. N. Eisenstadt and M. Lissak (eds), *Zionism and the Return to History: A Reappraisal* [Hebrew], Jerusalem: Yad Ben-Zvi Press, 1999, pp. 249–76.

5 Ibid., p. 250.

6 Ibid., p. 254. By 'ambivalent' Raz-Krakotzkin means that Christians recognize a shared source of authority with Jews, but deprecate the Jewish refusal to recognize the Message.

7 Ibid., p. 255.

8 Ibid., p. 265.

9 Ibid., p. 266.

10 M. Vereté, 'The Restoration of the Jews in English Protestant Thought 1790–1840', *Middle Eastern Studies*, 8/1 (January 1972), pp. 3–51. For another discussion of the same theme see R. Sharif, 'Christians for Zion, 1600–1919', *Journal of Palestine Studies*, 5/3–4 (Spring–Summer, 1976), pp. 123–41.

11 Vereté, 'Restoration', pp. 3–5.

12 Ibid., p. 13.

13 Ibid.

14 Ibid., p. 14.

15 Ibid., p. 15.

16 Ibid., p. 16.

17 Ibid., p. 17.

18 Ibid., p. 22.

19 Ibid., p. 25.

20 Ibid., pp. 26–7.

21 Ibid., pp. 27 8.

22 Ibid., p. 29.

23 Ibid., p. 33. Vereté uses the italics to emphasize that these are the words employed in the original discourse.

24 M. Vereté, 'Why Was a British Consulate Established in Jerusalem?', *The English Historical Review*, 85/335 (April 1970), pp. 316–45.

25 M. Vereté, 'The Balfour Declaration and Its Makers', in E. Kedourie and S. Haim (eds), *Palestine and Israel in the 19th and 20th Centuries*, London: Frank Cass, 1982, pp. 60–89. The article was written in 1967.

26 Ibid., p. 72.

27 Ibid., pp. 69–70.

28 A. Schölch, 'Britain in Palestine, 1838–1882: The Roots of the Balfour Policy', *Journal of Palestine Studies*, 22/1 (Autumn 1992), pp. 39–56. The article was published posthumously.

29 Ibid., p. 46.
30 Ibid., pp. 50–1.
31 Ibid., p. 47.
32 See above, Chapter One, p. 39–40.
33 Schölch, 'Britain in Palestine', p. 50
34 Ibid.
35 L. M. C. van der Hoeven Leonhard, 'Shlomo and David in Palestine, 1907', in W. Khalidi (ed.), *From Haven to Conquest: Readings in Zionism and the Palestine Problem until 1948*, Beirut: The Institute for Palestine Studies, 1971, pp. 118–19.
36 See J. Press, 'Same-Sex Unions in Modern Europe: *Daniel Deronda, Altneuland*, and the Homoerotics of Jewish Nationalism', in E. Kosofsky-Sedgwick (ed.), *Novel Gazing: Queer Readings in Fiction*, Durham, NC: Duke University Press, 1997, pp. 299–330.
37 E. Said, *The Question of Palestine*, New York: Vintage Books, 1979, pp. 60–8. Said's starting the book with Eliot is of course meant to lead to Herzl.
38 Ibid., p. 64.
39 T. Herzl, *Die Judensache (The Jewish Cause). Diaries 1895–1904*, 3 vols [Hebrew], Jerusalem: Mossad Bialik and the Zionist Library, 1997–2001, introduction by Sh. Avineri, Hebrew translation by J. Wenkert, editorial notes by M. Heymann, vol. 1, p. 78. See also Avineri's allusions on p. 27.
40 Ibid., p. 108.
41 Ibid., p. 259.
42 Ibid. p. 262.
43 Ibid., p. 446.
44 Z. Herzog, 'Deconstructing the Walls of Jericho', *Haaretz* [online edition], 29 October 1999. (The Hebrew title is 'The Bible: No Facts on the Ground'.)
45 Here are a few examples: J. Barton (ed.), *The Cambridge Companion to Biblical Interpretation*, Cambridge: Cambridge University Press, 1998; J. Barr, *History and Ideology in the Old Testament: Biblical Studies at the End of a Millennium*, Oxford: Oxford University Press, 2000; I. Finkelstein and N. Na'aman (eds), *From Nomadism to Monarchy: Archaeological and Historical Aspects of Early Israel*, Jerusalem: Yad Izhak Ben-Zvi and Israel Exploration Society, 1994 (the Hebrew edition appeared in 1990); Sh. Ahituv and E. D. Oren (eds), *The Origin of Early Israel – Current Debate*, Beer-Sheva and London: Ben-Gurion University Press, 1998; L. I. Levine and A. Mazar (eds), *The Controversy over the Historicity of the Bible* [Hebrew], Jerusalem: Yad Ben-Zvi and Dinur Center, 2001; *Zemanim, A Special Issue: Archaeology, Bible, History*, 94 (Spring 2006) [Hebrew].
46 For this feud I draw mostly on Sh. Geva, 'The Beginning of Israeli Biblical Archaeology [Hebrew]', *Zemanim*, 42 (Summer 1992), pp. 92–102, N. Abu Al-Haj, *Facts on the Ground: Archaeological Practice and Territorial Self-Fashioning in Israeli Society*, Chicago: The University of Chicago Press, 2001, pp. 99–130, and 'Reflections on Archaeology and Israeli Settler-Nationhood', *Radical History Review*, 86 (Spring 2003), pp. 149–63.
47 For an excellent and politically aware presentation of the Alt/Albright differences see Whitelam, op. cit., pp. 71–121.

48 B. Kuklick, *Puritans in Babylon: The Ancient Near East and American Intellectual Life, 1880–1930*, Princeton: Princeton University Press, 1996, pp. 185–93.

49 J. Barr, *Fundamentalism*, London: S.C.M. Press, 1981 (second edition).

50 See especially Whitelam, op. cit., pp. 80–1.

51 A. El-Haj, *Facts on the Ground*, pp. 101–23.

52 Whitelam, op. cit., p. 83.

53 See J. M. Sasson, 'On Choosing Models for Recreating Israelite Pre-Monarchic History', *Journal for the Study of the Old Testament*, 21 (1981), pp. 3–24, and especially 14–15. A more forthright casting of the argument is offered by K. Whitelam, 'The Search for Early Israel: Historical Perspective', in Ahituv and Oren, op. cit., p. 51.

54 Geva, op. cit., pp. 99–100.

55 For a succinct rendering of the ethnicity theme see Z. Herzog and O. Bar-Yosef, 'Different Views on Ethnicity in the Archaeology of the Negev', in E. D. Oren and Sh. Ahituv (eds.), *Aharon Kempinski Memorial Volume*, Beer-Sheva: Ben-Gurion University of the Negev Press, 2002, pp. 151–82, and especially pp. 159–61.

56 Z. Herzog, 'The Scientific Revolution in the Archaeology of Ancient Israel', in Levine and Mazar, op. cit., pp. 61–3.

57 For the full reference see again n. 45 above. Although most references are made to the volume's 1994 English edition, it is important to note that the Hebrew original had already appeared in 1990.

58 Herzog, 'Scientific Revolution', p. 52.

59 The focuses are summarily presented in pp. 54–61.

60 Ibid., p 55.

61 See N. Na'aman, 'The "Conquest of Canaan" in the Book of Joshua and in History', in Finkelstein and Na'aman, op. cit., pp. 218–82.

62 Herzog, 'Scientific Revolution', pp. 56–7.

63 Ibid., p. 58.

64 Ibid., pp. 59–61.

65 I. Finkelstein, 'The Rise of Early Israel: Archaeology and Long-Term History', in Ahituv and Oren, op. cit., p. 8

66 Herzog and Bar-Yosef, 'Different Views on Ethnicity', pp. 172 3.

67 P. R. Davies, *In Search of 'Ancient Israel'*, Sheffield: Sheffield Academic Press, 1992; for Whitelam see n. 2 above.

68 I am basically informed by the most recent and thorough book on this topic, though other studies will also be alluded to; T. Römer, *The So-Called Deuteronomistic History: A Sociological, Historical and Literary Introduction*, London: T&T Clark, 2005. See a detailed review by a foremost scholar of the same field, John Van Seters, in *Review of Biblical Literature*, 9 (2006).

69 Römer, op. cit., p. 50.

70 Ibid.

71 Ibid., p. 107.

72 Ibid., pp. 21–7.

73 Ibid., pp. 27–9.

74 I. Finkelstein, 'Archaeology and Bible: Neither Black nor White', in Levine and Mazar, op. cit., p. 145.

75 On the Persian redaction in particular see Römer, op. cit., pp. 165–85.

76 Ibid., pp. 45–9.
77 Finkelstein, 'Archaeology and Bible', p. 145.
78 See Römer, op. cit., pp. 82–3, and Sh. Ahituv (ed., comm.), *The Book of Joshua* [Hebrew], Tel Aviv: Am Oved and Jerusalem: Magnes, 1995, p. 9.
79 Römer, op. cit., p. 75.
80 Ibid., pp. 84–5. See also Na'aman, 'The "Conquest of Canaan"', p. 281.
81 Römer, op. cit., p. 90.
82 R. T. Nelson, 'Josiah in the Book of Joshua', *Journal of Biblical Literature*, 100/4 (1981), pp. 531–40.
83 Ibid., p. 537.
84 Ibid., pp. 534–7.
85 Ibid., p. 539.
86 A. Shapira, *The Bible and Israeli Identity*, Jerusalem: Magnes Press, 2005, p. 25.
87 For which see above, p. 285, n. 56.
88 Herzog, 'Scientific Revolution', pp. 64–5.
89 Ibid., p. 65.
90 Reproduced as Appendix 9 in Shapira, *The Bible*, pp. 133–4.
91 For discussion of which, see above, Chapter Three, p. 97.
92 Shapira, *The Bible*, Appendix 11, p. 146.
93 Ibid., p. 158.
94 In regard to the Old Testament, we have a thorough and stimulating study by Ronald Akenson, who compares (i.e., shows similarities and differences of) the ways in which what has undergirded three settler communities is a 'covenantal grid'. The communities he studies are the Afrikaans, the Ulster Protestants (initially Presbyterian Scots), and the Zionist Israelis. See his *God's Peoples: Covenant and Land in South Africa, Israel, and Ulster*, Ithaca: Cornell University Press, 1992.
95 M. Keren, *Ben-Gurion and the Intellectuals: Power, Knowledge, and Charisma*, Deklab: Northern Illinois University Press, 1983, pp. 100–18, and A. Shapira, 'Ben-Gurion and the Bible: The Construction of a Historical Narrative', *Alpayim*, 14 (1997), pp. 207–31. Shapira's essay was amply discussed in the previous chapter.
96 Keren, op. cit., pp. 100–1.
97 D. Ben-Gurion, *Biblical Reflections* [Hebrew], Tel Aviv: Am Oved, 1969, pp. 243–52, and *Ben-Gurion Looks at the Bible*, trans. J. Kolatch, New York: Jonathan David Publishers, 1972, pp. 113–26.
98 Ben-Gurion, *Ben-Gurion Looks at the Bible*, p. 124.
99 Ibid., p. 125.
100 See Keren, op. cit., pp. 107–11.
101 Ibid., p. 108.
102 In the Hebrew original these appear as separate essays in pp. 50–92, 104–26, 145–63 and 164–83. In the English edition two of the essays on the ancientness of the Hebrews in the land are grouped into one with two parts, pp. 55–110, and the other two appear in pp. 138–65 and 190–214.
103 For Kaufmann, see above, Chapter Three, p. 103–5.
104 Tel Aviv: Devir, 1947–56. Translated and abridged by M. Greenberg as *The Religion of Israel: From Its Beginnings to the Babylonian Exile*, Chicago: University of Chicago Press, 1960.

105 See B. Evron, *National Reckoning*, Tel Aviv: Dvir, 1986, p. 37.
106 Ben-Gurion, *Ben-Gurion Looks at the Bible*, p. 190.
107 Ibid.
108 Ibid., p. 193.
109 For the point on Chapter 24 see Römer, op. cit., pp. 180–1 and p. 181 n. 31.
110 Ben-Gurion, *Ben-Gurion Looks at the Bible*, p. 199.
111 P. 153 (Hebrew) and p. 201 (English).
112 Ben-Gurion, *Ben-Gurion Looks at the Bible*, pp. 200–1.
113 Ibid., p. 157.
114 Ibid., pp. 86–7.

# Index

"*The Returns of Zionism* is a sharply critical intellectual and literary history of the Zionist movement and its principal progeny, the State of Israel. The book represents a milestone in the study of Zionism. Unlike the great majority of writers in this crowded field, Gabriel Piterberg is concerned both with the intentions of the Zionists and with their actual impact on the native population of Palestine. He breaks down the familiar mould and rearranges the pieces. Many of the Hebrew texts cited in this book are not available in English. The author uses the whole panoply of sources in all the relevant languages to brilliantly illuminating effect. The result is a book which advances very considerably our understanding of the origins of the State of Israel. It is a magnificent accomplishment of original research and far-reaching historical reinterpretation." **Avi Shlaim, FBA, St Antony's College, Oxford**

"This thoroughly researched and engaging book provides an intellectual, cultural and literary fulcrum from which Zionist ideology and practice can be read afresh. While addressing the fundamental myths of Zionism, it collapses taken-for-granted distinctions with regards to time, space, and conflicting ideological camps. This book is an essential reading for everyone who is interested in the history of Zionism as well as the history of national movements." **Yehouda Shenhav, Professor of Sociology at Tel-Aviv University and author of The Arab Jews**

"A subtle and excitingly original effort of intellectual reconstruction, which explores many new ways of capturing the essence of the Zionist project. Gabriel Piterberg has pioneered an approach which, from many different starting points, and through exploring many different connections, demonstrates how Zionism developed its cohesion, its character and its blindness towards those it displaced in Palestine." **Roger Owen, A.J. Meyer Professor of Middle East History at Harvard University**

In this original and wide-ranging study, Gabriel Piterberg examines the ideology and literature behind the colonization of Palestine, from the late nineteenth century to the present. Exploring Zionism's origins in central-eastern European nationalism and settler movements, he shows how its texts can be placed within a wider discourse of western colonization. Revisiting the work of Theodor Herzl and Gershom Scholem, Anita Shapira and Ben Gurion, and bringing to light the writings of lesser-known scholars and thinkers influential in the formation of the Zionist myth, Piterberg breaks open prevailing views of Zionism, demonstrating that it was in fact unexceptional, expressing a consciousness and imagination typical of colonial settler movements. Shaped by European ideological currents and the realities of colonial life, Zionism constructed its own story as a unique and impregnable one, in the process excluding the voices of an already-existing indigenous people – the Palestinian Arabs.

HISTORY

www.versobooks.com
$29.95/£16.99/$33CAN

ISBN 978-1-84467-260-8

9 781844 672608

Design: **BRILL**
Cover photograph © Micha Bar-Am/Magnum Photos